PRAISE FOR JIM GILLIAN. ....

"Jim Gilliam's place in baseball lore has been largely overlooked until Steve Dittmore lifts him out of the shadows in *The Forgotten Dodger*. Well researched, fast paced, and entertaining, this illuminating biography shows just how important Gilliam's contributions were to seven Dodger World Series teams and chronicles the pioneering role he played as a Major League player and coach. With a franchise as storied as the Dodgers, it's hard to believe Gilliam's story isn't already better known. But that was the case all along for a very good player—1953 Rookie of the Year, five-time All-Star between the Negro and Major Leagues—whose contributions always seemed to be overshadowed by those of his better-known teammates. A long overdue tribute to Gilliam and a treat for fans of the game's history."

—Andrew Maraniss, *New York Times* bestselling author of *Singled Out: The True Story of Glenn Burke*

"Steve Dittmore's Jim Gilliam biography is a riveting story about an all-time great Dodger that time forgot. One of the few players to win a Negro League Championship and a World Series ring, Dittmore convincingly makes the case that the unheralded Gilliam, who grew up in Jim Crow Nashville, should have his rightful place next to the greats like Jackie Robinson, Roy Campanella, and Sandy Koufax."

—Dr. Louis Moore, author of *We Will Win the Day: The Civil Rights Movement, the Black Athlete*

"The stories of the Brooklyn and Los Angeles Dodgers have been told in many forms and in many places. Steve Dittmore has made a significant contribution to this already rich literature with his great new biography of Jim Gilliam. He shows how essential Gilliam was to the success of the Baltimore Elite Giants as well as the Brooklyn and Los Angeles Dodgers. Moreover, he situates Gilliam's life within the context of the communities where he spent his 49 years and 356 days with great nuance. This is one of the best baseball books of 2025."

—Clayton Trutor, author of *Loserville: How Professional Sports Remade Atlanta and How Atlanta Remade Professional Sports*

"Every generation there are a handful of baseball stars whose stellar, unfussy, consistent play too often is overshadowed by their flashier counterparts. Jim Gilliam was one of them. As integral as Gilliam was to those great midcentury Dodgers teams, his quiet demeanor and workmanlike attitude hindered him from receiving his full due. Until now. Steve Dittmore capably gives Gilliam the biographical treatment he so richly deserves, shining the spotlight on an essential player who rarely sought it."

—Luke Epplin, author of *Our Team: The Epic Story of Four Men and the World Series That Changed Baseball*

JIM GILLIAM: THE FORGOTTEN DODGER

STEPHEN W. DITTMORE

**August
Publications**

Jim Gilliam: The Forgotten Dodger

August Publications
215 10th Av. S., Unit 621
Minneapolis, MN 55415
augustpublications.com

Library of Congress Control Number: 2024939361

ISBN 978-1-938532-82-5 (Print)
ISBN 978-1-938532-83-2 (eBook)

9 8 7 6 5 4 3 2 1

Designer (cover): Natalie Nowytski. Photo licensed from Associated Press.

To Andrea and Andrew. Trust the Process always.

CONTENTS

INTRODUCTION

No one offered better descriptions of Dodger players through the years than the legendary team announcer Vin Scully. It didn't matter if it was during the course of a game or as the emcee at one of countless public events where Dodger players were in attendance.

Vin's words introducing a Dodger player were always well thought out and with meaning because, as much as anyone, Vin knew his subject. I think of this as I think of my friend, Jim Gilliam, and Vin's introduction at one Dodger event.

The description was brief but totally on point and spoken with the greatest of respect: "Jim Gilliam, baseball player."

That, indeed, was Jim and his public perception. And yet there was so much more to Jim and a life that ended all too soon after nearly 50 years. A life so well lived and yet so unknown by fans until Stephen Dittmore's wonderful writing in *Jim Gilliam: The Forgotten Dodger*.

A life in which a young boy established a dream to spend his life in the game he loved, baseball. A dream that seemed against all odds for a youngster from the South, where an equal playing field didn't exist. At best, even with early and unquestionable talent, the dream seemed to be limited to the Negro Leagues.

Jim Gilliam, as he would describe later in his life, was all about loving the game, learning the game, and playing to the best of his ability. Who could possibly imagine that this young man would find the light of his future turned on by a man he would later know as a close friend and team-mate, Jackie Robinson?

Former Los Angeles Dodgers GM Fred Claire.

When I joined the Dodgers' front office in 1969, Jim was in his early years as a coach on the team under manager Walt Alston. It didn't take long to see that Jim was a total professional in everything he did. It also was obvious he had the total respect of everyone in the organization.

From a personal standpoint, a few things remain in my mind about the friendship we developed.

I recall being in the clubhouse after a game and listening to Jim talk to a young Dodger player who had just told a reporter in a postgame interview what pitch he had hit for a home run.

Jim was befuddled by the response. "Why would you tell a reporter what type of pitch you hit for a home run?" Jim inquired of the player. "Don't ever give away any information related to the opposition."

A small point, perhaps, but not to Jim.

In the game and in his life, Jim was the ultimate perfectionist. I recall a round of golf I played with a group of Dodgers, including Jim and Don Newcombe. After six holes, Jim told Newcombe he was leaving.

"Where are you going?" asked Newk. The answer by Jim: "If I can't play any better than I am at this time I need more practice."

Jim, the perfectionist in baseball, fun times, and life.

Jim would be a model for how best to wear a baseball uniform and in his civilian clothes he was an immaculate dresser. I once went with Jim to a sportscasters luncheon and one of the popular TV announcers who was known as a great dresser saw Jim and asked, "Jim, you look great. What do you do with your old clothes?"

The reply, typical of Jim: "I'm wearing them."

Paying attention to detail, wanting to be his best, and doing so at a low-key level.

Walt Alston gave the best description of Jim on the playing field: "He didn't hit with power, but he did the little things to win ball games. He never griped or complained. He was one of the most unselfish ball players I know."

Gilliam's contributions as a player helped the Alston-managed Dodger teams win four World Series and seven pennants during a 14-year playing career.

On October 8, 1978, Jim Gilliam passed away of a massive brain hemorrhage while serving as a Dodger coach. It was just two days before the Dodgers were to open the World Series against the New York Yankees at Dodger Stadium. It was a dark time in the glare of the World Series limelight.

I well recall a meeting to discuss how we best deal with such a loss. Two days after Jim's passing the announcement was made that the number 19 would be retired.

Jim Gilliam, baseball player, always a Dodger, thus joined the greatest Dodgers of all time.

Fred Claire
Los Angeles Dodgers
Executive VP and General Manager, 1969-1998
Author, *My 30 Years in Dodger Blue* **and** *Extra Innings: Fred Claire's*
Journey to City of Hope and Finding a World Championship Team

1

THE FORGOTTEN DODGER

SCATTERED CLOUDS AND LIGHT RAIN WERE PREDICTED THROUGHOUT THE DAY IN the Twin Cities on Thursday, October 14, 1965. The *Minneapolis Tribune* advised the 50,000 spectators attending Game Seven of the 1965 World Series between the Los Angeles Dodgers and the Minnesota Twins later that day to grab their raincoats. Indeed, in the "wee small" morning hours, as Vin Scully described it to a nationwide television audience on NBC, the Minneapolis-St. Paul metropolitan area was hit by a storm producing heavy rains.

But the weather passed, helicopters dried the field at Metropolitan Stadium in the Minneapolis suburb of Bloomington, and temperatures in the 50s moved in accompanied by, according to Scully, "bright, blue skies." Perhaps this would be a good omen for the Dodgers, who were much more at ease playing under sunny skies than the dreary, cloudy skies of a Minnesota fall.

Reading off the Los Angeles lineup to the television audience that day, Scully began, "Let's take a look at those fellows whose names are printed boldly on the Dodger lineup card. Shortstop Maury Wills opening it up. Jim Gilliam at third base. There are no surprises today, for either team." That the Dodgers were even taking the field for Game Seven of a World Series and that Jim Gilliam was in the starting lineup at third base were, in truth, both surprises.

When the season began, Gilliam was the team's first-base coach, having retired following the 1964 season, his worst season statistically. He hit .228 in 116 games with just 390 plate appearances, all career lows. After sweeping the New York Yankees in the 1963 World Series, the Dodgers limped to an 80-82 record in 1964, good for sixth place in the National League.

Newspaper writers suggested toward the end of the 1964 season that Gilliam's skills had diminished and it was time for him to retire. As early as mid-August, *Los Angeles Times* columnist Paul Zimmerman blamed the team's slump from 1963 World Series champions to 1964 also-rans on the poor hitting of Frank Howard, Tommy Davis, and Gilliam. "In other seasons, somewhere along the line, Gilliam has taken over to patch things up."[1]

Sid Ziff, columnist for the *Los Angeles Times*, identified a number of possible fall guys on September 14, including questioning whether "age caught up with Jim Gilliam?"[2] Gilliam turned 36 shortly after the 1964 season ended, having played competitive professional baseball each summer since 1945, when he was 16 years old. His speed and reactions, qualities for which he was well known, had indeed slowed.

As if Gilliam's presence was not enough of a surprise, the Dodgers found themselves in third place, 4.5 games out of first, on September 15, 1965, a mere two-and-a-half weeks before the end of the season. The odds of Los Angeles catching both the San Francisco Giants and the Cincinnati Reds to win the pennant seemed pretty long at that point.

But Gilliam had faced pretty long odds throughout his life and had a knack for overcoming them. His father died when he was less than a year old. He was raised by his mother in segregated Nashville, Tennessee, attending, but never graduating from, Pearl High School. He rode buses through the Jim Crow south as a member of the Nashville Black Vols and Baltimore Elite Giants, Negro Leagues teams in the 1940s. He spent two years with the Montreal Royals, the Dodgers' top minor-league team, ostensibly because it was easier for the Dodgers to keep mediocre white talent on its big-league roster than face the scrutiny of fielding a team with five Black players.

Jim never commanded the spotlight, yet was influential in the Dodgers reaching seven World Series, winning four, during his career. He never had a permanent position and was frequently the subject of trade rumors. He is remembered more as a role player, someone who sacrificed his statistics for the good of the team. A company man.

Teammates and executives often talked about Gilliam's baseball intelligence, or IQ. "Walt (Alston) said Jim never made a mistake on the field," said former Dodgers owner and president Peter O'Malley. "I mean, it is incredible. Jim was always aware of the situation. Prepared. Knew what to do whether the ball was hit to him or someone else. He was in it. His head was totally in the game."

And so here was a role player with the incredible baseball IQ, three days shy of his 37th birthday, batting second and readying to play third base in yet another Game Seven. For Gilliam, October 14, 1965 represented his 37th start in a World Series game for the Dodgers franchise. It was his third magical Game Seven, one in which the winning team captured the title and the losing team was resigned to waiting for next year. At the time, just 18 of the 62 Series to that point had gone the full seven games, and Gilliam had played in one of every six that had gone the distance.

Third base had long been a problem position for the Dodgers. Dating back to 1947, Jackie Robinson's first year with the club in Brooklyn, the Dodgers had used 14 different Opening Day starting third baseman through the 18-year period ending in 1965. The hot corner would continue to function like a hot potato until Ron Cey emerged to hold down the position from 1973 to 1982.

Gilliam grew up as a third baseman on the sandlots of Nashville, but learned to play second base in the Negro Leagues. He made his first Major League appearance at third in 1958, the year the Dodgers franchise moved from Brooklyn to Los Angeles. During his career, Gilliam appeared in 761 games as a third baseman, starting 598. His only Opening Day start at the position occurred in 1960. Gilliam also opened the 1955 season as a left-fielder, in addition to six Opening Day starts at second base. The only other Dodger players in 115 years of franchise history through 2024 to start at three different positions on Opening Day were Bill Buckner (left field, right field, and first base) and Pedro Guerrero (right field, first base, and third base). Gilliam would play wherever his long-time manager Walter Alston needed him to play.

The Dodgers were clinging to a 2-0 lead in the decisive Game Seven as the game went to the bottom of the fifth inning. Sandy Koufax, starting on two days' rest, was struggling with his command, relying exclusively on his fastball. The Twins had two runners on base and one out with their MVP shortstop Zoilo Versalles at the plate. The right-handed-hitting Versalles jumped on a Koufax fastball and pulled it sharply down the third-base line. The ball seemed ticketed for the corner, possibly tying the game if both runners scored.

Gilliam, remembering Versalles' previous at-bats in the Series, was cheating toward the line, something Scully noticed and announced to the television audience: "Ground ball backhanded by Gilliam! To the bag for a force. Oh what a play! That would have been a double and at least one run batted in....Gilliam was guarding the line to cut down on the chance of an extra-base hit and it turned out to be the play. He did not have any other play, except to go to the bag."

Jim Gilliam's key play in the 1965 World Series. Photo by John Croft,
Minneapolis Tribune, *via Getty Images.*

Indeed, Scully's observation was prescient. "I was playing Versalles close to the line, and it was a good thing because the ball was hit pretty hard,"[3] Jim said after the game. He confirmed what was evident to everyone in attendance and watching on television: tagging third was the automatic play.

"I remembered Versalles pulled the ball pretty good the other day when he bounced one off my arm. I could also see that Sandy didn't have his real good curve," Gilliam added, demonstrating his baseball intelligence. "Anyway, I cheated to the line a few feet, or I never would have come up with the ball. Versalles hit it good. I guess it was a fast ball he hit."[4]

From across the diamond at his defensive position at first base, Wes Parker remembers not being surprised by the play. "I had seen him do it before. The Devil (Gilliam's nickname among his teammates) could outfox his opponents. He could out think and out smart them. What impressed me the most was his decision. A less experienced player might have tried to do more than the play called for and thrown to second to try for a double play. He didn't overdo it."

Future Dodger Derrel Thomas, 14 years old at the time, remembers watching the play on television at his home near Crenshaw and 29th Street in Los Angeles. "I can see it like it was yesterday," he said nearly 60 years after the fact. "He never got a lot of credit for his defensive ability. He was a steady fielder. If Brooks Robinson would have made a play like that then it would have been on every highlight film, especially for the World Series."[5] The implication in Thomas' comment being that baseball preferred to highlight the exploits of a star white third baseman rather than a Black player.

The play allowed Dodger defenders to relax slightly with two outs. "We all knew two guys weren't going to hit Sandy hard in a row,"Parker remembered. Indeed, Joe Nossek grounded harmlessly to short to end the inning. As the Dodgers prepared to bat in the top of the sixth, Scully told the television audience that Koufax had "his bacon saved" by Gilliam.

The player who saved Koufax's "bacon," and quite possibly the entire World Series, was lifted a few innings later for, of all things, defensive purposes and would watch the ninth inning from the Dodgers clubhouse. The moment was emblematic of Gilliam's playing career. He was not the outspoken player who commanded headlines. He did not hit many home runs. He was not flashy. He merely went about his business playing wherever his manager needed him.

So silent was Gilliam that his name is rarely mentioned alongside his Dodger contemporaries on World Series-winning teams in Brooklyn and Los Angeles. Roger Kahn's legendary 1972 memoir has assured that history remembers the 1950s-era Brooklyn Dodgers as baseball's *Boys of Summer*. The one-word names are familiar to baseball fans of all ages: Jackie and Campy, Pee Wee and Gil, Oisk and Skoonj, Duke and Newk,

Preacher and Billy. Yet Gilliam's name is often overlooked in conversations about the great Dodger teams of the 1950s and 1960s.

It seems history has largely ignored the contributions of the role player whose seven total World Series teams is tied for the most in team history with Pee Wee Reese and Carl Furillo. He was not profiled in Kahn's memoir, a book ostensibly about the 1952 Dodgers, the year prior to Gilliam's debut, but featuring stories of later years. Nor did his name appear regularly in Peter Golenbock's oral history of the Brooklyn Dodgers, *Bums*, which was published after Gilliam's death. Maury Allen's 50-year anniversary book about the 1955 World Series champion Dodgers team, *Brooklyn Remembered: The 1955 Days of the Dodgers*, did not commemorate Gilliam with an individual profile, as was done with other members of the team. Playing as he did on a 1955 team stocked with six future Hall of Famers, he seems easy to overlook.

His career as a player and a coach with the Dodger franchise spanned three decades from 1951-1978. He often entered spring training without a permanent position in the lineup or as trade bait, but still averaged 140 games played over 14 seasons, including two seasons as a player-coach. Gilliam would have likely surpassed half a century or more with the organization had he not died from complications of a brain hemorrhage at age 49, on the eve of the 1978 World Series where he was slated to coach first base. Like his teammates Jackie Robinson and Gil Hodges, Gilliam failed to live into his mid-50s.

Jim's fingerprints are ubiquitous on memorable moments across Dodgers history. He ranks third in team annals in plate appearances, fifth in at bats and games played, and fourth in runs scored. He is eighth in franchise history in Offensive WAR, using modern-day statistical evaluations. His uniform number 19 was retired by the Dodgers after his death, the only non-Hall of Fame player in team history to receive such an honor until the Dodgers announced in January 2023 the team would retire Fernando Valenzuela's number 34.

Gilliam did all this while standing at various gates designed to limit the role of Blacks in organized baseball. When future roommate Jackie Robinson integrated baseball in 1947, the First Gate was opened. Keeping Gilliam in the minors until 1953 was the product of the Second Gate, an unspoken "quota" on the number of Black players on a given team.

Jim helped open the Third Gate when he became the first Black base coach in baseball history. Although he was frequently discussed as a potential big-league manager, he would never be afforded the opportunity. It was Frank Robinson, appointed as manager of the Cleveland Indians in

1975, who finally burst through the Fourth Gate, nearly 30 years after Robinson debuted for the Dodgers.

Preaching at Gilliam's funeral on October 11, 1978, the Reverend Jesse Jackson described the challenges Gilliam faced throughout his life, from growing up in segregated, Depression-era Nashville, to staying in separate hotels from his teammates, to being passed over for managerial opportunities. "Jim Gilliam's life was against a headwind," Jackson said. "He was a first-class man and a second-class citizen."[6]

2

NASHVILLE

"You might say I was born on a ball field," Jim Gilliam wrote in Jackie Robinson's 1964 book, *Baseball Has Done It*.[1] In some ways, that statement is not as hyperbolic as it appears. Gilliam lived near a baseball field, played on the sandlots of Nashville, and baseball was in his parents' bloodlines.

In actuality, James William Gilliam, Jr. was born not on a ball field but at George W. Hubbard Hospital at Meharry Medical College, one of the few Black medical colleges in the United States, in Nashville, Tennessee on October 17, 1928, to parents James Gilliam, Sr. and Katherine Duval Gilliam.[2] A front-page story in the October 28, 1928 *Nashville Tennessean* extolled the benefits of higher educational institutions in Nashville, characterizing the Meharry Medical College as a "negro institution of note. Negro students in medicine and dentistry receive thorough training."[3]

Originally opened in 1912, the two-story Hubbard Hospital, located between 18th and 21st Avenues and bordered to the south by Albion Street, was expanded in 1923 to include a third floor that housed, among other facilities, a "delivery room, an eight bed children's ward, a nurses ward, a ten bed infant ward, a ten bed obstetrical ward, and 17 private beds."[4] It was likely here on the third floor that Gilliam was born. Today, the hospital is 11 stories and operates as Nashville General Hospital, on the grounds of Meharry Medical College, across the street from Fisk University, an Historically Black College founded in 1866.

The Black magazine *Our World* reported in August 1953, as did the

Nashville Tennessean in December 1965, Jim's official name was James Malcolm Gilliam, Sr.[5] while other media outlets printed his middle name as William.[6] His mother, Katherine, however, stated emphatically in 1953, "His name is just James Gilliam."[7] Gilliam's second wife, Edwina, confirmed Jim Gilliam, Jr.'s middle name was, indeed, William.

Jim's grandfather, Tim Gilliam, married Mattie Bender on January 8, 1900 in Gallatin, Tennessee, the county seat in Sumner County, 34 miles northeast of Nashville. The couple had six children, Callie born in 1900, Arthur born in 1904, Samuel born in 1905, William born in 1910, Richard born in 1910, and James, Jim's father, born in 1912. Records also indicate a son, Forster Gilliam, born to Tim and Mattie on June 30, 1907, who passed away on January 26, 1908.[8]

Katherine Duval was born on Cowan Street in East Nashville, just east of the Cumberland River, on May 12, 1911 to parents Edward and Millie Duval.[9] Her birth certificate spelled Katherine with a "C," but most other references had it with a "K." Her father's occupation was listed as "laborer" and her race listed as "colored" on her birth certificate. Within a few years of Katherine's birth, the Duval family moved to 419 Jefferson Street in North Nashville, on the west side of the Cumberland River, according to U.S. Census records from 1920.

Jefferson Street was, and still is, a major connector between North Nashville and East Nashville. A Parker Truss bridge built across the Cumberland River in 1910 joined the two growing Nashville neighborhoods, housing much of the city's Black population.

A marriage license from Davidson County, Tennessee dated July 24, 1928 confirms matrimony between Katherine Duval and James Gilliam. Gilliam was listed as 20 years old, while Duval was 19 on the marriage certificate, but that would appear to be inaccurate on both counts. Katherine's birth certificate indicated she was born May 12, 1911, which would have made her 17 at the time of marriage, and contradicts a later comment from her in which she said she married at the age of 14. James was born in 1912, making him just 16 at the time of marriage. That Katherine would give birth less than three months later suggests a marriage of necessity.

Shortly after Jim was born, his grandfather, Tim Gilliam, died February 8, 1929 at the age of 49. Cause of death was listed as hemorrhoidal hemorrhage due to a rectum injury sustained in a fall.[10] A few months later, Jim's father, James, died at 6 p.m. on June 11, 1929 when Jim was only seven months old. A Tennessee death certificate listed the cause of James Gilliam, Sr.'s death as "acute pulmonary phthisis," more commonly known as pulmonary tuberculosis.[11] James Gilliam, Sr. was just 17 at the time of his passing.

According to a death notice in the *Nashville Tennessean*, James Gilliam, Sr.'s funeral service was held at 1 p.m. on June 14 at First Street Baptist Church in Nashville, with interment following at Greenwood Cemetery. He was survived by his mother, Mattie, sister, Calli Ward, and brothers William, Richard, Arthur, and Daniel, although no birth certificate for Daniel exists. Evidence strongly supports James Gilliam, Sr.'s passing in June 1929 when Jim would have been seven months old. However, as an adult, Jim Gilliam often stated his dad died when he was two, a fact contradicting the death certificate and newspaper obituary. The deaths of Jim's grandfather and father at young ages foretold a common thread among the Gilliam men.

By all accounts, Jim and Katherine went to live with the Duval family following James Sr.'s death. The 1940 Census records list a 28-year-old Katherine Gilliam and a 12-year-old James Gilliam residing at 1008 7th Avenue North, a few blocks from her parents' Jefferson Street residence. Katherine's brother, Leon Duval, was listed as head of household at 7th Avenue North. Leon's occupation was as a gasoline station attendant while Katherine's occupation was as a housekeeper. Three other men were listed as lodgers in the house.

Katherine worked 17 years in a barbecue pit[12] (or as a maid;[13] stories vary as to her occupation), and never remarried. Jim had no brothers or sisters. By the 1950 Census records, 39-year-old Katherine Gilliam was living alone at 311 Madison Street in North Nashville, a few blocks north and east from the 7th Avenue residence. Her brother, Leon, had passed away on September 20, 1948 from an unknown cause, according to a death certificate. He was 38 years old.[14]

The Duval family, including Katherine, were active baseball players. "(Jim) got his ball-playing from my side of the family," Katherine proudly recalled in 1953. "I played on a girl's team myself. I married at 14 and I played baseball right on up to his birth."[15]

In 1953, Gilliam told writer Charles Dexter he grew up "mostly outdoors because my dad died when I was two and my mother had to go out to work and I was living with my grandmother and played a lot on the lots near her house."[16] Which grandmother is not clear, though his paternal grandmother Mattie stated in 1953, "I raised James. He said he was going to be a ball player, and he always did what he said he would."[17]

If Jim was raised by Mattie then one of them would have needed to cross the Cumberland River regularly. Mattie Bender Gilliam was listed as head of 125 Mark Street on the 1940 census, the same address of her parents, Jim and Maggie Bender, in the 1920 census. The 1940 census lists Mattie's son, Richard Gilliam (Jim Sr.'s brother), and her brother, James Bender, as residing there as well. Born in 1910, Richard was working as a laborer when he died of bronchial pneumonia on February 17, 1944 at just 34 years of age.[18]

The house on Mark Street no longer exists, razed in the name of progress, replaced by a new subdivision in east Nashville, between Dickerson Pike and Ellington Parkway, north of Spring Street. A 1908 map from the Nashville Public Library Metro Archives indicates 125 Mark Street—labeled on the map as "Marks"—was just east of the Indiana Lumber Company Yard, a space now occupied by Interstate 24.[19]

Jim's grandmother, Mattie Bender Gilliam, passed away on December 5, 1955 at 533 Ramsey Street in East Nashville at 75 years of age. She was buried in the same Greenwood Cemetery as her husband, James Gilliam Sr.

GROWING UP IN NASHVILLE

Growing up in Depression-era North Nashville in the 1930s and early 1940s, Gilliam lived primarily in a Black neighborhood, playing outdoors with other kids. Beginning when he was seven years old, Gilliam played sandlot baseball at a field on the block where he lived in Nashville, and on one next to the school he attended.[20] He learned to play baseball with a brown stick and a rag ball made by his mother, because he could not play with the local youth baseball league.[21] He also played some sandlot football with other kids in his Black neighborhood, but baseball was his passion, playing "wherever and whenever a group of youngsters of his race could get together with a bat and a ball."[22]

In that way, Gilliam was not much different than other young Black boys in Nashville in the 1930s and 1940s. A future Negro Leagues teammate, Henry Kimbro, also grew up in Nashville, albeit several years earlier than Gilliam. "Every part of Nashville had a park. We played sandlot. Every community had a team and we'd play from one park to another all in the summertime," Kimbro told author Brent Kelley.[23]

Those parks may have included a designated field at Fisk University, the historically Black college in North Nashville, which played against area teams, including Pearl High School. An actual baseball diamond was rare, said Kimbro's daughter, Harriet Kimbro-Hamilton, who has authored two books on her father and Negro League players from Nashville. "They didn't necessarily play, as my father said, in organized ball because you had so many open fields you could play anywhere," she said.[24]

Life in North Nashville with the Duval family was not integrated, but that did not mean families were lacking. "North Nashville was considered the Black downtown. It was a lot more progressive than people think," recalled Kimbro-Hamilton, who grew up in Nashville. "It was a town within a town. Very vibrant with clothing stores and restaurants. You were able to make a good living."[25]

"Although I lived in a Negro neighborhood, I had a lot of contacts with white boys playing ball. There was a barrier—we couldn't go to school or lunch counters together, but on the ball field we were equals," Gilliam wrote in 1964.[26] His interaction with white boys likely occurred while visiting Mattie on integrated Mark Street in East Nashville, though schools were still segregated.

Harold "Buster" Boguskie, who was white and would play more than 1,000 minor-league games in the 1940s and 1950s, played sandlot ball with Gilliam. "Every time I ran into him, whether it was at spring training or later in his career, we'd always stop and talk about the guys we grew up playing baseball with in Nashville," Boguskie told *The Tennessean's* David Climer in 1995.[27]

Gilliam had a one-track mind, focused on baseball. "I never did anything but play baseball, ever since I was knee-high to a duck," Gilliam said in 1956. "Oh, I used to play pool around Nashville and play a little billiards now and then. I read comic books and Westerns, but how're you going to do anything but baseball if that's your life."[28]

"He always was crazy about baseball," his mother, Katherine, recalled. "When he was a little boy he fell out of a tree and broke his wrist. While he had that wrist in a cast, I went out in the yard and caught him batting a tin can."[29]

According to Jim, that accident, which occurred when he was 12, helped him later when he learned how to switch-hit. "They put my right arm in a sling. But I didn't want to give up baseball, so I stood there and swung the bat one-handed, with my left hand. After that, I always knew I could do it."[30]

School was not nearly the priority for Gilliam that baseball was. Baseball provided Gilliam a chance at an education in life. "In our segregated school I had learned to read and write, but not algebra or sciences and all that. Baseball gave me a chance to meet people in life, to know whites in mixed games, boys of my own age and older fellows."[31]

Because this was the period pre-*Brown v. Board of Education*, Jim attended all-Black Ford Greene Elementary School and Washington Junior High in North Nashville, near Fisk University and the Meharry Medical Center where he was born. Gilliam would attend Pearl High School, but not graduate. He played third base on the baseball team and was a star halfback in football, but "football doesn't pay off like baseball. So I gave it up," he said.[32]

School and sports did not leave a ton of free time for Gilliam. "I had one job," Gilliam said in 1953. "I guess I got $19 or $20 a week as a sort of porter in a five-and-ten-cent store in Nashville."[33]

That five-and-ten-cent store was Nashville's now-famous Woolworth store, located at 221 5th Avenue North.[34] More than 15 years after Jim worked there, in 1960, the store would be the site of a key moment in the civil rights movement as area Black college students repeatedly staged nonviolent sit-ins at the lunch counter. The Black students were denied service and arrested when they refused to leave the property. Today, the building is a registered historic site as part of the Fifth Avenue Historic District in Nashville for its role in the civil rights movement.[35] When reporting to work, Gilliam would enter a side door to Woolworth's with a sign overhead that read, "Employees Only." Each day's activities were the same: sweeping the floor and carrying the trash to a dumpster.[36]

While his Woolworth's job paid better, Gilliam's real avocation was playing baseball. "Baseball was the only way to make an honest living. I picked up $5 now and then in sandlot games." Gilliam wrote in 1964. At age 14, during the summer of 1943, he was playing with the Nashville Crawfords,[37] likely a Black sandlot team so named as a way to honor the powerful Pittsburgh Crawfords of the Negro Leagues.

"Paul Jones, a fellow with the Nashville Black Vols, had been watching me for quite a while and offered me $150 a month to join his club," Gilliam said in 1953.[38] He would later claim the salary was $175 per month.[39]

"I didn't need the money. I wanted it," Gilliam said in 1963. "I had got to the 12th grade (sic)—and I did pretty well in school, too. We had what we needed. We ate all right (sic), and I liked school. But I was 16, and I had begun to look at girls. I liked baseball, and I'd been playing on the sand-lots, so when the man asked me to play for his team, it seemed like a good idea."[40]

Jim's mother, Katherine, established some ground rules for allowing Jim to drop out of school. "When he told me he wanted to leave school, he was in the 11th grade. I told him I didn't want him leaving school and running the streets. I said, 'If you join the ball club, you can leave school, but I don't want to see you on the streets.'"[41]

That Gilliam would go on to become a Major League player and four-time World Series champion was not something anyone in 1944 Nashville would have predicted, especially those who played alongside him.

"I don't think anybody would have looked at Junior Gilliam and said, 'There's a superstar in the making,'" Buster Boguskie said in 1978. "He did his job without saying much and you hardly noticed him until the game was over. Then you realized he had a couple of hits and had made the key defensive play."[42]

THE CENTER OF NASHVILLE BASEBALL: SULPHUR DELL

Organized baseball was first played in a downtown area of North Nashville near Fourth and Fifth Avenues as early as 1866, 10 years before the formation of the National League. The site was used by early pioneers to assemble, trade goods, and gather water. Deer and buffalo made the area their home. It was also the site of a sulphur spring, considered useful for medicinal purposes. It would become the future home of a ballpark initially called Sulphur Springs Bottom and, later, simply Sulphur Dell.[43]

With the arrival of the professional Nashville Americans of the Southern League in 1885, renovations to Sulphur Springs Bottom park were needed. At the time, one outfield fence was a reported 362 feet from home plate, while another was 485 feet away.[44] (During the Deadfall Era, home runs were not a major factor anyway, so fence distances were irrelevant.) Beyond right-sizing the fences, an enclosure was built for fans to park their "horses and carriages" along with bathrooms featuring "water possessing excellent quantities for this purpose."[45]

The Sulphur Dell grandstand, with seating for 7,500, was completed before the 1927 season began. The Vols ballclub and ballpark were purchased at the end of the previous season from owners who found they could not maintain the expense of supporting the team. Two of the four new investors co-owned *Southern Lumberman* magazine but, interestingly, they built the new grandstand mostly from steel and concrete. (The biggest threat to ballparks of the era: fire.) The dimensions were quirky: 334 down the left field line, 421 to dead center, and 262 down right. The entire outfield had terraces across the outer perimeter in lieu of a warning track, but the terrace height was most pronounced in right. For example, if the right fielder stood at the base of the fence, his feet were 22 1/2 feet above the playing surface. Other improvements included rooms for players, directors, scorers, and reporters.[46]

Sulphur Dell, 1950s. Courtesy State of Tennessee.

Legendary sportswriter Grantland Rice is acknowledged as the person responsible for shortening the name of Sulphur Springs Bottom park to Sulphur Spring Dell in a 1908 column published in the *Nashville Tennessean* newspaper. Eventually, the name was further truncated to Sulphur Dell.[47] Sulphur Dell was demolished in 1969, but its site is part of the parcel hosting the present-day First Horizon Park, home to the Triple-A Nashville Sounds, currently an affiliate of the Milwaukee Brewers.

The success experienced by the Nashville Americans continued in the early 1900s with the formation of the minor-league Nashville Vols, which competed from 1901 to 1963. Concurrent with that was the growing influence of Black baseball in the segregated south. The architect of the professional Black baseball movement in Nashville for the first half of the 20th century was Tom Wilson, owner of the Nashville Elite Giants, who would "mold Nashville into a mecca for Black baseball by recruiting the best local talent."[48] Negro Leagues stars Henry Kimbro and Thomas "Turkey" Stearnes were both among the Nashville natives who started their careers on Wilson's teams.

Nicknamed "Smiling Tom," Wilson "built his wealth on activities both legal and illegal."[49] He owned the Elite Giants from 1918 to 1947, competing in the Negro Southern League until 1929 when the team joined the Negro National League. The Elite Giants were successful enough to allow Wilson to finance the construction of 8,000-seat Tom Wilson Park in 1928, the first Black-owned ballpark in the South. The ballpark was located along 2nd Avenue South in Nashville's largest Black community—Trimble Bottom, south of downtown Nashville. A double-sided historical marker was erected in 2003 to commemorate both Wilson and the park. It reads, in part, that the "facility was one of two African-American owned professional ballparks" (the other: Pittsburgh's Greenlee Field, home of the Pittsburgh Crawfords and Homestead Grays) and stars like Babe Ruth, Lou Gehrig, and Roy Campanella once played there.

A LAMB ON THE DIAMOND

Young Jim Gilliam had been hanging around Sulphur Dell since the age of eight, serving as the visiting team bat boy until he became too big for the job. The park was no more than four blocks from his house on 7th Avenue North. As he got older he transitioned to the clubhouse. It was in these roles that he first met his future big-league teammate, Roy Campanella, who played for the Elite Giants from 1937-45.

"I've been watching you fielding grounders during batting practice, Junior," Campanella reportedly told him. "You're gonna be a great ballplayer some day."[50] Campanella's quote was attributed in 1953, after Gilliam's nickname of "Junior" was firmly established. No evidence exists to suggest Campanella had any role in bestowing the moniker on him, however. In fact, Gilliam would not receive the nickname until after Campanella had left the Elite Giants following the 1945 season.

Despite proximity to Black stars, Jim's fandom in the mid-1940s, however, was directed not at a Negro Leagues player but at a Major League player. "Roy was great even then. But my hero was Joe DiMaggio. I worshipped that man," said Gilliam, a Yankees fan growing up.[51]

Willie White was the clubhouse manager at Sulphur Dell during this period. Nashville baseball historian Skip Nipper recalled his father, Virgil, who grew up in the area and often made his way to Sulphur Dell to play, telling him, "Willie White is the guy who held the keys to Sulphur Dell. It didn't matter if you were Black, white or purple, he would let you play."[52]

"(Gilliam) was one of my lambs around Sulphur Dell...a bashful fellow," White said in a 1953 article in *The Sporting News*. "He was a member of the Sulphur Dell Giants and we played games when the Vols were on the road. He was a natural from the very start. He was fast and could do everything."[53] White, who reportedly gave Gilliam his first baseball glove and his first pair of baseball spikes,[54] also told Fred Russell of the *Nashville Banner* in 1953, "Gilliam started off as a catcher, but he could run so fast that I changed him to an infielder quick."[55]

When Gilliam passed away in 1978, White told *The Tennessean*'s Jeff Hanna, "All I can tell you about Junior Gilliam, he was one of those youngsters down at Sulphur Dell where Black boys and white boys played together and were friendly. I remember Junior didn't drink or smoke and didn't have any bad habits, except maybe he played some pool."[56]

Jim reconnected with White in December 1965 at "Jim Gilliam Day" in Nashville. Gilliam told Tom Powell, a reporter with the *Nashville Tennessean*, how influential White was to him. "Willie White actually had integration here long before anybody else. Our teams at Sulphur Dell had lots of Negro kids plus white boys like Pinky Lipscomb, Mickey Kreitner, and Buster Boguski (sic)."[57]

It was at Sulphur Dell that Gilliam developed his initial baseball knowledge and work ethic, even as a 14-year-old. Jim was rarely satisfied with his performance unless it was perfect. "The thing that stands out in my mind was that Junior recognized when he was still a youngster that he was not going to be a power hitter," said Mickey Kreitner, a former Nashville Vols player. "So when he was still just a kid, he was choking up on the bat and hitting to right field. Later on, he used that all the time for the Dodgers, hitting behind Maury Wills. He started it right down on Sulphur Dell as a 14-year-old."[58]

Speaking in 1978, Kreitner understood why Gilliam became a successful player and coach. "We had to run him out of the clubhouse at night because I'd show him some little point about his bunting technique and he'd go right out and work on it until it was too dark to see. I can understand why the players on the Dodgers loved him so much."[59]

3

"JUNIOR"

AFTER NEARLY TWO DECADES OF COMPETITION, THE NEGRO SOUTHERN LEAGUE (NSL) ceased to exist in 1937-44 due, in part, to World War II, but also to the formation of the Negro American League (NAL) as a companion to the original Negro National League (NNL). A collective desire of southern Black businessmen, from Little Rock to Atlanta, to resurrect the NSL led to a meeting at the Colored YMCA on 4th Street in Nashville on February 4, 1945.[1]

A month later, representatives from eight teams settled on a schedule in which each team would play 40 games in two halves of a split season, followed by playoffs. The eight teams: the Asheville Blues, Atlanta Black Crackers, Chattanooga Choo-Choos, Knoxville Grays, Little Rock Greys, Mobile Black Bears, Nashville Black Vols, and New Orleans Black Pelicans.

According to William J. Plott, author of the definitive 2015 book, *The Negro Southern League: A Baseball History, 1920-1951*, the NSL "never came close to achieving the status of the NNL....Yet the Negro Southern League made a significant contribution to what is recognized as 'major league' Black baseball. The NSL sent a number of players on to that higher level, drawing them from cotton fields and steel mills alike."[2]

Dr. R. B. Jackson served not only as owner of the Black Vols, but also as the NSL president in 1945. His club, which was renamed the Nashville Cubs for the 1946 season, would function as a minor-league affiliate of sorts with Tom Wilson's Baltimore Elite Giants of the NNL.

And so it was that the 16-year-old high-school dropout Gilliam, educated about baseball at Sulphur Dell, began his professional baseball career in 1945 playing in the resurrected Negro Southern League.

The date for Gilliam's professional debut for the Black Vols is not known. He claimed he played third base in his first game for the Vols at Chattanooga and hit a triple, but few details exist regarding Gilliam and the 1945 Black Vols season.[3] Plott's exhaustive research concluded, "Statistically, there is probably less information available on the 1945 season than any other in the Negro Southern League. No box scores were published, and even line scores were scarce and often incomplete."[4]

Standings published in the *Birmingham News* on July 8, 1945 and included in Plott's book show Atlanta on top of the final first-half standings with a record of 29-9. Nashville placed fifth with a record of 14-16. The Black Vols started the season's second half strong, sitting in first place in early August with a 12-3 record. A series between Atlanta and Nashville at Sulphur Dell during the first weekend of August resulted in Nashville losing every game, all by shutout, and falling to third place. Atlanta would win both halves of the split season, negating the need for a playoff.

Plott did find evidence of a scheduled game between an all-star team of Negro Southern League players and a Birmingham city industrial league team on September 16, 1945. At stake was a possible matchup against the Birmingham Black Barons of the Negro National League should the all-stars win. It is unclear whether the games were played as Plott could not find information regarding an outcome. But he did find the projected starting lineup for the all-stars. Batting second and playing third base was "Jim Gilliam, Nashville."[5]

Still a month shy of his seventeenth birthday, Gilliam was already recognized as a baseball talent. Playing on the Black Vols allowed Gilliam to continue his life education. "The Black Vols traveled as far east as Asheville, North Carolina, so I saw the world, so to speak, and what the segregated South was really like,"[6] Gilliam wrote.

THE FIRST GATE OPENS

Six days after Gilliam turned 17, on October 23, 1945, Jack Roosevelt Robinson walked into the offices of the Montreal Royals in Quebec, Canada. He was joined by the head of the Brooklyn Dodgers' farm system, Branch Rickey Jr., and the president of the Royals, Hector Racine. In those offices, Robinson signed a contract to play for the Royals in 1946. The terms of the contract included a signing bonus of $3,500 and a monthly salary of $600.[7]

For decades, Black baseball players had been forced to stand outside the gate of the Major Leagues. Owners conspired to thwart integration of their teams. As a result, Black baseball flourished as a segregated sport for nearly 30 years. Robinson's signing swung open ever so slightly the gate holding back integration, offering some measure of hope that Black baseball players would be welcomed in "organized" baseball. Robinson had walked through the First Gate.

As he was for many Black youngsters in the era, Robinson became an immediate inspiration for Gilliam, who had already turned his sights to what lay directly ahead. "Before Jackie was signed and made it, the only place for us to go was the Negro National and American Leagues. My aim then was to make the Elite Giants. I knew I was to have the tryout, but I was young. I had a lot to learn about baseball. I wasn't sure I would make the Baltimore team. I didn't have a right to think about any more."[8]

SPRING 1946: A PROMOTION TO BALTIMORE

Spring training for the Baltimore Elite Giants began April 1, 1946 at Sulphur Dell in Gilliam's hometown Nashville. On the day before camp opened, the *Nashville Tennessean* ran a brief story about the Nashville Cubs, previously the Black Vols, beginning practice and indicating "James Gilliam" would be returning to the Nashville team at third base.[9]

Twenty-one players were on the Elites roster as of April 11, with the *Baltimore Evening Sun* reporting "Tommy Butts and Frank Russell have been performing smoothly at shortstop and second base and are expected to open the league season at those posts the first week in May."[10] At just 17 years old, and with established veterans around the Elites infield, Gilliam, should he be called up to the Elites, figured to be nothing more than "organizational depth" for owner Tom Wilson's club.

Jim Gilliam with the Baltimore Elite Giants. Courtesy SABR.

During camp, however, Jim caught the eye of Baltimore's backup first baseman and coach, George Scales. Little did Gilliam know at the time, but the relationship he forged with Scales that spring training would forever change the trajectory of his career. Gilliam learned to switch hit, he was given a nickname, and he acquired a lifelong mentor.

George Walter Scales was born August 16, 1900 in Talladega, Alabama. Throughout the course of his 33 years in the Negro Leagues, Scales played all four infield positions as well as the outfield, and also served as a manager. Scales was a powerful hitter who amassed career statistics of a .312 average with 59 home runs and 502 RBI in 743 games. Bill James ranked Scales as the third-best second baseman in Negro Leagues history in his 2001 *New Bill James Historical Baseball Abstract.* James described Scales as a power hitter who "was both fast and quick, but tended to put on weight (he was called "Tubby")."[11]

Robert Peterson, author of the sensational book, *Only the Ball Was White*, originally published in 1970, contradicted James's assessment of Scales' speed, describing him as a strong hitter and good fielder "who compensated for lack of speed with intelligence and alertness."[12]

Scales, who broke into professional Black ball in 1919 as a member of the Montgomery Grey Sox, shared the field with nearly every great Negro Leagues player. Nominated on the Early Baseball Era Ballot in 2022, Scales received just four of the required 12 votes necessary for the Baseball Hall of Fame.[13]

On April 2, 1938, Scales found himself at Wilson Park in Nashville, site of spring training for the Baltimore Elite Giants, assuming the role of player-manager, following a stint with the New York Black Yankees.[14] After the season, Scales rejoined the Black Yankees as their manager for 1939, while Wilson installed Felton Snow as Elites manager. Scales returned to the Elites as a player just prior to the 1940 season. In a relationship which seems reminiscent to that of George Steinbrenner and Billy Martin in the 1970s, Wilson once again tabbed Scales as player-manager for the Elites for the 1943 season, only to ship him back to the Black Yankees for the 1945 season. Scales returned to Baltimore for the last time prior to the 1946 season, serving as a coach. He managed the Elites in 1947 and 1948 before transitioning to become the team's road secretary for the 1949 season.[15]

By all accounts, Scales was a likeable, successful manager, with decades of experience in the Negro Leagues. Long-time Elite shortstop Tommy "Pee Wee" Butts, a perennial Negro League all-star, recalled Scales' managerial demeanor.

"Scales was a little hard on you, but if you'd listen you could learn a lot. I used to have trouble coming in on slow balls. I'd have to come up to throw. He said, 'No, Pee Wee, that's not the way a good shortstop does.'

He drilled me hard until I finally caught on to it. He hollered, 'There, now you got it.' And it came to me just like that....Scales could get what he needed out of you."[16]

Scales would get plenty out of Gilliam that spring. "Well, it's true, I'm the one gave (sic) Junior Gilliam his chance. I forced them to play him," Scales said. "Gilliam was a kid had (sic) come up from Nashville with the team as a third baseman. The manager had a friend he brought up to play second, but that guy was nothing. So I went to Vernon Green, the owner, and said, 'Make that man put Gilliam on second,' and he did, and that was it."[17] Green, however, did not become the Elites owner until the 1947 season.

The "nothing" player to whom Scales referred presumably was Frank Russell, the player mentioned as the preseason starter in the *Baltimore Evening Sun*. Russell, also a former Black Vol, played second base for the Elite Giants in 1943 and 1944, but shifted to third base in 1946. He hit only .182 in 55 at bats in 1946.

During spring training 1946, Scales was watching the right-handed hitting Gilliam flail at curve balls thrown by right-handed pitchers. "I couldn't do anything with curve-ball pitchers. I figured I'd lay back and wait for the fast ball, but the pitchers in the Negro National League were smarter than me. They just threw me curves,"[18] Gilliam recalled in 1953.

Having seen enough, Scales is purported to have yelled, "Hey, Junior, get over on the other side of the plate."[19] At 45 years old, Scales was old enough to be Gilliam's father, and the nickname fit. His teammates, many of whom were a decade older than Gilliam, adopted it as well, and so the moniker stuck. Jim Gilliam was now Junior Gilliam.

Gilliam's version of the exchange with Scales, however, suggested it was more advice than a command. According to Gilliam, Scales approached him one day and asked, "You ever hit left-handed?"

"When I was a kid," Gilliam replied. "I broke my right arm when I was 12 but I still played with the other fellows. I'd hold my bat in my left arm and the other one, it would be in a cast."

"Then why not try it that way," Scales said. "You're not going any place this way."[20]

"This way" was a reference to being a right-handed-hitting utility man, his likely unofficial position in 1946, his first season with Baltimore. "George told me that if I'd learn to switch-hit, I'd never go through life as a utility man," Gilliam said to Bob Hunter for a 1964 *Sporting News* story.[21] Ironically, Gilliam's Dodger career would be remembered by many as just that—a utilityman, appearing at every position except pitcher, catcher, and shortstop in his 14 seasons with Brooklyn and Los Angeles.

Scales got a pitcher in camp to begin throwing to left-handed-batting Gilliam. "It was awfully awkward at first," Jim said in 1965. "But by the middle of the season I began to feel more at ease. Then I began to see an improvement. It helped me get down to first base better."[22]

If anyone in the Negro Leagues could mentor Gilliam on how to hit a curve ball, it was Scales. Negro League star and Hall of Famer Buck Leonard told John Holway, "That curve ball has sent more youngsters back than any other thing. That's right—that curve ball. George Scales knew how to hit it a T! Josh Gibson knew it to a T. They hit a curve ball farther than they hit a fast ball. I saw George Scales hit a curve ball four miles!"[23]

Scales' tutelage was successful. "When I first got over there I was afraid I couldn't duck," Gilliam remembered. "The first thing a switch-hitter's got to know is to duck. But by the end of 1946 I was making the full switch all the time and I found I was able to follow the curve."[24]

Pee Wee Butts believed Jim was actually a better hitter from the left side than the right. "George Scales is the guy who taught Gilliam all he knew. Gilliam was a right-handed batter, but Scales turned him over to be a switch-hitter. That's how Gilliam evened up his hits. I really think he was a better left-handed batter than he was right. Right-handed he was stronger, but he wouldn't get as many hits. When Scales switched him over, that's when Junior started hitting."[25]

Not much is known about the Elites spring training but the team logged exhibition victories in Birmingham, Knoxville, Asheville, and Statesville.[26] Gilliam impressed enough to be added to the Elites roster, but not in a starting capacity. The team's infield figured to be anchored by Butts at short and Russell at second, sharing time with Clyde Parris. Johnny Washington was a fixture at first. Third base was unsettled with Opening Day starter Manuel Stewart, Russell, and even manager Felton Snow occupying the hot corner.

1946 SEASON: YOUTH IS SERVED

Spring training 1946 had provided Gilliam a nickname and a new hitting approach. Now, if only he could figure out a way to dent the Elite Giants lineup. Complete box scores of Negro Leagues games are difficult to come by, and baseball historians vary in their compilation of individual statistics. The daily *Baltimore Sun* regularly printed line scores of Elite

Giants games during 1946, but full box scores were infrequent. The *Baltimore Evening Sun* often reported projected lineups, but rarely box scores. As a weekly newspaper, the *Baltimore Afro-American* almost never printed box scores of the hometown Negro Leagues team. In fact, its coverage of the Negro Leagues began to wane considerably in 1946 as the *Afro-American* devoted much of its attention on Jackie Robinson and other Black players in the Major Leagues' minor-league system.

Gilliam's only known appearance in the first half of the Negro League season occurred on Sunday, May 26, in a game against the New York Cubans. Clyde Parris, released a week later on June 4, started at second and was 0-for-2. With the Elites down 4-3, Snow sent first-year Puerto Rican Luis "King Kong" Villodas, a catcher, to bat for Parris. Villodas made an out, but the Elites added a run to tie the game at 4-4.

When the Elites took the field for the top of the ninth, Gilliam, according to the box score, was at second base. The Cubans added three runs, the majority off starter Bill Byrd as he was tagged with the loss. Gilliam's roommate, Joe Black, recorded the final three final outs, inducing a 6-4-3 double play, Butts to Gilliam to Luis Enrique "Tite" Figueroa, another rookie from Puerto Rico, who had replaced Washington at first.[27] It would be the first of many such twin-killing hookups for Butts and Gilliam. "They were out of sight as a double play combination," said teammate Lennie Pearson, a member of the 1949 Elite Giants. "Good hands, both of them, and both of them loved the game."[28]

No play-by-play exists for the bottom of the ninth, but the box score lists Gilliam as going 0-for-1. Luis Tiant, Sr., throwing in his 16th season, pitched the ninth inning for the Cubans, so Gilliam's first known NNL at-bat occurred against a three-time Negro League all-star. The box score does not indicate Tiant struck out anyone, thus it is unknown how Gilliam was retired.[29] At the age of 17 years, seven months, and nine days, Gilliam had made his Negro National League professional baseball debut.

In an attempt to settle the infield, and apparently thinking Gilliam was still too young, the Elites turned to two Negro League veterans when they released Parris on June 4, signing Sammy Hughes to play second and Willie Wells to play third. Hughes, recently discharged from the Army, appeared in six Negro League all-star games from 1934-39, all with the Elite Giants.

Wells, who began the 1946 season with the New York Black Yankees, made his rookie debut in 1924 and was now 41 years old. Playing with the St. Louis Stars in 1930, Wells won the Negro National League Triple Crown when he hit .411 with 17 home runs and 114 RBI in 90 games. He also led the league with 112 runs scored, 34 doubles, and 18 stolen bases. The two players provided needed stability and offense throughout the rest of the season.

At his peak, Hughes was one of the Negro Leagues' premier second basemen. Bill James had him ranked fourth, right after Scales, in his list of all-time Negro League second basemen, comparing him to Cubs Hall of Famer Ryne Sandberg.[30] He was recognized as "a good hitter, crack fielder, and real baserunner."[31] But, at age 35, Hughes had begun to slow when he joined Baltimore. He hit just .252 with only six extra base hits in 42 games.[32] Hughes retired at the end of the 1946 season.

Even older at 41 (he turned 42 in August 1946), Wells had a reputation as one of the finest infielders in Negro League history. James ranked him second overall at shortstop, commenting he "did everything outstanding except throw."[33] Peterson noted in his book, "Wells used his speed, good hands, and an accurate though not strong arm to achieve preeminence as a shortstop."[34] Moved to third base in 1946 with Baltimore, Wells turned in a remarkable offensive year for the Elites, hitting .325 with 42 RBI in 53 games as a 40-year-old.[35] He was elected to the Baseball Hall of Fame in 1997.

On Friday June 14, the *Baltimore Evening Sun,* as it often did, printed projected lineups for that evening's Elites game, this one at Bugle Field against the Homestead Grays. For the first time all season, Gilliam was listed, though not as a starter, but rather with "ut." after his name indicating utility.[36] He also appeared as "ut." in the projected lineup for the June 18 game against the New York Cubans. That his name continued to appear indicated that his confidence was improving and Snow's faith in him was increasing.

Baltimore finished the 1946 season's first half with a record of 14-17, placing it fifth out of six teams. Only the lowly New York Black Yankees, with their woeful 3-24 mark, saved the Elites from the basement.[37] Gilliam's name was absent from all of the available box scores from the first half of the season, so as the second half began, he could not have anticipated much playing time, despite appearing in projected lineups as a utility player. A five-paragraph story, a lengthy one by *Baltimore Sun* standards, previewed the Elites second half but did not mention Gilliam.[38] Thanks to the additions of Hughes and Wells, optimism abounded for the second half.

Indeed, the Elites' hopefulness was rewarded as the team jumped out to a fast start in the second half, opening with a 4-1 record to occupy first place in the NNL. The team was paced by centerfielder Henry Kimbro, hitting in the third spot and batting .366. Butts occupied the two hole, sporting a .313 average. Mid-season signee Wells was batting .344 in the cleanup spot.[39]

Finally, according to the July 17, 1946 *Baltimore Evening Sun*, Gilliam cracked the starting nine when the Elites hosted the New York Cubans at Bugle Field on Tuesday, July 16. Lining up at second base and batting eighth with his friend and roommate Joe Black on the hill against the Cubans, Gilliam's official line was 0-for-3 with a sacrifice against Cubans pitcher Dave Barnhill.[40] The Elites won the game 5-3, their seventh straight victory. Defensively, the box score revealed another 6-4-3 double play, this time Butts to Gilliam to Washington.

Although his name resurfaced in the *Baltimore Evening Sun* as a utility player in early August, Gilliam's name would not appear again in a box score until Sunday, August 18 when the Elites swept the Newark Eagles in a doubleheader, 7-3 and 7-1, in front of 3,000 at the Bloomingdale Oval in West Baltimore, the site on which current Leon Day Park exists. The park was dedicated in 1997 for the Baltimore resident and Negro League legend, Leon Day, who died six days after his induction into the National Baseball Hall of Fame in 1995.[41]

In the first game, the only one for which a box score exists, the Eagles gave their double play combination of future Hall of Famers Larry Doby and Monte Irvin the day off.[42] Starting at shortstop to spell Butts, Gilliam went 1-for-3 with a double and a run scored. His double came off Charles England, who surrendered all 12 hits to the Elites in 7.2 innings that day. England's entire Negro League career consisted of two starts, in which he allowed 17 hits and 13 runs in 9.2 innings.[43]

As the 1946 season continued, it was clear the 35-year-old Hughes was wearing down. His time in the Army had taken a toll, creating a dilemma for Snow, Scales, and owner Wilson. Scales approached Gilliam with an idea of focusing only on second base, rather than utility. "We got to have a second baseman to go with Butts," Scales said. "Sammy was all right (sic), but the Army took it out of his legs. He can't get around. You try it, Junior."[44]

Butts told John Holway, "(Gilliam) really liked third base, but George Scales said, 'No, you'd make a better second baseman.' And I think he did. They said he had a weak arm, but he really could get rid of the ball and make those double plays. He wouldn't stumble over the bag. Sometimes I'd say he wouldn't even touch it."[45]

Jim quickly became a fixture in the Elites lineup at second base, officially replacing Hughes, who retired at season's end. Gilliam started at second on August 27 against the Cubans, batting second, a spot in the order that would become quite familiar to him over his career. He went 2-for-5, batting against Tiant again.[46] A week later, Gilliam posted a 2-for-4 performance with a triple and RBI on September 2 in a 6-1 loss to the Homestead Grays, featuring Negro League legends Josh Gibson, Buck Leonard, and James "Cool Papa" Bell.

The highlight of 1946 for Gilliam occurred on September 13 as the Elites downed the Cincinnati Clowns of the Negro American League, 10-6. The *Baltimore Sun* wrote the next day that "Johnny Washington, Junior Gilliam, and Hem (sic) Kimbro were the big guns for the victors."[47] Gilliam went 4-for-5 with a double, stolen base, and two runs scored in front of 1,600 fans at Bugle Field. The reference to "Junior" in the September 14, 1946 *Baltimore Sun* article is the first known appearance in print of the nickname Scales bestowed upon Gilliam.

A BASEBALL EDUCATION

After their hot start to the second half, the Elites scuffled and finished in third place in the NNL. The Newark Eagles closed on a 15-2 run to win both the first- and second-half pennants. Baltimore ended the second half in third place with a 14-14 mark. Combined, the Elites won 28 and lost 31 in 1946.[48]

As the 1946 Negro Leagues season wound down, the Elites renewed an annual series of home games against local all-stars, comprised mostly of Baltimore Orioles, the Triple-A affiliate of the Philadelphia Phillies. In its series preview on September 22, the *Baltimore Sun* did not list Gilliam among the Elite players, although he would be a starter.[49]

The Elites would win the series, five games to four. Future Dodgers Roy Campanella and Don Newcombe had been brought in to supplement the Elites roster. Gilliam played second base most of the series, but struggled offensively. A week later the Elites played a twinbill against the Sherry Robertson All-Stars, a barnstorming team fronted by the utility player for the Washington Senators and featuring future Hall of Famer Early Wynn. Baltimore handily won the first game, played on Sunday, October 13 at Bugle Field, 11-2, while notching 15 hits. The nightcap, started by Wynn, ended in a 2-2 tie. While no box score of the game was available, it is safe to assume based on Gilliam's playing time in the All-Stars series earlier in the month, it is likely he batted at least once against Wynn.

Four days after the end of the season on October 17, 1946, Gilliam turned 18. He had batted .292 in 48 at bats with the Giants. With two seasons of professional baseball behind him, Gilliam would likely have been enthused about the 1947 season for several reasons. He seemed to have developed a rapport with Butts, which would lead to the pair being considered the Negro Leagues' premier double-play combination. Luke concluded in his book on the Elite Giants, "Other than Gilliam's and Butts's performance, neither the Elites as a team nor any individual players had much to cheer about" at the end of the 1946 season.[50]

Gilliam's education in baseball had continued on a team featuring some of the great Black players of all time who never had a shot at the Major Leagues. In hindsight, it is amazing to consider the 1946 Baltimore Elite Giants featured Pee Wee Butts, Willie Wells, Sammy Hughes, and Henry Kimbro, plus George Scales in a nonplaying role. In their prime, those five players were all talented enough to play Major League baseball. Gilliam had been mentored by some of the game's finest players, all denied an opportunity to play against whites.

JACKIE ROBINSON COMES TO TOWN

According to Bob Luke's well-researched 2010 book *The Baltimore Elite Giants*, barely 2,500 fans were in the stands "on a chilly Saturday night to see Jackie Robinson's initial game in Baltimore as minor leaguer" as the Montreal Royals played their first game against the Baltimore Orioles on April 27, 1946.[51] However, 10 times that, 25,306, showed up the next day to see Robinson and Royals pitcher John Wright, a veteran of the Homestead Grays, play in a doubleheader.[52]

It is not likely Jim Gilliam or any Elite players attended the game. The *Baltimore Evening Sun* reported on April 30 the Elite Giants would return from spring training in Nashville that day to prepare to open their season on Sunday, May 5.[53] The next time Montreal would visit Baltimore was June 6-8, but Robinson only appeared in part of one game due to a nagging leg injury. The Elites were in town, playing two games against the Philadelphia Stars on June 9, leaving open the possibility that players were spectators for one of the games.

Negro League baseball was to be forever changed the next year. On April 15, 1947, a Black man started at first base for the Brooklyn Dodgers in Major League Baseball, officially opening the First Gate of integration. Over the next several years, Major League owners raided the Negro Leagues of talent, often providing little-to-no compensation to Negro League owners. Spectators now had a choice: watch Black stars in the

Majors or attend Negro League games, and they increasingly chose the former. Even the Black press directed their attention more to Robinson and other Black Major Leaguers than to the Negro Leagues. Gilliam's baseball education was being shaped by men who never had the chance to play in the majors, while a future teammate and roommate whom he did not yet know was breaking down a gate.

4

BLACK BASEBALL

IN JANUARY 1947, TOM WILSON WAS REMOVED AS NEGRO NATIONAL LEAGUE (NNL) president, a role he had held since 1936, after his fellow owners determined a clear conflict of interest existed by having a league president who was also a team owner.[1] Columbia University graduate Reverend John Howard Johnson was voted president, and he immediately began to advocate for standardized contracts, balanced schedules, a revised constitution, and an affiliation with the Major Leagues.[2] Two months later, Wilson sold longtime partner Vernon Green a half-interest in the Baltimore Elite Giants in March 1947. Shortly after the season began, on May 17, 1947, Wilson died of a heart attack at age 61. Wilson's son, Tom Jr., sold the remaining half of the Baltimore club to Green, who promptly removed manager Wes Barrow in favor of Felton Snow, Elite Giants manager the previous two seasons. For the first time in a quarter century, the Elite Giants franchise would operate under different ownership.

Previewing the 1947 Elite Giants season, the *Baltimore Evening Sun* reported "Junior Gilliam, second-base understudy last season, has won a starting job this season."[3] Gilliam wore uniform number 18, the same as his age, and batted eighth in the lineup. By June 20, however, he had moved up to second, behind speedy outfielder Henry Kimbro and ahead of Pee Wee Butts. He was not yet, however, a recognizable name. The *Baltimore Afro-American* frequently spelled his name "Gillam."

The Elites finished 41-40 with two ties, good for third place behind the Newark Eagles and the New York Cubans. A young Gilliam hit .257 in everyday duty in 59 games. His 26 walks tied Henry Kimbro for the team lead, quite an accomplishment for a young and eager 18-year-old player. While his offensive numbers did not cause heads to turn, he did get noticed for his defense and his speed. Sam Lacy wrote in the *Baltimore Afro-American* he believed Gilliam was the fastest Elite player in circling the bases, quicker than Butch Davis or Kimbro.[4]

Bob Luke, author of the definitive book on the history of the Baltimore Elite Giants, noted, "Wilson's death left the Elites without the guidance of the man who had founded the original team, in Nashville in 1921; but their play on the field improved over that of recent years, and many thought the team was poised for a stellar year in 1948."[5]

LIFE IN THE NEGRO LEAGUES

To suggest that a baseball life in the Negro Leagues was challenging would be a gross understatement. Jim Crow dominated the South in the late 1940s. Teams traveled primarily by bus, slept in segregated hotels or in the bus when a hotel could not be located, and ate second-rate food, when they could find a lunch counter to serve them. In addition to regular league games, teams often played exhibitions in towns along the way to the next city.

Roy Campanella made his Negro League debut in 1937 as a 15-year-old and played with the Baltimore Elite Giants franchise from 1937-45. He recalled the days on the road in his autobiography, *It's Good to be Alive*, "Rarely were we ever in the same city two days in a row. Mostly we played by day and traveled by night; sometimes we played both day and night and usually in two different cities. We traveled in a big bus and many's the time we never even bothered to take off our uniforms going from one place to another. We'd pile into the bus after the game, break open boxes of sandwiches and finish the meal with some hot coffee as we headed for the next town and the next game. The bus was our home, dressing room, dining room, and hotel."[6]

As James Hirsch described in his 2010 biography of Willie Mays, who played for the Birmingham Black Barons in 1948-50, "Cross-country bus rides became part of the romantic lore of the Negro Leagues, a celebration of male bonding and roadside adventure that satisfied the wanderlust of any ballplayer. But the rides were also grueling marathons marked by cheap hotels, lousy food, and--particularly in the South—racial indignities."[7]

While Campanella and Mays both had the opportunity to travel as major leaguers in comfy Pullman train cars and, later, by airplane, scores of Negro League stars never had that opportunity. The bus was the only home they knew.

"We had the same problems, just like everybody else had," Henry Kimbro, Elite Giants star and Gilliam teammate, said. "Traveling conditions wasn't exactly good. We played a [Sunday] doubleheader in New Orleans and the next game was on Tuesday night in Baltimore. We got there that morning about one or two o'clock, somewhere along in there. In the meantime, we had to ride, eat, and everything. We'd stop in the grocery store and eat—buy food. You couldn't go in no restaurant or nothing. People wouldn't let you in a restaurant, so we'd stop and buy cold cuts in the store, put in the bus, ride that night, eat, get to where we were going the next day."[8]

Cities like Philadelphia and New York had hotels where the Elites could stay, but in other towns the team bus became the hotel. "We'd get on that bus and let that seat back," Kimbro said. "They bought a 40-something-thousand-dollar bus."[9]

Life on the road did not seem to bother Gilliam. In fact, throughout the years that followed, Gilliam always spoke fondly of the Negro Leagues experience. Speaking to Dodgers announcer Vin Scully on a 1966 record distributed by Union 76 as a promotional giveaway, Gilliam recalled, "In the Negro Leagues you had to travel a lot by bus. You got some eating money, about two dollars a day. Eating expenses weren't that high. One thing I'd say is it taught you how to play baseball."[10]

1948 SEASON: ALL-STAR RECOGNITION

Fifteen games into the 1948 season, Gilliam was batting .331. His evolution as a hitter was likely aided by his teammate and fellow Nashville native, Henry Kimbro. The combination of Kimbro, Gilliam, and Pee Wee Butts formed a potent top third of the order in 1948. Kimbro led the club with 54 runs scored, followed closely by Gilliam's 48, and 44 from Butts. Kimbro also led with 59 walks in 59 games, with Gilliam second on the club with 35 free passes.

Gilliam and Kimbro had a lot in common. Both grew up in Nashville. Neither finished school, although Kimbro only made it through sixth grade, while Gilliam went through 11th grade. Both lacked a father growing up.

"I talked to my dad about those that went on to do great things and he told me that Gilliam was raw talent. Came to the team with great talent, but raw talent," said Kimbro's daughter, Harriet Kimbro-Hamilton. "Individually he was a more standbackish-type person. People that tend to not have great confidence in themselves usually stand in the background. And my dad was one of them because he felt like he needed more education than the sixth grade. I think he identified with Gilliam in that his education wasn't complete either."

While George Scales was influential in Gilliam's early development, Kimbro influenced and refined Gilliam's approach at the plate. "Henry was a great leadoff man for the Elite Giants. He told me the one thing I must learn was the strike zone. He wouldn't swing at a ball an inch off the plate," Gilliam recalled in 1964.[11]

"I know my father was very good at trying to tell people to wait for their pitch. Wait for your pitch. My father loved being lead off. He could not stand being two, three or clean up. His job was to get on base," Kimbro-Hamilton said.

Indeed, the tendencies of Gilliam as a hitter throughout his career—patience, speed, drawing walks, and hitting behind runners—mirror Kimbro's reputation at the plate. Another Nashville native and Elite Giant teammate, Butch McCord, said of Kimbro, "I never saw him swing at the first pitch."[12]

As a team, Baltimore won the NNL first-half pennant but narrowly lost the second half to the Homestead Grays, setting up a championship series. In his book on the history of the Elite Giants, Bob Luke described the bizarre sequence of events awarding the title to the Grays. Homestead won the first two games, and the teams were tied 4-4 in Game Three when the game was declared a tie after it passed the Baltimore city curfew of 11:15 p.m. on a Friday night. Baltimore won the fourth game but after the game, NNL President Rev. John H. Johnson ruled the chief umpire in Friday's game had erred and the ninth inning, which had begun prior to the curfew, should have been completed.

Baltimore had deliberately stalled in the ninth inning hoping for a tie. Johnson ruled the stalling "was unsportsmanlike and therefore grounds for the game to be forfeited to the Grays, 9–0. His decision gave the pennant to the Grays."[13]

EAST-WEST ALL-STAR GAME

Negro League historian Larry Lester wrote the East-West All-Star Game represented an opportunity for high-quality Black baseball to be shared with all Americans.

"With Black league play normally ignored by the white press, the East-West attraction offered an excuse for white America to see Black baseball's best performers under one tent. Except for a radio broadcast of a Joe Louis fight, this game was the biggest sporting event in Black America."[14]

Baltimore Afro-American writer Sam Lacy told Larry Lester in 2001, "It was a holiday for at least 48 hours. People would just about come from everywhere, mainly because it was such a spectacle. It was better than our present all-star game because the interest was focused purely on Black folks. Train, bus, automobile, very little flying, somehow fans managed to get there. I would go on my vacation during all-star week so that I could be there the entire week. I didn't want to miss anything!"[15]

Eastern All-Stars, 1948 Negro Leagues East–West All-Star Game, Comiskey Park, Chicago. Front row: Buck Leonard, Bob Harvey, Marvin Barker, Frank Austin, Pee Wee Butts, Minnie Miñoso, Luis Márquez, Lou Louden, Bob Romby, Jim Gilliam. Back row: Lester Lockett, Monte Irvin, Rufus Lewis, Henry Miller, Luke Easter, Bob Griffith, Pat Scantlebury, Wilmer Fields, Bill Cash, Vic Harris, and manager José María Fernández. Via Wikimedia Commons.

In 1948, the East-West Game was a two-game series, with Game One played at Comiskey Park on August 22. Gilliam and his Elite teammate Pee Wee Butts formed the middle infield combination for the East, a team featuring Buck Leonard and Luke Easter of the Homestead Grays, Monte Irvin of the Newark Eagles, and Minnie Miñoso of the New York Cubans. In total, 14 future Major League players appeared in the 1948 East-West All-Star Game, the most in the game's history. Gilliam was installed in the sixth spot in the order and strode to the plate against pitcher Bill Powell of the Birmingham Black Barons. Powell, already 29 years old but only in his third Negro League season due to World War II service, spent 10 years in Minor League baseball with five organizations but never appeared in the big leagues.[16]

With the West already holding a 2-0 lead in the bottom of the second, Gilliam's instincts figured into an unusual double play. Powell hit a ground ball to Gilliam with runners on second and third. Reports in the *Pittsburgh Courier* and *Chicago Defender* vary as to the exact sequence of events, with the *Courier* reporting that rather than concede the run, Gilliam threw home to catcher Bill Cash, who caught Neil Robinson in a rundown between home and third. Cash fired to Miñoso at third, who tagged out Robinson as well as Quincy Trouppe, who was caught between second and third.[17] The *Defender* reported the sequence as Gilliam to catcher Louis Louden (likely correct), who tagged Robinson and threw to Gilliam, who threw to Miñoso to retire Trouppe.[18] Whatever the sequence, it was a rare double play involving only the second baseman, catcher, and third baseman.

Offensively, Gilliam went 1-for-3 at the plate as the West won 3-0 in front of 42,099, 10,000 fewer spectators than had watched Satchel Paige nine days earlier shut down the Chicago White Sox as a member of the Cleveland Indians.[19]

Two days later, the All-Star Game spectacle moved east to Yankee Stadium in New York for a rematch in front of a much smaller crowd, reported at 17,928. Declining attendance at the Negro Leagues' signature event was an ominous sign for the future of Black baseball.

Once again, Gilliam played second and hit sixth for the East squad, which avenged the loss two nights previously by winning, 6-1. With the East already holding a 4-1 edge in the bottom of the eighth inning, George Crowe of the New York Black Yankees and Gilliam singled. Both would score on Cleveland Buckeyes third baseman Leon Kellman's error, cementing the East victory. Baltimore teammate Joe Black earned the save with three shutout innings.

Gilliam again finished 1-3 at the plate but this time with a run scored and a stolen base. It was, however, another defensive play that caught the attention of the media. Writing in the *New York Amsterdam News*, Swig Garlington observed, "But the play of the night was may (sic) by Gilliam, who made a backhand stop of a drive and started a double play in the fifth to cut down any idea of a threat the visitors might have had."[20]

"PEE WEE" BUTTS

Still a 19-year-old, Gilliam was making a name for himself as a standout ballplayer by the end of the 1948 season, not only with his defensive ability in the East-West games, but by batting .289 with 48 runs scored in 58 games for the Elites. The long hours on the road afforded Gilliam an opportunity to bond with his double-play partner, Tommy "Pee Wee" Butts. The two developed a close friendship, one resembling a big brother-type relationship. Just as George Scales is credited with teaching Jim to switch-hit and Kimbro influenced his approach at the place, it was Butts's mentorship that molded Gilliam into an above average fielder.

Butts was born August 27, 1919 in Sparta, Georgia, making him nearly a decade older than Gilliam. Like Gilliam, Butts dropped out of high school to play professional baseball, joining the Atlanta Black Crackers in 1936 before jumping to the Elite Giants in 1939. Butts's arrival coincided with the Giants winning the 1939 Negro National League championship on a team managed by Felton Snow. Throughout the 1940s, Butts anchored a Baltimore infield that included George Scales or Red Moore at first base, manager Snow at third, and second basemen Sammy Hughes and Frank Russell. Roy Campanella handled the catching duties behind the plate. This core group constantly competed against a standout Homestead Grays squad in the 1940s. The Grays dominated the NNL, winning the league championship every year from 1937-45 except 1939. The Homestead squads had several future Hall of Famers, including Cool Papa Bell, Josh Gibson, Ray Brown, and Buck Leonard.

Campanella served as Butts's roommate for six years, as Elites owner Tom Wilson deliberately paired the two teenagers. Campanella was 17-years-old during the 1939 season, while Butts was 19 at the beginning of the season. The two young personalities did not initially get along, with the quiet Butts finding Campanella's talkative ways disruptive.[21] "He'd say, 'Come on, Pee Wee, let's talk about this,'" Butts recalled. "I'd say, 'Okay, go ahead,' and he would talk me to sleep."[22]

Eventually, Butts and Campanella developed a lifelong friendship, with Butts giving the younger catcher the nickname "Pooch." Campanella was effusive in his praise for Butts, "I'd compare Butts with (Pee Wee) Reese or (Phil) Rizzuto or anyone I've seen in the big leagues. Butts could do everything. He just didn't get the opportunity to go to the majors."[23]

Butts recalled visiting Campanella after the catcher's car accident left him paralyzed. "'Well, Pee Wee, I guess I'll be in this wheelchair the rest of my life.' I could feel the wetness in my eyes. I said, 'Aw, Pooch, you'll walk again.' He said, 'No, Pee Wee, I don't think I will.'"[24]

As might be guessed, Butts earned his nickname as the result of his stature, five-foot-nine and 145 pounds. As such, he was never considered a power hitter, known much more for his fielding than his hitting. "What a fielder," Kansas City Monarchs shortstop Othello Renfroe said. "Nothing flashy, he just made the plays, he'd just get you at first. Everything two hands, everything cool. Down in Cuba and Puerto Rico they called him Cool Breeze."[25] He was ranked by Bill James in his *The New Bill James Historical Baseball Abstract* as the sixth-best shortstop in Negro League history: "He was a decent hitter with some pop, probably as good a player as Gilliam."[26]

Baltimore Afro-American sportswriter Sam Lacy highlighted the burgeoning friendship between Butts and Gilliam in a September 4, 1948 article. "Pee Wee's readiness in offering suggestions to the ambitious Junior and the latter's willing to listen and profit by the criticisms have been responsible for the development of a close friendship between the two," Lacy wrote.[27]

The article included several pictures, showing Gilliam and Butts eating together, as they frequently did before for a game, and sitting next to one another on the team bus, with George Scales looking on from the row behind them.[28]

"The kid's a comer," Butts told Lacy about Gilliam. "For a long time (with the slower moving Sammy Hughes and Harry Williams, Gilliam's predecessors), I had to go to the other side of the bag a lot to help out. But with Junior, I don't have to worry about his side of second. I just take care of my territory. He's got good hands and learns fast. And once you tell him something, you can forget about; (sic) he never does."[29]

The two players complemented one another nicely and developed a rapport on the field. "I don't know how to explain, but when a ball comes to me, I just seem to know where Pee Wee is and do what is natural. I don't have to look for him," Gilliam remarked.[30]

Years later, Butts recalled, "We got to be pretty good together. I think Gilliam was better than Hughes. Sam was tall, and a taller man playing with a short one don't go together. Hughes would throw a little high to you, but Gilliam would keep it down. That's the way you make double plays. We got to know each other pretty well and that made it a lot better."[31]

Time, however, was not on Butts's side. He had turned 29 in August 1948. Meanwhile, Lacy speculated that Gilliam's time with the Elite Giants was limited with several Major League clubs showing interest in him.

"There is little doubt in the mind of this writer that, had he been fortunate to (sic) enough to possess about 10 more pounds, Butts would have been one of the first NNL players sought by the major league outfit," Lacy wrote. "But with only 146 pounds on his frame—wringing wet—Butts is much too small to serve efficiently as a major league shortstop. This, to the writer's way of thinking and this alone has kept him from being a big league player today. Judging by present standards, it would be this scribe's view that the Gilliam-Butts combination could demand a $100,000 price tag on the majors' market."[32]

Unfortunately, there were no Major League buyers at that price, or any other, in 1948, nor would there ever be a buyer for Butts. Gilliam's suitors were still more than a year away. "I don't know what kind of credit Junior Gilliam might give anybody, but Butts worked with him just like he was his own son and developed him into one of the top infielders of the Negro National League," Renfroe said.[33]

PUERTO RICO: INTERNATIONAL PLAY

Gilliam's mentor from the 1946 Elite Giants, George Scales, had been playing baseball in Puerto Rico during the offseason for years and, during the winter of 1948, he helped convince his protege to pursue the path similar to many other Negro Leaguers. Gilliam initially joined the Almendares Scorpions in the Cuban league, where he played before joining the Aguadilla Sharks in Puerto Rico. Puerto Rican baseball scholar Tom Van Hyning noted the Puerto Rican season began eight days after the Cuban season, on October 16, 1948, helping explain the switch.[34]

Two of Gilliam's Aguadilla teammates would be future Dodger teammates as well, third baseman Don Hoak and catcher Dixie Howell. It was, however, the presence of several Negro League players that aided Gilliam's transition to the island. In particular, the duo of Willard Brown from the Kansas City Monarchs and Bob Thurman of the Homestead Grays impacted Gilliam's career in subsequent winter seasons. Jim batted .273 in 161 at bats for the Sharks, who finished fifth out of six teams with a record of 32-48. Joe Buzas, a middle infielder who played in 30 games for the New York Yankees in 1945, became Aguadilla's manager midway through the season and was immediately impressed with the young Gilliam.

"You could tell Gilliam was special," Buzas would say years later. "He studied the game; asked questions; was very polite, yet determined. I had managed Artie Wilson with Mayagüez, in 1947-48, and Fernando Díaz Pedroso, with San Juan, 1949-50. But Gilliam had something extra as a 20-year-old...he was headed for greatness in the 1950s and beyond."[35]

Although Gilliam had played with white kids on the sandlots of Nashville, his Aguadilla experience represented the first time in Gilliam's professional career in which he played alongside white teammates or had a white manager.

DECLINE OF BLACK BASEBALL?

The institution that was Black baseball began to see cracks in its foundation almost immediately after Jackie Robinson debuted with the Dodgers on April 15, 1947. The Cleveland Indians signed Larry Doby of the Newark Eagles, while Hank Thompson and Willard Brown both enjoyed brief stints with the St. Louis Browns. Prominent Negro Leaguers Roy Campanella and Satchel Paige made their debuts in 1948 with the Brooklyn Dodgers and Cleveland Indians, respectively. Black ballplayers were increasingly being given an opportunity to play in the Major Leagues, providing hope and inspiration to young Black stars, facts not lost on Gilliam.

"Before Jackie was signed and made it, the only place for us to go was the Negro National and American Leagues," Jim said in 1953. "Now every kid can think as big as he wants. All he's got to do is play that big and his dreams can come true."[36]

The first fissures in the facade of the Negro Leagues were pointed out by one of the institution's biggest supporters. Writing in a January 1948 column, sportswriter Dan Burley of the *New York Amsterdam News* decried the Negro Leagues' "lack of organization, exhibitions mixed in with regular league games, failure to keep the public informed as to what's going on, diffident attitudes towards such highly important programs as building future fans from kids. The way things look, Negro baseball will make the same mistakes of the head in 1948 because the newspapers haven't heard a thing from its various officials since the end of the 1947 season. Newspapers are the vehicles in which they get their publicity. If we don't know what is going on, how is the paying public to know?"[37]

In some ways, Burley's thesis at the beginning of 1948 was misguided. The "withering" of Negro baseball could be viewed from multiple lenses. After Jackie Robinson broke the color line in 1947, clubs like the Dodgers, Indians, and Browns began raiding the Negro Leagues of talent, often doing so for little or no compensation to Black owners. A few months later, Robinson publicly critiqued Black baseball in a three-page bylined article in the June 1948 *Ebony* magazine titled, "What's Wrong with Negro Baseball." In Robinson's view, his five months playing in the Negro Leagues led him to the conclusion, "the game needs a housecleaning from top to bottom."[38] Specifically, he called out low player salaries, inconsistent umpiring, and questionable business relationships of team owners.

Historian Neil Lanctot drew parallels between Robinson's comments and criticisms Dodgers General Manager Branch Rickey had voiced three years earlier when Brooklyn signed Robinson in August 1945. "Viewed from the comfortable perspective of the major leagues, the country's most prosperous professional sports organization, Black baseball was clearly heavily flawed....Yet both Rickey and Robinson demonstrated little sympathy for the previous decades of struggle to establish the industry and largely failed to acknowledge the impact of inadequate financing and revenue. Like most African American businesses, Black baseball had long faced the fundamental problem of catering to a limited and impoverished customer base."[39]

One of the biggest emerging issues for financially challenged Negro League owners was compensation for players. Before Robinson had played a game in the Dodgers organization, Rickey struck deals for two other Negro League players in April 1946: Don Newcombe of the Newark Eagles and the Elite Giants star catcher Roy Campanella. Rickey's compensation to Baltimore for Campanella was the same as his offer to the Monarchs for Robinson: nothing. While Elite Giants owner Tom Wilson let the issue pass, some Negro League team owners voiced displeasure with the practice of signing their players without compensation. On the one hand, owners wanted to see Black players succeed in the majors. But on the other hand, the owners felt entitled to some remuneration for the players showcased for Major League scouts.

As Black players experienced success in the Major Leagues, the Black press—which had covered Negro League baseball for many years—began to devote precious column inches to the exploits of Black stars in the Major Leagues, leaving little space for Negro Leagues coverage. In that sense, Burley's claim in January 1948 that newspapers were the conduit to publicity can appear hypocritical. Simultaneous to this, attendance at Negro League games began to suffer, further eroding owner revenues. In order to stay financially solvent, Negro League owners were increasingly open to selling players in an attempt to cover for decreasing gate receipts. Future Major League players like Sam Jethroe and Al Smith of the Cleveland Buckeyes, as well as Minnie Miñoso and José Santiago of the New York Cubans, were all sold during the 1948 season, prompting Lanctot to conclude, "player sales to Organized Baseball provided the only positive financial development in either" the Negro National League or the Negro American League.[40]

When the Homestead Grays defeated the Birmingham Black Barons four games to one in the 1948 Negro World Series, it marked the end of a seven-year run of competition between two leagues. Facing uncertainty and financial challenges, the Negro National League ceased operations after the 1948 season with four clubs—the Baltimore Elite Giants, the New York Cubans, the Philadelphia Stars, and the Houston Eagles—joining the Birmingham Black Barons, Chicago American Giants, Indianapolis Clowns, Kansas City Monarchs, Louisville Buckeyes, and Memphis Red Sox to form a new ten-franchise Negro American League divided into East and West divisions. The Elites were placed in the East with the Cubans, Clowns, Stars, and Buckeyes.

Despite the uneasiness beginning to form around the long-term viability of the Negro Leagues, Gilliam had to feel optimistic. He had made the Negro Leagues East-West All-Star game in 1948, impressed in winter ball, and developed a reputation as a solid defender. Plus, with Major League teams increasingly purchasing Black players, Gilliam, at just 18 years old, seemed to have a real shot at following in the footsteps of Jackie Robinson, Roy Campanella, and others.

1949 SEASON: MORE RECOGNITION

Gilliam was the first member of the Elite Giants to sign a contract for the 1949 season, doing so at the home of owner Vernon Green on Tuesday, February 22, 1949.[41] However, like the team's previous owner, Tom Wilson, Green also passed away during a season, succumbing to a heart condition on May 29, 1949. Ownership was passed to Green's wife, Henryene, the third owner in four years, who appointed Richard Powell vice president and general manager.[42] In subsequent years, Powell would play a pivotal role in selling off the team's best players in an effort to remain financially solvent.

Prior to his passing, Green sought to strengthen his club by acquiring more Negro League veterans for the Elites roster. Baltimore resident Leon Day took over in center field, bumping Henry Kimbro from center to right and Lester Lockett remaining in left field. Green also added Lennie Pearson at first base and Henry Baylis at third. The *Baltimore Afro-American* predicted those two combined with Butts and Gilliam gave the Elites their best infield since the 1939 NNL championship. Pearson was entering his 13th year in the Negro Leagues, most with the Newark Eagles (now in Houston). He would finally get a chance at integrated ball in 1950 and 1951 when he played for the Boston Braves' Triple-A affiliate Milwaukee

Brewers. But, like so many of Gilliam's teammates, Pearson would never see a big league diamond.

Day was a Negro Leagues legend, having joined the Baltimore Black Sox in 1934 as a 17-year-old. Like a lot of Negro Leaguers, he developed a reputation as a two-way star, both as a pitcher and batter, playing second base and the outfield. With the Black Sox having financial challenges, Day jumped to the Brooklyn Eagles in 1935, where he would stay during the team's move to Newark through 1945. In 1937, Day went 13-0 as a pitcher with a 3.02 ERA, while also batting .320 and slugging eight home runs.[43]

On March 8, 1995, the Veterans Committee of the Hall of Fame inducted Day into Cooperstown, becoming just the 12th Negro Leagues player to receive that recognition. Day received the news while sick in the hospital. He passed away five days later at the age of 78. "I think Leon gave up after he made it. I really do. That's what he's been waiting for all these years," Day's sister Ida May Bolden told Brad Snyder for the *Baltimore Sun*, where news of induction, and his death, both warranted front-page treatment.[44]

EAST-WEST ALL-STAR GAME AGAIN

The 1949 season marked the first year Black players participated in the MLB All-Star Game, taking some wind out of the East-West Game's sails. Four ex-Negro Leaguers—Jackie Robinson, Roy Campanella, Don Newcombe, and Larry Doby—all saw action in the MLB game, played July 12. Robinson was the only Black starter, playing at second base in front of a partisan crowd at Ebbets Field in Brooklyn. Robinson scored three runs, but it was not enough as the American League won, 11-7. Newcombe pitched 2.2 innings, giving up two runs. He was the losing pitcher.

One month later, the East-West classic returned to Comiskey Park in Chicago on August 14. Once again, attendance waned as the game drew just 31,097, according to the *Chicago Defender*.[45] The East team cruised to a 4-0 shutout. Gilliam again started at second and again batted sixth, but this time he was 0-for-4 at the plate. The East pitching was so strong that only six balls made it to the outfield. Gilliam recorded eight assists and two putouts.

The declining attendance was concerning. Prior to the game, Wendell Smith wrote in the *Pittsburgh Courier*, "It is the biggest sports event ever promoted by Negroes and has been a box office hit from the start....More than a half million fans have turned out for these classics down through the years and paid in the neighborhood of a million to watch the cream of the crop in Negro baseball perform."[46]

But a week later, his publication was wondering out loud, "Is the East-West game a barometer to the waning of the popularity of Negro baseball? Is the game meeting its Dunkirk? Why did the game lose 11,000 fans from last year?"[47]

Smith perceived the presence of Major League Commissioner Happy Chandler at the East-West Game to throw out the ceremonial first pitch as an ominous sign. "By participating in the ceremonies, Chandler is giving the game his unofficial sanction and recognition. It is another step in the campaign to place Negro baseball under the jurisdiction of organized ball. Eventually that will happen. Some day, if the Negro owners are able to weather the current financial storm, Negro teams will be a part of the organized baseball world and participate in its workplace."[48]

MLB SCOUTS ARRIVE

The success of players like Robinson, Doby, and Campanella prompted some, but not all, Major League teams to seek young Black players to add to their farm system. Gilliam was not immediately grabbing the attention of scouts, though Rodger H. Pippen, then sports editor of the *Baltimore News-Post*, recalled recommending Gilliam to the hometown Baltimore Orioles following one of the fall series against the Elite Giants. "I was so impressed I recommended Junior to the Orioles....The Birds, however, permitted him to get away without a look. It was like tossing a hundred thousand dollars into an ash can," Pippen said in 1954. [49]

In early August 1949, Gilliam was hitting .304 with a league-high 54 runs scored, prompting Wendell Smith to write in the *Pittsburgh Courier*, "They've been scouting Gilliam ever since the season started. He can hit, run and field. He's young, aggressive and seems to know exactly what the game is all about. Don't wait to see him later on, or even next season. Somebody's going to grab him, but quick." Smith does not say who the scouts were.[50]

Many MLB teams hired retired Negro League players as scouts. Bill Yancey was one of those who filled this role. A shortstop during the 1930s, Yancey played with several different clubs, including the Philadelphia Stars, New York Black Yankees, and the New York Cubans. Yancey, a Philadelphia native who lived in New Jersey after he retired, was a scout for the New York Yankees in the late 1950s when he signed Al Downing, a young Black pitcher from Trenton, New Jersey. Downing would pitch against the Dodgers in the 1963 World Series and later join the team in 1971, pitching parts of seven seasons in a Los Angeles uniform.

Downing recalled a story Yancey told him about scouting Gilliam a decade earlier, in the late 1940s. Former Pittsburgh Crawfords star Judy Johnson, perhaps the greatest Negro League third baseman of all-time, told Yancey he needed to come to Baltimore and check out the second baseman, Gilliam. "The kid can really fly," Johnson said. With Yancey and Johnson in attendance at an Elite Giants game against the Birmingham Black Barons, Gilliam reached second and seemed destined to score on a base hit to left center. As Gilliam is rounding third, the Barons' center-fielder fires a strike to home plate. "Gilliam is thrown out by 15 feet," Downing recalled.

Who is that in center field? Yancey wondered. Johnson responded, "Some guy named Willie Mays."

A FIRST CHAMPIONSHIP FOR GILLIAM

The new offensive punch Green added to the Elite Giants prior to his death propelled the Baltimore club to first-place finishes in the East division for both the first and second halves of the season. Their opponent in a best-of-seven game Negro American League Championship was the Chicago American Giants of the West division. The *Afro-American* previewed the series lineups, highlighting Gilliam's season in which he hit .301 and led the NAL with 85 runs scored and 12 triples.[51] Gilliam was one of five Elite players to bat over .300, joined by Henry Kimbro, Bob Davis, Lennie Pearson, and Ed Finney.

The first two games were in Baltimore and the Elites held serve, winning 9-1 on Friday, September 16, and 5-4, Sunday, September 18. After Baltimore captured Game Three, 8-4 in Norfolk, Virginia on Monday, September 19, Game Four shifted to Comiskey Park in Chicago on Thursday, September 22. Baltimore won 4-2 to capture the Negro American League Championship. Nashville native and Elite Giants outfielder Butch McCord remembered the post-game celebration. "Some had some beer. We didn't throw the beer on each other. We drank the beer. I drank OJ."[52]

McCord, born in Nashville three years earlier than Gilliam, in 1925, attended Tennessee State University, a Historically Black College, in Nashville where he played football. Tom Wilson signed McCord in 1947, but Wilson's death put a hold on his debut with the Elite Giants. Instead, McCord played for the Nashville Cubs in 1947 before joining the Elite Giants in 1948.

"We had such a good team in Baltimore. We had Joe Black, Leon Day, Pee Wee Butts, Henry Kimbro, Junior Gilliam, and Lennie Pearson with us. That was the best team of all the teams I played for," McCord said. "My first game in 1948 with Baltimore was against the Homestead Grays. Buck Leonard was at first base, Sam Bankhead was at shortstop, Luke Easter was in the outfield and Luis Marqüez was in center field. I hit a ball to the left side, a slow ball down the left side. I was a left-handed hitter, so I thought, 'I got this one made.' I thought I could run. He [Bankhead] threw me out by about two steps! I said to myself, 'Welcome to the Negro Leagues!'"[53] Like many of his Elite Giants teammates, McCord never made it to the Major Leagues, despite playing 11 seasons in the minors from 1951-1961.

FAMILY: MARRIAGE AND CHILDREN

The story of how Jim and wife Gloria White met has not survived history, but it is safe to assume they met somewhere in East Baltimore, near the Baltimore Elite Giants' home park. Bugle Field was located at the intersection of Federal Street and Edison Highway, just a few blocks south of Baltimore Cemetery and approximately one-and-a-half miles off what is now I-895.[54] According to author Bob Luke, a majority of the residents of East Baltimore were poor, working-class Blacks, with many on public assistance.[55]

Originally built in 1912, Bugle Field, named for the Bugle Coat and Apron Supply Company, Maryland's largest laundry, was the early home of the Baltimore Black Sox, a charter member of the Eastern Colored League in 1923. After the club won the 1929 American Negro League championship, Black Sox owner George Rossiter sold the club to Joe Cambria, chief scout for the Washington Senators.[56]

The field's orientation was nontraditional, with the first-base line running north-south, parallel to Edison Highway, and the third-base line running east-west, parallel to Federal Street. Home plate was situated in the southeast corner of the field.[57] Outfield signs featured competing beer brands with Gunther's Beer, "Maryland's Favorite Beer By Far," in the left-field corner, and Globe Brewing Company's Arrow Beer, "the great *new* beer," above the field-level scoreboard in right field. Spectator capacity was around 6,000, though long-time Elite Giants employee Richard Powell told the *Baltimore Sun* in 1994, "we could squeeze in 7,000."[58]

The ballpark sat just to the east of what is referred to today as the Baltimore East/South Clifton Park Historic District, an area added to the

National Register of Historic Places in December 2002. As the outfield signs suggested, breweries were an important aspect of the area. The five-story American Brewery building on North Gay Street, approximately a mile west of Bugle Field, is a historic landmark.[59]

About two miles west of Bugle Field was Eden Street. It was at 819 Eden Street, according to 1940 U.S. Census records, that Gloria Arlene White, born May 4, 1933, lived with her parents, James and Mary White.

Gilliam was 20 and Gloria was not quite 16 years old when she gave birth to James Malcolm Gilliam on April 16, 1949. Jim and Gloria married later that year on December 27, 1949 as Jim opted not to return to Puerto Rico in the winter of 1949. The ages of the newlyweds—Jim was 21 and Gloria was 16—was similar to Jim's parents when he was born in 1928. Jim's dad, James, was 16 when he became a father and Jim's mother, Katherine, was 17. Census records for 1950 show Gloria living with her mother, Mary, at 246 North Bethel Court (likely North Bethel Street), less than a mile south of 819 Eden Street. Gloria's entry lists her age as 16 with her last name crossed out and Gilliam written over it. Also residing at 246 North Bethel was a grandson, "James M." His age was listed as April.

Breaking the pattern of teenage pregnancies in the Gilliam family would become something Jim and Gloria's daughter, Katherine Mary, born less than a year later (August 26, 1950), would seek to accomplish.

"My mother was so young when she had us. I wanted to stop the cycle of teenage pregnancies in our family," Katherine said. She broke the trend by holding off on marriage until she was in her 20s, after experiencing the women's liberation movement during her teenage years in the 1960s. When Katherine did give birth to a daughter in 1974, Gurushakti, Katherine was a practicing sikh.

END GAME FOR BLACK BASEBALL?

The 1950 Negro American League season was set to begin under tremendous strain. Interest in the league was diminishing, creating financial problems for several teams. Author Neil Lanctot wrote that by 1950 "Black baseball could offer precious few selling points to consumers, as much of the best talent was now in the major or minor leagues. Moreover, unlike the Depression, officials had virtually no reason to anticipate future improvement in the industry's fortunes."[60]

Additionally, Lanctot observed, "Player sales, extensive barnstorming, budget cutting, and continued Southern segregation had prolonged the industry's survival, but the increasingly anachronistic all-Black teams faced the almost impossible task of operating in an environment less favorable to separate enterprises and newly transformed by television."[61]

Long-term sustainability of the League seemed in serious jeopardy—the Louisville Buckeyes folded after the first half of the 1950 season. Meanwhile, the Baltimore Elite Giants were confronting their own financial troubles and looking for a new home. After the first two games of the 1949 Negro American League Championships were played at Bugle Field, the owners of the property began demolition of the ballpark in preparation for sale of the land. A hastily assembled field on a plot of land in the Westport section of Baltimore was to be erected. Matt Reinhold of the Gallagher Realty Company told Elites president Richard Powell the site, owned by his company, was "good enough for Negroes."[62] The field, as it turned out, would not be ready until July 2, so the Elites played mainly on the road with a few home games in Baltimore's Memorial Stadium.

When it was ready, the Westport facility was hardly good enough for any team. The field drained poorly. The grandstand had no roof. And it was not readily accessible via public transportation. Powell summed up the situation as a, "terrible field in every respect....I can't find words to say how bad it was. It only looked like a baseball diamond."[63]

The easiest way for Negro League clubs to infuse revenue into their coffers was by selling their star players to Major League teams. The standard price tag was anywhere from $5,000 for a Negro League All-Star—Monte Irvin, Sam Jethroe, or Minnie Miñoso—up to the $30,000 the Cleveland Indians paid the Kansas City Monarchs for Satchel Paige, including a $10,000 bonus directly to Paige.[64]

With much of the top talent already sold to the Major Leagues, Baltimore was holding one of the few remaining player assets, 21-year-old All-Star Junior Gilliam. As Sam Lacy reported in the *Baltimore Afro-American* just before spring training, the Boston Braves "got suddenly deaf" when the Elite front office asked for $15,000 for Gilliam.[65]

5

THE MAJORS CALL. TWICE.

HAINES CITY, FLORIDA RESIDES IN THE HEART OF THE STATE, NEARLY equidistant from the east and west coasts, northeast of Winter Haven, and about 20 miles from Disney World. According to a 1940s era postcard, Haines City was "a beauty spot situated among orange groves and lakes." The city's lone 1940s baseball field, Yale Athletic Field, was named for Jed Yale, a resident of Haines City who donated the property on the northeast shore of Lake Eva as a remembrance of his son, Hugh, who died on his way home from France after World War I.[1]

In addition to use by the Haines City High School, the facility served as the 1940s and 1950s spring-training home for the Baltimore Orioles, minor-league affiliate of the Philadelphia Phillies, and the Kansas City Blues, minor-league affiliate of the New York Yankees. Future Hall of Famers Yogi Berra, Joe DiMaggio, and Phil Rizzuto all played on Yale Field. Today, the Yale Field site is a paved parking lot for patrons of the Lake Eva Aquatic Center.

Like most rural Florida towns at the time, segregation was the rule. In fact, when Luis Marquez of the Newark Eagles was given a tryout with the New York Yankees in 1949, it was the first time in the town's history when colored fans were admitted to Yale Field.[2] According to *Baltimore Afro-American* writer Sam Lacy, workers at the facility quickly erected a makeshift "colored" seating area, and when he asked about a colored restroom, Lacy "was directed to a tree about 35 yards off from where the rightfield foul line ended."[3]

It was here, in the heart of segregated Florida, where Jim Gilliam and six other Negro League ballplayers reported on March 10, 1950 hoping to secure a spot in the Chicago Cubs organization, preferably with the team's new farm club at Springfield, Mass.[4] The *Chicago Defender* and the *Baltimore Afro-American* both reported the Cubs paid $7,500 for Gilliam and $5,000 for his Elite teammate Leroy Ferrell on February 22.[5] The two were joined at the tryout by Bob Thurman and Earl Taborn of the Newark Bears, Triple-A affiliate of the Yankees, Gene Baker of the Kansas City Monarchs, Bill Ricks of the Philadelphia Stars, and Lorenzo Cabrera of the New York Cubans.[6]

Dan Burley of the Black newspaper, *The New York Age*, wrote the Cubs could have integrated a few years earlier, but got cold feet. "The Cubs slated to be the second team behind the Dodgers to hire Negro players three years ago, but Wrigley got his fill when the Negro American League played a doubleheader at Wrigley Field and players and fans tried to mob an umpire for an unpopular decision. Conduct of the fans and players prompted Wrigley to bar Negro promotions from his park."[7]

Consistent with the times, the Black players were "quartered" away from their white teammates, staying at the home of George Atchison on Church Avenue north of Yale Field. Each player was "provided with a separate room, all of which are clean and neatly furnished,"[8] and "the best meals in the United States."[9]

Stan Hack was the Springfield Cubs manager, and while he was impressed by the older Baker (whom the Cubs signed), he was not willing to take a chance on the younger Gilliam. Baker was 24 years old on the day of the tryout. Gilliam was 21. "(Ferrell and Gilliam) are both young and still have a lot of time to develop. I'd say Gilliam hasn't hit his stride yet."[10]

Rather than take a chance on when Jim might hit that stride, the Cubs released both Gilliam and Ferrell on March 31, 1950, after just three weeks of evaluation. A letter from John T. Sheehan, president of the Cubs' minor-league system, to Elites owner Richard Powell explained Gilliam's release thusly, "Gilliam has been in training about three weeks and up until this time does not look as though he will be able to hit well enough to stay in this classification."[11]

To say Jim was shocked at his release would be an understatement. "To this day I don't know what it was all about," Gilliam said in 1953. "I thought I played well enough to make it. I thought I was set, except that nobody said anything to me about a contract or salary. One day they called me into the office. 'We're sending you back to Baltimore,' I was told. I wanted to know why and they didn't tell me. It bothered me. Not because I didn't think I got a fair chance, but because I knew then I was good enough."[12]

Joe Black, Gilliam's teammate and roommate on the Elite Giants since 1946, blamed his friend's failed tryout on insecurities. Gilliam's tryout was his first exposure to integrated professional baseball in the United States, and, according to Black's biographers, Gilliam withdrew, often sitting in the corner alone. "I couldn't integrate,"[13] Gilliam told Black.

Of the seven-player group, the Cubs added Thurman, Taborn, and Baker for the 1950 season.[14] Thurman landed in the Majors with the Cincinnati Reds five years later at age 38. He would amass 733 plate appearances over a five-year big-league career. Taborn, a catcher who had previously played with the Kansas City Monarchs, did not appear in the Cubs organization in 1950 and would spend the next 11 seasons plying his trade in the Mexican League.

Baker spent 1950 with three different Cubs minor league affiliates, including Springfield, where he went 1-for-9. He dented the Cubs lineup late in 1953, at age 28, and shared the middle infield duties with Ernie Banks until 1957, when Baker was traded to the Pirates. Thurman and Baker played a combined 964 games in Major Leagues, less than half of the 1,956 games in which Gilliam would play.

Gilliam lost out on an opportunity to play for a Major League organization and the Elite Giants lost out on a potential $7,500 of sorely needed cash. Nonetheless, the ever-optimistic Gilliam reminisced that things worked out just fine for him. "The day before the season opened, they sent me back. I don't know why. I know it made me feel pretty bad at the time, but it was the greatest thing that ever happened to me,"[15] he told *Sport* magazine's Jack Mann in 1963.

1950 SEASON: A FINAL HURRAH WITH THE ELITE GIANTS

In his first game back with Baltimore, Gilliam seemed intent on sending a message to the Cubs. Playing the Philadelphia Stars in front of a "large, enthusiastic crowd"[16] of 10,000 fans at Memorial Stadium on May 7, the Elites opened their home season as the defending Negro American League champions. On the mound for Philadelphia was none other than Bill Ricks, also fresh from the failed Cubs tryout. Baltimore scored in the bottom of the first when Butts walked and moved to third on Gilliam's single. Butts came home on Butch Davis' infield ground out to make it 1-0. The game would see-saw back and forth for the next eight innings, with Philadelphia knotting the game 3-3 in the top of the ninth.

Will Dumpson replaced Ricks on the hill for Philadelphia to pitch the bottom of the ninth. Butts reached first base to open the home half, bringing up Gilliam, who promptly doubled, scoring Butts. Jim finished the game with three hits in five at bats, including the walk-off triple. The headline in the *Chicago Defender* blared, "Elite Giants Defeat Stars in Ninth, 4-3; Gilliam Returns To Pace Attack on Two Pitchers."[17] The message was delivered via newspaper in the local market: the Cubs missed by not signing Gilliam.

Two months into the season, Powell released veterans Bill Byrd and Leon Day, citing salaries "far in excess of their rapidly declining market value."[18] Later that summer, seemingly in financial desperation, Powell wrote letters on July 3 to the Elmira (New York) minor-league club offering to sell Ferrell's contract for $2,500 and Gilliam's contract for $5,000.[19]

Sam Lacy reported a slightly different series of events in the July 1, 1950 *Afro-American*. The Brooklyn Dodgers, he wrote, were "expected momentarily to purchase" the contracts of Gilliam and John Coleman, a left-handed pitcher, after Dodgers scout George Sisler watched both players in Washington, D.C. Lacy speculated they would be assigned to the Dodgers Single-A affiliate in Elmira.[20] Lacy continued reporting the Dodgers-Gilliam courtship in the July 22, 1950 *Afro-American*, suggesting Brooklyn took a 10-day option on Gilliam and Ferrell, but failed to pick up on it.[21]

Years later, in 1956, Dick Young, writing in *The Sporting News*, stated without context or attribution that the Phillies could have snared Gilliam and Joe Black for a total of $2,500, but declined. Philadelphia became the last National League team to integrate when the team pinch-ran John Kennedy on April 22, 1957 in Brooklyn.

For the third year in a row, Gilliam was selected to participate in the East-West All-Star Game on August 20. The impact Major League integration had on the game was evident as only slightly more than 24,000 fans, half of the attendance from two years earlier in 1948, were in the stands at Comiskey Park. Gilliam, playing second base again for the East, stroked a solo home run off Vibert Clarke of Memphis in the second inning. Wendell Smith of the *Pittsburgh Courier* described it as a fast pitch to Gilliam, who "socked it high and far into the leftfield stands, 353 feet away for a homerun."[22]

Despite the star power of the East-West game, home runs were not common. Throughout the entire decade of the 1940s, only three round-trippers were hit: two by Buck Leonard (1941 and 1943) and one by Ted "Double Duty" Radcliffe (1944). Gilliam was never a serious long-ball threat, making the feat all the more remarkable. In fact, statistics kept at *Baseball Reference* do not reflect that Gilliam had ever homered as a member of the Elite Giants. It would be the last home run hit in an East-West All-Star Game until James Banks homered in the 1957 game.[23] By that time, most major league-caliber talent was competing in "organized" baseball.

Six days after the All-Star game, the Gilliam family grew as Katherine Mary Gilliam, named after Jim's mother, entered the world on August 26, 1950. Jim was just 21 years old while Gloria was 17.

FAREWELL, BALTIMORE

Still battling financial difficulties, Powell followed the lead of clubs in Houston, Birmingham, and Memphis by agreeing to pay players a percentage of gate receipts in lieu of salary, beginning with a Labor Day weekend matchup against the Philadelphia Stars, featuring former Negro League legend, turned World Series champion, turned Negro League star Satchel Paige. The move did not sit well with several Elite Giants players, including Pee Wee Butts, who refused to play. Powell suspended Butts and four others indefinitely.

A "disappointing" crowd of 2,000 turned out during the holiday weekend to see the Stars dominate the depleted Giants, 15-4. Paige started and went three innings, allowing one run on three hits. Gilliam, batting third, went 3-for-4 with two runs scored. How Gilliam fared against Paige in the first inning and, possibly again in the third is unclear, although it would seem likely he had at least one hit off the legendary Hall of Famer.[24] The matchup was likely the first, and only, time Gilliam batted against Paige in a non-barnstorming game.

A little more than a month later, on October 9, Gilliam was scheduled to make what would be his final appearance at Westport Stadium as a member of the Negro Leagues, participating on what was billed as a Negro American League All-Star team. The opposition that day was to be the champion Indianapolis Clowns, who added three current major leaguers to its roster: Jackie Robinson, Roy Campanella, and Larry Doby. Gilliam, it appeared, would play the same position on the same field opposite the player who broke the Major league color barrier.[25] Unfortunately, rain prevented the matchup from occurring. Gilliam would need to wait a little longer to take the field with Robinson.

BROOKLYN CALLS

Throughout the 1950 season, Brooklyn Dodgers general manager Branch Rickey was embroiled in a bitter battle with Walter O'Malley for operating control of the club. Rickey, of course, is credited with spearheading the team's efforts to break the major league color line, the First Gate, when it signed Jackie Robinson in October 1945. O'Malley would later boast to New York sportswriter Red Smith, "You know how Rickey has always said he was the one who broke the color line with Robinson? Well, Red, the true story is that it wasn't his idea. It was mine."[26]

After months of negotiating with O'Malley on a stock buyout, Rickey officially resigned from his post with the Dodgers on Thursday, October 26, 1950. The announcement occurred in Room 40 of the Hotel Bossert at 98 Montague Street in Brooklyn. Tommy Holmes described the two protagonists this way, "Walter O'Malley walked into the room, looking bland and relaxed. A few moments after came Branch Rickey, who seemed almost radiant."[27] Shortly thereafter Rickey agreed to become the general manager of the Pittsburgh Pirates.

How the Brooklyn Dodgers came to purchase the contracts of Jim Gilliam, Joe Black, and Leroy Ferrell from the Baltimore Elite Giants during this period is unsettled. Differing accounts of the acquisition create confusion as to when the Dodgers signed the players and who was responsible for signing them.

Rickey's resignation in late October 1950 is significant as it calls into question whether Rickey had any role in signing the players. Two of Rickey's biographers, Jimmy Breslin and Murray Polner, both reported the signing occurred as the result of a conversation between Rickey and his longtime assistant Mickey McConnell concerning the challenges of having a consistent second baseman for the Montreal Royals, the Dodgers top minor-league affiliate. Montreal was open to Black players, having hosted Jackie Robinson, Roy Campanella, Dan Bankhead, and others as members of the Dodgers organization. "When Mickey McConnell heard Rickey complaining about Montreal's second-base problem he mentioned a young Black 'borderline prospect who might become a utility infielder on a major league team,'" Polner wrote.[28] Gilliam was that infielder.

A September 7, 1979 *New York Times* story by Red Smith quoted a letter McConnell wrote to Rickey, although Smith's article provides no information about when the letter was written. Smith excerpted from the letter,

"Rickey told me to see whether Gilliam could be purchased. I asked how much he would pay and he said, 'Try to get him for $4,000.'

"I called the elite (sic) owner and he said he was interested but said he needed $5,000 to pay some bills and buy a new bus. He said he would throw in a pitcher named Joe Black if we would pay $5,000. I hadn't seen Black pitch, and I said I would call him back.

"Rickey made a counter-proposal to pay $4,000 for Gilliam and $500 to look at Black in spring training, with the provision that we would pay $1,000 more if we kept Black. We did retain Black and the ailing Giants were paid $5,500 for both men, who played with Montreal in 1951. The rest of the story is known, with both of them playing beyong (sic) our expectations and building remarkable careers."[29]

Breslin indicated in his biography of Rickey the Dodgers paid $5,000 for Gilliam, the amount determined by Baltimore's need for a new bus. Consistent with Smith's version of the events, Breslin wrote, "Baltimore threw in a pitcher named Joe Black."[30] Clyde Sukeforth, the scout who signed Jackie Robinson, told Rickey he got two World Series players for $5,000.

"Luck," Rickey responded, "is the residue of design."[31]

Neither biographer's version of the events, nor Smith's story of McConnell's letter, establish when this transaction took place, and none mention Ferrell. Rickey's involvement would mean, of course, the purchase would have occurred prior to his resignation in late October 1950. Other accounts of the signing contradict this version of the events, both in terms of timing and the amount.

Rickey's replacement as general manager was Buzzie Bavasi, who held the same title for Montreal from 1948 to 1950. As might be expected, Bavasi's recollection of how Gilliam and Black came to the Dodgers organization differs greatly. Writing in his autobiography, *Off the Record*, Bavasi offered this version, "Spencer Harris, a Dodger minor league executive, called to tell me the Elite Giants needed money and that I could buy some players at a discount. For $11,000, I purchased Gilliam, Joe (sic) Farrell, and Joe Black. When I called Mr. Rickey, he was furious that I had spent $11,000 of his money. 'You did what?' he said when I told him. In the end, it proved to be a pretty shrewd deal."[32] Again, Rickey's purported involvement suggests the transaction occurred some time in October 1950.

A third account of the signing, this one involving Dodgers front-office executive Lafayette "Fresco" Thompson, provides yet another interpretation of how Gilliam and Black came to the organization. In his definitive history of the Royals, *Baseball's Fabulous Montreal Royals*, author William Brown credits Thompson, a former Montreal player and manager, with engineering the purchase prior to the 1951 season. "Thompson bought two young ball players from the Baltimore Elite Giants of the Negro Leagues; pitcher Joe Black and second baseman-outfielder Jim 'Junior' Gilliam. A smooth fielder and a switch-hitter, Gilliam fit right into the Royals' lineup at second base, occasionally playing the outfield."[33]

Writing in the *New York Daily News* on October 5, 1952, Dick Young stated Thompson was central to negotiations with Elites owner Ed (sic) Powell, which focused on Black and Ferrell. "All you have to do is pay $500 apiece for the look and if you keep them we'll talk money. Oh, and you might as well take an infielder we have; kid named Jim Gilliam."[34]

Ferrell went into the Army, but Young reports Thompson liked what we saw with Black and Gilliam and paid $5,000 for each. In this account, however, Gilliam, not Black, is considered the afterthought. The total price tag of $11,500, $500 to try out each player, and $10,000 to purchase both Black and Gilliam, appears to be the most accurate accounting of the cost to the Dodgers.

Bob Luke, while also acknowledging the conflicting prices for the players,[35] wrote in his book on the history of the Baltimore Elite Giants that the final amount was $10,000, or $5,000 apiece. "In an April 16, 1951, letter from Montreal Royals' general manager (Guy) Moreau, to Powell, Moreau said he was enclosing a $10,000 check representing final payment for Gilliam ($5,000) and Black ($5,000). Earlier, in a December 12, 1950, letter, Moreau had sent $1,500 to cover the option to purchase both players' contracts. Both were assigned to the Montreal Royals."[36]

Thompson's involvement in the signing is not mentioned anywhere in his memoir, *Every Diamond Doesn't Sparkle*. If Thompson, who would later become the Dodgers general manager in 1968, was directly involved in signing Black and Gilliam, the absence of the event in his book is conspicuous given the magnitude of the signings and their collective impact on the Brooklyn Dodgers. Black and Gilliam would win back-to-back National League Rookie of the Year awards in 1952 and 1953.

Perhaps the clearest explanation to the question of who the Dodgers desired more—Black or Gilliam—comes directly from Joe Black, who told Roger Kahn in an interview for the *Boys of Summer*, "The Dodgers wanted to buy Gilliam and they put me in the deal and that was it."[37] Kahn, however, left that out of his book's final manuscript.

Black's biographers stated, "Joe believed they (the Dodgers) were convinced that all he (Gilliam) would need in order to get comfortable was a roommate he knew. Joe Black was the perfect choice."[38]

Jim's departure from the Elites meant he and long-time friend Pee Wee Butts would no longer occupy opposite sides of second base. "I sure was glad for Gilliam when he finally did make it. I was glad. But I hated to see him go. We had to get another second baseman and start in all over again. I don't think Gilliam wanted to leave, himself. I had to coax him. 'Get up there, Gilliam, you gotta go. You'll be making more money and everything,'" Butts reminisced. "We used to lay in bed talking about that. He was wishing he could go, but after he got the chance he didn't want to go. I pushed him on. I said, 'You better go.' George Scales said, 'Here's your chance, you better go. Here's your chance to make money.' That was the main thing."[39]

When asked about his time in the Negro Leagues by John Wiebusch for *Baseball Digest* in 1969, Jim recalled how he was lucky, rattling off names of players like Josh Gibson, Willie Wells, Pee Wee Butts, and Jonas Gaines, who never had a chance to play Major League Baseball. "See why I am lucky? Most of them are dead. Most of them never got a chance. They were making $275 a month like me. And you know what? They never thought it would happen. They never thought a Black man would play in the white leagues. Most of them were happy doing what they were doing—playing baseball and making a buck."[40]

THE "BLACK SEA" IN PUERTO RICO

Santurce is a barrio in the city of San Juan on the northern coast of Puerto Rico. First shown on a map in 1519, Spanish officials began calling the Santurce area "Cangrejeros," the Spanish word for crab, due to its crab-shaped layout on a map. The area's influence with the United States dates back to World War I, when the U.S. Army used portions of the area for training soldiers.[41]

Shell Oil executive Pedrín Zorrilla founded the Santurce Cangrejeros in the 1939-40 season and enjoyed some early success, thanks to the contributions of "imports" such as Josh Gibson and Roy Campanella. Santurce would share Escambrón Stadium, later to be renamed Estadio Sixto Escobar in honor of Puerto Rico's first world boxing champion, with crosstown rival San Juan for 23 seasons.[42]

By the mid to late 1940s, Santurce had emerged as a "league anchor" with a loyal fan base and an offensive-minded duo of Negro League stars, Willard Brown and Bob Thurman.[43] Beginning with the 1947-48 season, Santurce strung together three straight winning seasons, but could never eclipse the Puerto Rican powers of Ponce, Mayagüez, and Caguas.

Ponce dominated Puerto Rican baseball, winning five league championships in the 1940s, all managed by Gilliam's early mentor, George

Scales. Puerto Rican baseball expert Thomas Van Hyning, author of the definitive book on the Santurce Cangrejeros, reported when Zorilla tabbed Scales to be his manager for the 1950-51 season, "Scales told Pedrín Zorrilla that Junior Gilliam would solidify the team's infield defense, and provide speed and good on-base percentage at the top of the line-up. Basically, get on base for the tandem of Willard Brown and Bob Thurman—the 'Babe Ruth-Lou Gehrig' of Santurce."

If that is indeed what Scales said, he was absolutely correct, and it was here that Jim first learned of his sale to the Dodgers while reading newspapers. Gilliam wrote a letter to Dick Powell, dated December 27, 1950, the night of the Puerto Rican All-Star game.

After asking about Powell's Christmas, Jim writes without punctuation, "I read in the the (sic) paper about me an (sic) Joe an (sic) Stub (sic) is it true it was in the paper here I am still waiting on your letter How are you coming how is the familly (sic) it won't be long before the season is over here an (sic) won't I be glad we are still in second place Tell everybody I said Hello Junior."[44]

JAMES GILLIAM

Jim Gilliam with the Santurce Cangrejeros, 1950-1951 winter season. Courtesy of Wade Carothers.

Gilliam thrived in his first season for Santurce, as the Cangrejeros placed second with a 48-30 record. Gilliam finished second in the league with 75 runs scored, and in stolen bases with 20. The season ended with a Santurce win over San Juan on February 1, 1951, giving the Cangrejeros the San Juan city championship. This was the first step in the ultimate playoff reward, dubbed the Trifecta—city championship, Puerto Rico championship, and the Caribbean Series.[45]

Santurce drew Ponce in the league semifinals and dispatched of the Lions four-games-to-one to earn the right to play Caguas for the league title. With the championship series tied at two games apiece, Gilliam's two-run single proved the difference as Santurce won Game Five, 2-1. Caguas would take Game Six, forcing a deciding Game Seven. Santurce's Pepe Lucas, a .243 hitter with two home runs, hit a walkoff home run to left center to win the game, 3-2. Gilliam tripled and scored Santurce's first run in the third inning. With the San Juan city championship and the Puerto Rican league championship on its resume, Santurce had now captured two legs of the Trifecta.[46] All that remained was the Caribbean Series.

Venezuela served as the host country for the 1951 Caribbean Series, which featured clubs from Havana (Cuba), Magallanes (Venezuela), Spur Cola (Panama), and Santurce. The Cangrejeros, led by future New York Giant star pitcher Rubén Gómez and current Brooklyn Dodger Luis Olmo, a Puerto Rican native, rolled to a 5-1 record and its first-ever Caribbean Series title.

Pedrín Zorrilla's wife, Diane, recalled, "All week long, the Cuban officials, fans and writers were bragging about how good they were…no other Winter League could come close to them. Pedrín put together the best possible team to represent Puerto Rico. He wanted to win this series for the people of Puerto Rico and Santurce's fans."[47]

For his part, 22-year-old Gilliam's contributions in Havana would look remarkably similar to how he would perform in several MLB World Series. Gilliam hit .240 in the Caribbean Series but with a .367 on-base percentage thanks to five walks. He scored seven runs and drove in four. Among his six hits were two doubles and one triple. And, he only struck out twice in 30 plate appearances over the six games. Plate discipline was a hallmark of Gilliam's career.

But beyond contributing throughout the season offensively, Gilliam's defensive skills were also noticeable enough that the Santurce fans gave him a new nickname, "Black Sea." Ron Samford, who was white and played shortstop for Santurce in the mid-1950s, told Van Hyning, "Santurce fans called me the 'White Sea' and Jim Gilliam the 'Black Sea' because we covered so much ground."[48]

Gilliam returned to the United States as Caribbean Series champion in March 1951, brimming with confidence. "The best players in the Triple A leagues are (in Puerto Rico) and I made out against them. I made out good. By then I learned the jump wasn't too much from the Negro National League to the Triple A leagues. The fellows still called me Junior, the way they did when I first started playing pro ball and I was the youngest on the team, but I wasn't a rookie in baseball any more," Gilliam said in early 1953. "From 1946 through 1950 with the Elites made me a veteran. I had my confidence I could do good against any team. I had my confidence I could do good in any league."[49]

6

THE MINOR LEAGUES

LIKE JACKIE ROBINSON WAS BEFORE HIM, GILLIAM WAS ASSIGNED TO THE Dodgers' top minor-league affiliate, Montreal, for the 1951 season. Montreal had finished the 1950 season 86-67, good for second place behind the Rochester Red Wings, affiliate of the St. Louis Cardinals. The Royals were managed by Walter Alston, a quiet, unexcitable Ohio native, who, over time, would forge a long, professional relationship with Gilliam. Beginning in 1951 and continuing every year for the next 25 years (except 1953), Alston and Gilliam would be connected in the same dugout. Alston immediately took to Gilliam, though it is unlikely they would have ever been considered friends, hailing from very different backgrounds.

Alston grew up in Darrtown, Ohio, a rural community in the southwest corner of the state with a population hovering around 500, and frequently returned home in the offseason. He graduated from nearby Miami University in Oxford, Ohio. Gilliam was Black, grew up in segregated Nashville during the Great Depression, and had dropped out of high school after the 11th grade. The two bonded primarily because both were quiet individuals who went about their business without fanfare, and because both were baseball lifers who would do whatever the Dodgers asked.

"That is why he and Walter Alston were so compatible. They were both company men," said Peter Golenbock, author of *Bums: An Oral History of the Brooklyn Dodgers*. "Alston was from some little town in Ohio. He would never invite an African-American over to dinner. They were not close friends. But they worked well together."

1951 SEASON: NORTH OF THE BORDER

The Royals opened their 1951 International League schedule on April 18 as a team replete with Major League experience. George "Shotgun" Shuba, who had spent parts of the previous three seasons in Brooklyn, was expected to lead the outfield, along with Al Gionfriddo, whose running catch against the left-field wall in Game 6 of the 1947 World Series robbed Joe DiMaggio of a home run. Jim Russell, a nine-year veteran of the National League (mostly with the Pirates), also figured prominently in Alston's plans.

Montreal's infield would be anchored by Gilliam at second; Bobby Morgan, an Oklahoman who spent all of 1950 in Brooklyn, at shortstop; and at third base, a 30-year-old Cuban Héctor Rodríguez making his United States debut. New Englander George Byam, playing for his third International League team in as many years, would man first base. The pitching staff featured several future Brooklyn contributors, including Joe Black, Tom Lasorda, Bud Podbielan, Chris Van Cuyk, and Jim Hughes. Despite the experience, as the season began, Alston expressed concern about an Opening Day lineup composed of banged-up players and one, Morgan, who was not yet with the club.

"If Morgan arrives in time, I'll play him at short and bat him fourth. That'll help a lot, but Shuba is out with the flu, Rodriguez has a bad tooth and (catcher Ken) Staples broke a finger," Alston said. "I doubt if our club is as strong as a year ago right now. The pitching looks good, but we'll need help. It's hard to say now about such players as Gilliam and Rodriguez. They've looked fine in camp, but I want to see them in stiff competition."[1]

The season's opening game was scheduled in a city all too familiar to Gilliam: his hometown of Baltimore. In 1951, the Baltimore Orioles were the Triple-A affiliate of the Philadelphia Phillies and played their home games at Memorial Stadium, the facility where Gilliam's Elite Giants had played a portion of their 1950 games. Jim and his family still had plenty of connections in Baltimore and were making it their offseason home. Regardless, the Baltimore fans were less than hospitable to their fellow resident, spewing a number of racial names at him. "I had played in Baltimore with the Elite Giants and never heard a word about my color. But when I came there with the Royals, the fans got on me. Hearing those names, I just bore down harder," Gilliam wrote in 1964.[2]

It was here, at 900 E. 33rd Street in Baltimore, that Gilliam made his integrated-baseball debut. That debut game ended up previewed how Alston viewed Gilliam and how he intended to use him. Gilliam was stationed in the number-two spot in the batting order, a position he would find himself in through his playing days in Los Angeles.

Left-fielder Al Gionfriddo hit leadoff and "lasted exactly thirty seconds."[3] Gionfriddo tossed his bat after being called out on strikes, and the home-plate umpire tossed him. With his depleted bench, Alston was forced to shift Gilliam to left field and install utility infielder Walter Fiala at second. "On opening day in Baltimore...Alston told me to go out left field. The manager tells you to do something you do it. It's the way I learned to play ball," Gilliam, employing the thought process of a company man, told *Our Sports* magazine in 1953.[4]

While the *Montreal Gazette* did not mention any fielding miscues, *Our Sports* magazine reported Gilliam dropped the first fly ball hit to him. "Thereafter he dropped few other chances and Gilliam's talent is proved in the way he was able to handle any job that was thrust his way in any emergency."[5]

At the plate, Jim's debut could not have been more impressive. Former Aguadilla teammate and future Dodger teammate Don Hoak and Gilliam both stroked home runs in the fourth inning to stake the Royals to a 5-1 lead. In the next inning, Gilliam came to bat with two out and the bases loaded, clearing the bags with a double. It was now 10-1. After Baltimore rallied to 10-5 through six innings, Gilliam received a gift as the Orioles right fielder lost Gilliam's drive in the lights for an RBI single, scoring Fiala. Starting pitcher Bob Alexander would go the distance for the Royals. Gilliam led the Royals hit parade, going 4-for-6 at the plate and driving in six runs in a 15-7 triumph.[6]

By mid-June, newspaper writers in New York City were beginning to take notice of Gilliam's exploits north of the border. Jimmy Powers was the first to mention Gilliam on June 14 in the *New York Daily News*, noting he was "being groomed to succeed Jackie Robinson."[7] The *Brooklyn Daily Eagle* devoted several column inches to a story about Gilliam, under the headline, "Brooks groom Gilliam on Montreal farm," the very next day. The article reported Gilliam was hitting "well over .310," prompting an Alston quote saying, "He's been carrying the club." The article noted Gilliam was moved to the outfield, where his play was "outstanding."

When asked about his ambition, he responded, "To play in the majors, of course, just like Robinson."[8]

As if he needed to give the scribes some validation for the hype, two days later on June 17, Gilliam went 8-for-8 with three walks in a double-header sweep at Buffalo. He capped off his otherworldly day with a grand slam in the ninth inning of the nightcap, won by Montreal, 11-4.[9]

Years later in 1965, Jim spoke of that day fondly. "One of my biggest thrills was when I was at Montreal and we played Buffalo in a double-header. I went 4-for-4 in each game. I walked once in the first game and twice in the second. I hit a grand-slam home run in my last trip. This has to stand out in my mind."[10]

Shortly after Gilliam's hitting display in Buffalo, Jimmy Powers wrote in the *Daily News* that St. Louis Browns owner Bill Veeck was interested in adding "colored" players to his team. "He's casting his eyes toward the great Montreal second baseman, Jim Gilliam. But the Brooks may like to keep the flashy fielder as eventual successor to Jackie Robinson."[11]

That the media stories of 1951 suggested Gilliam as an eventual replacement to Robinson, and not someone who would line up next to Robinson, provided the first evidence of the Second Gate—how many Black players would a Major League team be willing to field in the same lineup? Or, stated another way, at what point would the largely white Brooklyn fan base voice displeasure at the idea of the Dodgers fielding a starting nine with a majority of Black players? "The Brooks" already had Robinson, Roy Campanella, and Don Newcombe as stars. The crosstown New York Giants were fielding a lineup with Monte Irvin, Hank Thompson, and a rookie named Willie Mays. Surely "the great Montreal second baseman" could find a way into the Dodgers lineup.

As great as Gilliam was in his first full season in organized baseball, it was his 31-year-old teammate Rodríguez who won the International League Rookie of the Year award in 1951 by a single vote over the 22-year-old Gilliam. Gilliam had acquitted himself well in Triple-A, batting .287 with 117 runs scored and 117 walks in 152 games. Rodríguez had batted .302 with a league-leading 95 runs batted in. After the season, the Dodgers traded Rodríguez to the White Sox, where he played the 1952 season as the team's primary third baseman. It was his only year in the bigs. Montreal won the International League title in 1951 but lost to the Milwaukee Brewers in the Junior World Series.

TENSIONS IN MONTREAL

For the most part, life in Montreal for Gilliam, Black, and other players of color on the Dodgers lacked any sort of drama or tension. Jackie Robinson, Roy Campanella, Don Newcombe, Sam Jethroe, and Dan Bankhead had all performed well during their stints with the Royals. But while Blacks were accepted in Montreal, that did not mean they were treated hospitably on the road—as Gilliam had experienced in Baltimore in their season's opening series.

One night in Buffalo, with the Royals ahead 2-1 and Black on the mound, Gilliam stepped in to diffuse an escalating situation. Black told Roger Kahn that on his way back to the dugout after executing a sacrifice bunt, Black heard from the Buffalo dugout, "You're dumb just like your dumb assed Black mother."

Back on the mound, Gilliam asked what was said, and Black told him. Gilliam inquired whether Black knew who said it. "Well we only got one more inning, I'm going to get him as soon as the game is over." Gilliam asked for clarification. "I'm gonna beat the living shit out of him."

Black retired the first two batters and got two strikes on the third batter when Gilliam walked to the mound. "Don't do it," Gilliam said.

"Don't do what?" Black responded.

"You're gonna throw the ball as hard as you can and then leave."

"You better believe it."

Black fired the ball in and headed for the foul line, conceding a hit if the batter had made contact. "He wasn't going to hit *that* one," Black told Kahn.

Black encountered the Buffalo team in the runway to the clubhouse where an unidentified player said to Bison pitcher Rudy Minarcin, "you shouldn't have said that to the big colored guy. He might get you and cut your head off."

Minarcin was a right-handed pitcher born in North Vandergrift, Pennsylvania, a rural community about 40 miles east of Pittsburgh. He was on track for the majors when a two-year stint in the army from 1952-53 derailed his plans. On the day before he was discharged, he tore his ACL playing football in Korea, and while he appeared in 70 games in 1955-57 for the Reds and Red Sox, he was never the same pitcher.[12]

"I wish that nigger would come here," Minarcin responded.

Black tapped him on the shoulder and said, "That nigger's behind you."

Gilliam intervened, imploring Black not to be violent. "We'll never get a chance to play if you hit him."

Black backed off but Minarcin ran into the clubhouse and returned with an ice pick. "Come on, nigger. You want to get me. Come on and try for a piece, nigger," Minarcin said.

Black threw his glove at him and pressed him against a wall. When Alston stepped in and asked Black to stop, he let Minarcin go. Two weeks later when the teams faced off again, Minarcin apologized to Black, "Negroes have the right to play. Sorry I said what I did about your mother."[13]

SANTURCE: EXCELLING IN PUERTO RICO

After the 1951 season ended, Gilliam again returned—this time with his family—to Santurce and the Cangrejeros, which opened its defense of the Trifecta on October 16. After a summer in Canada and the United States, the prospect of a winter on a Caribbean island must have sounded agreeable to Jim, Gloria, and the kids.

Despite an overall record at 41-31, the Cangrejeros entered the Puerto Rican Championship series in February 1952 as third seed, playing Caguas. Santurce swept Caguas, 3-0, to earn a spot against San Juan in the finals on February 9, 1952. But the Senators downed Santurce, four games to two.[14] (It was a somber series for the Senators. Players wore black crepe on their uniform sleeve to commemorate Hiram Bithorn, the island's first major leaguer, who was shot to death by a policeman in Mexico on December 29, 1951.) Santurce would not capture any legs of the Trifecta.

Gilliam, one of the six imports allowed on a Puerto Rican team roster, enjoyed a fine season, leading the league in runs scored with 63 and was second to Carlos Bernier of Mayagüez in stolen bases with 14.[15] He finished second in Player of the Year voting. He also played in the league All-Star game, which his Import team won 2-0 over the Native team. In a pre-game activity, Gilliam placed second in a contest to see who was fastest in circling the bases. Luis "Canena" Márquez of San Juan won in a time of 13.5 seconds.[16]

QUOTA: THE SECOND GATE

Jackie Robinson's breaking the color barrier in 1947, and the subsequent successes of Larry Doby, Roy Campanella, Satchel Paige, Monte Irvin, and Don Newcombe, had blown the First Gate of integration wide open. While not yet universally accepted on Major League rosters, Black players had demonstrated they belonged on the same field as white players. Now, Black players stood at a Second Gate of integration—an unofficial quota.

On October 1, 1949, Brooklyn sold Major League-ready outfielder Sam Jethroe to the Boston Braves. Jethroe, signed by Branch Rickey for $5,000 from the Cleveland Buckeyes midway through the 1948 season, batted .326 with 19 triples and 154 runs scored in 153 games with Montreal in 1949. Rickey sold Jethroe, who would become the National League's Rookie of the Year in 1950, for a sum reported as high as $125,000, quite a return on Brooklyn's initial investment.[17] While the sale of Jethroe helped integrate another team—he became the first Black player to play for the Braves—a question existed as to whether Rickey's motivation was merely a financial return, or whether he concerned about backlash from fielding a lineup with four Black players. To that point, no Major League team had fielded a lineup with more than three Black players.

Rickey addressed this very question in a 1957 *Ebony* magazine article in which he discussed several aspects of Black players in baseball, including the trading of Jethroe. "I was on the fence on the question" of whether the Dodgers had too many Black players, Rickey said. "Five of the directors thought we had too many, but I said, 'I don't think we have too many.' I wanted the best players to keep on winning the pennant and I told them if a man kept me from winning, I wouldn't hire them regardless."[18]

Author Bryan Soderholm-Difatte observed in his book on 1950s integration of Major League Baseball that the first wave of Black players, such as Robinson, Campanella, Doby, and Mays, were all superstars:

"Without in any way diminishing the importance of the Black players who were so superb in the 1950s, and especially the importance of Jackie Robinson, because their excellence ensured there was no going back to segregated major-league baseball, integration could not be considered consolidated until *any* (emphasis in original) Black player with major-league ability, not just those with superior talent, could realistically compete with white players of similar major-league ability for big-league starting jobs, may the best player win."[19]

Essentially, what Soderholm-Difatte pointed out was that until teams opened their rosters to Black players of average to above-average ability, integration would not be complete. In order for that to occur, teams needed to be open-minded to fielding a lineup with more than half the players Black. Jethroe was one of those players who had Major-League ability, but at age 33 was not likely to be a superstar, so, he was expendable.

About the Dodgers specifically, Soderholm-Difatte wrote, they "appear to have been risk-averse to giving an opportunity to a Black player of far more pedestrian major-league ability—someone like the Giants' Hank Thompson—than their trio of Black stars. It was not until 1952 that the Dodgers began to expand their horizons about which Black players would be given a chance in the major leagues."[20]

Despite Gilliam's success in 1951, little evidence exists to suggest he figured in the team's plans in 1952. The Dodgers relied heavily on their "big three" Black players in 1951: Robinson, Campanella, and Newcombe. Instead, the catalysts for the inclusion of more Black players on the Brooklyn roster turned out to be the departure of Newcombe for a two-year stint in the military in February 1952 and the collapse of the Dodger bullpen in 1951, culminating in Bobby Thomson's walk-off home run in Game Three of the 1951 National League playoff. By turning to former Negro Leaguer Joe Black in 1952, the Dodgers solved not only their bullpen woes, but they were able to rationalize adding a Black player because Newcombe was gone.

In 1952, the Dodgers, Indians, and Giants would all regularly play three former Negro League stars. The Dodgers had Robinson, Campanella, and Black. The Indians fielded Doby, Luke Easter, and Harry Simpson. The Giants had Irvin, Hank Thompson, and Willie Mays, until the Army took him away. To that point, none of the teams regularly fielded four Black players.

As such, Gilliam's chances of making the Brooklyn roster in 1952 were slim despite his outstanding 1951 season at Montreal. Author Steve Treder evaluated Brooklyn's decision to keep Bobby Morgan and Rocky Bridges as backup infielders in 1952 instead of Gilliam. Both Morgan and Bridges were capable of backing up Pee Wee Reese at shortstop, a position which Gilliam did not play. But in keeping both, "the Dodgers deprived themselves of a backup infielder who could swing from the left side of the plate, and they were also sending down the fastest man of the three, and the best hitter."[21]

While Treder initially critiqued the decision from a pure baseball perspective, Brooklyn's decision to send Gilliam back to Montreal in 1952 looks even worse when race is considered. "The reason it took the Dodgers so long to find a place for Jim Gilliam on their roster was not that they had better players available," Treder concluded. "No one would seriously argue that Bobby Morgan or Rocky Bridges was a better player than Gilliam. Had he not been African American, it is inconceivable that

Gilliam would have had to wait until 1953 to get his first Major League at bat."[22]

Here was the Second Gate.

DODGERTOWN: "THE DEVIL" EMERGES

After experimenting with holding spring training overseas in Cuba (1947) and the Dominican Republic (1948) to lessen the impacts of racism, the Dodgers returned to Florida in 1949, ending up at the Vero Beach complex known as Dodgertown.

During the 1950s, Vero Beach was a community of approximately 5,000 people in highly segregated Indian River County on the Atlantic Ocean and, like much of Florida at the time, whites and Blacks did not intermingle.

From owner Walter O'Malley's perspective, Dodgertown allowed all of his Dodger players, white and Black, to live alongside one another on the complex, something they could not do off complex. As Jackie Robinson wrote in his autobiography, *I Never Had it Made*, this arrangement worked out well enough, provided Black players did not want to go into town. "It was like being confined to a reservation, and it was the only reason that we were quartered along with the whites."[23]

Once off the "reservation," Black players were subjected to the Jim Crow laws of the time, which meant patronizing restaurants and barber shops designated for Blacks only and transportation in colored-only taxis. Catcher John Roseboro, who joined the Dodgers nearly a decade after Dodgertown had opened, recalled the challenges. "For the Black players while I was there it was still Florida, Dixie, the deep South, a bad place to be."[24]

The unincorporated community of Gifford, separated from Dodgertown by the Vero Beach airport to the south, served as a safe haven for Black players seeking entertainment and diversion. As a predominantly Black community, Gifford thrived in the 1950s and 1960s as businesses catering to Black customers, from laundromats to barber shops, prospered. The team ran a bus from the complex into town in the evenings, dropping white players and their families in Vero Beach, while continuing across the railroad tracks into Gifford for the Black players.

One of the most popular pastimes among players and coaches during spring training was billiards, a sport at which Gilliam excelled and through which he acquired another nickname. As the story goes, one night during spring training in a year not recalled by anyone, Gilliam walked into a pool hall in Gifford. No one was playing, but several people were in the hall. Gilliam placed a twenty-dollar bill onto a table and, chalking up a cue, proclaimed, "Who wants a piece of 'The Devil?'" From that point forward Gilliam was known to his teammates and coaches as "The Devil," or even more simply, "Devil."

When asked about the legend in 1963, Gilliam admitted there were no takers, but if someone had called his bluff, "I'd have snatched that twenty and run the hell out."[25]

While Gilliam may have downplayed his ability, future teammate John Roseboro recalled Gilliam as a pool shark. Regarding the pool competition at spring training, Roseboro wrote in his memoir, "Walt Alston and Jim Gilliam were the best. Alston had a hand for it and could do it all, but The Devil was sneaky-good, playing perfect position and just tapping the ball so it barely fell in. They had a kid catcher in those camps who made money hustling at the tables, but the skipper and The Devil did him in."[26]

1952 SEASON: A RETURN TO MONTREAL

Gilliam was reportedly one of the first Royals players to sign a 1952 contract, demonstrating an eagerness to reach the Major Leagues. He recorded a hit in each of the Royals' first 16 games, as the team jumped out to a 12-4 start en route to winning the International League regular-season title for the second straight season. Gilliam batted .301, led the league in runs scored and stolen bases, finished second with 112 RBI, and was named the International League's MVP in 1952. Similar to the previous year, the Royals failed to win the Junior World Series, falling in six games to the Rochester Red Wings.[27]

1952 Parkhust card for Jim Gilliam, promoting Frostade, a Canadian competitor to Kool-Aid.

The *New York Daily News* reported in early August 1952 that Brooklyn manager Charlie Dressen, mindful of his team's August collapse in 1951 when they lost the pennant to the Giants, was lobbying for the club to bring up "the fine Negro infielder" Gilliam to help during the pennant stretch.

"I'd like to have a guy like that around, so that I can give my regulars a few days rest," Dressen told writer Dick Young. "I could put him in for Robinson if Jackie gets a little tired or sore in the legs. I might be able to use him for Reese, or even in the outfield if I want to get some more left-handed hitting in the lineup."[28] Dressen already viewed Gilliam's value as a utility player capable of filling in just about anywhere.

1952 insert from Montreal's French-language La Patrie *daily newspaper. Courtesy Wade Carothers.*

On the day the *Daily News* article ran, Brooklyn held an eight-game lead over the Giants. *The Sporting News* reported Gilliam's average at .309 with 92 runs batted in. The crosstown rival Giants would once again narrow the gap into September, but Brooklyn held on to first place and went to the World Series, where they lost in seven games to the Yankees after being up 3-2.

The front office never acquiesced to Dressen's lobbying for Gilliam, likely due to several factors, not the least of which was the number of Black players already on the team. In addition, by keeping Gilliam in Montreal, Brooklyn did not yet need to add him to the club's official roster. He was still Brooklyn property but, according to *The Sporting News*, he was getting noticed. The weekly publication reported in its August 27, 1952 issue, Boston Braves scout Billy Southworth advised the Braves that "Jim Gilliam, the Royals' fleet Negro infielder, is the No. 1 prospect in the (International) league. The Chicago White Sox also are said to be interested in Gilliam."[29]

If Jim had performed somewhat anonymously to that point, the cat was out of the bag a few weeks after the season ended when *The Sporting News* ran a story with the attention-grabbing headline, "Gilliam tabbed Robinson's successor with Brooklyn."[30] The problem with the declaration was that it was not attributed to anyone in an official Dodger capacity. Again, the media narrative centered on Gilliam as a replacement for a Black player, not as an additional player worthy of a starting role.

As far as Gilliam knew, he still needed to secure a Major League roster spot. And, so, accompanied by Gloria, Malcolm, and Kathy, he once again traded the French-speaking city of Montreal for the Spanish-speaking city of San Juan.

SANTURCE: AN ALL-STAR, CHAMPIONSHIP SEASON

George Scales did not return as Santurce manager for the 1952-53 season, a task falling to James "Buster" Clarkson, the team's shortstop each of the last several seasons. While the team was again led by outfielders Willard Brown and Bob Thurman, Gilliam at second, and Rubén Gómez on the mound, several new faces figured to inject enthusiasm in the lineup as play began on October 15.

Dodgers farmhand Billy Hunter, who spent 1952 in Double-A ball with Fort Worth where he won the league MVP and roomed with future Major Leaguer Don Zimmer,[31] was added to replace Clarkson at shortstop. The Dodgers wanted Hunter to team with Gilliam up the middle as a possible double-play combination. Hunter was enjoying his "working vacation," playing beach volleyball and lounging by the pool at one of the island's higher-end hotels, the Condado Beach Hotel. One morning, while eating breakfast with his wife Bev, he read a newspaper headline announcing he had been traded by the Dodgers to the St. Louis Browns, whose owner, Bill Veeck, wanted him to return to the United States. "I can't," Hunter replied. "I'm making more money—$1,200 a month—than at any time in my life."[32] Veeck agreed to increase Hunter's salary to $1,000 and give him a $1,000 bonus to return home. Two days later, his "vacation" ended.

Also joining the team was pitcher Alva Lee "Bobo" Holloman, who spent the 1952 season with the Syracuse Chiefs of the International League, compiling a 16-7 record and a 2.51 ERA. Gilliam played against Holloman many times that year, and he recommended Holloman play for Santurce that winter.[33] Holloman would gain immortality on May 6, 1953, when he threw a no-hitter in his Major League debut for the St. Louis Browns, a 6-0 win over the Philadelphia Athletics.[34]

The final addition to the Cangrejeros roster makeover occurred when they added an 18-year-old backup outfielder and Puerto Rican native named Roberto Clemente. He was the 23rd and last player to join the Santurce club, signing for $40 per week.[35] Offensively, Clemente contributed little, hitting just .234 during the season, and he became a spectator in the postseason.[36]

Although Santurce had won the city series with San Juan, 11-7, San Juan captured the regular season title with Santurce finishing second, matching the Cangrejeros with the Ponce Lions in the semifinals. Gilliam had once again led the league in runs scored with 55 and tied for third in stolen bases with 16. But it was Gilliam's overall batting that stood out, as he hit .312, good for fourth in the league.[37]

Santurce swept Ponce, 3-0, setting up an inner-city matchup with San Juan for the island championship. Santurce prevailed four games to two, thanks to strong pitching from Gómez and Holloman, and the power of Thurman, who drove in seven runs in Game Five alone. Prior to Game Five, Gilliam visited with Jackie and Rachel Robinson, who were vacationing in Puerto Rico and watched the game on February 14 in which Gilliam collected four hits and played "flawlessly" at second base.[38] When asked by a reporter from El Mundo how Gilliam was doing, Robinson said, "Just fine."[39] One can only speculate what Robinson meant in his response. Did he anticipate the prospect of Gilliam taking his job in a month?

The 1953 Caribbean Series took place in Cuba and featured Santurce, Havana, Chesterfield (Panama), and Caracas (Venezuela). The pivotal game of the six-game round-robin Series occurred on February 22, 1953 between Santurce and Havana in front of 16,700 partisan fans. Havana had rallied from a 3-1 deficit with three runs in the eighth inning and another in the ninth to lead 5-3. With no one left to pinch-hit, pitcher Cot Deal doubled for Santurce with two outs and scored on a single by Luis "Canena" Márquez. Gilliam singled Márquez into scoring position and Vic Pellot, a powerful first baseman who would become a six-time MLB All-Star and seven-time Gold Glove winner under the name of Vic Power, singled home Márquez, moving Gilliam into scoring position.

With the score tied, Rubén Gómez strode to the plate and drove in Gilliam to win the game. He had entered as a pinch runner for Willard Brown earlier in the game and stayed in to play left field. As Deal told Puerto Rican baseball expert Van Hyning, "The Cuban fans got all over him [Gómez]...listed as a pitcher on our roster. When Gómez drove in Gilliam with the winning run on a base hit, they [the Cuban fans] got quiet all of a sudden."[40]

José "Pepe" Seda, a Puerto Rican baseball pioneer, general manager, scout, and writer, described the emotions of the game in the February 26, 1953 *El Mundo* newspaper:

"When the score was 5-3 (in favor of Havana) and with two outs, I accepted defeat like a presidential candidate when the partial number of votes come in...when Cot Deal lit the match and Canena and Gilliam kept it alive, I thought about our battling citizens who struggle to overcome their problems. The game-winning and miraculous hit by Gómez was emotionally satisfying to all Puerto Ricans."[41]

Three days later, Gilliam helped Santurce beat Havana again, 7-3, with a home run, his second in the Series, and cement a perfect 6-0 mark for the Cangrejeros. Gilliam went 12-for-22 (a .545 average) in the Series and was named to the All-Star team at second base. His teammate, Willard Brown, was the MVP with his four home runs and 13 RBI.[42]

After a year in which he was the International League MVP and Caribbean Series All-Star, Gilliam had more than shown himself ready for the Brooklyn Dodgers as he arrived in Florida in March 1953. He was ready to knock on baseball's Second Gate.

7

MOVING JACKIE

JACKIE ROBINSON'S TRIP TO PUERTO RICO TO SEE JIM GILLIAM IN MID-February 1953 was as much a scouting mission as it was a vacation. Robinson was sizing up the first real competitive threat to his second base job in Brooklyn. Upon reporting to Vero Beach on February 28, Robinson was asked to provide his assessment of Gilliam's abilities. "He is a fine ball player," Robinson said. "But I don't think he's good enough to take my job away from me—yet."[1]

Rumors about Jim's fit on the Dodgers' Opening Day roster began while he was still in Puerto Rico. *The Sporting News* anointed him "most likely to succeed" in its January 7 issue. "Junior is the guy who so often has been referred to as Jackie Robinson's successor, but he might be somebody's successor in the outfield."[2] It was the first time the media began to advance a narrative that Gilliam and Robinson might both be in the Dodgers' lineup.

Perhaps anticipating a domino effect, Dodgers vice president Buzzie Bavasi created a hole in left field when he traded Andy Pafko to the Boston Braves on January 17 for minor-league infielder Roy Hartsfield and $75,000 cash. Pafko appeared in 150 games in 1952, second on the club behind Gil Hodges. Bavasi positioned the trade of 32-year-old Pafko as a way for the Dodgers to get younger. Among Dodger regulars, only Duke Snider and Hodges were under the age of 30 entering the 1953 season. "We can't sit still and watch the team collapse of old age," Bavasi said. [3]

"The whole point," Bavasi told *The Sporting News*, "is that we're conscious that players get older, and when they're 32 or more they get older mighty quick sometimes. We hope, and we believe, that we've got the replacements that will be ready made when the time comes, either suddenly or gradually."[4]

The *New York Daily News* quoted Bavasi similarly. "This was a deal in itself, with one purpose in mind. To make room for some younger player."[5] Newspaper writers immediately speculated that the younger player would be Gilliam, now 24 years old, but reasons existed to think otherwise. Starting right fielder Carl Furillo and backup outfielders George Shuba and Dick Williams had all undergone offseason surgery.[6] Shuba appeared in 94 games in 1952, while Williams logged 36

Undated Jim Gilliam pinback. Courtesy Wade Carothers.

appearances. Both men hit over .300 in their brief MLB stints, and while both seemed capable replacements for Pafko, their status for the 1953 season was in doubt. Outfield depth suddenly seemed precarious.

Others in the mix for outfield playing time included Bill Sharman, Don Thompson, and Bill Antonello. Sharman hit .294 for Triple-A St. Paul in 1952 and was 26 years old. Thompson appeared in 80 games for Brooklyn in 1951 and hit .345 for Triple-A Montreal in 1952. He was the oldest of the group at 29. Antonello, 26, hit .290 for Double-A Mobile in 1952. Yet another possibility was Jim Pendleton, a former Negro Leaguer who could play both outfield and third base. Pendleton, 29 years old, had played four years in Triple-A, three with St. Paul and the 1952 season with Gilliam in Montreal. He consistently hit around .290 with decent power numbers and decent speed.

Baseball's reserve clause in effect at the time allowed teams to stockpile players like Pendleton and Gilliam in the minors without fear of another team signing them. The deep Brooklyn farm system built by Branch Rickey in the late 1940s drew cover story attention in *The Sporting News* on February 25, 1953. The article's banner headline read, "Kid Crop Backs Dodger Flag Dynasty" with a subheadline of "Enough good young talent for eight to ten years."[7]

"We are top heavy in good infielders and outfielders. We have fine kid pitching prospects whom I believe to be two-three years from the majors," Fresco Thompson, vice president of minor-league operations, boasted.[8]

Bavasi leveraged that depth, and further narrowed the field for Pafko's replacement, when he traded Pendleton in February to the Braves, joining Pafko. As part of a four-team deal, the Dodgers also sent utility infielder Rocky Bridges to the Cincinnati Reds, receiving veteran pitcher Russ Meyer from the Philadelphia Phillies. The surplus of young talent afforded the Dodgers the opportunity to increase cash flow by nearly $200,000 by selling infielder Billy Hunter in October and Pafko in January. In addition, the club added a key arm in Meyer, all without changing the core of the team.

Gilliam, among the youngest of the prospects at age 24, certainly would infuse youth into the lineup. And while he played outfield on a semi-regular basis with Montreal the previous two seasons, appearing in 50 games there in 1952, Jim's true position was second base. If he were to wrestle that job away from Robinson, where would Jackie play? Save for six appearances at third base in 1948, Robinson's entire big-league career had been at either first base or second base. When a reporter asked Robinson in Vero Beach about Gilliam's prospects as a good outfielder, he replied with a broad grin, "He'd better be if he wants to make this club."[9]

No matter how good Gilliam performed in camp, the possibility of him returning to Montreal was very real for two reasons, one more easily rectified than the other. First, Gilliam was still not on the Dodgers' 40-man roster. As easy as it seems to fill the roster spot, teams did not always have an incentive to do so. Writing in the March 1953 *Baseball Digest*, Norm Nevard called players like Gilliam "illegitimate rookies," players physically in camp but not rostered. In a veiled shot at the reserve clause, Nevard wrote, "If they don't make good, they report back to the farm club just like the regularly certified rookies who don't make good. The only difference is that, through this ruse, a big-league club can take more than its legal quota of 40 players."[10] If a player was sent back to minors, the club had saved an option on the player while retaining control.

The second reason was much more complicated: Gilliam's skin color. Star pitcher Don Newcombe was in military service in 1953, meaning Brooklyn's Black players were Robinson, Campanella, and 1952 Rookie of the Year Joe Black. Adding Gilliam would create the possibility of featuring Dodgers four Black players on the diamond at a time. This would not be groundbreaking: the New York Giants rostered four Black players with Willie Mays, Monte Irvin, Ray Noble, and Hank Thompson. During the 1951 World Series, the Giants had started an all-Black outfield against the Yankees. In the American League, the 1952 Cleveland Indians rostered six Black players in Luke Easter, Harry Simpson, Larry Doby,

Dave Pope, Quincy Trouppe, and Sam Jones during the season, with all but Pope appearing in games on May 3 against Washington and May 4 at Boston.

Nonetheless, on the eve of training camp, the *Daily News'* Dick Young felt it necessary to address the issue in his column. "Nobody will say so out loud, but it is generally believed that neither Junior Gilliam nor any other Negro will make the Dodger club until Jackie Robinson is through. There is an unwritten racial ratio at this stage of social progress and the Brooks have reached the saturation point—so they'll sell surplus colored players, just as they did with Jim Pendleton."[11]

Young was saying out loud what baseball was trying to keep quiet regarding integration—a Second Gate awaited Black players. The First Gate, designed to keep Black players out of Major League Baseball entirely, was blown open by Robinson in 1947. The Second Gate limited the number of Black players on any one team. Brooklyn's trade of Pendleton, an outfielder capable of filling a hole in the team's lineup, could be viewed from multiple perspectives heading into the 1953 season. It could mean the Dodgers were more confident in the younger Gilliam than in Pendleton despite the position differences. Or, it could mean the Dodgers were not ready for six Black players on their roster.

Baseball's "Great Experiment" with integration had occurred seven springs prior in 1947. Twenty-eight Black players had appeared in a Major League game since that time. Still, only 30 Black players were present in training camps in 1953.[12] And while that number did not include players like Mays and Newcombe, who were in military service, the reality was only eight of the 16 Major League clubs had integrated. With the wealth of young prospects, a vacancy sign in left field, and the continuing specter of race in the newspapers, the Dodgers' 1953 spring training promised to be one of intrigue.

A REUNION WITH JOE BLACK

Gilliam's appearance in Brooklyn's Major League camp brought with it a welcomed reunion with his good friend Joe Black. When Black reported to the Baltimore Elite Giants spring training in Nashville in April 1946, one month after his army discharge, he was assigned to room with 17-year-old Gilliam. It was as unlikely a pairing as possible. Gilliam was a teenager who had not graduated high school. Black was 22 years old, had served in the military during World War II, and was on his way to earning a degree from crosstown Morgan State University, which he eventually did in 1950. Gilliam was quiet and reserved. Black was outgoing and gregarious.

Neither man could have predicted how intertwined their lives would become. The two players played together with the Elites in 1946-1950. Their contracts were purchased together by the Dodgers, and the two spent part of 1951 together as teammates with Montreal. Black joined the Major League club in 1952 and won National League Rookie of the Year, the first baseball season in which the two men did not share the same dugout. Black was quoted in a 2015 biography jointly authored by his daughter Martha Jo Black and sportswriter Chuck Schoffner, saying of Gilliam, "If he had a dollar, I had a dollar and vice versa. We bared our souls to one another."[13]

Black believed Gilliam was cognizant of his lack of formal education, and perhaps that contributed to his quiet demeanor. As a college man, Black encouraged Gilliam to spend time reading more than the newspaper sports page, which Gilliam did. This, Black was convinced, translated into Gilliam becoming more confident and talkative. It was Black's assertion that the only reason the Dodgers were interested in him was because of Gilliam. Black's biographers wrote, "Joe believed they were convinced that all (Gilliam) would need in order to get comfortable was a roommate he knew."[14]

Recalling Gilliam's quote to her father that Gilliam could not integrate the Cubs in 1950, Martha Jo Black reinforced the idea that Gilliam needed her father. "The Dodgers wanted Gilliam, but he was not comfortable around whites. Dad was more equipped to deal with that. 'I couldn't have been Jackie,' he told my dad."

The two developed such a close friendship that Gilliam would become godfather to Joe's son. Born May 26, 1952 in Brooklyn, Joseph Frank Black would forever be known as Chico, a name the older Joe Black picked up playing winter ball in Cuba where Chico was conceived. The earliest memory Chico has of Gilliam is that he struggled to say his name. "I called him JuJu. I just couldn't say his name. Years later I would talk to him and say, 'It's JuJu,' and he knew exactly who it was," Chico Black remembered.

SPRING TRAINING

Having shuttled Gloria, Malcolm, and Kathy from Baltimore to Puerto Rico and Montreal, Jim brought the family to Vero Beach in the spring of 1952, intent on making the big-league club. However, the family would continue to live in Baltimore to be close to Gloria's parents.

Training camp opened March 1, 1953, but Gilliam did not report until March 5, taking a week off after the Caribbean World Series. He did not practice until March 6 because "his uniform was still packed in the trunk."[15] That uniform bore the assigned number 35. Once Gilliam was settled in camp, Dodgers manager Charlie Dressen quickly put to rest any possibility that Gilliam would compete for an outfield spot.

"The next thing you know, we will have nothing but left fielders on this club," Dressen told the media. "Besides, if he is going to replace Jackie Robinson one day on the Dodgers that's where he ought to be playing—second base. I don't want him to go to the outfield."[16]

Not many secrets in spring training, apparently, as Jim Gilliam (right) overhears a discussion of his future with (l to r) Dodgers manager Charlie Dressen, Pee Wee Reese and Jackie Robindon. Via Wikimedia Commons.

Gilliam's first workout at second base on March 6 was "sensational," according to Fresco Thompson. The account in the *Brooklyn Daily Eagle* proclaimed the way "Gilliam scampered around his sector of the dirt was a revelation to the rest of the Dodgers players, watching from the side-lines."[17] The Dodgers played their first exhibition game on March 7 against the Boston Braves in Miami. Gilliam's debut was rather unremark-able as the Dodgers won, 8-4. He entered the game in the sixth inning, replacing Robinson at second base. At the plate, Gilliam was 0-for-3. In the field, Gilliam was middle man on a double play and "shooed his outfielders off" an Eddie Mathews pop fly, which fell to the ground between Snider, Carmen Mauro, and himself for a double.[18] Gilliam notched his first Dodger hit the next day when, after once again replacing Robinson at second, he singled off Lew Burdette of the Braves. He settled in after that.

Two weeks later, Dressen had seen enough to know what he was going to do, telling Dick Young of the *Daily News* his plan to make reigning third baseman Billy Cox a utility player in order to keep Gilliam and Robinson in the lineup. Gilliam would not be replacing Robinson so much as he was moving Robinson. The problem, according to Cox, the player being replaced, was Dressen had not told him of the switch.

"TROUBLE ON THE DODGERS"

Following the 1947 season in which Robinson broke the color barrier, Branch Rickey traded Dixie Walker, who had started a petition in spring training 1947 asking to not play with Robinson, to the Pittsburgh Pirates for Cox and pitcher Preacher Roe, an Arkansas native. Cox had been a fixture at third base for Brooklyn every year since. Now, at age 33 and eight months younger than Robinson, the popular Cox was being replaced in the lineup.

Writing in the *New York Herald-Tribune*, Roger Kahn addressed the issue directly. "When Don Hoak and Bobby Morgan worked out at third base nothing was said by the other players. When Gilliam moved to second and Robinson to third, resentment grew. The reason is nearing the surface and remarks by some Dodgers in the clubhouse and at their hotel indicate that the problem of Negroes in baseball is still to be finally resolved."[19]

Kahn's insinuation: when Hoak and Morgan—both white players— were competing for the position, everything was fine. But once Gilliam moved Robinson from second to third, sending Cox to the bench, a problem arose.

Morgan, who was born in Oklahoma City, had spent the previous five seasons shuttling between Montreal and Brooklyn. He had shown power with 14 MLB home runs in under 400 at bats, and versatility, playing three different positions. He also had a reputation as someone not comfortable around Black players.

"Oklahoman Bobby Morgan, for example, was never happy with playing with Blacks and, being tough and able to handle himself, wasn't afraid to say so. He once stood up in the dugout and, spotting a Black player on the other team, said, for all to hear: 'Why isn't he a Dodger? He's Black enough.' Bobby was a good utility man at several positions but the days for remarks like that in the Brooklyn dugout were gone, and soon so was he, to make room for players like Amorós and Gilliam. Bobby had to go because he was one of the 'Klan contingent' and, unlike a few others, he wasn't valuable enough to the team to get away with it," Rudy Marzano wrote in his book, *The Last Years of the Brooklyn Dodgers*.[20]

Indeed, Kahn alluded to Morgan's membership in the "Dodger Klan contingent"[21] in his statement for Peter Golenbock's *Bums: An Oral History of the Brooklyn Dodgers*. Asked about the 1953 spring training nearly 66 years later, Morgan denied any controversy around Black players took place. "What are you talking about? What occurred? I don't remember any of that. I don't know how Roger Kahn could remember it either because he wasn't around that much. You know these sportswriters write things that happened in the airplane or a place like that and, hell, they weren't even on the airplane. I don't know how they get these stories when they are not even there."

As might be expected, the story lingered for several days in the media. A headline splashed across the back page of the *New York Post* on Monday, March 23, read, "The Inside Story of Trouble on the Dodgers," with the last four words in bold font stretching across the width of the page. The accompanying article, written by Milton Gross, addressed the issue of racial discord on the Dodgers directly.

"Officially, the Dodger brass says the stories of the issue were exaggerations; that the half-dozen players who spoke in sympathy, resentment, confusion and shallow humor have given their assurances no race problem existed and never will exist.

"Yet Negro baiting remarks were made, not all in jest, and several questions remain unanswered: Is it dead or merely buried alive? Has discretion become the better part of bigotry? And—most important of all—why and how could this have happened on a team which served the classic demonstration that whites and Negroes can work side by side, not with tolerance but with respect?"[22]

For his part, Bavasi spoke directly with his team and declared the incident to be a non-issue. "I met with a few members of veteran players and I am satisfied," Bavasi said. "The whole thing has been exaggerated. There is no racial problem on the club and I assume there never will be."[23]

However, in his famous ode to the 1950s Brooklyn Dodgers, *The Boys of Summer*, Kahn, who years later referred to this period as "the Gilliam incident,"[24] wrote about a coffee-shop conversation he had at the McAllister Hotel in Miami in March 1953 with Cox and Roe about Gilliam and his impact on the team dynamic.

> "What do you think of Gilliam?" Cox said.
>> "Helluva ball player."
>> "How would you like a nigger to take your job?"...
>> "I guess I wouldn't like a nigger to take my job."
>> "Ya see," Cox said, to Roe.
>> "Can Robinson play third?" I said.
>> "I don't mean Jack," Cox said.
>> "Robi'son's one hell of a man," Roe said.
>> "I mean the nigger, the kid," Cox said.
>> "They got as much right to play as anyone else," Roe said, "but now they're pushin' Billuh around."
>> "The ball club's doing it, not Gilliam, not Robinson."
>> "I don't know," Roe said. "It's pretty fucked up."
>> "It sure is," I said.
>> "Ah," Billy Cox said. "Fuckit. But what the fuck they want a guy to do."[25]

Kahn, who was beaten on the original story by Young, was determined to get the last word in on the race issue. Writing for *Our Sports* magazine in the same June 1953 issue that featured a profile of Gilliam, Kahn initially added fuel to the fire under the headline, "What white big leaguers really think of Negro players." He quoted three unnamed Dodgers making disparaging comments during spring training. "How come that guy isn't on our club," one player is quoted as saying after seeing a Black minor-league player walk past the Major League field. "It's all right to have Negroes in the game, but now they're taking over," said a second player. "I don't know how Billy Cox feels, but I wouldn't want a n----- to take my job," said a third.[26]

Dressen engaged with Kahn in a question-answer segment in an article designed to put to bed the discussion of whether there was a race problem on the Dodgers. "What will happen when your best team consists of five Negroes and four Whites?" Kahn asked.

"Then that's the way it'll be. The nine best guys will play and anyone who doesn't like it can quit," Dressen responded. "But they won't quit and they'll start to like it when they see the Negro ball players getting them into the World Series and $5,000 extra."[27]

The story eventually spilled over into the Black press, where a headline on the front page of the *Pittsburgh Courier* read, "Gilliam key to spat on Bums' team." Bill Nunn, Jr. wrote, "The fact that the Dodgers may play three Negroes in their lineup...four when hurler Joe Black is on the mound...is considered one of the basic reasons behind the steady tension that has been built up over the past week."[28]

While Gilliam declined to comment on the situation, Robinson did speak to Nunn, acknowledging, "I know Cox is upset, but I don't think it's anything personal....Someone has moved him out of his position and he has a right to be upset. I don't think it makes any difference to him whether that someone is white or Negro."[29] Kahn's version of the story in *Boys of Summer*, in which he quoted Cox as saying, "How would you like a nigger to take your job?" suggested that it did matter if the someone was white or Negro.

Whether real or imagined, the damage caused by the articles and comments had been inflicted, so much so that Marzano titled his chapter about 1953 in his book, *The Last Years of the Brooklyn Dodgers*, "Race was always a problem."

"Bringing up Gilliam was another matter. Jim had impressive credentials but he wasn't worth risking tearing the club apart for. For that's what almost happened and it's a wonder the team won the pennant with the dissension that seethed below the surface," Marzano wrote.[30]

NASHVILLE HOMECOMING

As the Dodgers continued north from Vero Beach toward Brooklyn, the club detoured through the south to play a series of exhibition games against the Milwaukee Braves. Because Major League baseball had not expanded further west than St. Louis and the Mississippi River or further south than Cincinnati and the Ohio River, these exhibitions allowed fans to see their favorite stars up close. It also afforded Black spectators in the south the opportunity to show their support for Black players, and no one drew a bigger crowd than Jackie Robinson and the Dodgers. The two clubs began their series on April 1 in Mobile, before heading to New Orleans, Atlanta, Chattanooga, Nashville, and finally concluding in Pee Wee Reese's hometown, Louisville.

An hour-plus rain delay at the start of the opening game in Mobile, Alabama did not dampen the "overflow crowd of 8,285"[31] at Hartwell Field, home to the Dodgers' Double-A affiliate. The Dodgers scratched out a 3-2 victory in 10 innings when former Bear Don Zimmer singled home

Ed Roebuck after Gilliam had been intentionally walked. Following an 11-3 Braves win in New Orleans, the clubs rode into Atlanta for a game at Ponce de Leon Park. By this point, Jim was firmly entrenched at second base and in the leadoff spot, but his performance at the plate still attracted skeptics. As the game began on April 3 in Atlanta, Gilliam was hitting a meager .200 on the spring.

Jim Gilliam publicity shot from the Brooklyn Dodgers, 1953.

Jim seemed nonplussed about his hitting woes. "I think I'll be all right (sic). I hit good last year and last winter in Puerto Rico I hit good. But when I got to Vero Beach I just quit hittin'. I don't know why. Nobody can figure slumps," he said.[32] Indeed, he was about to bust out of his slump in a big way.

"Junior Jim Gilliam," as Howard Burr called him in the *Brooklyn Daily Eagle*, "lashed on three hits, one a double, and drew a base on balls to add

26 points to his percentage"[33] as the Dodgers squeaked out a 9-8 victory. Gilliam told Burr after the game he was "mighty grateful to Mr. Dressen for keeping me in there when I wasn't hitting a lick. He had me out in the morning at Atlanta for some special instruction. He told me I was swinging with my hands too close to my body."[34] The hitting continued the next day in Chattanooga when Gilliam went 1-for-4 with two runs scored as the Dodgers fell to Milwaukee, 9-8.

The Dodgers woke up on Easter Sunday, April 5, 1953, in Gilliam's hometown, Nashville. As might have been expected, a huge crowd turned out to see one of Willie White's "Lambs" play as a Major Leaguer, including Gilliam's mother, Katherine, and grandmother, Mattie. A crowd of 12,059 crammed into Sulphur Dell to watch the teams play—a record for an exhibition game—including a reported 6,259 "paying colored fans."[35] A photo in the next day's *Nashville Tennessean* showed fans seated eight rows deep in front of the left-center field scoreboard, a rope-and-stanchion separating the crowd from the field of play. The previous year, 1952, the Dodgers-Braves exhibition game in Nashville drew just 6,506. The hometown star was worth nearly 6,000 fans.

The anticipated game featured Braves ace Warren Spahn against Dodger newcomer Russ Meyer. Brooklyn opened the scoring in the bottom of the third when Gilliam, batting right-handed against the lefty Spahn, delighted the crowd with a single behind third. Zimmer singled to right center, and Snider singled to score Gilliam. In the bottom of the seventh, the suddenly hot Gilliam singled from the left side of the plate against right-handed Virgil Jester as the Dodgers won, 3-1.[36] Three days later, on April 9, the Dodgers announced they had purchased Gilliam's contract from Montreal, despite him hitting just .240 during the spring.

Once Jim had secured a spot on the Dodgers for 1953, Gloria moved back to Baltimore with the kids, now 3 and 2, and settled in the Cherry Hill area at 611 Cherrycrest Road, Apartment F. This allowed her to be closer to her parents, who could provide assistance.

JACKIE ROBINSON: ACT LIKE A CHAMPION

Comparisons to Jackie Robinson were inevitable. Gilliam was moving Robinson to third base, a position at which he had played just 36 innings in 1948—or was it the other way around? Robinson's biographer Arnold Rampersand wrote, "Robinson had moved to help Gilliam, with whom he roomed for a while, and liked a great deal, and their club."[37]

The Black magazine, *Our World*, set a high bar for Gilliam with its unbylined August 1953 article titled, "Will Gilliam top Jackie? Call Him the Boy with the Magic-Eye. But Can His Magic Equal Robinson's Exploits." *Our World* was a premier publication, covering contemporary topics from Black history to sports and entertainment, founded by John P. Davis and published from 1946-1957. The August 1953 magazine cover featured a color photo of Robinson and Gilliam in the upper right corner, with a cutline of "Will Gilliam Top Jackie?". A smiling headshot of "Howard U co-ed Sylvia Blackburn" dominated the rest of the cover. Setting the tone for what fans should expect from Gilliam as he lined up alongside Robinson, the article suggested, "Gilliam isn't a powerful sensational player, yet he matches Jackie on his playing ability. He's fast, he can hit and he can field.

"With a long career ahead of him, Gilliam may yet outdo Jackie's baseball feats. But he may never equal Jackie Robinson as a symbol to Negro kids everywhere. Anyway you look at it, Gilliam has a tough row to hoe to surpass Jackie Robinson."[38]

Around the same time, May 1953 marked the debut of *Our Sports* magazine, a short-lived publication focused on Black sports that listed Jackie Robinson as its editor. Over the course of five issues, the publication struggled with its positioning in the marketplace. The May issue stated it was "A New Monthly Magazine Feature Negro Athletes." The June issue billed itself as "The Negro's Own Sports Magazine." By August, the tagline had become, "The Great New Negro Sports Magazine." None of those worked. By November, the magazine ceased publication.

The June issue featured Giant outfielder Monte Irvin on the cover, but sandwiched between articles on Josh Gibson and Little League Baseball's role in teaching racial unity was an non-bylined article, "Meet Junior Gilliam!"

Essentially an interview, the article documents Jim's respect for the pioneer. When asked what he thought when he heard Robinson had signed with the Dodgers seven years earlier, Gilliam said, his humble nature already showing, "All I could think was that if Jackie made good maybe some others would get a chance and maybe if I got good enough I could be one of them. But how could I figure it would be me to take his place. I still am not sure now."[39]

The article continues with the anonymous author stating, "As we talked, I could sense the tension, excitement and expectation in Junior. There was the hope he would make it and the fear he would not."[40] Given the article's split focus between Gilliam's past and potential, and Robinson's legacy, it is not hard to conceive the anonymous article was written by Robinson himself. Or, at the very least, he had significant editorial input.

"People ask me if I tried to pattern myself on Jackie, if I tried to imitate the way he plays. Guess it would be a better story if I said I did, but it just wouldn't be so.

"They forget I was a second baseman before Jackie was. (italics in original) They forget I broke into the Negro leagues (sic) Jackie broke into organized baseball. If I was going to imitate anybody it would have to be somebody who was an older player in our own league. Maybe my heart was with Jackie, but my eyes had to be with me."[41]

Jackie Robinson believed it was his job to mentor Gilliam in his rookie season, and to that end, he chose to room with the shy youngster, a decision Roger Kahn recalled to Peter Golenbock. "Jackie roomed with Jim Gilliam, who usually had less to say than anyone. Even when he could have roomed with Joe Black, a fairly sophisticated college man, he chose Gilliam."[42]

Teammate Don Newcombe, himself a former Negro Leaguer, remembered Robinson's mentorship of the rookie. "Jackie felt it was his responsibility to talk to him. The first thing Gilliam did was sit down and talk to the godfather. Jackie told Junior what he was supposed to do as a human being, a person, a player. And not to do Uncle Tom 'yes, sir!'/'no, sir!' shit. Instead it was 'Act like a champion, carry yourself like a professional.' Jackie nursed Gilliam along so that he overcame his shortcomings and became a star player himself."[43]

To suggest Gilliam respected Robinson would be an understatement. By all accounts, Gilliam revered Robinson and understood the sacrifices he had made on behalf of all Black ballplayers. "He (Gilliam) and Jackie got along fine," former Negro League player and Giants star Monte Irvin said. "He didn't have any problem because he would go along with whatever Jackie wanted to do."[44]

Author Harvey Frommer quoted Gilliam, without time context, "one of the greatest things in my life was coming to the Brooklyn Dodgers and rooming with Jackie Robinson. I learned a lot about life on and off the field from him."[45]

As Jim stood on the precipice of replacing a pioneer at second base, he told the anonymous *Our World* author, "Every one of us who got the chance to play in the big league, or at least the chance to try for it, owes it to Jackie because he made it. Do you realize what it will mean to be the one who follows him in his job?"[46]

8

A STRONG MLB DEBUT IN 1953

In its preview of the upcoming 1953 season, the *Brooklyn Daily Eagle* anointed Jim something of a savior to the club. "The outstanding artistic development of the team this year was the performance of junior (sic) Jim Gilliam after this lithe and fleet-footed young Negro reported from Puerto Rico. Even allowing for the fact that Gilliam had played all Winter and reported in top shape, his skill as a second baseman was a remarkable revelation," columnist Tommy Holmes wrote on April 3.

"Nobody in the major leagues today plays second base better than this fellow....Gilliam switches at the plate and shapes up as an adroit and competent hitter. He, of course, doesn't carry Jackie Robinson's bat up to the plate. And this, in turn, means Gilliam in the lineup doesn't mean Robinson out of it."[1]

The beginning of Gilliam's big-league career mirrored that of Robinson's experience in 1947, one of high expectations and a lackluster opening game. Robinson went 0-for-3 with a sacrifice bunt, and a ground out into a double play on April 15, 1947 against the Boston Braves. He did reach on an error and score the go-ahead run in the seventh to help Brooklyn win. Gilliam's debut six years later on April 14, 1953 included a single to open the bottom of the fifth off Pittsburgh pitcher Murry Dickson. Gilliam, too, would score a go-ahead run on a Duke Snider home run two batters later, as Brooklyn won its 1953 opener.

"Junior Jim Gilliam was making his big league debut. He got only one infield hit, took a third strike and on his other three trips to the dish he couldn't get the ball out of the infield. He seems a little uncertain going back for popups. But fielding conditions were atrocious and his hit started the downfall of Dickson in the fifth," Harold Burr wrote in the next day's *Brooklyn Daily Eagle.* [2]

Things improved considerably for Gilliam after that first game: he started the Dodgers' first 74 games, leading the club to a 46-28 record. Following a 3-for-3 performance on May 4, Gilliam was hitting .344 with a .506 on-base percentage. He reached base safely by hit or walk in his first 24 games in a Dodgers uniform.

But the grind of non-stop, year-round baseball set in, and his offensive performance steadily declined until Dressen benched him just after the Fourth of July. His average had fallen to .238 after a 20-6 loss to the Giants on July 5. Dick Young of the *Daily News* suggested Gilliam was "so fast that he ran into the 'sophomore jinx' in his rookie year." [3]

1953 Jim Gilliam Topps baseball card. Courtesy Wade Carothers. Copyright Topps, all rights reserved.

The *Brooklyn Daily Eagle* remarked Gilliam's "eight-game rest proved to be quite a tonic." [4] He reentered the starting lineup on July 16 and promptly cracked seven hits in his first 13 at bats. He did not exit the lineup for the rest of the season. A six-game road stretch in St. Louis and Chicago from July 28-August 2 saw Gilliam hit safely 14 out of 27 trips to the plate, raising his average to .272, where he stayed the rest of the season.

From July 19-August 26, Jim reached base safely in 39 straight games, the longest such stretch of his career. During that period, his slash line was .365/.473/.545.

"I know I was tired," Gilliam said toward the end of the season. "My hitting improved, and I think it will keep on improving as I find out a little more about the pitchers and how they work on me. Then I can figure out a way to counteract them." [5]

When the campaign ended, Jim had hit .278 for his rookie season with a .383 on-base percentage. He led all of baseball with 17 triples and the National League with 710 plate appearances, despite his eight-game benching in July. His 100 walks were second behind Stan Musial and tied with Ralph Kiner, setting a National League mark for most walks in a season by a rookie. His 21 stolen bases in 1953 ranked him third, but his 14 times caught stealing was tops in the National League. He crossed home plate 125 times, good for fourth in the National League.

Duke Snider relayed the story that Jim had said at the beginning of the year: "I am going to have fun leading off for this team because I love to run so much." Snider and his teammates were happy to oblige, telling him they would "run his tail off." By July, according to Snider, Gilliam said, "Man, you guys were right. I need a couple of days off."[6]

1953 WORLD SERIES: AGAIN, THE YANKEES

The 1953 World Series was a repeat of the 1952, 1949, and the 1947 series. Brooklyn would again face crosstown rival Yankees, who had captured four titles in a row, and five of the last six. New York City was the epicenter of the baseball world in October 1953, and it would stay that way until Brooklyn and the New York Giants left for California after the 1957 season. In all but one year between 1947 and 1957, at least one of the three New York City teams—Yankees, Giants, and Dodgers—appeared in the World Series. Six times in those 11 years the matchup was between the Yankees and the Dodgers.

"Never before and never again would teams and the players on those teams dominate the sport, the psyche of fans, and the spirit of a city as did the New York City baseball teams of the era,"[7] wrote Harvey Frommer in *New York City Baseball: The Last Golden Age, 1947-1957*.

The 1953 Series opened at Yankee Stadium on September 30 in front of 69,734 spectators, quite possibly the largest crowd Gilliam had seen, much less played before. On the mound for the Yankees was Allie Reynolds, pitching in his sixth and final World Series with the Yankees. In his career, he amassed a 7-2 record in 15 career World Series games, good for a tie for second place in career World Series wins. To this day, he ranks third in career World Series strikeouts and is top 10 in career starts, innings pitched, and shutouts.

Round one of the classic veteran versus rookie matchup went to the rookie. Gilliam opened the game with a ground-ball single to center, but was stranded at second base. The Yankees jumped all over Dodger starter Carl Erskine in the bottom of the first, scoring four times, punctuated by a bases-loaded triple from Billy Martin.

Gilliam had struck out to open the top of the third against Reynolds. The score stayed 4-0 Yankees until the top of the fifth. Round three went to the rookie, as the left-handed-hitting Gilliam stroked a one-out home run to deep right field, putting the Dodgers on the scoreboard. Brooklyn tied the game at 5-5 in the top of the seventh, but surrendered four runs in the seventh and eighth innings to fall, 9-5. Jim finished 2-for-3 against Reynolds, but was 0-for-2 against Johnny Sain, who pitched the final 3.2 innings for New York.

Gilliam's recollection of the game years later had the sequence of events slightly off. "In my rookie year I hit a home run off Allie Reynolds the second time up in the World Series," he told the *Tennessean*, grinning. "I walked back to the bat rack with my bat the next time. Man, he really reared back and threw the ball past me."[8]

Game Two didn't go much better for the Dodgers, falling 4-2 to Yankees' starter Eddie Lopat. Gilliam struggled, going 0-for-5. He was now hitting just .200 in two World Series games, and the Dodgers trailed 2-0 in the Series as it headed to Brooklyn.

The Dodgers started Erskine again in Game Three, as he had lasted just one inning in Game One. This time the Indiana native was on point, limiting the Yankees to two runs in nine innings, as Brooklyn won 3-2 thanks to a go-ahead home run from Campanella in the bottom of the eighth. Gilliam was 1-for-4 with a caught stealing.

Jim's fortunes changed the next day, October 3, when he greeted left-hander Whitey Ford, who would later become the winningest pitcher in World Series history, with an opposite-field ground-rule double to right. Gilliam scored two batters later on a Robinson single. In the second, Gilliam doubled with two out off Tom Gorman, who had replaced Ford, but was stranded. In the fourth, Gilliam doubled again, his third of the game, scoring Carl Furillo and giving Brooklyn a 4-0 lead.

Batting in the sixth against Sain, Gilliam lined to Mickey Mantle in right, scoring Cox and increasing Brooklyn's lead to 6-2. (Inexplicably, Gilliam was not awarded a sacrifice fly.) In his final at bat in the eighth, Gilliam flew out to deep center. Officially he was 3-for-5 with three doubles, but he had hit the ball hard each time. Brooklyn won 7-2 and evened the Series at two games each.

Mantle's second-inning grand slam, plating four unearned runs, was the difference in Game Five as the Yankees rolled to an 11-7 win and 3-2 Series edge. Gilliam's hot hitting continued as he went 2-for-4 with a single and a ninth-inning home run off lefty Bob Kuzava. In doing so, Gilliam became the first player in World Series history to hit a home run from both sides of the plate in the same Series. Mantle would duplicate the feat the next day.

Gilliam was also hit by a pitch and scored two runs. After his slow Series start, Gilliam had enjoyed the home field at Ebbets, raising his average to .348 with five extra base hits, as the Series moved back to Yankee Stadium

The Yankees won Game Six, and the Series, in walk-off fashion on October 5, 4-3. Gilliam's offensive struggles in the Bronx continued as he posted an 0-for-4, lowering his final average to .296. His five extra-base hits, along with five from the Yankees' Martin, tied Babe Ruth's 1923 World Series performance and that of Chick Hafey in 1930 for most in a six-game Series. Reggie Jackson's 1977 six extra-base hits in yet another Yankees-Dodgers World Series would surpass Gilliam and Ruth's record for most in a six-game Series.

ROOKIE OF THE YEAR

When Jackie Robinson won MLB's first Rookie of the Year honors in 1947, the award was given to just one player across both leagues. Alvin Dark of the Boston Braves won the award in 1948, after which it was split into two awards, one for each league. In the more progressive National League, the next five winners were all former Negro League stars: Don Newcombe, Sam Jethroe, Willie Mays, and Joe Black. Would Jim Gilliam continue the streak?

Whereas Mays and Black had each won with greater than 70 percent of the vote, Gilliam's case was not as clear cut. St. Louis Cardinals' pitcher Harvey Haddix won 20 games and posted a stellar 7.3 wins above replacement (WAR). He even received nine votes for the National League Most Valuable Player award. As good as Gilliam's season was, his 3.9 WAR was just seventh on his own team, and he did not garner any MVP consideration. Nonetheless, Gilliam received 11 first-place votes, tallying 46 percent, to finish ahead of Haddix's four votes, surprising Gilliam. "I certainly thought Harvey Haddix would win the award. He won 20 games you know,"[9] Gilliam said.

Haddix's eligibility for the award was up for debate. He joined the Cardinals after military service in August 1952 and appeared in seven games, totaling 42 innings pitched. His manager, Eddie Stanky, stated bluntly in early September, "Haddix isn't a rookie." For his part, Haddix believed he qualified for the status. "I think I am a rookie, but I would like to know."[10]

The Sporting News, the organization awarding the honor, addressed the controversy in its October 1, 1953 issue, establishing "a clear cut definition for a major league rookie as any player who has not had more than 45 days in the big leagues, regardless of the number of games played."[11] Previously, a player who appeared in more than 10 games would have been ruled ineligible for rookie status the following season. As a pitcher, Haddix appeared in just seven games in 1952, despite being on the roster for nearly 45 days.

BARNSTORMING WITH ROY CAMPANELLA

Gilliam's Rookie of the Year season afforded him, presumably, his pick of postseason barnstorming teams fronted by his teammates, one led by Roy Campanella and one led by Jackie Robinson. Postseason barnstorming tours, part of the baseball landscape for decades, served multiple purposes, both similar to the preseason exhibition games. First, it afforded non-Major League towns, primarily in the south and the west, the opportunity to see big league players up close. Second, principally before the Major Leagues integrated, it encouraged Black players to play with and against white players, though this posed some problems in southern cities. And finally, it allowed players to exercise their own individual capitalism by collecting, and often sharing, ticket revenue.

Following the 1953 season, Gilliam signed on with Campanella's All-Stars, as opposed to Robinson's squad, for reasons not completely clear. Perhaps it was the presence of Jim's long-time friend, Joe Black, who would play with Campanella. Or, perhaps it was the fact that Campanella's team featured all Negro players, while Robinson had invited white players, including Dodgers Gil Hodges and Ralph Branca, to tour. Or, perhaps it was as simple as money. Robinson's approach was to guarantee each player a fixed share of revenue from the tour, with Robinson pocketing the extra. Campanella had a different approach: equal shares for everyone.

"That's why some of us turned down guarantees to go with Jackie Robinson's team," Black told Neil Lanctot. "We liked Campanella's plan. Everybody gets the same."[12]

Campanella's team featured Gilliam, Black, and Newcombe from the Dodgers, paired with Larry Doby, Harry Simpson, Dave Hoskins, Bob Boyd, Connie Johnson, Othello Renfroe, and three Milwaukee Braves players, Bill Bruton, George Crowe, and one-time Dodger minor leaguer Jim Pendleton.[13] The tour began October 11, six days after the World Series, in Memphis, Tennessee and ended November 6 in Pensacola, Florida.[14] In between, the team played 25 games in 11 states across the deep south, Hawaii, and California.

The tour's second stop on October 12 was in Jim's hometown of Nashville, where mayor Ben West had declared the evening, "Junior Gilliam Night." The game, played at Sulphur Dell, included festivities at the end of the fifth inning in which West and Nashville councilman Robert E. Lilliard presented Gilliam a scroll and a key to the city.[15] Campanella, whose team defeated a squad of Negro League players, 8-2, in front of 3,000 fans, told the local media about Gilliam, "You bet they like him up there in Brooklyn. Why not? He had a great year."[16] Gilliam rewarded the fans with an RBI double in the sixth.[17]

Most games were against Negro League teams, but it was the series of games played in the U.S. territory of Hawaii (it would not gain statehood until August 21, 1959) drawing the stiffest competition, a team of white Major League All-Stars led by New York Yankees pitcher Eddie Lopat. Othello "Chico" Renfroe was a 30-year-old journeyman from the Negro Leagues, who had made his debut in 1945 on the same Kansas City Monarchs team as Jackie Robinson. He also played for the Cleveland Buckeyes and the Indianapolis Clowns before retiring after the 1953 season, a year spent in the independent Manitoba-Dakota League. He recalled his excitement when Campanella asked him to join the barnstorming club as a backup catcher. "I got a letter from Campanella asking me if I want to go barnstorming with him. 'Would you go and help me catch?

"'Gosh!' I said. 'Would I!'....I was the only minor leaguer on the team....We played all the big parks, made tremendous money. But this is when Campanella proved that he was a champ. He got $1,000 a man guarantee to go to Honolulu to play three games against an all-star team that had Nellie Fox at second, Harvey Kuenn at short and Enos Slaughter in right. He said, 'I'm going to take this guy with me, and he's going to get the same cut we get.' He made everybody on the team take enough money out of their cut to make me make the same,"[18] Renfroe told John Holway in 1971.

The series opened on October 18 with a 7-1 Lopat win, behind two Jackie Jensen home runs, both off of Dave Hoskins. The second game went to extra innings, with Campanella's team coming out on top, 4-3. In the final game on October 20, Newcombe "threw aspirin tablets," scattering three hits over nine innings. Campanella's team slugged three home runs, including a solo shot from Gilliam in the eighth, to coast to a 7-1 win, and a 2-1 series advantage.[19]

Despite the presence of big-league stars like future Hall of Famers Yogi Berra, Slaughter, Eddie Mathews, Bob Lemon, Fox, and Robin Roberts on Lopat's team, it was Campanella's team garnering the newspaper headlines. A photo credited to Gordon Morse in the *Honolulu Advertiser* the day after their arrival shows Campanella's team lined up outside the Pan American Stratocruiser at the airport. Players were smiling, dressed in suits and ties with leis around their necks. Gilliam is standing between Doby and Renfroe, wearing a light-colored suit and a white Panama-style hat.[20]

That Gilliam was smiling in a *Honolulu Advertiser* photo after a long flight over the Pacific Ocean was surprising for a member of the Dodgers' "no-fly" club. After the Braves moved to Milwaukee for the 1953 season, airplane travel became the norm for the Dodgers. Owner Walter O'Malley even purchased a team plane. Over the years, this was speculated to be a problem for Gilliam and a few other players, notably Carl Furillo, Sal Maglie, and Don Newcombe. This "no-fly" group declined to fly, preferring the serene train rides in between cities.

Furillo claimed flying "provoked air sickness" and successfully used this excuse, combined with a medical procedure his wife was to have, to get out of a post-season goodwill trip to Japan two days after the 1956 season. Furillo, who had served in the Pacific in World War II, had additional incentive to not want to fly across the Pacific Ocean. "I want no part of it. I've seen Japan (during the war) and there's nothing there that I want to see again,"[21] Furillo said.

Newcombe's fear of flying was informed by witnessing two plane crashes near his New Jersey home in 1951, killing 84 people. He became so unnerved he refused to fly and was given permission to travel by train. When the club moved to Los Angeles, Newcombe turned to hypnotism to conquer his fear.[22]

While Gilliam preferred trains, he had learned that flying was necessary, particularly if he wanted to make extra money early in his career. As spring training for Gilliam and the Montreal Royals concluded in 1952, Walter Alston approached Dodgers farm director Fresco Thompson about Gilliam's reluctance to fly.

"Alston appealed to me for help with his problem. I told him that when he held his team meeting tomorrow I would come over and have a little chat with Junior and square away the problem.

"Cornering Gilliam, I said, 'Junior, I understand you have some objection to flying.'

"He nodded.

"'What did you do last winter?' I questioned.

"'I played ball in Puerto Rico,' he said.

"'Oh?' I questioned. 'How did you get there? There's no bridge, no railroad.'

"'I flew, Mr. Thompson,' he admitted.

"'Well,' I said, after due deliberation, 'I think the only decision that we can make is that if you fly to Puerto Rico for Junior Gilliam to make a buck, I think you'll have to fly to Newport News for Mr. Rickey.'

"He flew—and I am very pleased for we would have been in bad shape without the great efforts of Gilliam since that occasion."[23]

The only problem with Thompson's recollection was that Branch Rickey left the Dodgers organization in October 1950, 18 months prior to Thompson purportedly convincing Gilliam to fly.

During a 1963 interview with Jack Mann of *Sport* magazine, Gilliam confessed he still did not like to fly. "Hell, no," he said. "I'll never get used to it. The greatest feeling in the world is when those wheels touch. Then I can breathe. I ain't ever gonna like it, but these days you fly or you don't play."[24]

Although barnstorming would continue for a few more years, this series would be one of the last to attract large crowds and so many star players. More than 24,000 fans paid to watch the three-game series showcasing eight future Hall of Famers, in addition to players who would win Most Valuable Player or Rookie of the Year awards.

Once the tour wrapped up, Jim returned home to Baltimore to rest with Gloria, Malcolm, and Kathy. "This season I felt the strain of year-round ball for the first time in my life. I finally had to be benched for seven or eight games to get back in stride,"[25] Gilliam remarked.

9

"THE NAME'S JIM"

GILLIAM'S OUTSTANDING DEBUT SEASON WITH BROOKLYN SERVED TO ingratiate him into the fabric of the team's fans, in much the same way the community embraced Jackie Robinson, Carl Erskine, Gil Hodges, and the others. The relationship between Dodger players and their fans was intimate, almost familial. Sons and daughters cheered for the Dodgers because their parents cheered for them. Stuart Wantman was eight years old in 1953, living in the Midwood section and attending P.S. 193, now named after Gil Hodges and bordering Gil Hodges Way, when his fandom took hold.

"We rooted for the team our dad rooted for and that was it," Wantman recalled. "They were ours. They lived near us but we didn't invade their privacy. Their kids went to our schools. It was part of everyday life in Brooklyn. The fans loved all the players, Black and white. Snider was my favorite player, but knowing what I know now, I should have chosen Jackie."

Wantman's father, Jack, passed away in September 1953, but his father's cousins owned Brooklyn-based Esquire Boot Polish, one of the many advertisers with a brightly colored outfield sign at Ebbets Field. Wantman's mother, Rose, obtained box seat tickets and, on September 10, 1954, took Stuart and younger sister, Blanche, to his first Dodgers game at Ebbets Field. It was a rain-shortened, five-inning Friday night affair against the Milwaukee Braves won by Brooklyn, 2-1. "Our seats were on the first base side. I had never seen grass so green, or lights lighting a field. It was magical," Wantman said.

He continued attending games at Ebbets Field, riding the subway, not an uncommon practice for a 10-year-old at the time, from Avenue J or Avenue M north to the park. He collected soda bottles to redeem for the money necessary to purchase a ticket, knowing ushers would allow spectators to mingle down to vacant seats closer to the field after the first inning. "It was sort of like what Disney is to many people. It was heaven," he recalled wistfully.

Baseball on television was still in its infancy, so the Dodgers were not on the tube as often as today. The way to experience the magic of Ebbets Field and the Dodgers was to go to games, an event filling the senses. "Going through the opening, I remember how green the grass was," remembered Matt Perlstein, who lived two express stops from Ebbets Field and attended P.S. 217 on the corner of Coney Island Avenue and Newkirk Avenue. "As you approached, you could smell the Bond Bread Factory nearby. The signs all seemed colorful."

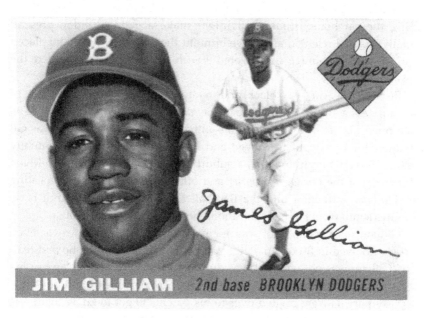

Jim Gilliam's 1955 Topps baseball card. RLFE Pix / Alamy Stock Photo

For Gilliam, as with many other Dodgers, the feeling of admiration for the fans was just as strong as the fans' affinity for the players. "They were the best. They knew the game for they had it for so long. They knew when a guy was in a slump. They knew when a guy was trying. You could come to Ebbets Field and watch a game but you couldn't say anything you wanted to about the Bums because their fans loved that team," Gilliam said. "I will always have a soft spot in my heart for Ebbets Field."[1]

Jim's fan appeal was not confined to the Brooklyn borough. Eight-year-old Dave Johnson first spied a stray black cat behind home plate at South Park Field in Monmouth, Illinois, near a water spigot where players on his father's softball team would get a drink between innings. It was early June 1956 in the small farming community west of Peoria, and south of Davenport, Iowa.

During the 1955 World Series, the first one young Dave watched on television, he became a Dodgers fan. "Everyone was for the Yankees, so I said I will be for the Dodgers," Johnson recalled. He was fascinated by nicknames, particularly the players on the Dodgers named Pee Wee and Junior. "I knew no one else named Junior."

Johnson's birthday was a week or two later in the summer of 1956 and he pleaded with his father that night at the softball game to allow him to bring the cat home, thinking it might make a good birthday present. Finally, his dad relented and Dave brought the cat home, where he placed it in a box in the garage and covered it with blankets. It was still there the next morning.

Because the cat was black and really fast, it reminded Johnson of Gilliam. As a result, "Junior" became part of the family, and Johnson continued his life as a Dodgers fan—although his favorite player was Gil Hodges. Johnson went to college and became a sportswriter, eventually settling in Newburgh, Indiana, a suburb of Evansville on the Ohio River. He wrote for the *Evansville Courier* and often penned columns advocating for Hodges' induction into the Baseball Hall of Fame. Newburgh is 35 minutes south from Hodges' childhood home in Princeton, Indiana.

Gilliam's Black skin color was not apparent to everyone, however, even those who lived in Brooklyn. Peter V. Trunk, Sr. recalled when he first realized Gilliam was not white. It was during the 1953 World Series when his older sister, by 15 years, had become engaged to someone from Brooklyn.

"My parents were invited over to his parents to get to know them. We went over there for dinner, I was 6 going on 7, 'Why don't you go upstairs, Peter, and watch the Dodger game. We will put it on the TV for you.' Gigantic TV, like 19 inches, of course it was black and white. I never saw a TV that big.

"I'm watching the Dodgers and Yankees and here comes Junior Gilliam coming up and I'm saying to myself, 'I never knew he was Black.' I went through the whole summer listening on the radio and following in the newspapers. I never knew he was a Black guy.

"I go running downstairs yelling, 'Pop! Pop! Guess what? Junior Gilliam is Black.' And my father goes, 'You didn't know that? Everybody knows that.'"[2]

Jim Gilliam and Jackie Robinson, undated. Alamy Stock Photo.

THE INEVITABLE SOPHOMORE JINX?

Following the 1953 season, Brooklyn manager Charlie Dressen asked Walter O'Malley for a two-year contract, something O'Malley was reluctant to offer. Player contracts were all one-year contracts. Manager contracts, O'Malley figured, should be, too. So Dressen was not rehired. To replace him, the Dodgers looked to their top farm team in Montreal to bring up the quiet, but successful, Walter Alston.

For Gilliam, one of 17 Dodgers who played for Alston in the minors, this was welcome news. He had enjoyed success in his two years under Alston at Montreal and expressed his excitement in the *Brooklyn Daily Eagle*. "Walt's a real good manager," Gilliam said. "He'd watch me hitting and pick out flaws. He noticed that sometimes I swing too hard and take my eye off the ball. Walt taught me how to play the outfield, too. I'd never played out there before, but every now and then we'd be a man short and he'd send me out there."[3]

Gilliam had thousands of other reasons to be excited prior to the 1954 season—seven thousand reasons, to be exact. He received a sizable raise from the $5,000 minimum contract in 1953 to $12,000 for the 1954 season.[4] The increase represented a rare moment of exuberance for O'Malley, the Dodgers' typically tight-fisted owner. The team brass was betting on Gilliam avoiding a sophomore jinx—a second-year slump—on which so many writers fixated.

A headline in the January 27, 1954 *The Sporting News* proclaiming, "Sophomore Jinx? It's Just Lotta Bunk to Dodgers' Gilliam,"[5] summed up the reigning Rookie of the Year's thoughts. "I don't believe in that. If I have a bad year it won't be because of that,"[6] he said.

In a nod to his eschewing a jinx, Gilliam chose not to play winter ball for the first time since skipping the 1949-50 season. But that did not mean he wasn't going to do everything he could to avoid conversations about a jinx. Gilliam was one of a dozen or so first-line Dodger players to report to Vero Beach early. His reasons were several. He intended to work with Tommy Holmes on slapping more balls to left field to improve his batting average. "I ought to hit around .300. I'm not a high-average hitter but I ought to get better this year. I know the pitchers now and that'll help me for sure."[7]

In addition to hitting, Jim intended to work with Dodgers coach Billy Herman, a former second baseman, on the double-play pivot and how to avoid having runners take him out with their slides. "The big fault with Gilliam was that he was too fast," Herman said during spring training. "He came charging in and then would be badly off balance. I told him to slow and kind of pussyfoot the rest of the way. Gilliam's got a second baseman's arm. It isn't a particularly strong arm. But he snaps the ball away nicely and quickly."[8] Questions about Gilliam's arm strength would dog him throughout his career.

Finally, the team wanted to work with Gilliam on baserunning, particularly sliding. The player judged by sportswriters as the fastest runner on the Dodgers stole 21 bases but was caught stealing a league-high 14 times in 1953. "Gilliam slides to hit the bag with his right leg. But he tends to bend the right leg too far back in the slide," Alston commented. "And most of the time his left leg, which is held straight, is past the bag before the right foot touches it."[9]

Reporting early could also be interpreted as Gilliam's way of telling Buzzie Bavasi he intended to hold on to his position at second base in the face of the Dodgers' continual influx of new talent. Major League Baseball's reserve clause did not permit free player movement and as the Dodgers assembled in Florida, the team appeared deep with infield players. In addition to Gil Hodges, Pee Wee Reese, Billy Cox, Jackie Robinson, and Gilliam, rookies Don Hoak and Don Zimmer were knocking on the door. Utility player Bobby Morgan was traded to the Phillies for Dick Young and $50,000 cash on March 28, 1954, eliminating one contender. Young, a .234 hitter in 77 career Major League at-bats, spent the next six seasons in the Dodger minor-league ranks without making it back to the bigs.

To add to the depth, and perhaps the pressure on Gilliam, Dave Anderson wrote in the *Brooklyn Daily Eagle* of a "Negro kid named Charley (sic) Neal." According to Dodger coach Mickey Owen, for whom Neal played at Caguas in Puerto Rico that winter, Neal would be pressing Gilliam for playing time as soon as next year. "Mark my words, Neal will give Gilliam competition in a year or two." Based on Owen's review of Neal, one would think he was the same player as Gilliam. "He's a good hitter. Not too many homers but lots of line drives. He's a good leadoff man, too. That's where I used him and at a quick look, he reminds you of Gilliam. He's 23 built about the same way, 5-11 and 160 pounds. But he makes the pivot better than Gilliam and has a better arm. Actually, he could play shortstop. He's that good."[10]

He could not have known it at the time, but for Jim, fending off would-be challengers for playing time would become an annual activity throughout his career.

Perhaps in an additional attempt to ward off any potential sophomore jinx, Junior Gilliam campaigned for a name change. "The name's Jim and Junior is just for kids,"[11] he told the Associated Press. After he retired, Gilliam discovered another advantage to being referred to as Jim: signing autographs. "I sign Jim because it's three letters and Junior is six. The Junior will never change to Jim, but I don't care what you call me as long as you keep on calling me for a few more years."[12]

Gilliam was always destined to have a nickname of some sort. He was Junior in the Negro Leagues and Black Sea in Puerto Rico. On the Dodgers, he would later answer to Sweet Lips, a reference to the way he pursed his lips while batting, or The Devil, a myth about his pool-playing ability acquired in spring training one year.

A DISAPPOINTING 1954 SEASON

As a team, Brooklyn disappointed in 1954, if one can call finishing 92-62 and five games behind the New York Giants a disappointment. That the hated crosstown Giants won a World Series in just their second attempt during the "Glory Days" of New York City baseball made the second-place finish even more miserable.

Gilliam began the season strong, batting .358 in April with a surprising four home runs, but he went into a 0-27 slide in May.

When the 1954 season ended, Gilliam's offensive numbers were remarkably similar to his Rookie of the Year campaign. He actually hit four points higher, at .282, and slugged 13 home runs, up from six as a rookie. He scored 107 runs and drove in 52, often hitting second behind Pee Wee Reese, but Gilliam's walk rate was down from 100 to 76.

As a result, Jim's 2.9 WAR was a full point below his rookie season, but still

1954 Red Heart Jim Gilliam baseball card. Courtesy Wade Carothers.

fifth-highest on the team, behind Snider, Reese, Hodges, and Robinson. He started 139 games at second base, plus three starts in right field and two in left field, a precursor of sorts for how Alston would use him in subsequent years.

THE SECOND GATE: QUOTA

The issue of a saturation point or quota of Black players on the field at any one point in time gained prominence during the 1954 season. The New York Giants won the 1951 National League Pennant with an all-Black outfield. The 1953 Dodgers regularly played four Black players—Robinson, Black, Campanella and Gilliam—but no team had not taken it further and fielded a starting lineup with more Black players than white players at any one time. Don Newcombe returned from the military for the 1954 season and Sandy Amorós, a Black Cuban who hit .353 for Montreal in 1953, forced his way into the lineup in left field. Gilliam and his teammates stood at a Second Gate of integration, one involving the total number of Black players.

National media discussion of this saturation point began when John Lardner wrote of the "50 per cent color line" in the May 10, 1954 *Newsweek*. He noted that Amorós had been scratched from starting a game in which Newcombe, Gilliam, Robinson, and Campanella were already in the lineup. "Behind the talk and thought is the implied suggestions that it is somehow sinister—that it would be bad judgment, at this time—to have too many Negroes playing simultaneously in big-league ball,"[13] Lardner wrote.

Perhaps inspired by Lardner's column, Fritz Pollard, who in 1920 became the first Black player in the NFL and the first Black coach in 1921, wrote in the May 15, 1954 *New York Age*, part of the Black press, "Saturation point? Who ever heard of a ball club having reached a point where it was saturated with good players? And the only Negro players on any team in the country are good players, and when they've been in the game everybody knows it."[14]

Author Bryan Soderholm-Diafatte's 2015 argument that true Major League integration would not be complete until teams opened their rosters to players of above-average ability was underscored by Pollard's observation that the only Black players on a team were the good players—the superstars. In order to get past the saturation point, a team must be willing to roster players who were part-time or role players.

Alston's desire to play Amorós, a left-handed hitter, only against right-handed pitching meant the Cuban fit the description as a part-timer. Each time Newcombe started on the mound, whether by coincidence or by purpose, Alston juggled the lineup. On some days, Robinson sat. On other days, Campanella was out of the lineup. When facing a left-handed pitcher, Amorós sat.

Robinson, writing a series of first-person articles in *Look* magazine in February 1955, commented on the strange lineup changes, including one instance in which Amorós was scratched on a day he would normally start. "None of us really believed, however, that Sandy was taken out of that game because of his color, but I wasn't certain. Sure enough, later in the season, Alston used all of Brooklyn's five Negro players as a unit on several occasions. That was enough to convince me that the Brooklyn management wanted to win ball games—period."[15]

The first of those occasions Robinson mentioned occurred on July 17, 1954 in Milwaukee, while playing a Braves team featuring a rookie outfielder named Henry Aaron. Alston wrote a lineup card with Campanella at catcher, Gilliam at second, Robinson at third, Amorós in left, and Newcombe on the mound. For the first time in Major League history, a team started more Black players than white players.

Media scarcely noticed the moment, however. *The New York Times* buried the fact at the end of the game story, noting Alston had intended on leaving Amorós on the bench but decided against it. Roscoe McGowen wrote, "The decision to play Amorós made a bit of major league history. For the first time it put five Negroes, Newcombe, Campanella, Gilliam, Robinson, and Amorós in a major league line-up. In previous games, when Amorós formerly was with the Dodgers, it always happened that he didn't play when Newcombe was the pitcher."[16] *The Sporting News* did not even mention the occurrence, even though it wrote about "saturation" in its April 21 issue.

The Dodgers won the game that day, 2-1 in 11 innings. Collectively, the five Black players were 0-for-18 at the plate, although Robinson scored the team's first run after drawing a walk in the second inning. Alston would use the five Black player lineup configuration three more times during the 1954 season, finishing the season with a 3-1 record in those games.

Ed Roebuck, Jim's teammate on the 1952 Montreal Royals and a member of Dodger teams from 1955 to 1963, was very aware of the Second Gate of integration. "By the early 50s there were a lot of Blacks in the minors. No one told the Black players and us white players in the Dodgers' system how to coexist. We just did it. We were very cognizant of the quota system, which meant that only a certain number of Blacks could make it to the majors, and that no team would have more than a few Blacks, and that some teams didn't have Blacks at all yet. So it was tough for the Black players."[17]

BARNSTORMING AGAIN WITH CAMPANELLA'S ALL-STARS

Gilliam once again joined Roy Campanella's All-Stars winter barnstorming team after the World Series, although this time without its front man, as Campanella stayed in Brooklyn to have surgery on his left hand. The squad was composed of all Black Major League players, including Monte Irvin and Hank Thompson of the Giants, Larry Doby and Dave Hoskins of the Indians, Minnie Miñoso of the White Sox, and Dodger teammates Don Newcombe and Joe Black.

The tour began October 8 in Baltimore at Westport Stadium, site of Gilliam's final days as a member of the Baltimore Elite Giants, and included 32 games in 31 days throughout the deep south as well as California and Texas.[18]

Gilliam returned to his home field in Nashville as the All-Stars played at Sulphur Dell in Nashville on October 18, the day after his 26th birthday, in what *The Tennessean* characterized as the top "colelction (sic) of Negro big league players ever seen in the Dell."[19] The paper did not cover the game as a homecoming for Gilliam, nor mention any local connection.

Interest in watching the barnstormers was inconsistent as poor weather plagued the stops in the south. By the time the club reached one of its final stops at Acadian Ballpark in New Iberia, Louisiana on November 4, an estimated 300 spectators attended, down from the 3,000-plus crowd in Charlotte in mid-October. In that Nov. 4 game, Gilliam slugged three hits, including a three-run home run, to pace team barnstormers to a 9-3 win over the American Negro All-Stars.[20]

TRADE RUMORS: CINCINNATI, PHILADELPHIA

Having reached the World Series the previous two seasons, the 1954 Brooklyn season was viewed as a disappointment by both the media and the team's fans. Almost immediately rumors began to fly about ways in which the Dodgers could improve their ballclub, and those rumors persisted throughout the winter months. The reserve clause prohibited free movement of players from one team to the next, so the only ways a player could be added or subtracted from a team was via trade, being released, or being drafted through the Rule V minor-league draft.

During baseball's minor-league meetings in Houston in late November, trade talks began to heat up between both the Dodgers and the Cincinnati Reds, and the Dodgers and the Philadelphia Phillies. Brooklyn still had holes in the lineup, particularly in left field and starting pitching, while the club had a surplus in the infield. In addition to Gilliam, Reese, Cox, and Robinson, Don Zimmer was ready to make an impact at shortstop. Don Hoak had emerged as a solid third-base candidate. Cuban Chico Fernández, and former Negro Southern Leaguer Charlie Neal, both infielders, had above average Triple-A seasons in 1954.

A perception existed that Gilliam had regressed from his Rookie of the Year season and rumors emerged he would be traded. The 1954-55 offseason would be the first time for such rumors, but certainly not the last, as Gilliam found himself confronting an uncertain future role with the

Dodgers. That it occurred just one year removed from winning the National League Rookie of the Year was a bit unnerving.

The first rumor to emerge was in late October 1954, involving some combination of Gilliam, Cox, and possibly Robinson going to Philadelphia for starting pitcher Curt Simmons. Dodgers general manager Buzzie Bavasi viewed Gilliam as expendable due to the plethora of infield prospects, but Alston reminded Bavasi that Gilliam, as a switch-hitter, might also be a valuable outfielder.[21]

A month later, Dave Anderson wrote in the *Brooklyn Daily Eagle* on Saturday December 4, 1954 that Gilliam and pitcher Bob Milliken would be traded on Monday, December 6 to Cincinnati for outfielder Wally Post and catcher Hobie Landrith.[22] From a baseball standpoint, the trade made sense: Trade from a position of surplus (infield) to fill a need (outfield). Post, a right-handed power hitter, had slugged 18 home runs in 1954 at age 24.

Dick Young of the *New York Daily News* wrote about the potential deal the next day (Sunday, December 5): "The deal was made because Gilliam is considered expendable and the Brooks must have catching insurance for Roy Campanella's physical impairment,"[23] a reference to Campanella's offseason surgery.

Three days later, however, the deal seemed off. Anderson wrote on December 7 the Dodgers were waiting for a counter offer from the Phillies, which never arrived.[24] Neither deal, with the Phillies or the Reds, would materialize. The next day, Anderson quoted Brooklyn vice president Buzzie Bavasi saying a deal was never imminent. "We never had a deal, we had an offer, that's all. We gave it a lot of serious thought, but...."[25] Further, Bavasi stated in his best public-relations spin, "In Gilliam, we know we have a good second baseman and a good outfielder to alternate with Amorós, so we've got protection at two positions. They asked if he was available. Naturally, anybody's available if you get a value in return and if you think you'll help your club. But it came down to this—we did not feel as secure without Gilliam as we did with him."[26]

Post would hit 40 home runs in 1955 and 36 more in 1956 for the Reds. Brooklyn used eight different players in left field in 1955, including Gil Hodges and Jackie Robinson. Collectively, they did not come close to 40 home runs. It is clear, in hindsight, that Post would have helped Brooklyn.

If Bavasi's comments gave Gilliam confidence he was not, in fact, expendable and would not be traded, that confidence was short-lived when Anderson reported in late December the Dodgers were still trying to "peddle" Gilliam to Philadelphia. The Phillies' interest in Gilliam was because the team needed a second baseman, and, Anderson wrote, the Phillies "want to introduce a Negro."[27]

Instead of introducing Gilliam as the team's first Black player in 1955, it would be two more full seasons before Philadelphia played a Black player. Infielder John Irvin Kennedy, who had spent time with the Kansas City Monarchs and the Birmingham Black Barons, pinch-ran in a game on April 22, 1957 at Brooklyn. Kennedy appeared in just five games before being sent to the minors. His career stats: 0-for-2 at the plate, with one run scored.

Despite the rumors, Gilliam signed his 1955 contract on January 17. The agreement called for him to be paid $12,500 for 1955, a slight increase over this $12,000 contract from the year before.[28] "Junior Gilliam, who had been tossed around like a bad penny in Dodger trade talks all winter, signed his contract yesterday and became an entry in the infield derby which will be contested at Vero Beach."[29] Or so Joe Trimble wrote as the lead paragraph in his January 18, 1955 *Daily News* story.

1955 SEASON: A UTILITY ROLE

Jim spent much of the offseason with his long-time friend from the Elite Giants and 1952 Rookie of the Year, Joe Black. Both former award winners were disappointed in their 1954 seasons—Black spent much of the year in Triple-A Montreal—and were determined to be in good physical shape for the 1955 season. The two worked out regularly at the Harlem YMCA, finding jobs selling autos in the Floral Park area of Long Island, just east of Queens.

The Dodgers opened the season on fire, winning their first 10 games and never looking back. On July 1, Brooklyn stood atop the National League at 52-20, 12.5 games ahead of the Chicago Cubs, led by a second-year former Negro Leagues shortstop named Ernie Banks. Gilliam, however, was not a reason for the team's offensive success. In fact, he was in full struggle mode. He had started the season's first 72 games at second base but was hitting just .213. Frank Graham, writing in *Sport* magazine in February 1956, remarked, "Gilliam wandered through the (training) camp like a little lost boy. He had heard that he was about to be traded and he believed it. He had good reason to."[30]

Despite generally fielding his position well, Alston decided to bench Gilliam on July 2 in favor of Don Zimmer, who would start 43 straight at second. Don Hoak, the other half of the "youthful Dons,"[31] as Dick Young referred to them, would start a similar string of games at third, creating a surplus of outfielders in Carl Furillo, Duke Snider, Amorós, Robinson, and Gilliam. Although Alston occasionally inserted Gilliam in as a defensive replacement at second, his opportunities to start in the next month and a half came in the outfield.

Gilliam started the second game of a July 6 doubleheader at Pittsburgh in right field for an injured Furillo, and found himself in right for four straight games. He responded by batting 6-for-20 during the stretch. But with Furillo healthy, Gilliam returned to the bench until he was needed to spell a sore Amorós in left. For the next month, while Amorós sat, Gilliam was a left fielder, except for a couple starts in center.

The benching and shift to outfield or utility role had helped Gilliam. By the time he finally started another game at second, on August 18, his average was up to .233, but still well below previous seasons. From that point on, Gilliam rarely missed a start as Alston settled on a rotation with Gilliam appearing in left field when the Dodgers faced a left-handed pitcher and at second when a right hander opposed them. Jim finished the season with a .249 average.

Gilliam's role on the team had transformed from a starting second baseman and Rookie of the Year to someone who could play multiple positions in just two seasons. Worse, despite playing in 147 games and scoring 110 runs, he was assigned the utility label in a World Series preview by the *Daily News*.[32] Gilliam would carry the utility stigma with him for his remaining 11 years as a player.

DISCORD AT HOME

A possible explanation for Jim's slow start and underperformance in 1955 might be traced to his home life. After making 611 Cherrycrest Road, Apartment F in the Cherry Hill area of Baltimore his offseason home in 1954, the Gilliam family purchased a home at 965 Thorn Street in Rahway, New Jersey for $11,000 on November 22, 1954. Originally built in 1927, the two-story home on the corner of Thorn and East Albert Street was just under 1,000 square feet. Joe Black's son, Chico, remembers visiting the Gilliams and playing with Jim and Gloria's children, Malcolm and Kathy. The neighborhood was mixed race, with an Italian family across the street. "People would say hello. But the kids did not play with one another," Chico remembered.

When exactly marital struggles began between Jim and Gloria is not known. On January 1, 1955, the children—Malcolm, five years old, and Kathy, four years old—were still very young. In court papers filed four years later during Jim and Gloria's divorce, Jim testified that in January 1955, "my wife was constantly leaving home for any purpose and would often stay out late night, many times until 2 or 3 a.m." Jim also testified Gloria, just 21 years old on January 1, 1955, would "leave our children uncared for" and "she would stay out all night drinking excessively, and then sleep all day the next day."[33]

Kathy remembers her grandmother and Gloria's mother, Mary White, coming from Baltimore, along with Mary's sister Helen, to help take care of the kids at some point in 1955. "They were gentle, nice people. But when mom left, they left," Kathy said. Marital struggles for the Gilliams would persist throughout the 1956 and 1957 seasons.

1955 WORLD SERIES: BREAKING THE STREAK

The 1955 World Series was a repeat of the 1953 Series and the World Series in 1952, 1949, and 1947, matching the Brooklyn Dodgers with the dreaded New York Yankees. Brooklyn fans, obviously, hoped the outcome in 1955 would be different than the previous four.

Each team maintained their respective home-field advantages, with the Yankees winning Games One and Two at Yankee Stadium, and Brooklyn sweeping Games Three, Four, and Five at Ebbets Field. The Dodgers stood on the precipice of a World Championship as the scene shifted back to the Bronx the next day, October 3 for Game Six. One win and they would no longer be Bums.

To this point in the Series, Alston had followed the platoon script, starting Gilliam in left against the Yankees' left-handed pitchers, and starting him at second against right-handed pitching. Gilliam's regular-season hitting struggles had abated in the first five games of the Series, compiling a .294 average and .478 on-base percentage in the leadoff spot.

Alston sent rookie sensation Karl Spooner to the mound for Brooklyn, the sixth different starting pitcher in as many games, to counter Yankee ace lefty Whitey Ford. Spooner was a revelation during the regular season, going 8-6 in 29 games as both a starter and a reliever. His 78 strikeouts in 98 innings were solid, though his 41 walks and eight home runs allowed suggested the Dodgers never knew which Spooner would be on the mound.

Spooner looked sharp in relief of Billy Loes in Game Two in Yankee Stadium, hurling three shutout innings of relief, yielding one hit and one walk while striking out five. Gilliam, playing Game Two in left field, aided Spooner's effort by nailing Irv Noren at third as Noren tried to go from first to third on a Yogi Berra single with one out in the bottom of the fifth.

For Game Six, Alston chose to deviate from his routine. With a nod to defense, Alston started Gilliam at second base, with the left-handed-hitting Amorós getting the call in left against the southpaw Ford. This meant Don Zimmer, the typical starter at second against lefties, would be on the bench. Alston's decision on the mound backfired in the first inning, and Gilliam was caught in the middle of it. Spooner struggled out of the gate, walking Phil Rizzuto to open the bottom of the first. Billy Martin struck out as Rizzuto stole second. As Glenn Stout described it nearly 50 years later, Rizzuto got a lousy jump but made the base when Gilliam was late to the bag, causing Campanella to double-clutch before the throw."[34]

Newspaper accounts the next day varied in their assessment of that particular play and the reason Rizzuto was safe. The *Daily News* published a photo from Charles Hoff showing Rizzuto sliding into second as Gilliam attempts to tag him. The photo's caption reads, "Junior Gilliam holds late toss as Rizzuto has already taken second on steal in 1st. Phil broke from 1st as Martin struck out. Gilliam hesitated before breaking to cover the bag and Campanella had to hold up his throw to wait for Junior to get there."[35]

But that caption contradicted the *Daily News* game story account authored by Joe Trimble, who wrote, "The Dodgers got a bad break when the ball stuck in the webbing of Campanella's glove and the catcher had trouble getting it out for the throw, which Rizzuto beat cleanly."[36]

Dodgers beat writer Dick Young broke down the play in more detail for the *Daily News*, noting both times Martin had fouled off a 3-2 pitch from Spooner, Rizzuto had broken for second, the clear inference being Gilliam should have cheated more toward second. "Again Rizzuto took off with the pitch. Again Martin cut. This time he foul-tipped ever so slightly. Campy caught in his webbing, reared up as if to fire, then hesitated; not once, but twice. Finally he fired to Gilliam, who only then seemed to be arriving at the base."[37]

After the game, Gilliam told Young, "I could have been there in time. I shortened up for Martin so I could go straight over without leaving a hole. I think the ball got caught in Campy's web."[38]

Campanella would deny the ball stuck in his glove. "I had the ball out. I feinted to throw twice to get him out of there. I can't figure it. Maybe he thought Martin was gonna hit that way."[39]

An anonymous Dodger told Young, "You gotta throw the ball whether anybody is there or not. It's not your fault if nobody covers. Let it go."[40] Spooner, however, would not let it go after the game, attributing his poor pitching performance to Gilliam and his late break to cover the bag. "All I know is that when a runner goes down to steal somebody had better cover second. Maybe I should have struck everybody out."[41]

Had the Dodgers executed the strike 'em out-throw 'em out double play, it would have brought Gil McDougald to the plate with no one on and two out. Young speculated in the *Daily News* the botched throw to second might have a "pronounced psychological effect on Spooner."[42] McDougald struck out twice against Spooner in Game Two, but on this day he walked, bringing Yogi Berra to the plate with two on and one out.

Berra hit a hard ground up the middle, to the right of second. Gilliam took a few steps to his right and planted for a backhanded grab of the ball and an attempted double play, only the ball never found his glove—scooting, instead, into the outfield and scoring Rizzuto and moving McDougald to third. Young described the ball's journey toward Gilliam as "taking distinct bounces at about knee-height, [but] suddenly 'stayed down' as Gilliam flicked his glove out. The ball, hugging the ground, rolled under the glove and on into center."[43]

After the game, Gilliam placed the missed opportunity on his shoulders. "I just didn't get the Berra hit. There was no bad hop."[44]

The next batter, Hank Bauer, singled to left for a 2-0 lead. Spooner then fell behind Bill "Moose" Skowron two balls and no strikes. The next pitch sliced over the right-field wall for a three-run home run and sent Spooner to the clubhouse. "The guy was down 2-0 with two on and only one out. I knew he would throw a strike. He threw a high pitch and I went after it," Skowron said.[45]

"It was high and outside," Spooner said after the game. "I didn't think he could reach it. I was setting him up for the inside pitch so I could get a ground ball and get out of the inning."[46] Russ Meyer and Ed Roebuck would shut down the Yankees down the rest of the way, but Brooklyn could not claw back, falling 5-1 to force another decisive Game Seven.

Afterward, Spooner and the Dodgers could not help but wonder what might have been had Alston stuck to his usual lineup against lefties, with Gilliam in left and Zimmer at second. Alston mused about what might have been. "If we could have had any one of those two double plays, Spooner would have been out of the inning, and who knows what would have happened? Maybe he would have straightened out. He had good stuff, I thought. It's just his control was off."[47]

Former *New York Post* columnist Maury Allen wrote in his 2005 book about the 1955 Brooklyn Dodgers, "It might have been Robinson who said it or Campanella or Snider or maybe even Reese, but a still-unidentified member of the team suggested that Alston didn't even put the best Brooklyn lineup on the field for the sixth game."[48]

Game Seven's lineup posed an additional challenge for Alston: Duke Snider was hurting. In the bottom of the third of Game Six, Snider had "stepped in something" while catching a Skowron fly ball in center. Snider was lifted for pinch-hitter Zimmer in the top of the fourth. Zimmer, ironically, would stay in the game at second, with Gilliam moving to left and Amorós covering Snider's ground in center. "I don't know what it was; all I know is I hit something, the knee buckled and popped," Snider said after the game, sipping a beer with his left knee wrapped in a sleeve. "I gotta play tomorrow. If I can walk, I'll play."[49]

The Yankees had endured most of the Series without their star, Mickey Mantle, who was bothered by a sore right leg, a reminder of the 1951 World Series when he stepped on a drain pipe in the outfield. Mantle had appeared only twice in the first six games, starting Games Three and Four, and logging just nine at bats. Now it was the Dodgers' turn to ponder a critical game without their star. Alston told reporters he was optimistic the Dodger slugger, who already had four home runs in this series, would be in the lineup. "It'll be the same lineup that we started today. If not, we'll have to wait and see."[50]

With left-handed-throwing Tommy Byrne scheduled to start Game Seven for the Yankees, a return to the "same lineup" meant Alston would use his typical lineup against right-handed pitching, leaving Zimmer on the bench and starting Amorós in left with Gilliam at second. Instead, Alston returned to the lefty pitcher lineup for Game Seven, Gilliam in left and Zimmer at second.

Johnny Podres started Game Seven on the mound for the Dodgers. A precocious left hander in his third season with the club, Podres was just a few days removed from his 23rd birthday when Alston gave him the ball for the biggest game of his life. He and Gilliam were teammates on the 1952 Montreal Royals team that won the International League title, and both opened the 1953 season with Brooklyn.

Podres was the lone Dodger starting pitcher with a losing record, 9-10, in 1955. But he had defeated the Yankees 8-3 in Game Three on September 30, his birthday.

Brooklyn broke the deadlock in the top of the fourth when Hodges singled home Campanella with two out for a 1-0 lead. A rather pedestrian set of circumstances arose in the top of the sixth that would change the course of the game, and the series. The Dodgers loaded the bases with one out for Hodges. Yankees manager Casey Stengel brought in right-handed

Bob Grim to replace Byrne. Grim induced a flyout from Hodges deep enough to score Reese from third. A walk to Don Hoak loaded the bases for Zimmer, who rarely hit against right-handed pitching.

Alston countered with left-handed slugger George Shuba, who pulled the ball to first base for the third out, missing out on a chance to blow the game open. To replace Zimmer, Alston inserted Amorós in left and moved Gilliam to second base.

"I have always said the Dodgers would never have won their only World Series in Brooklyn if Alston hadn't had the good sense to take me out of the game,"[51] Zimmer wrote in his autobiography.

Clinging to their 2-0 lead, the Dodgers took the field in the bottom of the sixth needing just 12 precious outs for their first World Series title. But Podres ran into trouble, walking Billy Martin and yielding a bunt single to Gil McDougald. The go-ahead run strode to the plate in the form of Yogi Berra. The story of what happened next has been told thousands of times and is forever ingrained in the memory of every Brooklyn Dodgers fan.

Now in left field, Amorós wore his glove on his right hand. Gilliam, now at second, wore his glove on his left hand. That little fact would be as central to the story as anything.

The Dodgers expected Berra, a left-handed batter, to pull the left-handed Podres, so Amorós was cheating toward left-center field, away from the foul line. Berra sliced Podres' offering on a high arc toward the line. Amorós sprinted from his position in left-center with his gloved right hand extended out toward the foul line. A few feet from the line, and the edge of the grandstand, Amorós caught up with the ball and made the incredible one-handed catch.

McDougald, anticipating the ball would drop in safely for a hit, had rounded second base. Pee Wee Reese called for the ball, received it, and fired across to Gil Hodges at first for the 7-6-3 double play. Instead of a tie game and Berra on second with a double and no one out, there were now two outs with Martin still on second. Most importantly, the score was still 2-0 Brooklyn.

Reflecting on the play in 1967, Gilliam said, "I'm sure I couldn't have caught Yogi's ball. Only a left-handed outfielder could've done it. Besides, Yogi is a pull hitter and I would have been shading him in left-center. There's just no way I could've caught it."[52]

The Yankees threatened again in the eighth, putting runners on first and third with one out. Podres induced Berra to fly out, this time to Furillo in shallow right, and struck out Hank Bauer. In the bottom of the ninth, Podres retired Bill Skowron, Bob Cerv, and Elston Howard in order. As

Hodges received Reese's throw from short to retire Howard, the Dodgers swarmed Podres and Campanella in front of the pitching mound.

Brooklyn had finally won the World Series. The *Daily News* page one headline screamed, "This is Next Year!" Podres, to no one's surprise, was named the World Series MVP.

Offensively, Gilliam rebounded from the up-and-down 1955 season to have one of his best World Series, batting .292 with a .469 on-base percentage, thanks to eight walks. Defensively, however, it was an uncharacteristic struggle. Following the miscue at second on the stolen base attempt in Game Six, Gilliam and Duke Snider miscommunicated on a fly ball from Berra early in Game Seven, and the ball dropped in between the players for a double.

Winning the World Series carried a financial bonus of nearly $10,000. When asked by an International News Service reporter how he intended to spend the money, Jim commented, "I have a wife and two children who have to be taken care of. The World Series dough will come in handy."[53]

10

LEAVING BROOKLYN

BEFORE THE STREETS OF BROOKLYN WERE CLEANED OF DEBRIS FROM THE WORLD Series celebrations, Gilliam was back playing baseball, this time as part of an all-Black barnstorming team billing itself as the Mays-Newcombe All-Stars. From a talent standpoint, the team was loaded. In addition to Willie Mays, Don Newcombe, and Gilliam, the All-Stars boasted Henry Aaron, Ernie Banks, Monte Irvin, Larry Doby, Roy Campanella, and Joe Black, among others. "I don't think it would have mattered who we played," Mays said in his biography. "That might have been the best team ever assembled."[1]

The team opened its schedule on October 7, 1955 in Chapel Hill, North Carolina, and finished a month later on November 6 in Los Angeles. Author Thomas Barthel, in his book on baseball barnstorming teams, summarized how dominant the team was. "This squad didn't lose a single game as they meandered first to Chapel Hill, N.C., and then south to Georgia, next west to Alabama, Louisiana, Texas, the barnstorming tour ending in California. The 32-game tour ended on November 6 with more than 100,000 paid admissions with $95,588.79 in total receipts. If we grant 50 percent to the promoter and with the usual twelve players on the team, each man could take home about $4,000 each."[2]

Combined with his World Series bonus, Gilliam would have made nearly $14,000 in less than six weeks, roughly doubling his annual salary.

Going national in the first rounds of the Cola Wars in a BBDO ad.

A NEW MARKETING STAR

The close connection between fans and Dodger players enhanced their attractiveness to brands seeking to reach these consumers. It did not hurt that, as baseball players in the cradle of the nation's advertising industry, Dodger players—like their Yankee and Giant counterparts—were often signed to endorsement deals, blending sports and Madison Avenue. Being Black did not hinder the ability of star athletes to profit off their image. Gilliam's soft-spoken nature, sense of style, and smile lent itself well to newspaper and magazine advertisements, particularly in publications focused on Black audiences.

Beginning with his 1953 rookie season with the Dodgers, Jim appeared in an *Ebony* magazine advertisement for Crosley televisions. "Make the TV side-by-side test. You'll agree: You can see it better on a Crosley," was the headline message in the August 1953 issue. One of the two dominant images of Gilliam is a portrait of him smiling in full Dodger uniform (before teams aggressively enforced their intellectual property rights in advertisements), with his hands on his hips. The other image depicts Gilliam fielding a ground ball framed in a Crosley television.

Much of the full-page ad's text was attributed to Gilliam, who mentions Gloria in the testimonial, painting a public image of Jim as a family man. "And you know, my wife and I are just getting settled in our new apartment—so my wife is extra-conscious about furniture. The rich-looking Crosley made a hit with her...it's finished in mahogany, and it really *makes* our living room."

Jim soon found himself pitching everything from cola products to chewing gum to cigarettes. In the summer of 1955, Batten, Barton, Durstine and Osborne (BBDO), a New York ad agency, prepared a full-page ad for "Negro Newspapers" showing a well-dressed, smiling Gilliam sitting in a chair holding a bottle of Royal Crown Cola. "RC is the cola I drink because RC tastes so good!" No visual association with the Dodgers is present.

That fall, an advertisement for Beech-Nut Chewing Gum in the September 1955 *Ebony* magazine told the story of a Gilliam slump through a series of cartoon-like panes. While riding the bench for a few games, the

A Beech-Nut ad targeted the Black press.

cartoon intimates, Gilliam was offered peppermint gum from a coach. He subsequently broke out of his slump in his next start.

"Yes, I almost didn't make it in the big time. I had to learn to relax, take it easy, forget the pressure. And I found that there's no tastier way to do just that than chewing Beech-Nut Gum. It definitely helps me ease the tension. It will help you too—at your job, or at sport. Try it for me,"[3] Gilliam extolled in the ad, which also appeared in the *Baltimore Afro-American*.

Full-page ads in the June 18, 1955 *Baltimore Afro-American* and *Chicago Defender* shows Gilliam in a plaid shirt holding a lit Lucky Strike. "First thing I do after a game," his testimonial reads, "even before I kick my spikes off is light up a Lucky. Why Luckies? I wish everything was that simple: Luckies just taste better than any cigarette I know of. When I light up a Lucky, I'm living!"[4]

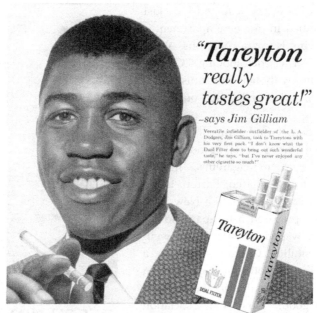

Jim Gilliam ad for filtered Tareyton cigarettes from the 1960s. He was not a smoker, but like many stars of the era he endorsed the product,

That he lent his image to cigarettes even though he was not a smoker was emblematic of the times. Nearly all Black major leaguers, including Hank Aaron, Ernie Banks, Jackie Robinson, and Willie Mays, were featured in cigarette ads in the Black press in the 1950s. A 1992 academic study comparing cigarette endorsers in *Ebony* and *Life* magazines from 1950-1965 concluded cigarette advertisements in *Ebony* used sports figures at a much higher rate than the predominantly white endorsers in *Life* magazine. "Athletes might have been used to appeal to the Black audience simply because Black consumers were thought by cigarette firms to be more influenced by sports heroes than by other role models,"[5] the authors wrote.

Later, in the early 1960s, Gilliam would lend his image to the "new dual filter" cigarettes from Tareyton, which also employed Black Los Angeles teammates Tommy Davis, Maury Wills, and Charlie Neal.

CONSTANTS AT SPRING TRAINING

During spring training in the 1950s, and before a suitable stadium was built at Dodgertown, the Dodgers often relocated from Vero Beach south to Miami to play exhibition games. The Black players would be housed at the Lord Calvert, built in 1951, while the white players stayed at the McAllister Hotel. *New York Daily News* writer Dick Young visited the players one day at their hotel but, because he was white, was not allowed upstairs. He phoned Gilliam in his room and the two met in the lounge.

"How are they treating you? Wouldn't you rather be with the club?" Young asked.

"Hey, we're doing just fine," Gilliam replied. "Campy is our traveling secretary. He takes care of the money. We don't have any bed-check like the other guys do. Don't louse it up for us. They give us a suite, best in the house. Treat us like kings."[6]

Indeed, the Lord Calvert, located at 276 NW. 6th Street in the Overtown section of Miami, was the place for Black entertainers in the 1950s. Promoted as the "Resort of the Stars," Nat King Cole, Lena Horne, Billy Eckstine, and Sammy Davis, Jr. all stayed there while in town to perform on Miami Beach. Many of the Black Dodger players, including Gilliam, developed friendships with the entertainers. A 1955 newspaper advertisement listed the hotel's many services, including nightly dancing and entertainment, free cocktails, social hostesses, and a weenie roast.[7]

Dodgers management did not like the optics, however, that its players were staying at separate hotels in spring training, a problem regularly confronting them in St. Louis during the regular season. Buzzie Bavasi claims he convinced the manager of the McAllister to allow Black players and their families to stay there. When Bavasi told the Black players, specifically Campanella, Newcombe, and Gilliam, they got upset. Bavasi finally visited the Lord Calvert and understood why the players did not mind the separate accommodations. "They each had suites by a swimming pool. The Lord Calvert was a beautiful hotel,"[8] Bavasi wrote in his autobiography.

TRADE RUMORS RESURFACE

Trade rumors involving Gilliam were another constant at spring training, with the New York media frequently quoting Buzzie Bavasi or Walt Alston about any potential trades. Rarely did the media seek comment directly from Gilliam who, when he did speak, often gave short answers that did not reveal much about how he was thinking or feeling.

Jim's reputation as a quiet figure began during his rookie campaign and was officially recognized after the season when *The Sporting News* published its annual poll of sportswriters in which they designate their "unofficial" team leaders. In addition to being voted as the Dodgers' fastest runner, Gilliam was also bestowed with the title, "Least Co-Operative with Writers."[9]

Brooklyn Daily Eagle beat writer Tommy Holmes took exception with the national vote, writing, "Tabbing Gilliam as the least co-operative Dodger with baseball writers seems like a bad rap here. I've always found Junior agreeable enough and willing to answer questions, although like a lot of other fellows, he doesn't volunteer much."[10]

That *The Sporting News* gave Gilliam the least cooperative "award" in the same issue it quoted him directly about winning the Rookie of the Year and improving in 1954 drips in irony. His quotes were buried on page 18, in a small four-paragraph non-bylined story, headlined "Gilliam figured Haddix would win rookie prize," while the story of "unofficial" team leaders was splashed across the front page.

The *Sporting News* article was written by C.C. Johnson Spink, son of J.G. Taylor Spink, longtime publisher (1914-1962) and for whom the Baseball Writers' Association of America (BBWAA) named its annual award for outstanding journalist. In early 2021, Ryan Fagan, senior baseball writer at *The Sporting News*, authored a lengthy piece lobbying for the removal of J.G. Taylor Spink's name from the award, citing systemic racism in the publication's coverage of Black baseball players.[11] Indeed, the award was renamed as the BBWAA Career Excellence Award later in 2021 "due to Spink's troubled history in supporting segregated baseball."[12]

After almost being traded to Cincinnati prior to the 1955 season, Jim again found himself the subject of offseason trade speculation, this time reportedly headed for the Philadelphia Phillies. Bavasi, using many of the same talking points as he employed the year before, told the *Daily News'* Dick Young, "There's always a chance for a trade if the offer is right. But I consider Gilliam a very valuable man on our club. He's four players in one: he hits lefty, righty…plays second base and left field.

"I am not saying we wouldn't trade him for, say, Del Ennis, but they wouldn't do that so why talk about it. Everybody thinks we have so many infielders we can give them away. Well, we don't. Of course, if Charley Neal makes the club, that could change things."[13]

Ennis was an interesting target for the Dodgers. The Phillies left fielder was coming off a 1955 season in which he hit .296 with 29 home runs and 120 runs batted in, good enough to start the All-Star Game and finish 13th in MVP voting. He would certainly provide a steadying presence for Brooklyn, even as he entered his age 31 season. And, Gilliam was likely to be pushed in spring training.

Charlie Neal (frequently referred to as "Charley" in marketing materials and baseball cards) was, in many ways, identical to Gilliam. Born in January 1931, he grew up in Texas and Louisiana, bouncing around semipro teams before playing briefly with the Atlanta Black Crackers of the Negro Southern League. The Dodgers signed him as an 18-year-old second baseman, and he began his pro career with the Dodgers in 1950, the year before Gilliam signed, with the Class-D Hornell Dodgers of the Pennsylvania-Ontario-New York (PONY) League, where he played alongside fellow future Dodger Don Zimmer. From there Neal rose steadily in the Dodger system, reaching Triple-A St. Paul for the 1954 season, batting .272 with 18 home runs, 20 stolen bases, and 101 runs scored.

Neal appeared ticketed for a roster spot on the 1955 Dodgers, but the numbers game dictated otherwise. Brooklyn had its core group of Black players in Jackie Robinson, Roy Campanella, Gilliam, Don Newcombe, Sandy Amorós, and even a rehabbing Joe Black. Neal was also competing for a spot with Black Cuban Chico Fernández, who had spent all of 1953 and 1954 impressing management in Montreal. The number of Black players in 1955 spring training did not go unnoticed by Dick Young, who wrote in his regular Sunday column on February 13, 1955, about prospect of a different "saturation point" as the Dodgers had eight "Negroes" in camp—Gilliam, Robinson, Newcombe, Campanella, Amorós, Black, Neal, and Fernández.

"Suppose you own a ball club and it represents about $3,000,000," Young speculated. "Everything you do in connection with the club must be done with an eye towards your investment. Suppose the club were to put nine Negroes on the field at the start of a ball game. Maybe nothing drastic would result. But as things now stand you must admit it would be taking a chance—and no man takes a chance with $3,000,000 when he doesn't have to."[14]

The inference from Young's speculative point is that having too many Black players was potentially bad for the financial side of the business. He conveniently omits any reference to on-field performance. "I honestly don't believe Major League Baseball is ready for that step right now. That is why I think Neal will be farmed out and Gilliam will be traded," he concluded. "Idealists may scream. But it is easy to be an idealist when you don't have $3,000,000 involved."[15] Young had gifted Bavasi the needed cover to trade Gilliam, but Bavasi did not take the bait. Instead, the Dodgers sent both Fernández and Neal to the minors. Six Black players began the 1955 season on the roster. Black was eventually traded to Cincinnati midway through the 1955 season, but he was not replaced by another Black player.

THE SATURATION POINT PERSISTS

Even with Joe Black gone, as spring training 1956 arrived, it was only natural that the media revisit the topic of Black players on the roster. Dick Young again opined in the *New York Daily News* that the Dodgers still had not figured out what the "point" was, a reference to the saturation point. "Only the Brook brass knows how many Negroes it wishes to keep on the club this season—and, of course, it would never say. Last year the number was five. At the moment there are eight. Neal, at a guess, would rank No. 6. If the 'point' is six, he should stick. If it is still five, Gilliam or Robinson or Amorós would have to go in order for Charley (sic) to make it."[16]

As it would turn out, the number would be six as Gilliam, Robinson, Amorós, Campanella, Newcombe, and Neal all made the team. Fernández, who was sent back to Montreal for his fourth season with the Royals, nearly quit. Robinson convinced him otherwise. "I told Buzzie Bavasi that I wasn't going, so he sent Jackie Robinson to talk me out of it," Fernández said in 2015. "Jackie said, 'Look, Chico, don't be stupid and go back to Cuba because Pee Wee maybe has one more year.'"[17] The Dodgers eventually recalled Fernández in July after Zimmer was beaned and Pee Wee Reese dealt with a sore hamstring. Fernández started 16 games for Brooklyn in 1956, none after August 16. After the season, he was traded to Philadelphia.

Five Black Dodgers, everyone except Amorós, were in the lineup on Opening Day: Gilliam in left, Robinson at third, Neal at second, Campanella catching, and Newcombe on the mound. Because Robinson, Gilliam, Neal, and Amorós all played essentially the same three positions, one player figured to sit each day. Even on the rare occasion when Gilliam or Amorós started in right field, the Dodgers still sat at least one Black player. April 29, 1956, the season's 11th game, was an example: Campanella was at catcher, Neal at second, Gilliam in left, and Amorós in center. Robinson, however, sat in favor of Ransom Jackson against the Pirates' Vern Law. It was Robinson's only day off in the first two months of the season.

Later in the season, Alston started Neal at second, Robinson at third, Amorós in left, and Gilliam in right for the second game of a doubleheader against the Giants' Al Worthington on September 2. However, because Campanella started the first game of the doubleheader, Alston elected to go with Rube Walker at catcher—although Campanella did later pinch hit in the seventh and stay in the game, briefly giving Brooklyn five Black fielders. Even if the "point" really was six, the Dodgers did not push past five.

1956 SEASON: ANOTHER SERIES

Opening Day for the 1956 season found the Phillies at Ebbets Field and Robin Roberts starting on the mound for Philadelphia. Roberts made seven straight All-Star teams between 1950 and 1956. From 1952 to 1956, the right-handed hurler led the National League in wins, innings pitched, and complete games. Twice during that stretch he led the league in strike-outs. But, for whatever reason, Gilliam enjoyed hitting against the future Hall of Famer. In 196 plate appearances against Roberts, the third-most for Gilliam against any pitcher, Jim hit .312 with an .816 OPS.

On April 17, 1956, with Brooklyn already trailing 7-3 in the bottom of the fourth, Gilliam sliced a liner to left field that should have dropped for a harmless single. As center fielder Richie Ashburn raced over to cut the ball off in left-center, the ball took an unexpected bounce and Ashburn fell flat on his face trying to reverse course. The ball rolled to the left-centerfield wall, where left fielder Del Ennis retrieved it and began a three-throw relay to home plate. It was too late: Gilliam had raced around for an inside-the-park home run. It was the first such home run at Ebbets Field, a notoriously confined park, since Carl Furillo had accomplished the feat in 1950. Interestingly, Duke Snider would also hit an inside-the-park home run off Roberts at Ebbets Field later in 1956.

Nearly a month later, on May 12, Carl Erskine hurled the second no-hitter of his career, this one a 3-0 shutout of the crosstown rival Giants at Ebbets Field. Erskine was efficient, walking only two batters and inducing several lazy pop flies. For Gilliam, who started at second, it would be the first of seven no-hitters in which he participated as a Major Leaguer.

Walter Alston managed the National League entry in the 1956 All-Star Game played at Griffith Stadium in Washington, D.C. on July 10, but no one from his Brooklyn squad was in the starting lineup voted on by fans. Five members of the Cincinnati Reds, who entered the All-Star break a game-and-a-half in front of Milwaukee and two games ahead of Brooklyn, were voted to start.

Four Dodgers—Duke Snider, Roy Campanella, Jim Gilliam, and Clem Labine—rode the bench to begin the game. Only Snider and Campanella got into the game, won by the National League, 7-3. For whatever reason, Alston opted to leave Gilliam on the bench, along with fellow backup infielders and future Hall of Famers Ernie Banks and Eddie Mathews in favor of an all-Cincinnati infield of Ted Kluzewski at first, Johnny Temple at second, Roy McMillan at short, and Gus Bell at third.

On July 21, the Dodgers took the field for a Saturday afternoon game at Busch Stadium in St. Louis. The game itself was unremarkable for Brooklyn, as the team blew a 3-1 lead and lost 13-6. However, Gilliam's name entered the record books after assisting on 12 of the 24 game's outs from his second-base position. His performance tied a record previously established by Fred Dunlap, player-manager of the Cleveland Blues, on July 24, 1882, and equaled by John Ward of the Brooklyn Grooms on June 10, 1892. The 12 assists by a second baseman in one nine-inning game remains a Major League record, tied seven additional times since Gilliam's 1956 game.[18]

With the Dodgers a half game behind Milwaukee and five games to play, lightning struck on September 25 in front of just 15,204 fans on a chilly night at Ebbets Field. Sal Maglie, acquired midseason from the New York Giants, took the mound. Staked to an early 5-0 lead after three innings, Maglie headed to the ninth inning having not allowed a hit. He recorded two quick outs before hitting Richie Ashburn in the foot, bringing up Marv Blaylock.

"I hit Ashburn in the foot, and he was the right man to put on base, because he was the one I thought was apt to get a base hit. He splatters the ball all over the place. And I didn't care that I hit him. The last batter was Marv Blaylock, the first baseman. In fact, the first time up, he hit the best ball, he lined out to Amorós in left field," Maglie told Peter Golenbock in his oral history of the Dodgers. "This time I threw him an outside curveball. He tried to pull it, and he hit a slow grounder to Gilliam. And I'll never forget the last ball hit down to second base. I didn't think it would ever get there for the second baseman to throw him out."[19]

Maglie had hurled the Dodgers's second no-hitter of the season. Brooklyn was rained out three days later, Friday, September 28, but Milwaukee's loss at St. Louis pulled the teams even in the loss column, with the Braves having one more win at 91-61 to 90-61. The rainout forced the Dodgers into a Saturday doubleheader against the Pirates. Brooklyn swept Pittsburgh 6-2 and 2-1 during the day and were aided that night when the Cardinals beat Milwaukee, 2-1, in 12 innings. The Dodgers now had a full one game lead on the Braves heading into the season's final day.

Brooklyn took the field at 2 p.m. Eastern, a full hour before the Milwaukee game would begin. Vern Law started for the Pirates, while Don Newcombe was on the hill for the Dodgers. Following a scoreless top of the first, Gilliam led off the bottom of the first by walking for the 95th time that season. Reese singled, Snider homered, and before Law had recorded an out, the Dodgers led 3-0. Although Newcombe struggled with his control, the Brooklyn bats were alive, tallying five home runs, two apiece from Snider and Sandy Amorós and one from Jackie Robinson, propelling the Dodgers to an 8-6 win and the National League pennant for the fourth time in five years. The opponent? The New York Yankees, of course.

1956 WORLD SERIES: MORE OF THE SAME

The 1956 World Series followed the same pattern as the 1955 Series, with the home teams winning the first six games. Brooklyn took a 2-0 lead to the Bronx, only to drop Games 3-5 to the Yankees. Game Five was historic as Don Larsen threw a perfect game, the first no-hitter in World Series play. The game also marked the third time Gilliam had played in a no-hitter.

Following his 0-for-3 against Larsen, Gilliam was batting just .059 in the Series entering Game Six at Ebbets Field. The game turned out to be a pitchers' duel for the ages between the Yankees' Bob Turley and the Dodgers' Clem Labine. The two hurlers matched zeroes through nine innings. Turley yielded four hits and six walks to Labine's seven hits and two walks. Labine set the Yankees down in order in the top of the 10th, setting the stage for the bottom half of the inning.

Labine led off the inning by popping out to second. Gilliam, after skipping batting practice in an attempt to change his fortunes, singled in the third and walked in the sixth. Now, in extra innings, Gilliam worked another walk on four pitches. Pee Wee Reese sacrificed Jim to second to bring up Duke Snider, who was intentionally walked in favor of Jackie Robinson. On Turley's second pitch, Robinson sent a line drive into left field that Enos Slaughter misjudged and let sail over his head, allowing Gilliam to score the game's only run.

Unfortunately for Brooklyn, it would be the last run the team scored in the Series as New York won Game Seven, 9-0. Just like in 1955, the winning team captured the Series with a shutout victory on the road. Gilliam finished with a disappointing .083 batting average and seven walks.

Despite the poor World Series average, Gilliam's 1956 season was his finest since joining the Dodgers. He established what would be career highs in both batting average, .300, and on-base percentage, .399. He scored 102 runs, the fourth straight season he eclipsed the century mark. His 6.1 WAR was second on the team, behind Duke Snider. He was second in the National League to Willie Mays with 21 stolen bases. He appeared in 153 games and led the Dodgers in plate appearances, 701, and at bats, 594.

Gilliam was named to his first National League All-Star game, though he did not play. And, he finished fifth in National League MVP voting with 103 points, behind Newcombe, Maglie, Hank Aaron, and Warren Spahn. Gilliam received four of a possible 24 first place votes, but was named only on 12 ballots.

A POSTSEASON JAPAN TOUR

Early in 1956, Dodgers' owner Walter O'Malley was invited by Matsutaro Shoriki, the founder of the Yomiuri Shimbun and the "father of Japanese professional baseball,"[20] to play a series of exhibition games following the 1956 season. O'Malley, with support from the U.S. government and President Dwight D. Eisenhower, moved forward with plans for the trip. The World Series ended on Wednesday, October 10. On Friday, October 12, the Dodgers flew to Hawaii for a series of three exhibition games before departing for Japan.

For Jim, the trip marked his second trip to Hawaii, a lengthy plane ride for someone with a stated aversion to flying. His first trip to the island territory was as part of the Roy Campanella All-Stars barnstorming tour after the 1953 season. The team departed on Tuesday, October 16 for Tokyo, with an intermediate stop in Wake Island, where they stayed for five hours to refuel and fix a tire problem.

Dodgers pitcher Fred Kipp, who had been called up by the Dodgers to pitch batting practice late in the 1956 season, detailed the layover in his memoir, "When the islanders heard about the delay, they declared a national holiday, and the whole island seemed show up (sic) at the airport to see us. We signed a bunch of autographs and talked with the locals."[21]

Jackie Robinson, Roy Campanella and Jim Gilliam on the 1956 Japan postseason tour. From the December 1956 issue of a Japanese Baseball Magazine via Wikimedia Commons.

According to Kipp's calculations, the team's trip from New York to

Tokyo covered 9,254 miles over 29 hours in the air, not counting the intermediate stops. When the team finally deplaned in Tokyo, the team was welcomed with a parade and flowers. Lots of flowers. "There were flowers everywhere," Kipp remembered. "We had to give them away. There were 50-60 bouquets of flowers in our room."

The team played a total of 19 games, going 14–4–1 in the exhibitions. Gilliam claimed the games played in Japan were more taxing than the regular season, primarily because of the need to get up by 6 a.m. to catch a train.

PROBLEMS PERSIST AT HOME

Jim's earlier marital problems from 1955 did not go away. In April 1957, Gloria sought the advice of Calvin J. Hurd, an attorney from nearby Elizabeth, New Jersey. News of the meeting between Gloria and her attorney made its way to Sam Haynes, a writer with the *Baltimore Afro-American*. Haynes reached out to all parties for comment. In his story, running on April 27, 1957, Gloria stated, "I have always had the highest respect for the AFRO and for the press in general. But I cannot comment on this matter until I have had further consultation with my lawyer."

Hurd told Haynes, "She (Mrs. Gilliam) was in to see me, but there is no truth to the report she has filed for either divorce or separation. Something may develop later." Jim Gilliam said simply that he had no comment.[22]

Three days after the article ran, on April 30, Gloria filed divorce papers in the Chancery Division of Superior Court. Gloria's suit contained six complaints, including admission of adultery, domestic abuse, and refusal to support, monetarily, herself and their children.[23] She suggested his abuse caused her to experience nervousness, weight loss, emotional strain, and nervous breakdown. The charges also alleged Jim used offensive language in front of Malcolm, 8, and Katherine, 6.[24]

Once again, Jim carried the strain of his personal life to the ballpark. After batting .300 in 1956, Jim started strong, hitting .370 in April 1957. Almost as soon as the *Afro-American* article ran in late April, he stopped hitting. Gilliam batted just .205 the entire month of May with as many strikeouts, six, as walks. It would be the only month as a regular player in his career in which he did not have more walks than strikeouts.

Six weeks later in mid-June, the *Afro-American* reported the Gilliams were considering reconciliation, primarily for the sake of their two children.[25] The potentially improved home situation allowed Jim to relax somewhat on the field, as he hit .238 in June and .248 in July, before finally returning to form in August when he batted .281 with a .366 on-base percentage and 26 runs in 30 games.

Circumstances changed again on Tuesday, August 13 when Rahway police were called to Thorn Street and found Gloria unconscious. Jim was some 30 miles north and east at the time, at the Polo Grounds, preparing to play the New York Giants. Gloria was rushed to Rahway Memorial Hospital at 11:25 a.m., where she was diagnosed as having overdosed on sleeping pills.[26] The *Baltimore Afro-American* reported Jim was informed of Gloria's condition prior to playing in that evening's game, a 4-2 Dodgers loss.[27]

Exactly when they split, daughter Kathy did not recall. Eventually, Jim's mother, Katherine, settled in the house in New Jersey to care for the kids while Jim was on the road.

A DISAPPOINTING 1957 SEASON

The Dodgers were never able to harness the magic of previous years during the 1957 season. After dropping three of four at home to Philadelphia, Brooklyn found itself in fifth place at the All-Star break. Cincinnati would be the opposition at Ebbets Field on July 11 when play resumed.

With his team ahead 1-0 in the bottom of the fourth, Reds starting pitcher Brooks Lawrence imploded, yielding a single to Gilliam, a home run to Duke Snider, a walk to Elmer Valo, and back-to-back singles to Gino Cimoli and Gil Hodges. Lawrence's day was done, and Raúl Sánchez entered and extinguished the fire. Sánchez had some history with the Dodgers, having hit Neal a month earlier with Brooklyn winning 7-0. Campanella had also been knocked down by Sánchez who, it appeared, was only wild against the Dodgers' Black players. Campanella's biographer, Neil Lanctot, wrote that Campanella said at some point, "That Cuban blankety-blank. I'll fix him."[28]

With Brooklyn now ahead 3-1 in the bottom of the fifth, things got interesting. Neal opened with a ground ball to ex-Negro Leaguer George Crowe at first. Crowe fed Sánchez for the out. Gilliam reached safely when his bunt was fielded by Sánchez, who tagged Gilliam out but dropped the ball. The Reds protested with several members of the team, including manager Birdie Tebbetts, crowding around first base umpire Augie Donatelli. Nothing additional ensued until the bottom of the seventh.

With two out, and Brooklyn now trailing 4-3, Sánchez knocked Gilliam down with his first pitch. On his second pitch, Gilliam again bunted, only this time the ball went into the air in foul territory. As Sánchez settled under the ball, Gilliam collided with him running toward first. The two players immediately exchanged punches, and both benches emptied.

A still photo from the event shows Sánchez and Gilliam wrestling on the ground with Roy Campanella reaching for them. Despite his earlier vow to "fix" Sánchez, Campanella claimed he was trying to break it up and "didn't punch nobody."[29]

Former Dodger Don Hoak, now the Reds' third baseman, ran in to defend Sánchez. Neal, who had burst out of the dugout to support Gilliam, decked Hoak with a punch. "Hoak, who had been on the boxing team in the marines, was actually trying to be a peacemaker as he leaned over the pile of bodies all wrestling on the ground. It was then that Neal caught him with a right hook under his left eye and sent flying onto the grass," wrote Don Zimmer years later in his autobiography. "As baseball fights go, this one was a dandy, one of the better ones I've ever witnessed."[30]

Gilliam, Neal, Sánchez, and Hoak were all ejected. John Roseboro hit for Gilliam and walked against the new pitcher, Tom Acker. Duke Snider followed with a home run, giving the Dodgers a 5-4 victory. All four of the ejected players were fined $100 by National League president Warren Giles.

LEAVING BROOKLYN

The end days of Ebbets Field and the Brooklyn Dodgers relocation to Los Angeles are well reported by scholars and authors. The team limped to an 84-70 record and a third-place finish. Attendance for the final game at Ebbets Field on September 24, 1957 reflected this overall feeling. A mere 6,702 showed up for the Dodgers' 2-0 win over the Pittsburgh Pirates. Gilliam started at second base and opened the bottom of the first with a walk. He scored two batters later on Elmer Valo's double, giving Brooklyn a 1-0 lead. Don Zimmer's seventh-inning single was the last Dodger hit in Ebbets Field.

Five days later, on September 29, Brooklyn finished its season in Philadelphia, losing 2-1. Gilliam's two-out, line-drive single to right field off left-handed Seth Moorhead in the top of the fifth would be the final hit in Brooklyn Dodger history. Journeyman outfielder Bob Kennedy, who played in a total of 19 games for the Dodgers, made the club's final out when he flew out to center field.

Perhaps because of his well-publicized marital difficulties, Jim had, statistically for him, a below average season in 1957, although he led the Dodgers in plate appearance and stolen bases. His .250 season batting average and 0.9 WAR were among the lowest marks of his career. Certainly his .205 average in May, during his well-publicized separation from Gloria, contributed to that. He played almost exclusively at second base, starting 148 of the team's 154 games there, second only to his 1953 rookie season in which he started 149 games at second.

Less than a month after the team's final game in Philadelphia, Gilliam walked off an airplane in Los Angeles as a member of the Los Angeles Dodgers.

11

HOLLYWOOD

WALTER O'MALLEY'S DECISION TO MOVE HIS FRANCHISE FROM BROOKLYN TO Los Angeles was akin to ripping the hearts out of one community, while simultaneously giving another community a heartbeat. But even that is not without controversy, as the methods by which the Dodgers received the land at Chavez Ravine have come under question and are well-documented by several scholars.[1]

The team arrived around dinner time on Wednesday, October 23, 1957 at Los Angeles International Airport amid much fanfare. The Convair 440 airplane with "Los Angeles Dodgers" painted on either side of the aircraft —where "Brooklyn Dodgers" had once appeared—taxied to the United Airlines terminal. Los Angeles media covered the plane's journey "in the same way that they followed Santa's sleigh on Christmas Eve,"[2] author Michael D'Antonio wrote in his biography of Walter O'Malley.

Several thousands applauded Walter O'Malley as he walked off the plane onto the tarmac, like a general who had just liberated a city in World War II. Wearing a double-breasted sport coat and fedora, O'Malley smiled broadly as he walked down the steps to be greeted by Los Angeles mayor Norris Poulson and other dignitaries. The Inglewood Boys Band played and UCLA's "Bruins Belles" tossed flower petals.

The lone Dodger to make the cross-country trip from LaGuardia Airport was Jim Gilliam. Given Gilliam's previously stated preference for train travel, playing on the West Coast and being subjected to long plane flights must not have seemed desirable. Harold Parrott, the Dodgers' business manager, put to rest any concerns about players refusing to fly. "There are a handful (Don Newcombe, Carl Furillo, Junior Gilliam) who don't like to fly, particularly, but they've never been adamant about it. That won't be a problem."[3]

Southern California native Duke Snider pushed his way through the crowd to greet his teammate and O'Malley. The contingent was subsequently whisked away to the Pacific Ballroom of the Statler Hotel, where tables were decorated with Dodger pennants and "piled high with peanuts, Cracker Jack, and soda pop."[4]

When asked about moving from New Jersey to Southern California, Jim said, "I've been moving all my life. Nashville is my real home but I haven't lived there in 10 years."[5]

TRADE RUMORS AGAIN

Jim stayed on the West Coast, an entire continent away from his kids, now under the care of Jim's mother, Katherine, at their home in New Jersey. Once again, he signed on to play a series of barnstorming games with his friend Willie Mays and the Willie Mays All-Stars in the month of November. Teammates this time included Gene Baker, George Crowe, Jim Pendleton, Elston Howard, and Joe Black. Games against Pacific Coast All-Stars occurred in Sacramento and San Francisco, while a series against a team fronted by Bob Lemon was contested at Wrigley Field in Los Angeles.

Shortly thereafter, Gilliam found himself in the familiar position of wondering whether or not he was trade bait. One December rumor had Jim, Randy Jackson, and Rube Walker being dealt to the Phillies for Rip Repulski, Willie Jones, and possibly Richie Ashburn.

Gilliam had started all but six games at second base in 1957 and led the National League with a .986 fielding percentage, but Dodgers management appeared intent on moving Charlie Neal from shortstop to second base in order to free up playing time for the patient Don Zimmer at short. This was the fourth spring training in which Neal and Zimmer were to supplant Gilliam and Pee Wee Reese in the middle of the Dodger infield.

As the Dodgers reported to Vero Beach for spring training in 1958, the team still had an abundance of infielders with Gilliam, Reese, Zimmer, Neal, Bob Lillis, Randy Jackson, and Dick Gray. After five years in Brooklyn as a second baseman and part-time outfielder, the veteran Gilliam might be tried out at the same position he was first assigned with the Baltimore Elite Giants a dozen years earlier, utility. "As for Gilliam, he is more valuable as a utility man than as a second sacker," Fresco Thompson, the team's vice president and farm director said in January. "He can play infield or outfield, is a switch hitter, a good pinch hitter, an exceptional base runner."[6] The suggestion that Jim was more valuable as a utility player than a second baseman was certainly odd considering Gilliam was, fielding percentage-wise, the best second baseman in the National League in 1957.

"Those reports are a lot of hooey," Vice President Buzzie Bavasi said, referring to the trade rumors swirling around Gilliam. "At this time we have no intention of disposing of Gilliam. It would take an overpowering offer, one that would insure a pennant, for us to think of disposing of him. Junior is three men in one. He bats both ways and he can play the infield or outfield. Besides that, he's possibly the best leadoff man in baseball."[7]

Over the years, Bavasi would use the same talking points to describe Gilliam. He was a switch-hitter, capable of playing multiple positions, and a valuable asset at the top of the lineup. His description of "disposing" of Gilliam made it clear Bavasi was running a business and even someone who was "three men in one" could be traded. It was a stigma that Gilliam had endured each offseason since 1954, and one that would continue in the team's new home in Los Angeles.

And yet, despite Bavasi's comments, when the Dodgers took the field for their first official game as the Los Angeles Dodgers, the 29-year-old Gilliam, "possibly the best leadoff man in baseball," was not in the lineup. Charlie Neal opened at second, Dick Gray started at third, and Duke Snider was in left. Gilliam did draw a walk in a pinch-hitting role in the ninth as the Dodgers lost 8-0 on April 15 to San Francisco in the first West Coast Major League game, played at the Giants' temporary home, Seals Stadium. Gilliam led off the next day while starting in left as the Los Angeles Dodgers won, 13-1. The "best leadoff man" went 2-for-5 with 2 RBI and a walk.

When the Dodgers made their home debut in front of 78,672 at the cavernous Memorial Coliseum on April 18, Gilliam was leading off and playing left. The Coliseum was not built for baseball, and the unique configuration, which included a 40-foot-high screen in left field, meant that spectators were not always close to the action. It represented a dramatic departure from the intimate confines of Ebbets Field. "I'd run a mile and still not see a fan,"[8] Gilliam quipped.

"There was definitely a feeling of culture shock going from New York to Los Angeles," Carl Erskine recalled. "As a professional you handle it because you have to."

In the bottom of the third of the opening game, Gilliam drew a walk, advanced to second on a Pee Wee Reese groundout, and scored on Snider's single. Jim had scored the next-to-last run at Brooklyn's Ebbets Field and the first run at the Dodgers' new home in Los Angeles.

The Dodgers' 1958 season went quickly downhill after that. As April turned to May, Los Angeles was already in seventh place in the National League, a spot they would hover around throughout the season. The remaining "Boys of Summer"—Gil Hodges, Duke Snider, Carl Furillo, and Pee Wee Reese—struggled to stay healthy. Reese would retire at season's end at 40 years of age. Furillo would play in only 58 more games across the next two seasons before retiring.

As such, Alston was constantly tinkering with his lineup. Frank Finch, Dodgers beat writer for the *Los Angeles Times*, likened Alston's lineup shuffling in August to a merry-go-round.[9] Despite not being in the Opening Day starting lineup, Gilliam led the team in moving around the carousel, starting 65 games in left, 39 at third, 26 at second, and six in right field. At the end of the season, Gilliam led the Dodgers in a variety of offensive categories, including at bats, hits, doubles, walks, and stolen bases. His 2.0 WAR was fourth-highest on a team finishing a distant seventh in the National League race.

Defensively, Gilliam played all three outfield positions plus second and third bases. He made his first appearance in center field since 1955, moving from right field for the bottom of the eighth inning at Philadelphia in a 7-4 loss to the Phillies on July 27. Jim played a total of 25 and two-thirds innings in center field for the Dodgers, fielding all 10 chances he had without making an error. The Dodgers would eventually finish in seventh place, 21.5 games behind the Braves, and just 2.5 games ahead of basement-dwelling Philadelphia.

A FINAL DIVORCE

As Jim and the Dodgers were settling into life in Los Angeles, Gloria moved home to Baltimore in early January 1958 to live with her parents after Jim asked his mother, Katherine, to move to New Jersey. The kids, however, did not follow either their mother or father, instead staying in New Jersey to be cared for by their grandmother. Divorce paperwork was initiated a second time. Sam Haynes of the *Baltimore Afro-American* once again covered the legal proceedings, characterizing it as a "bitter battle over property rights and custody and support of their two children."[10] The *Afro-American* headline read, "Jim forces wife out, mother in."

Calvin J. Hurd, Gloria's attorney, appeared before Superior Court Judge Nicholas A. Tomasulo in Elizabeth, New Jersey on February 14, 1958. He asked the court to grant Gloria $250 per week, an annual amount of $13,000, for support of herself and the two children. Hurd presented evidence that Jim earned $17,000 per year with the Dodgers, plus an estimated $5,000 on post-season barnstorming exhibitions.[11] Hurd also claimed that Gloria was forced out of the house when Jim brought his mother to live with them.[12] The process continued throughout the summer of 1958 with the kids in New Jersey, Gloria in Baltimore, and Jim playing baseball, primarily on the West Coast. With no National League team in New York in 1958, the closest Jim would get to his kids during the summer was Philadelphia.

As the 1958 season ended, Jim stayed in Los Angeles, except for a brief trip to Alabama in December with his friend, Willie Mays. The two players had become friends during their time in New York, and Gloria told reporters that she and Mays' wife, Margherite, often shopped together in New York.[13] Jim officially filed his divorce paperwork, using 860 60th Place in Fairfield, Alabama, Mays' hometown, as his residence. The *Baltimore Afro-American* reported this was the address of a lawyer and that Jim stayed at an unnamed Birmingham hotel during the divorce proceedings. Attorney George Young of Birmingham represented Jim, while Gloria's representative was listed as Lillian Ulass, a notary public from New York.[14]

In his filing, Jim charged that Gloria had "voluntarily" abandoned him on January 1, 1955 and stayed away "for more than one year" since he initiated separation proceedings. Jim stated in his testimony that "at sometime prior to January, 1955, my wife was constantly leaving home for any purpose and would often stay out, late at night, many times until 2 or 3 a.m." Jim added that Gloria would "leave our children uncared for" and "she would stay out all night drinking excessively, and then sleep all the next day."[15]

Jim's charges present an opposite perspective from Gloria's assertions in 1957 in which she alleged Jim was the one who was negligent toward family duties and engaged in infidelity.

The petition was filed on December 15 and granted three days later by circuit judge W. A. Jenkins, Jr. based upon abandonment. The court record indicated Gloria denied the abandonment charge. Terms of the settlement, as reported by the *Afro-American*, stipulated that, "Mrs. Gilliam (1) relinquish any right to tangible property—and effects; (2) Give custody of the two children, James Malcolm Gilliam, 10, and Katherine

Gilliam, 8; and (3) Gilliam pay his divorced wife $1,500, plus $50 a week for five years."[16]

The *Pittsburgh Courier* reported Gloria was under doctor's care in New York due to a "rundown and nervous condition." As a result, her attorneys agreed to allow Jim custody of the children.[17]

Marion E. Jackson, writing in the *Alabama Tribune* on January 16, 1959, provided the most detailed account from Jim's complaint. "Many times she would stay out all night drinking excessively and then when I ordered her to stay home, she moved out and started living on the second floor of the house. During that time I had to get her mother, Mrs. Mary White, to care for the children. In January 1957, she moved out of our home an (sic) set up residence at the YWCA in New York."[18]

Jackson also wrote, "Gilliam said his wife did not want the children nor the house."

LIVING THE HOLLYWOOD LIFE

In carrying on the precedent set in New York, businesses wasted little time calling on the new Dodgers to help pitch products. In anticipation of the 1958 debut season, Packard-Bell employed Walter Alston, Gil Hodges, and Gilliam (along with four Giants who had moved from New York to San Francisco) in a series of advertisements for televisions and hi-fi radios. Each player was depicted on a postcard-size picture card with the player likeness on the front, and the Dodgers schedule and a short testimonial pitch on the back side. Gilliam's testimonial read, "I like music and I like the way it sounds on my Packard-Bell Hi-Fi. It's got AM-FM radio and it *looks* as good as it sounds, too!" His signature, "James Gilliam," was underneath the copy.

Packard-Bell supplemented the schedule cards with a series of tri-fold advertisements and a poster with the saying, "We came west and found the best." The experienced pitchman from New York, Jim, identified as Junior Gilliam, is depicted with a smile and his left thumb pointing over his shoulder at a Hi-Fi floor radio box resting on four legs.

This marriage between Dodger players and popular culture was a natural fit. The movie industry was taking off and nearby Hollywood served as the epicenter for it. Being seen at Dodgers games became the "in" thing for movie stars. "The stands were sprinkled with celebrities. Danny Kaye. Bing Crosby. They were always there. I remember guys gawking over the dugout at Lana Turner," Erskine said.

It was only a matter of time, therefore, that players would cross over into cameo roles in movies and television. A week before Christmas 1958, Paramount Pictures released *The Geisha Boy*, starring Jerry Lewis as Gilbert Woolery, a magician sent on a USO mission to Japan to entertain troops in the Pacific. Woolery attends a baseball game between the Los Angeles Dodgers and a Japanese team, shot on site at Wrigley Field in Los Angeles. Erskine served as the Dodgers' player representative at the time and negotiated with Lewis to allow the comedian to choose which nine players he wanted in the film.[19] Gilliam was selected for a cameo as the Dodgers' third baseman. A copy of a "day player agreement" for Hodges specified a payment of $500 to Hodges for his role in the movie.[20] It is reasonable to think Jim earned the same.

1959 SEASON: MORE UNCERTAINTY

Gilliam entered 1959 spring training confronting the same uncertainty as previous seasons, namely questions about whether he would be traded. One prominent rumor had him going to two-time defending National League champion Milwaukee Braves in exchange for outfielder Joe Adcock.

"The Braves are the team to beat, so why should we help them by dealing Gilliam? Junior is three men in one. He bats both ways and he can play the infield or outfield. Besides that, he's possibly the best lead-off man in baseball,"[21] Buzzie Bavasi repeated, echoing the comments he voiced prior to the previous season.

Bavasi was even more superfluous while discussing Gilliam in the *Los Angeles Sentinel* in February 1959. "I don't think of Jim as just one ball player. He can do too many things. He's one of the best lead-off men in the business. He's a switch hitter. He can play infield or outfield equally well. That's like four men rolled into one as far as I'm concerned."[22] Jim's presence had grown from being three men, as Bavasi articulated in 1958, to four men.

ENTER EDWINA FIELDS

Born in 1935 in St. Louis, Missouri, Edwina Fields was a college student at Spelman College, a Historically Black College for women in Atlanta, when she and some friends were at a club in Birmingham during a break from their studies some time in the 1950s. It was at the club where she met a baseball player.

"A gentleman came over and said Jim Gilliam wanted to meet me and I didn't know who he was because I wasn't into baseball. I said ok and he and Satchel Paige came over," Edwina recalled, although she did not remember the exact year. During a 1965 interview with *The Tennessean*, Edwina remarked five years passed before she and Jim were married, which would place their introduction in 1954.

After their initial meeting, Edwina moved back home to St. Louis, where she received a degree in medical records from St. Louis University in 1956. She began working as a medical record librarian at the Veterans Hospital on North Grand Boulevard in St. Louis and reconnected with Jim when he would call while the Dodgers were in St. Louis. A friendship developed first and moved on from there.

As the 1959 season began, Gilliam and Fields made plans to marry while the Dodgers were in St. Louis, choosing Saturday, April 25 as the date. But when a change in the schedule moved the game from evening to day, wedding plans needed to be adjusted as well.[23] Fields' parents, Edward and Hannah, lived in a two-story brick house at 6 Lewis Place in the Fountain Park area of St. Louis, just a few miles from Forest Park and St. Louis University. It was here, at 10 a.m. following a Dodgers 3-2 extra-innings win the night before, Jim and Edwina were married by Minister James E. Cook in front of many of Jim's teammates and Edwina's family. Dodger infielder Charlie Neal served as the best man, while Edwina's older sister, Dorothy, served as maid of honor. An Associated Press photo shows Jim and Edwina smiling in the back seat of a vehicle with manager Walt Alston, coach Pee Wee Reese, and teammate Clem Labine peering through an open window. Jim sported a white carnation as a boutonniere.[24]

After the ceremony, the players traveled the two-plus miles to the original Busch Stadium (the former Sportsman's Park), where the Dodgers and Cardinals played a day baseball game, won by the Cardinals, 6-5. Gilliam was 0-for-3 on the day with two walks and a run scored while starting at third base. Once the game ended, the players convened back at the Fields house for a 6 p.m. catered reception. Several Dodger beat writers were pictured with the bride and groom at the reception, including Bob Hunter of the *Los Angeles Herald-Examiner*. Hunter would become a staunch supporter of Gilliam throughout his tenure in Los Angeles.

The Dodgers beat the Cardinals, 17-11, in a day game on Sunday. Alston gave Gilliam the day off after his wedding reception. The team left town after the game for a three-week road odyssey taking Los Angeles to Pittsburgh, Philadelphia, Cincinnati, Milwaukee, and San Francisco before finally returning to the Coliseum on May 11. Edwina stayed in St. Louis for several months to work before moving to Los Angeles at the end of the baseball season.

Whether coincidental or not, by leaving St. Louis as a married man, Gilliam embarked on one of the most productive offensive streaks of his professional career. He was batting just .214 entering play on May 1. By the time the season's first All-Star Game rolled around on July 7, Gilliam's average had improved to .349 with a .462 on-base percentage, thanks to a .430 average in the month of June. His .349 average tied him with St. Louis first baseman Bill White for second in the league, behind Milwaukee's Hank Aaron, who was batting .370.

During a 10-game home stretch from June 22-July 2, Gilliam reached base safely to open the bottom of the first inning in each game, as the team went 8-2. All told, Gilliam reached base safely in 35 straight games from June 3-July 9, the longest such stretch of his career. Inexplicably, however, he was left off the National League All-Star roster for the July 7 game at Pittsburgh's Forbes Field. It took an injury to a Dodgers teammate to get Gilliam added to the National League roster for the second All-Star Game on August 3 at the Los Angeles Memorial Coliseum.

Beginning in 1959 and running through 1962, Major League Baseball played two Midsummer Classics. The controversial proposal was approved, in large measure, to increase revenues, with *The Sporting News* estimating a potential for an additional $500,000. Players, however, were less certain of the need for two games. Only nine of 16 clubs voted in favor of two games. The Dodgers, host of the second game, voted unanimously in favor of the new format.[25]

Gil Hodges, the Dodgers' long-time slugging first baseman, was batting .293 with a .948 OPS on July 23 when he pulled a muscle in his right leg sliding into second base, requiring hospitalization. Fred Haney, Milwaukee Braves manager and skipper for the National League team, officially named Gilliam to replace Hodges on the National League roster. Despite his .319 average, many who followed the Dodgers were distraught that Gilliam's best man, Charlie Neal, was not selected.

"While Gilliam is a sound selection, we think it is a downright dirty shame that second baseman Charlie Neal wasn't added to the squad. Charlie's the best man at his position in the league, and certainly deserved a break. But that's politics, or somethin',"[26] Frank Finch wrote in the *Los Angeles Times*, without elaborating on the perceived politics or "somethin'."

Three days before the game Finch and others received their wish, when Neal was added to replace an injured Bill White on the roster.

Gilliam was a reserve on the National League All-Star team in 1956 but did not appear in the game, so although his inclusion in the 1959 Game was his second selection, it would be the first time he actually played in the game. He became the seventh former Negro League All-Star to appear in a Major League All-Star Game, preceded by (in order) Jackie Robinson, Roy Campanella, Larry Doby, Minnie Miñoso, Satchel Paige, and Ernie Banks.

With the American League on top 3-2, National League manager Fred Haney sent Gilliam to the plate in the bottom of the fifth to bat for Reds second baseman Johnny Temple. Facing future Hall of Famer Early Wynn, Gilliam drew a two-out, one-on walk batting left-handed. Ken Boyer followed with a walk to load the bases for Hank Aaron, who grounded out to Pete Runnels at first.

Gilliam would bat again in the bottom of the seventh with two outs and the National League now trailing, 4-2. This time he would face the Baltimore Orioles' Billy O'Dell, a lefty. Since moving to Los Angeles, Gilliam's power numbers had dropped. In five seasons at Ebbets Field, Gilliam averaged more than 40 extra base hits per season. During the 1958 year, Gilliam tallied just 32 extra base hits and fell off to only 25 in 1959, his All Star season.

"I'm a line-drive hitter. When the Dodgers were in Ebbets Field those short fences were tempting, but I know I don't have the power to hit the long ball consistently. Besides, I bat mostly left-handed in the Coliseum, so I don't get many chances to shoot for that left field screen,"[27] Gilliam said.

Throughout his professional career, Jim hit just 65 home runs, roughly two-thirds as a left-handed batter against a right-handed pitcher. But here he was, batting right-handed in the All-Star Game with his team trailing, 4-2, and the left-field screen beckoning him. Gilliam worked a 3-2 count on O'Dell before lifting the payoff pitch high into the air toward left-center field. Outfielders Tony Kubek and Al Kaline converged on the spot where the ball might come down, but watched it sail over the screen for a home run. It was the first National League home run in an All-Star Game since 1952. In so doing, Gilliam became the first and only player in baseball history to hit a home run in both a Negro League and Major League All-Star Game.

Gilliam came up again in the bottom of the ninth against righty Cal McLish, who had allowed Frank Robinson and Wally Moon to reach base, before retiring Hal Smith and Smoky Burgess, in a 5-3 game. Gilliam represented the potential winning run but hit a ground ball that first baseman

Vic Power, Jim's teammate on the 1953 Santurce team that won the Caribbean Series, fielded and won the race to the bag.

On the season, Gilliam batted .282 with a league-leading 96 walks for a .387 on-base percentage.

OCTOBER BASEBALL RETURNS

For a franchise accustomed to playing baseball in October, three years without doing so can seem like an eternity. During the past decade, since the 1949 season, the Dodgers had played in the World Series as many times as not: five. Following third- and seventh-place finishes the previous two seasons, competing in October 1959 would be a welcome return to normalcy.

The Dodgers finished the regular season with an 86-68 record, the same as the Milwaukee Braves, forcing a best two-of-three playoff series. Los Angeles won Game One, 3-2, in Milwaukee, and rallied to win Game Two, 6-5 in 12 innings, in Los Angeles and advance to the World Series. The previous five trips to the Fall Classic had all been against the New York Yankees. This time, however, the opponent was the Chicago White Sox.

Chicago jumped all over Los Angeles in the opener at Comiskey Park, winning, 11-0. After that, however, it was all Dodgers, who would take the series in six games. Gilliam was fairly quiet, batting .240 (6-for-25). His best game occurred in the Dodgers' 1-0 Game Five loss, when he tied a World Series record with four straight hits, all singles. The winning team share was $11,231.18, nearly two-thirds the amount Jim earned in salary in 1959.[28] When asked about her plans for the money, Edwina told the *Los Angeles Sentinel*, "We just fixed our new apartment, so I don't need anything really at the moment. I guess I will just put it in the bank, temporarily anyway."[29]

MOVING FROM THE SPORTS PAGE TO THE SOCIAL PAGE

Baseball players in the late 1950s and early 1960s frequently took offseason jobs as a way to supplement their income while simultaneously helping promote the team. As a recognizable name from the Brooklyn days, Gilliam was a willing and reliable participant for the Dodgers public relations staff throughout his time in Los Angeles.

The team had yet to take the field as the Los Angeles Dodgers when Gilliam signed with Roy King, "the slick-talking public relationist," in March 1958 to arrange personal appearances once the season was over. Jim had already been featured by Packard-Bell, and King reported "several fat offers for the services of Gilliam,"[30] even before he played a game.

During one of those appearances at the Southern Area's Dodger Ball, Jim, alongside Charlie Neal and John Roseboro, signed autographs and shook hands with everyone who stopped by, wrote Brad Pye, Jr. in the *Los Angeles Sentinel*: "From where we sit this is an important move by the Dodgers."[31] Over the next two decades, Pye, who passed away in 2020, would report a lot about Gilliam in the *Sentinel*, a Black newspaper founded in 1933 and still publishing today, as well as other Black-focused media.

King's pitching of Gilliam as a pitchman was immediately successful, particularly in the *Sentinel*. In the June 25, 1959 issue, Gilliam was pictured seated next to Willie Mays, Elston Howard, and Mike Gordon, proprietor of Mike's Shoe-O-Rama on Crenshaw Boulevard. Mike, the copy said, "owns the only complete, name-brand family shoe salon operated by Negroes in America."

Six weeks later, Jim was promoted alongside teammates Neal and Roseboro for an appearance at Nat Diamond's Empire Furniture Stores at 46th and Central. The three Dodger teammates would be signing autographs as Nat Diamond celebrated his 48th birthday sale with "big hit values." In an early form of pay-for-play journalism, the ad ran on page A8 while a non-bylined story, reading more like a press release, ran on page B8. "So many youngsters never get an opportunity to meet their heroes like Neal, Roseboro, and Gilliam in person," Diamond is quoted. "And we are going to give them this chance on Saturday."[32]

Give Diamond credit—he knew how to maximize a news cycle. Nearly a month later, on September 3, the *Sentinel* ran a photo from the event in which Diamond is standing behind the three Dodgers and Mittie Lawrence, crowned "Miss Bronze '59."

Gilliam parlayed the 1959 World Series title and All-Star Game performance into a sales representative position with distiller Hiram Walker and Sons, at its offices at 3460 Wilshire Boulevard. His official duties included servicing customers by promoting Canadian Club whiskey and Walker's DeLuxe 8-year-old bourbon.[33] His unofficial duty, however, was to dress in a suit, smile, and get his picture in the local media with clients. He proved particularly adept at this unofficial role, especially in the Black press.

Less than a month after his employment with Hiram Walker, Gilliam and teammate Charlie Neal were honored at a pre-Thanksgiving Testimonial Banquet at Ish's Sportsmen's Club, where they were presented plaques for their "invaluable contributions" to the Dodgers. The Black newspaper *California Eagle* published a series of pictures from the event with a caption imploring readers to "remember there is no better way in which you can say thanks for a job well done than to pick up on a Milford Company taste handled by Gilliam."[34] The paper gave Neal equal time, encouraging readers to patronize Hamlin W. Nerney Ford, offseason employer of Neal.

Gilliam's image in the *California Eagle* continued through December, appearing in print ads next to a recipe for Walker's DeLuxe Bourbon Punch. Curiously, the ads identified him as "'Junior' Gilliam, World's Champion third baseman of L.A. Dodgers and stellar sales representative of the Hiram Walker Distilleries."

A photo in the December 24 paper shows Gilliam with four other Milford Company executives in the company's Beverly Hills office celebrating the sales of Hiram Walker's 8-year-old bourbon and Canadian Club whiskey hitting a new high in the Southern California market.[35] Much like his endorsement of cigarettes, Gilliam was not a regular consumer of the product. He was nothing more than a social drinker.

Gilliam's status as a newlywed, 1959 World Series champion, and alcohol sales representative was fame enough for him to be featured regularly in the social sections of newspapers. Two photos of him entertaining guests at the home of Hildegarde Bostic during a farewell party, sponsored by Hiram Walker, for the New York Rinkeydinks ran on the *California Eagle's* Social News pages in January 1960. Newspaper articles from the 1950s identified the Rinkeydinks as a "club composed of musicians' wives."[36] Bostic was married to saxophonist Earl Bostic, whom it is believed had a huge influence on John Coltrane. Earl died from a heart attack in 1965 and was buried at Inglewood Park Cemetery, not far from Jim Gilliam's ultimate resting spot.

Others listed as in attendance included Catherine Basie, second wife of Count Basie who, in 1958, became the first African-American to win a Grammy. Also in attendance was Ruth Bowen, wife of Billy "Butterball" Bowen, a former member of The Ink Spots, a vocal group that welcomed various members from 1934-1954. Bowen was with the group from 1944 to 1952. In 1989, the original Ink Spots were inducted into the Rock & Roll Hall of Fame.

As a fan of jazz music, Jim undoubtedly enjoyed mixing with this crowd, as one of his favorite performers was Billy Eckstine. Gilliam continued to rub shoulders with the Black celebrities of the era, joining, among others, Nat King Cole, Ella Fitzgerald, Johnny Mathis, and Dinah Washington, as well as Roseboro and Neal, at the Hill Toppers Charity

Guild benefit for the NAACP on January 25. The event, which took place at the famous Cocoanut Grove inside the Ambassador Hotel on Wilshire Boulevard, generated $2,500 for the education fund of the NAACP and was attended by, according to the *Sentinel*, "the cream of Los Angeles society."[37]

Three days later, Jim signed his 1960 Dodgers contract for $22,000, a $4,000 raise over 1959.[38] In the two years since the franchise moved to California, Gilliam won a World Series, hit a home run in the All-Star Game, got divorced and remarried, appeared in a Jerry Lewis movie, became an effective pitchman for the Dodgers, and held a lucrative job with a liquor company. The palm trees of Hollywood seemed to fit Gilliam well.

Jim Gilliam photo card, part of the 1960 MacGregor Advisory Staff of Champions series.

12

BLACK BEVERLY HILLS

A QUICK 5-1 START HAD LOS ANGELES IN FIRST PLACE IN 1960. THE TEAM, however, followed that with an 8-18 stretch that dropped the club into sixth place by May 20, nine games out of first. The Dodgers recovered enough to finish the season with an 82-72 record, good for fourth place, but well behind the champion Pirates and a disappointing finish after winning the World Series in 1959. Offensively, Gilliam hit only .248 but drew 96 walks with a team-high 96 runs scored. His 4.4 WAR was third on the team, behind starting pitchers Don Drysdale and Johnny Podres.

The usually quiet Gilliam did cross off a new item on his list of baseball accomplishments when, on May 7, he was ejected by umpire Ed Vargo for arguing a call at third base. With the score tied 1-1 against the Phillies at the Coliseum, Alvin Dark attempted to go from first to third on a single to right by Ed Bouchee. Gilliam pleaded his case that Tommy Davis' throw and the subsequent tag applied by Gilliam nabbed Dark. While pleading his case, Vargo implied Gilliam pushed him, to which Gilliam replied, "Horsefeathers."[1]

The next day, Gilliam expanded on his version of events. "All I said was, 'he never got to the bag.' Vargo then turned around and said, 'you're out of the game.' I asked him 'What for?' and he said, 'you pushed me.' I never touched the man, and I didn't curse either."[2]

By September 1, the Dodgers were entrenched in fourth place and seemed to be riding the season to its conclusion. Gilliam started 119 of the first 129 games at third base, before giving way to Triple-A star Charley Smith, who had paced Spokane in 1960 with a .322 average, 20 home runs, and 106 RBI. The move provided early fodder to the annual hot stove rumors regarding Gilliam's future with the team. Brad Pye, Jr. wrote in the *Los Angeles Sentinel* on September 15, "While all sorts of trade rumors will be flying before the 1961 campaign gets underway, the only Negro player on the present Dodger roster who may not be back is probably James 'Junior' Gilliam. Jim is one of the most versatile players on the club, and he's also one of the key players most of the other clubs want, too."[3] The context of this rumor was the Dodgers' pursuit of New York Yankee Elston Howard, but also the possibility the team would seek to trade its young Black outfielders, Tommy Davis and Willie Davis.

The *Los Angeles Times* reported on October 8 the Washington Senators (soon to be the Minnesota Twins) were "making discreet inquiries about the availability" of Gilliam, although General Manager Buzzie Bavasi was quick to dismiss the rumor, "I don't know who they've got that we would want, unless it would be Earl Battey, Camilo Pascual, or Harmon Killebrew, and I doubt that they're going to turn those fellas loose."[4]

In December, the Dodgers were reported to be on the cusp of trading for the Tigers' slugging outfielder Rocky Colavito, who had hammered 118 home runs in the previous three seasons. Bavasi had offered Don Demeter, Johnny Roseboro, and Bob Lillis to Detroit, but was willing to provide

JIM GILLIAM
INFIELDER—LOS ANGELES DODGERS

Jim Gilliam's 1960 Leaf baseball card. Topps controlled rights to cards distributed with gum, so Leaf cards were distributed with bags of Sports Novelties, Inc. marbles.

Gilliam instead of Lillis if that would close the deal. "Ordinarily, Buzzie would be reluctant to pawn off versatile players like Lillis and Gilliam, but they're not exactly indispensable,"[5] wrote Frank Finch. The deal never materialized. Bavasi finally acquired Colavito in late spring 1968. He batted just .204 with three home runs in 113 at bats for the Dodgers before being released in July 1968.

Bavasi was also reportedly rebuffed in an attempt to deal Demeter, catcher Joe Pignatano, and Gilliam to the last-place Phillies for pitcher Dick Farrell.[6]

On December 6, Major League Baseball, with cooperation from Dodgers' owner Walter O'Malley, announced an expansion franchise, the Los Angeles Angels, would begin play in the American League the following season. Angels owner Gene Autry declared during a press conference at Wrigley Field, site of the team's home games, in December 1960, "I wish like hell we had Jim Gilliam on our club. We are going to try like hell to get him. He is a fine gentleman and an outstanding ballplayer."

Autry was quoted by Brad Pye in the *Sentinel*. Pye offered his own spin on the many trade rumors. "With every passing day there seems to be some rumor that the Dodgers have Gilliam on the trading block. But nothing ever seems to jell," Pye wrote, suggesting that if the Dodgers simply wanted cash, a deal could be made.

"If Buzzie Bavasi will give him up, I will buy him tonight,"[7] Autry said.

Gilliam, meanwhile, did his best to ignore the rumors and focus on his offseason job as a liquor sales representative. A photo taken by Jack Davis that ran in the December 1 *Los Angeles Sentinel* shows Jim meeting with Arnold Hoffman of Arnold's Liquors, 3894 S. Western Avenue in Los Angeles. The caption said Jim was "batting .1000 (sic) as a salesman for Hiram Walker."[8] The same photo ran in the December 24 *Chicago Defender* with a caption describing Gilliam as "batting 1000 in the winter league" as he had "just sold one of the largest orders ever taken for Christmas gift-wrapped liquor in Southern California."[9] Jim's off-field business success was getting nationwide attention.

The off-field success was beneficial as the Gilliam family was growing. Yvette Renee Gilliam was born to parents Jim and Edwina on January 22, 1961 at Cedars of Lebanon Hospital at 4833 Fountain Avenue.[10]

MORE UNCERTAINTY IN 1961 SPRING TRAINING

Having once again survived the various trade rumors, Gilliam entered the 1961 season as the third-longest tenured Dodger after Gil Hodges and Duke Snider, signing a $25,000 contract on February 2, just in time to head to spring training at Vero Beach where once again he would compete for playing time on a crowded Dodger roster.

Frank Finch of the *Los Angeles Times* prefaced his story by noting Gilliam "gets on base more and strikes out less than 95% of the players in the National League....As usual, the sharp-eyed veteran will go Florida

Feb. 20 to fight-off challengers to his third base job....Upstarts don't bother the Nashville native who now makes his home here."[11]

Finch was correct. In 1958, Charlie Neal started at second base with "upstart" Dick Gray at third base. Gray spent parts of 1958 and 1959 with Los Angeles until he was shipped to St. Louis on June 15, 1959. In 1959, Neal was again at second with Jim Baxes at third. Baxes only made it until May 22 when he was traded to Cleveland. Even though he began 1960 as the team's starting third baseman, Gilliam still wound up splitting time with Charley Smith, Bob Lillis, and 36-year-old Gil Hodges.

Smith was the odds-on favorite "upstart" as spring training began in 1961, but Tommy Davis emerged as the camp darling, securing the starting job and forcing Gilliam into a presumed full-time utility role in 1961. As the season approached, it was apparent to the media that Jim would begin the season on the bench; a "traditional rite of spring," which columnist Jim Murray lamented in the April 6 *Los Angeles Times*, less than a week before the season.

"Junior Gilliam has been not making the Dodgers in spring ever since he joined the club in 1953," Murray wrote. "He starts every season in the dugout. He sleeps every night with his bag packed at his feet and rumors of a trade swirling around in his dreams. He lives his life in a kind of limbo midway between the Dodgers and the rest of the National League."[12]

As if accustomed to the treatment, Gilliam expressed a level of ambivalence toward the prospect of sitting on the bench when he spoke to Murray. "I'll just have to set here and see what turns out. I've never seen a ball club with so much talent on it. But sometimes talent develops trouble hitting the curve ball or stopping the ground ball, too."[13]

Gilliam rarely said anything about segregation or conditions he faced during his career in the Negro Leagues, minor leagues, or with the Dodgers. So it was a bit surprising in spring 1961 when he, along with fellow Black teammates John Roseboro, Tommy Davis, and Willie Davis, addressed a concern to Peter O'Malley, the son of Dodgers owner Walter O'Malley, who was in charge of the spring-training facility at the time. While the barracks at Dodgertown were integrated, the bathrooms at Holman Stadium—where the team played its games—were not. Nor, for that matter, were the stands integrated, with Black patrons confined to the right-field bleachers.

When the players mentioned it to Peter O'Malley, his response suggested it never dawned on him that might be the case. The next day, all of the segregated signage was gone. Signs that previously said "White

Women" and "White Men" now read simply "Women" and "Men."[14] "We had to physically take the Black people to set them in other spots around the stadium," Tommy Davis recalled. "When we had an exhibition game we went and took the people out of the right field area and told them to sit in left field, sit behind home plate, sit over there. And they wouldn't believe us....That was the integration of Holman Stadium."[15]

A 1961 REGULAR-SEASON COMEBACK

The emergence of Sandy Koufax as a dominant pitcher helped Los Angeles improve to 89-65 in 1961, good for second place, four games behind the Cincinnati Reds. The starting pitching quartet of Koufax, Drysdale, Podres, and Stan Williams combined to post a 64-40 record with 810 strikeouts in 917.2 innings pitched.

Gilliam's 439 at bats in 1961, while fourth highest on the team, were the fewest in his career since joining the Dodgers. His 144 games played, also a career low, was second behind Maury Wills with 148. Jim split his time primarily at second base with Neal and at third base with Tommy Davis and veteran Darryl Spencer, acquired midway through the season. Jim also started several games in left field. Offensively, however, Gilliam struggled, batting a career-low .244 with just 74 runs scored, another career low.

As for Charley Smith, the minor-league star supposed to push for playing time, he struggled in limited action with the Dodgers in 1960 and 1961, hitting just .190 in 84 at bats while striking out once every four at bats. He was traded to Philadelphia on May 4, 1961 and bounced around baseball for the rest of the decade, playing for six additional big-league clubs before retiring in 1969.

Jim Murray's preseason column proved prescient. "Then the season starts and some 'phenom' begins to leak at the seams, the stuffing oozing out of him at every trip to the plate," Murray wrote on April 6. "The manager sets up a hysterical search amid the bat bags, locker room towels, and press clippings of his wunderkind—and there sits Jim Gilliam, waiting."[16]

Jim turned 33 after the season's end. Coming off career lows in virtually every statistic, it was not hard to wonder what his future with the Dodgers looked like.

A JOURNALIST'S PLEA

Dating back to his time in the Negro Leagues—when he was covered favorably by Wendell Smith of the *Pittsburgh Courier* and Sam Lacy of the *Baltimore Afro-American*—Jim always had advocates in the Black press. Brad Pye, Jr. of the *Los Angeles Sentinel* emerged as another ally immediately after the team moved to Los Angeles, as did magazine writer and occasional *Sentinel* columnist Andrew Spurgeon "Doc" Young.

Echoing the sentiments of not just the Black press but many fans as well, Young directed a preemptive strike of sorts to Buzzie Bavasi. As part of his "Refreshing World of Sports" column on August 10, 1961, sponsored by Hamm's Beer, Young authored an "Open Letter to Bavasi," using Bavasi's own words against him.

You told the story yourself when you said, 'Keep in mind that Gilliam is four players in one—he's a switch hitter who can play outfield or the infield....

"Every fall, winter and spring, reporters ticket for Philly, Milwaukee, or Chicago. Always there is some 'phenom' who is going to bench him. Yet, despite the Dodgers' long bench and their deep freeze never a season comes when they don't fall back on 'Ol Reliable Mr. Gilliam. And this true major leaguer never fails to take up the slack in the Dodger line. Here is a guy who is one of the most under-rated players of all time. His pay-check proves it. Perhaps it is partially due to the fact that, as one observer has said, he doesn't bend everybody's ear with superfluous conversation....All Junior Gilliam brings to the game is...talent!"[17]

Young's column restated much of what *Times* columnist Jim Murray had written prior to the 1961 season. That two journalists, one Black and one white, would author similar sentiments in defense of the player *The Sporting News* anointed as "Least Co-Operative with Writers" in 1954 spoke to Gilliam's evolution and maturity as a player and person. Writers, at least those in Los Angeles, respected Gilliam as a company man who did everything asked of him without complaint. He did not seek the headlines, they found him.

Whether by coincidence or as a result of the stories from Young and Murray, a flurry of articles in the years to follow told the same narrative, only now it was being shared with a national audience. New York sportswriter Jack Mann first shared Gilliam's story across the country with his January 1963 article in *Sport* magazine titled, "Gilliam brings three gloves and waits around." Bob Hunter of the *Los Angeles Herald-Examiner* and *The Sporting News* would later take up the campaign with an April 1964 article in *The Sporting News* calling Gilliam "unsung and unsurpassed."

In December, the Dodgers sold second baseman Neal, Gilliam's roommate and best man in his wedding to Edwina, to the New York Mets for $100,000 and utility player Lee Walls. Gilliam, it seemed, would once again be a second baseman, unless another "upstart" or "phenom" challenged for playing time. "We won't be hurting at second base," general manager Buzzie Bavasi said. "Jim Gilliam played the spot on three pennant winners at Brooklyn, and while he can't play every day any more, we've got an adequate replacement in Larry Burright."[18]

For the first time since 1954, Gilliam was not the subject of trade rumors in the offseason. Perhaps Bavasi had taken to heart Murray and Young's thoughts that the 33-year-old Gilliam, despite his track record as a consistent and valuable team member, was being typecast as someone who could not play every day. Whether Burright could do what Neal, Baxes, Smith, and others could not, remained to be seen.

BLACK BEVERLY HILLS

Shortly after they were married, Jim and Edwina purchased a duplex at 1067 South Redondo Blvd., between Hancock Park and Beverly Hills, in the Wilshire district. The Gilliams lived in one half of the duplex and rented out the other half.

Malcolm and Kathy remained at the Thorn Street house in New Jersey with their grandmother, Katherine, until Jim sold the New Jersey home later in 1961 and moved his mother and kids to Los Angeles. Jim's mother settled in Altadena, north of Pasadena and bordered by the San Gabriel Mountains, while Jim's children joined him and Edwina and their infant daughter at their house. Los Angeles was officially home for the entire Gilliam family.

Jim's stature on the Dodgers certainly aided his ability to buy a home in a largely white part of Los Angeles. "I had white tenants for a long time, and a few more Negroes have moved into the neighborhood since then," he said in 1964. "That doesn't mean there's no housing problem in L.A., or in New York, for that matter. I had no trouble buying a house because I was a Dodger."[19]

When established in the 1920s, Hancock Park was one of several Los Angeles neighborhoods placed under a 50-year restrictive covenant, which stated non-whites could not live in the neighborhood, unless they were servants.[20] Nat King Cole and his wife, Maria, made an offer on a house in Hancock Park in July 1948 but when local residents learned of their skin color, an attorney representing the homeowners association told Cole's attorney if Cole rescinded the sale of his home, they would give Cole his money back with a profit.[21] The Coles balked at the offer, as they were intent on living in Hancock Park and helping to integrate the community, similar to how Willie and Margherite Mays bought a home on Miraloma Drive and integrated the exclusive planned community of St. Francis Wood in San Francisco in the late 1950s.

Cole, with whom Gilliam had become friendly during his days at the Lord Calvert in Miami, asked the Gilliams to buy a house in Hancock Park. With the family growing, the Gilliams sought a bigger home and moved south across the Santa Monica Freeway to 4926 Valleydale Avenue in the View Park-Windsor Hills section of Los Angeles, south of Baldwin Hills. Once referred to as the Jewish section, the entire area quickly became the "Black Beverly Hills," as Kathy Gilliam-Belway referred to it. Many affluent Black families settled there in the 1960s, fleeing the increasingly turbulent streets of South Central and Watts to the east and south across the 110 freeway.

Black families in this part of Los Angeles were generally much better educated than their South Central counterparts, with just over 71 percent of all employed African Americans in Baldwin Hills classified as white-collar workers.[22] The Gilliams' neighbors, within a couple of blocks, included singers Nancy Wilson, Ray Charles, Ike and Tina Turner, and assorted other Black doctors, lawyers, and psychiatrists. Fellow Major Leaguer Curt Flood lived a block away.

The new home had four bedrooms, five if one counted the temporary partition that occasionally separated the room where Kathy and Yvette slept. The back yard had a pool, while the front yard had a basketball hoop. Darryl, who was born in 1964, remembered the house being a center of activity for himself and neighboring kids. "Everybody knew everybody. We were always outside playing football or basketball or baseball or riding bikes. We were the sports block," he said.

Malcolm, 12, and Kathy, 11, attended John Burrows Junior High School, where Malcolm briefly dated Natalie Cole, daughter of Nat King Cole. From there, the two oldest children attended Los Angeles High School, where Malcolm starred in both football and baseball.

Malcolm first garnered media attention as an athlete in the summer of 1962 when he was just 13 years old. The *Sentinel's* L.I. "Brock" Brockenbury noted Malcolm was hitting above .300 and that he might soon compete with Maury Wills' sons (including future Major Leaguer Elliott "Bump" Wills) for a future Dodgers team. "With Wills' two sons wanting to play short and Gilliam's son after the same spot, the 1972 Dodgers are going to be overloaded at the position, or somebody will have to move over to second or third."[23] Malcolm was already being cast in the same mold as his father.

As Malcolm grew into high school, he was moved to center field. In his sophomore year at L.A. High in 1965, Malcolm hit .395 and was voted a first-team All-League outfielder. "I love baseball, and not just because my dad played in the major leagues,"[24] Malcolm said in March 1965. (The past-tense "played" reflected the fact Jim had temporarily retired after the 1964 season.)

As Jim was enjoying a bit of a renaissance season after his brief retirement, an article in the July 1965 *Valley Times* speculated that Jim and Malcolm could be the first father-son duo to play together in the Major Leagues.[25] Malcolm competed against future Dodger Derrel Thomas, a member of the 1981 World Series champion team. Thomas played for rival Dorsey High School.

"When I made the varsity team, we went to play L.A. High School. In the stands, Jim was there. Just before he went to spring training. That was the first time I met him, because of Malcolm," Thomas remembered. Years later Jim would offer Thomas batting tips while Thomas was a member of the San Diego Padres before he joined the Dodgers.

Malcolm also starred as a defensive halfback on the L.A. High football team that went undefeated and won the 1965 all-city title during his junior season. During his senior baseball season, 1967, Malcolm was named a second-team All-League outfielder. After high school, Malcolm attended a Dodgers tryout at the Rancho Cienga playground near Baldwin Hills on June 27, 1968 but was not signed.

During this time, the Gilliams employed a housekeeper, Nina, a Black woman who also cooked for the family. Jim preferred traditional Southern soul food, but Nina abruptly switched to healthier foods one day, things such as wheat bread and whole grains. Apparently, a doctor had ordered a diet change. Jim had been diagnosed with high cholesterol, but he did not tell many people.

RETURNING TO THE SOCIAL PAGES

Using a misogynistic tone reminiscent of the early 1960s, Doc Young wrote about baseball wives in a January 1962 *Los Angeles Sentinel* column: "Like all marriages, a baseball marriage can have its trying moments. But it's not the worst sort of life in the world, not by a long shot...

"You travel more, you see more of the world; you meet more famous people than the average housewife; you are lionized yourself, quite often, by the social clubs and the social climbers; you usually wear nice clothes and drive a big car and eat well because if your husband's any kind of ball-player at all, he's making a five-figure salary every year he plays.

"If you're a baseball wife, you're a pretty special sort of breed. I mean, chances are, you are a wonderful woman."[26]

The arrival of the Dodgers, prominent Black players, and their wives, provided the local Black press much desired content as it sought to put into practice what Young had written. Edwina was just 24 years old when she and Jim married in 1959. Edwina was not merely a housewife. She graduated from St. Louis University and worked as a medical records librarian in both Missouri and New Jersey. Like Jim, Edwina had a reputation as being well-dressed. That she was extremely photogenic aided in making her a favorite of the *Los Angeles Sentinel* and its social pages.

On March 1, 1962, the *Sentinel* published its annual elaborate spread highlighting the 10 Best Dressed Women, "a salute to the thousands of fashion conscious Negro women of the west, well groomed women, with the ability to select and wear beautiful clothes."[27] Edwina, identified as "Mrs. James Gilliam, Homemaker," was one of the 10 women featured. Nearly 60 years later, all Edwina would say about the honor was, "It was a nice compliment."

The *Sentinel* had planned to stage a photo of the "charming Edwina Gilliam" with new Dodger Stadium in the background, but she was visiting her parents in St. Louis while Jim was at spring training. As such, "the photo in the Best Dress layout was not posed, but caught in action by Howard Morehead a season ago as Edwina watched the Dodgers play."[28]

Edwina's favorite colors were reported as black and gray, and a preference for basic dresses that may be dressed up or down was noted. "Once in a while she ventures into the realm of extreme high fashion, for a special occasion dress, but this is rare. She treats the extreme new hair styles with the same caution, wearing them only when a special occasion demands it.

"Simplicity in hair styles and wearing apparel is practiced by this young winsome wife of Jim Gilliam, who stands out as fashion conscious person in a ballgame crowd, or in the quiet circle of her immediate friends."[29]

Edwina appeared on the society pages two months later when the *Sentinel* ran a photo spread of Dodger wives for Mother's Day, along with

Shirley Davis, wife of Tommy Davis, and Jeri Roseboro, John's wife. None of the players were pictured, and the article noted the team would be in St. Louis on Mother's Day. Edwina is featured with a smiling 15-month-old Yvette, along with personal information revealing she is a "member of St. Paul's Catholic Church, and is also affiliated with Talley Pals Bridge Club and East-West Coasters Social Club."[30]

Dodger spouses continued to provide content opportunities for the *Sentinel*. Edwina, Shirley Davis, and Jeri Roseboro were featured answering phones during a fundraiser for the Exceptional Children's Foundation, sponsored by KGFJ radio.

Even as the Dodgers would trade both Black players Tommy Davis and John Roseboro, and Gilliam would transition into retirement later in the 1960s, the *Sentinel* continued to highlight Edwina in its society pages. Whether modeling the latest fashion or attending fundraisers, Edwina was a consistent presence in photographs, pictured alongside Camille Cosby, wife of actor and comedian Bill; Wanda Lomax, wife of journalist Louis; actress Jayne Meadows; and Ruth Cosgrove, wife of comedian Milton Berle.

Reprinted with permission from the Los Angeles Sentinel Newspaper.

ENTERING THE 1962 SEASON

As the calendar flipped to January 1962, Murray began a *Los Angeles Times* column, "To fully appreciate Jim Gilliam's value to the Dodgers, you have to dig deeper than the home-run, RBI and batting-average columns. It is the 'little' things the versatile vet does at the plate and afield that have won Gilliam recognition as one of the game's real pros."[31]

Murray trumpeted Gilliam's ability to avoid swinging at bad balls, creating a number of walks and low number of strikeouts. He extolled Gilliam's ability to sacrifice, noting he was a perfect 13-for-13 in that endeavor in 1961. "If I had eight Gilliams in the lineup there wouldn't ever be a need to flash a sign,"[32] Alston told Murray.

As spring training was wrapping up, *The Sporting News*, which had covered the Dodgers' second-base battle in each issue that spring, highlighted Burright prominently in its "Rookie Roundup" in late March. Labeled the "heir apparent" to the second-base job, Larry Burright was receiving assistance from Gilliam on how to "cheat" on batters and cover the bag on certain runners.[33]

That Gilliam was in the starting lineup on Opening Day 1962, playing second base and batting second behind Maury Wills, was news in and of itself. This would be the club's fifth season in Los Angeles and Gilliam's only prior Opening Day start was in 1960 at third base. In fact, Gilliam had ceased being primarily a second baseman when the team relocated. In 1958, Gilliam played more games in the outfield and at third base than at second. During the 1959 and 1960 seasons, Gilliam was almost exclusively a third baseman. In 1961, Gilliam split his time between third and second, with a few outfield starts.

DODGER STADIUM

The *Los Angeles Times* alternately referred to the $18 million stadium as the Dodgers' new "playground" or the "Golden Gulch." The symmetrical field dimensions, a departure from the short left-field fence at the Coliseum, meant different things for different hitters. Gilliam was one of the players who expected to benefit from it: "It figures to help me. I have got a lot of space now,"[34] he said.

The team opened its new home on April 10, 1962 in a day game against the Cincinnati Reds. The pregame festivities were replete with all the "fuss and feathers," as Vin Scully would say, of Opening Day, including a parade through downtown Los Angeles. Walter O'Malley was introduced to the capacity crowd of 52,000 and escorted onto the field through the left-field bullpen by Gilliam. Jim was not the only Brooklyn Dodger on the roster—Duke Snider, Johnny Podres, Sandy Koufax, John Roseboro, and Don Drysdale had all logged time in Flatbush—so his selection to escort

O'Malley over World Series heroes Snider and Podres provides insight into Jim's relationship with the owner. O'Malley valued loyalty and company men, and Gilliam embodied that throughout his career.

JAMES GILLIAM

Jim Gilliam was part of Nicholas Volpe's 1962 series of Dodger players, with prints given away at Union 76 filling stations. RLFE Pix / Alamy Stock Photo

Despite the pomp and circumstance, the opener at Dodger Stadium was less than memorable for the home team, at least from an on-field perspective. The Reds led 1-0 only three batters into the game before Los Angeles rallied in the bottom of the fourth. Gilliam opened the frame with a line-drive single to right and scored the first Dodger run in Dodger Stadium on a two-out double by Ron Fairly. The Reds would blow open a 2-2 game in the seventh when Wally Post blasted the first home run in ballpark history, a three-run shot off Johnny Podres. Cincinnati won the game, 6-3.

Los Angeles exacted revenge the next day. Following a Wills triple to open the bottom of the third of a scoreless game, Gilliam sent a Moe Drabowsky pitch deep over the left-field fence for the first Dodger home run in Dodger Stadium. Los Angeles cruised to a 6-2 win behind Sandy Koufax.

Jim was truly the bridge between Brooklyn and Los Angeles. He recorded the last hit in Brooklyn Dodger history, scored a run in the final game at Ebbets Field, scored the first Dodger run in both the Los Angeles Coliseum and Dodger Stadium, and blasted the first home run in Dodger Stadium.

June 30, 1962 represented another Dodger first at Dodger Stadium, as Sandy Koufax hurled the first of four career no-hitters. Interestingly, it was not the first no-hitter at the new stadium, as Bo Belinsky of the Los Angeles Angels, who leased Dodger Stadium from 1962-65 while waiting for Anaheim Stadium construction to be complete, no-hit the Baltimore Orioles on May 5.

On this night, however, Koufax struggled but still blanked the woeful New York Mets, 5-0. He needed 138 pitches to accomplish the feat, walking five and running the count full on nine batters. Koufax struck out 13, but none in the ninth as he induced a series of three consecutive ground-ball forceouts after walking Gene Woodling to open the inning.

For Gilliam, who started and played the whole game at third base, it marked the fourth no-hitter in which he had been a participant, and his first since the three games in 1956. For Koufax and Gilliam, there would be several more.

A DISAPPOINTING FINISH TO THE SEASON

The end of the 1962 season proved to be eerily reminiscent of the fateful 1951 season, when the New York Giants rallied from 13 games back in August to tie Brooklyn for the National League pennant and force a three-game playoff. The Giants, of course, won the playoff with Bobby Thomson's "Shot Heard 'Round the World" in Game Three of the playoff.

Los Angeles led the National League by four games with seven to play when the team inexplicably stopped winning. A 1-6 stretch allowed the Giants to tie and, once again, force a three-game playoff. San Francisco won the first game, 8-0, at home before the series shifted to Los Angeles, where the Dodgers pulled out an 8-7 walk-off win in the bottom of the ninth. As in 1951, a decisive Game Three awaited on Wednesday, October 3 at Dodger Stadium.

The Dodgers carried a 4-2 lead into the top of the ninth and were, once again, three outs away from a World Series. And, once again, all hell broke loose. *Washington Post* writer Michael Leahy, in his book *The Last Innocents*, describes in detail the horror which would unfold in front of 45,693 fans at Dodger Stadium that afternoon.

Larry Burright was one of those "phenoms" who would challenge Gilliam for playing time in 1962. Indeed, the 24-year-old Burright made the Opening Day roster and appeared in 115 games, mostly as a second baseman. His presence in the lineup allowed Alston to slide Gilliam to third base, where the collection of Daryl Spencer, Tommy Davis, and Andy Carey had struggled.

With the Dodgers ahead 3-2 in the top of the seventh, Burright entered Game Three defensively at second base, with Gilliam switching to third base. As was the case in Game Seven of the 1955 World Series, Gilliam could only watch as the teammate who replaced him for defensive purposes factored into a key moment of the game. This time, however, the outcome would not be in the Dodgers' favor.

The Giants began the top of the ninth against Dodger relief pitcher Ed Roebuck, who saved the Dodger bullpen in 1962, posting a 10-1 record and a 3.09 ERA in 119 relief innings pitched. Now, Alston had turned to his ace reliever to bail out starting pitcher Johnny Podres in the sixth inning. As Leahy described, Roebuck did not throw hard, relying on "guile and a repertoire of pitches that included a sinker and an excellent slider."[35]

That Alston left Roebuck in for his fourth inning was somewhat controversial. He had pitched each of the first two games of the playoff series. According to Leahy, "players wondered whether he had enough left to work the ninth inning. Yet Alston's options were few....No one else in the bullpen looked like any more of a reliable bet than Roebuck."[36]

Matty Alou opened the ninth with a single, bringing up Harvey Kuenn. Burright inexplicably moved closer to first base, away from the second-base bag, prompting, as reserve catcher Norm Sherry told Leahy, the "haunting" question, "Who moved Burright?"[37]

Kuenn hit a two-hop perfect double-play ball to Maury Wills at short, but because Burright was so far from the base, the only out Los Angeles could record was the force at second. After Roebuck issued back-to-back walks to Willie McCovey and Felipe Alou with one out, Willie Mays came to the plate with the bases loaded. Mays singled to narrow the score to 4-3 with the bases still loaded and one out.

Alston replaced Roebuck with Stan Williams, who surrendered a game-tying sacrifice fly, a wild pitch, and two walks. Los Angeles now trailed 5-4 with two out and the bases loaded. Ron Perranoski came on for the Dodgers to face José Pagán, who hit a ground ball that Burright fumbled, allowing another run to score. The Giants won, 6-4.

Gilliam, like teammates Maury Wills and Duke Snider, the *Los Angeles Times* reported, was "grimly silent." In the third inning of the game, Gilliam had committed an error, allowing a Giant run to score. His relay of a throw from Snider hit Kuenn in the back as Kuenn attempted to slide back safely to first.

Years later, Dodger outfielder Ron Fairly summed up the team's play in his memoir, "We gave the Giants five outs in what was the worst inning we played all year."[38]

As the curtain fell on the 1962 season, Gilliam could lay claim to a dubious distinction: having led the Dodgers in games started at two different defensive positions—96 at second base and 60 at third base. In total, Jim appeared in 160 of the team's 165 games, behind only Wills and Tommy Davis. At age 33, he hit .270 with a .370 on-base percentage in 702 plate appearances. He led the Dodgers with 93 walks and 15 sacrifice hits and was credited for helping Wills steal 104 bases and allowing Davis to drive in 153 runs, the most in the National League since the Cardinals' Joe Medwick knocked in 154 in 1937.

But the team disappointed, having come so close to a return trip to the World Series.

MARITAL TROUBLES AGAIN

As if the end of the 1962 season did not hurt enough, Jim and Edwina separated on October 30, with a petition for divorce filed in early November. In the petition, Edwina, now 27 years old, alleged "extreme cruelty" on the part of Jim, asking for custody of Yvette. She also sought a restraining order against Jim in order to "prohibit his molesting her or their shared community property."[39] The complaint requested monthly alimony of $840, plus equity in the home on Redondo Boulevard and community property.[40] Jim was presumably still paying Gloria the alimony she had been awarded in 1959.

Jim was ordered to pay $300 per month to support Edwina and $125 per month to support Yvette by a Los Angeles Superior Court commissioner. Nine months later, in August 1963, Superior Judge Elmer D. Doyle removed the case from the calendar when neither party appeared for the trial. Jim's attorney announced the two had reconciled. The 1963 Dodgers were clicking on all cylinders in August 1963, and Jim was in the middle of one of his finest seasons in baseball. 1963 would be a year to remember.

13

BENCH TO MVP CANDIDATE

LESS THAN TWO MONTHS AFTER THE DODGERS' NINTH-INNING IMPLOSION IN
the decisive 1962 playoff game, Buzzie Bavasi packaged infielders Larry
Burright and Tim Harkness in a trade with the New York Mets for pitcher
Bob Miller. The November 30, 1962 deal was designed to bolster the
Dodgers relief corps, but it also allowed the team to move on from 1962.
Burright, who was front and center in the Dodgers' collapse in Game
Three of the 1962 playoff, had started the 69 games at second base that
Gilliam did not, but was deemed expendable as the Dodgers, of course,
had another youngster waiting to force his way into the starting lineup.

Signed by Los Angeles in 1959 at the age of 18, Nate Oliver's path to
the Dodgers in spring 1963 bore a striking resemblance to the one Gilliam
journeyed down a decade earlier. Like Gilliam, Oliver came from a baseball lineage. His father, James "Jim" F. Oliver, played for the Cincinnati
Clowns of the Negro Leagues from 1941 to 1942, and also the Birmingham
Black Barons in 1945, ending his professional baseball career the year
before Gilliam began his. Nate's older brother, also Jim, played baseball as
well.

"Dad had had his fill," Oliver recalled. "He wanted to spend time at
home with us."

Gilliam and Oliver possessed similar physical characteristics. The 1963
Dodgers yearbook listed Gilliam at 5-11, 180 pounds, while Oliver was 5-
10 and 160 pounds. Just as Gilliam had his own diminutive nickname,
"Junior," so, too, did Oliver, who had somewhere along the way, acquired

the moniker "Pee Wee." Fifty years later, Oliver still did not know the origin of the nickname. "I have no idea. I think it had to do with my stature. I was 5-8, 150 pounds soaking wet," Oliver said. "I'm not sure when or where it started, but it stuck."

Oliver graduated from Gibbs High School in St. Petersburg, Florida. Opened in 1927, Gibbs High was Pinellas County's first public secondary school for Blacks. White students began attending the school in the early 1970s after Florida integrated its public schools. Among its prominent alumni were former Major League infielders Ed Charles, the oldest member of the 1969 New York Mets, and George Smith of the Boston Red Sox, along with the Pittsburgh Steelers' Steel Curtain standout safety Glen Edwards and Houston Oilers wide receiver Ernest Givins. Oliver's father, Jim, was responsible for instructing and developing those players.

Jim Gilliam, undated Los Angeles Dodgers publicity shot.

Today, Gibbs High sits in the heart of St. Petersburg, visible from the west side of Interstate 275, two miles from Tropicana Field, home of the Tampa Bay Rays. Across Interstate 175 to the south of Tropicana Field is Oliver Field at Campbell Park, named for Pee Wee's father.[1] Oliver Field was the first field to be refurbished under the Rays Field Renovations program in 2006.

As the Dodgers had done with so many of their Black players in the 1950s, including Gilliam, the team assigned Oliver to an integrated city in the North. In Oliver's case, this meant the Class B Green Bay Bluejays and, later, the Fox Cities Foxes in nearby Appleton. Predictably, the young Oliver struggled being so far away from home. In 1960, however, he blossomed, batting .329 with 15 triples and 30 stolen bases for the Class C Great Falls Electrics, even earning a brief promotion to Triple-A St. Paul. Oliver was on the fast track from there, batting .266 for Triple-A Spokane in 1961, where his teammate was 35-year-old Don Newcombe, trying to get back to the Major Leagues after his release from the Cleveland Indians in January 1961.

At the age of 21, Oliver hit .317 for Spokane in 1962, playing second base alongside future Dodger teammates Dick Nen at first base, Dick Tracewski at shortstop, and John Werhas at third base. Just as Gilliam had done 10 years earlier, Oliver would spend that winter honing his craft in Puerto Rico, forcing the Dodgers to find a place for him in the big-league lineup.

As was the norm in baseball in the early 1960s, the Dodgers had two Triple-A minor league affiliates. In addition to the Spokane Indians, managed by Preston Gómez, the Dodgers also had an agreement with the Omaha Dodgers, managed by Danny Ozark. By the 1965 season, both Gómez and Ozark would serve as coaches for Dodger manager Walt Alston. The 1962 Omaha club boasted another hot, young Dodger prospect in Ken McMullen, a native of Southern California. McMullen, who turned 19 midway through the 1961 season, tore up Class C Reno, batting .288 with 21 home runs, 109 runs scored, 96 RBI, and 107 walks while playing exclusively at third base. In Omaha in 1962, however, McMullen split time among third base, first base, and the outfield. He hit .282 with 21 home runs, good enough to earn a September call-up to the big league Dodgers, where he logged 11 at bats.

As the Dodgers sought to get younger, the 22-year-old Oliver certainly figured into the team's plans going into Vero Beach in spring 1963. Bob Hunter noted in *The Sporting News* the Dodgers, even with 32-year-old

Moose Skowron at first base instead of the 20-year-old McMullen and Oliver at second, could field a starting nine with an average age of 26.[2]

Predictably, Hunter's hypothesized lineup did not include Gilliam. Finding himself once again without a position heading into spring training, 34-year-old Jim Gilliam's future with the club looked cloudier than ever, despite his solid 1962 season.

"Every year there's been some pheenom (sic), repeat pheenom, who was gonna take his job. None of them has yet. It never shakes him up. Gilliam brings three gloves and waits around and says, 'Well, I'm gonna play some place.' So you'd play the pheenom all spring and Gilliam would get in 152 games anyway,"[3] Dodger manager Walter Alston told Jack Mann for *Sport* magazine in its January 1963 issue.

Alston's quote resonated so much with the *Sport* magazine editors, they titled the article, "Gilliam Brings Three Gloves and Waits Around." The article's author, Mann, was a national sportswriter specializing in baseball, serving as sports editor at *Newsday* and would eventually write for *Sports Illustrated* from 1965-67. He was effusive in his assessment of Gilliam's abilities, and inabilities, calling him "the finest mediocre ballplayer who ever walked...and walked....and walked. There will be no votes (except one) for Gilliam's admission to the Hall of Fame. He has been a great player, not because of the talents he has but in spite of the talents he hasn't."[4]

In 1953, Gilliam moved Jackie Robinson from second base to third base and sent Billy Cox to the bench. Charlie Neal moved Gilliam to left field in 1956, and later to third base in 1959. Now, in 1963 after Gilliam had reclaimed second base, Oliver and McMullen were forcing the same domino effect. Their presence, along with that of Tommy Davis, created a surplus of options for Gilliam's primary positions: second base, third base, and left field. Gilliam was, once again, without a home, wrote Hunter in *The Sporting News*. "While Gilliam has no job, it's the same old story for him. He never has a job—until the day the season opens, then he's in there some place."[5]

As training camp wore on, the possibility of an opening increased as the experiment with Davis at third base failed. A sore arm contributed to eight spring-training errors, most on errant throws, forcing Alston to reevaluate his options. He would turn first to McMullen as a potential starter at third, knowing veterans like Gilliam, Daryl Spencer, and Don Zimmer (reacquired via trade with the Cincinnati Reds in January), still existed on the roster, as did the slick-fielding, 28-year-old Dick Tracewski.

With one week to go before Opening Day in Chicago on April 9, Alston was still unsettled as to who would play third, but Oliver was now entrenched at second base. Not only had he taken Gilliam's defensive spot, but Oliver now occupied Junior's spot in the batting order. "Pee Wee still has to prove he can hit big league pitching seven days a week, but if we opened today he would be my No. 2 hitter,"[6] Alston told the media on April 2.

Alston authored a bylined scouting report on his Dodgers on Monday, April 8, the day before the season began. Whether he wrote it or it was ghost-written is up for debate, as the language reads more like a sports-writer than a manager. In the article, Alston expressed cautious optimism for Oliver at second, "Oliver seems to have what it takes—savvy, good hands, plenty of range and good wrist action at the plate. Whether he can be a capable No. 2 man in the batting order, behind leadoff man Maury Wills, remains to be seen. That's a tough assignment because Jim Gilliam was one of the best."[7]

Similarly, Alston was uncertain about third base, where he iterated confidence in McMullen, but acknowledged the presence of Gilliam, Spencer, and Zimmer. "It would be nice to have the job settled, but we may have to wait a bit before we say, 'That's it.'"[8] Alston wrote.

The manager could not have scripted the opening inning of the opening game of the 1963 season any better. Wills opened the top of the first at Wrigley Field with an infield single off Cubs starter Larry Jackson. Oliver worked the count to 3-1 before stroking a single to right, sending Wills to third where, one out later, he would score on a ground out. Oliver, playing the role of Jim Gilliam by batting second and playing second base, had recorded his first major-league hit in his first major-league at bat. Oliver collected two hits on the day and McMullen contributed a two-run double in the top of the ninth, adding insurance to a 5-1 victory for starting pitcher Don Drysdale.

Through the season's first nine games, Gilliam was relegated to pinch-hitting duties with an occasional appearance at third base late in the game. Finally, in the season's tenth game on April 19, Gilliam was in the starting lineup, batting second and playing third base. Gilliam led off the bottom of the seventh against Houston's Turk Farrell with a double, his first hit of the season, and scored two batters later when Frank Howard homered. The Dodgers won, 2-0, behind Sandy Koufax's two-hit shutout. It was Gilliam's 1,500th career game played.

THE BUS INCIDENT

The Opening Day success notwithstanding, the entire Dodger team seemed to struggle to begin 1963. Oliver started the first 22 games at second, but after his sparkling debut, his bat cooled. An 0-for-9 stretch had dropped his average to .218, and he had struck out five straight times.

Playing sparingly, Gilliam was batting just .167 when he made his first start of the season at second in Pittsburgh on May 3. At the same time, Alston moved Tommy Davis to third base, replacing the combination of McMullen (who was sent to Spokane on May 8 with a .205 average), veteran Spencer (released on May 10), and Gilliam.

Following a 7-4 loss at Pittsburgh on May 6, the Dodgers' record stood at 12-14. Los Angeles held a 4-2 lead headed to the bottom of the sixth in that game when things went sideways. Ted Savage opened the inning with a ground ball to Gilliam, whose wild throw from his second-base position allowed Savage to reach safely in front of Pirates sluggers Willie Stargell and Roberto Clemente. The Pirates would score four runs in the inning, three of them unearned because of Gilliam's miscue.

The club was now in eighth place, ahead of only the New York Mets and expansion Houston Colt .45s, and tempers on the club were beginning to flare. According to the *Los Angeles Times'* Frank Finch, Alston had "built up a head of steam and blew his lid"[9] as the team rode a bus to the Pittsburgh airport where they would fly to St. Louis. Players were reportedly complaining "vociferously" about cramped conditions and lack of air conditioning on the bus. Some began yelling at traveling secretary Lee Scott, who responded, "If you guys would win some games, instead of kicking 'em away, you might deserve an air-conditioned bus."[10]

Alston, seated in the front seat, instructed the bus driver to pull over to the side. Alston stood up and first chided Scott for his comments about losing, and then offered to cede bus procurement to any of the players. "Can everybody in the back hear me?" Alston asked. "Ok, I've heard enough wrangling about what kind of busses we use. Does anybody want to volunteer to check the bus we get in St. Louis?" There was silence.[11]

Alston was just beginning. "I kept getting angrier—and hotter," he wrote. "I said if nobody liked the new arrangements we could handle the complaint any way they liked—by talking it out privately, or in front of everybody, or if they weren't satisfied right now, I'd be glad to step out on the sidewalk and have it out. I concluded by emphasizing, 'What I've just said goes for everybody.'"[12]

No one took Alston up on his offer to handle bus procurement, nor to discuss the matter further. While the speech was prompted by a literal bus, the metaphor for getting the team on the right bus seemed appropriate. Writers noted the "Bus Incident," as Alston called it, was the turning point of the season. Even though things would immediately improve for the Dodgers, Alston wrote, "it was strictly coincidental."[13]

The *Los Angeles Times* reported the bus awaiting the Dodgers in St. Louis was air conditioned.[14] Coincidental or not, the Dodgers jumped on the Cardinals the next day, May 7, scoring nine runs in the first four innings en route to an 11-1 win behind a strong start from Koufax.

Around the same time, Alston switched the lineup again, starting Tracewski at short and shifting Wills to third, with Gilliam now ensconced at second. "A lot of the guys on the team, and Jim Gilliam in particular, wanted me to play shortstop and move Maury to third base," Tracewski said years later. "It actually happened for a while and I was playing fairly good as I remember. One day I came back into the clubhouse and looked at the lineup that was posted and Maury was back at shortstop."

That day was June 29 when Wills resumed his role at short, McMullen starting at third, and Gilliam at second. The lineup tinkering continued the rest of the season, with Lee Walls and Marv Breeding also getting shots in the infield.

Following The Bus Incident, Gilliam went on an offensive tear, collecting five hits in 12 trips in St. Louis, including his first home run of the season. He did not know this at the time, but Gilliam was in the midst of a 15-game hitting streak, the second longest of his career. His consecutive games streak of reaching base safely hit 30, the fourth longest of his career.

When May ended, Jim had hit in 22 of 25 games played during the month, raising his average from .167 to .297. He batted .348 (32 hits in 92 at bats) with 11 walks and 18 runs scored. Midway through the streak, though, Gilliam commented, "I can't remember what my longest hitting streak was. What you did last year and the year before that you can forget. This is another season."[15]

More important than Gilliam's individual accomplishments was the team's turnaround with him entrenched in the lineup. The Dodgers vaulted from eighth place before The Bus Incident, to third place, just two-and-a-half games behind San Francisco on May 31.

On the season, Alston would use seven different starting third baseman and four different starting second baseman. Gilliam made 110 starts at second and 27 more at third. Alston would also run seven different players out in left field. Los Angeles used 21 different position players in 1963, an unusually high number for that era, necessitated by player injuries, slumps, and transactions.

"There was criticism of the manager from time to time because of his 'refusal' to stick with a set lineup. I was accused of carrying platooning to extremes. My only answer was that if it took a lot of players to win, that's how it had to be. Nobody would have enjoyed playing a regular eight more than the skipper of the Dodgers if he could have found enough consistency in his crew,"[16] Alston wrote years later.

Tracewski was one of those players moved around by Alston, until the end of the season. After starting 24 games at shortstop in June, Tracewski started 16 games the rest of the season, with five of those starts at second base, not his normal position. When Alston started Gilliam at third, Wills at short, and Tracewski at second on the last day of the season, September 29, it was only the second time all year the triumvirate had played the infield together. One week later, they played every inning together and were World Series champions.

NO-HITTER #5

Ladies' Night at Dodger Stadium was held May 11, with *Los Angeles Times* writer Frank Finch predicting "plenty of dolls will be on-hand for the hurling heart throb, Sandy Koufax."[17] Koufax would be opposed by Giants star Juan Marichal. During their 1960s rivalry, Gilliam logged 96 plate appearances against Marichal with little success, hitting just .224 with 10 walks. Marichal struck out Gilliam nine times in their career, about one out of every 11 confrontations. Over the course of his career, Gilliam struck out only 416 times in 8,322 plate appearances, a ratio of once every 20 trips to the plate. Marichal definitely gave Gilliam problems.

On this night, however, in front of more than 55,000 spectators, Marichal struggled once the game reached the sixth inning. A Wally Moon home run to open the second had given Koufax a 1-0 lead. That score held until the bottom of the sixth, when Gilliam laced a line-drive single to right, his second hit of the game off Marichal. One out later, Tommy Davis singled Gilliam to second. Moon followed with a line-drive single to right fielder Felipe Alou, scoring Gilliam. After an intentional walk to Ron Fairly loaded the bases, Roseboro singled in two more runs. A fifth single in the inning, this time an infield hit from Tracewski, chased Marichal. The Dodgers now led 4-0.

With a comfortable lead, Alston decided to go to his bench in the top of the seventh, earlier than normal. Just as he had done the night before,

Gilliam moved from second to third, with Tommy Davis replacing Moon in left, and Oliver inserted at second. Koufax had retired all 18 Giant batters he had faced. He was nine outs away from a perfect game.

After retiring Harvey Kuenn on a fly ball to right to open the seventh, Felipe Alou's blast to left was caught by Tommy Davis with his back against the bleachers. Willie Mays then "slugged a screamer which Jim Gilliam speared on the fly at third base."[18] Melvin Durslag of the *Los Angeles Herald-Examiner* described it as a "blistering liner which Jim Gilliam stabbed behind the third base bag."[19] Sportswriters believed Gilliam's defensive play was one of the game's key moments. It would not be the last time in his career that Gilliam would boost Koufax with his defense.

Six outs to a perfect game. Orlando Cepeda led off the eighth for the Giants. With a 1-0 count, Cepeda hit a sharp grounder back up the middle, deflecting off Koufax's glove right at Oliver, who threw to first for the out. Five outs to go.

Nearly 60 years later, Oliver recalled not feeling nervous as the ball caromed to him. "The adrenaline flow during a no-hitter is unbelievable. You can't wait for the ball to be hit to you," Oliver said. "We would say, 'if the ball comes this way, the guy is going to make a right turn.'"[20]

Koufax lost the perfect game when the next batter, Ed Bailey, worked a walk on a full count. Koufax would go full on Jim Davenport before getting him to bounce to a Tracewski-Oliver-Fairly double play. Koufax still had the no-hitter, facing the minimum number of batters. The Dodgers padded their lead in the bottom of the eighth when, with two outs and Gilliam batting, pitcher John Pregenzer balked home Tracewski. Gilliam worked a walk to load the bases. All three runners scored on Fairly's double to right, giving Los Angeles an 8-0 lead and one question. Would Koufax get the no-hitter?

Joey Amalfitano and José Pagán each flew out to open the ninth, when Willie McCovey strode to the plate to bat for the pitcher. Koufax threw four straight balls to issue his second walk of the game. Kuenn hit a bouncer back toward Koufax, who fielded it, ran toward first, and carefully lobbed the ball to Fairly for the final out. Koufax had his second career no-hitter. For Gilliam, it was the fifth time in his career in which he had participated in a no-hitter.

THE NEGRO PROBLEM

Just as the Dodgers began rolling in the summer of 1963, a *Jet* magazine cover story in June revisited a topic covered back in 1954, regarding how many Black players in a lineup was too many. Titled "Do the Dodgers have a Negro problem?" the magazine cover featured photos of six Black Dodger regulars: Maury Wills, Willie Davis, Tommy Davis, John Roseboro, Nate Oliver, and Jim Gilliam. The article, authored by longtime Black sportswriter Andrew S. "Doc" Young, was a response to an article written by syndicated *New York Post* columnist Milton Gross a month earlier. Nearly 10 years earlier, in March 1953 Gross had authored an article, "The Inside Story of Trouble on the Dodgers," initiating conversations about race after Gilliam was named starting second baseman, relegating white infielder Billy Cox to the bench.

In 1963, Gross quoted an unnamed white Dodger player as saying the Dodgers do not field their best lineup because six of the players would be Black. "Are you nuts?" the player responded to Gross's inquiry. "The front office doesn't want to have six out of eight colored players starting a game."[21] Dodger general manager Buzzie Bavasi, clearly no fan of Gross, told Young in *Jet* magazine, "I consider the source it comes from. I know Milt Gross. He's doing it to attract readers and doesn't care whom he hurts....If we had eight Jackie Robinsons, we'd play all eight of them every day."[22]

Whether Bavasi was serious about playing eight Black players is unclear in part because no team in the early 1960s was keeping extra Black players on their roster. It was the same situation as a decade earlier, when the Dodgers kept Gilliam in the minors for two years instead of having him on the bench as a utility player. The Black players teams kept were superstars, not bench players. Recalling those 1960s Dodger teams, Tommy Davis wrote, "There weren't too many Black players who sat on the bench. Either you started or you went back down to the minors or moved on to another organization or went home.

"Think about it in terms of the Dodgers back then. Maury Wills and Jim Gilliam were both really important parts of that team. Willie Davis played. I played. Roseboro played. Who's sittin on the bench who's Black? No one."[23]

Los Angeles did have a few Black bench players at different times during the 1960s. Infielder Nate Oliver averaged 60-plus games played between 1963 and 1967. The addition of Lou Johnson in 1965 after Tommy Davis suffered a season-ending injury created an extra Black outfielder in

1966. The team also added 34-year-old journeyman outfielder Wes Covington in 1966, but Covington batted just .121 in limited action on his last stop in the majors. Teenage outfielder Willie Crawford logged 51 plate appearances between 1964 and 1967 and even recorded a hit in the 1965 World Series as an 18-year-old.

Outside of those four players, Tommy Davis' comments were accurate. Black players on the Dodgers during this period were either starters or minor leaguers.

KILLER INSTINCTS

By late July 1963 the Dodgers had built a comfortable lead over second-place St. Louis and were in Milwaukee to play the Braves. Koufax started for Los Angeles, but was replaced in the sixth by Ron Perranoski. Now, with the Dodgers holding a slim 5-4 lead in the bottom of the ninth, seldom-used Braves outfielder Don Dillard was sent to first base to pinch run for Joe Torre. With two out, Mack Jones hit a grounder back to the mound, deflecting off Perranoski and carrying toward Maury Wills at short. With no chance to get Dillard, Wills rifled the ball toward first. Dillard's path to second had taken him in the line of Wills' throw and the ball hit Dillard above the right eye, knocking him out, short of the base.

The ball caromed back toward Wills. Gilliam, playing second that day, alertly called for the ball and tagged Dillard, who had staggered across second and was lying unconscious on the ground not touching the base, for the game's final out.

"Everyone was worried he had been killed and went to him, except Gilliam, who was playing second. Gilliam was only worried about the out, and he went to the ball and tagged the unconscious player to make sure he was out," John Roseboro wrote in his memoir. "'That's the first time I tagged out a dead man,' chuckled The Devil."[24]

Dillard left the field on a stretcher and was taken to a local Milwaukee hospital for "repairs to his damaged features."[25] The *Los Angeles Times* reported he suffered no fractures and needed seven stitches to close the wound. Dillard missed the next week of action.

SEASON STATS: A MODEL OF CONSISTENCY

The 34-year-old Gilliam finished the season with a .282 average, the third time in his career he would hit exactly .282. Though not a stat at the time, his 5.2 wins above replacement would be the second highest in his career, behind a 6.1 WAR in 1956, and was second highest on the team, behind Koufax's ridiculous 9.9 WAR. As had been foretold prior to the season, Gilliam had merely waited around and was presented a chance to play. He had withstood, for now, the challenges of "pheenoms" and eclipsed 600 plate appearance for the 10th time in his career.

Jim's season splits showed how steady his season was: a .281 average in the season's first half and a .283 average in the second half. His home and away splits, .288 and .277, were also basically equal. He excelled against the league's top contenders, batting .312 against the runner-up Cardinals and .319 against the third-place Giants.

1963 WORLD SERIES: THE YANKEES AGAIN

Los Angeles found itself playing a familiar foe in the 1963 Series: the New York Yankees, who sported a 104-57 record, finishing 10.5 games ahead of the Chicago White Sox. New York entered the Series as the two-time defending World Series champions and in the middle of appearing in four straight Fall Classics.

New York boasted a potent lineup of sluggers, including Elston Howard, Joe Pepitone, Tom Tresh, Roger Maris, and Mickey Mantle, who missed 61 games due to a broken foot. On the mound, the Yankees were led by Whitey Ford and a rookie left-handed pitcher and future Dodger, Al Downing.

"We should have won in '62. We were the best team in '62. But we didn't win," Dick Tracewski said. "In '63 our club was so focused it was unbelievable. When we went over the Yankees, they had Maris, Mantle, (AL MVP) Elston Howard…and Pepitone. They just had a complete nine guys who were All-Stars."[26]

Two legendary lefties, Sandy Koufax and Whitey Ford, were matched in Game One at Yankee Stadium on October 2. Los Angeles plated four runs in the second inning, punctuated by a three-run home run by John Roseboro, and won the game, 5-2.

Game Two of the World Series also featured two lefties, the Yankees' Al Downing against the Dodgers' Johnny Podres, the next day in the Bronx. Los Angeles struck swiftly in the first when Wills opened with a grounder through the mound, which Downing, more than 50 years later, contended he should have fielded, "The ball just stayed down." Downing figured he had an advantage on Wills—who had never seen his pickoff move—and, on Wills' first move, Downing fired to first baseman Joe Pepitone. The subsequent throw to second base was too late; Wills had stolen second. Downing now turned his attention to Gilliam at the plate.

"Jim was hard to pitch to. He understood what his job was. Whatever the situation called for, he would do. That was the mark of a solid ballplayer,"[27] Downing said. In this instance, Gilliam's job was to get Wills to third, which he executed perfectly by singling to right field, where Roger Maris fielded the ball and threw home. But Wills held at third and Gilliam, always thinking, took second on the throw. Willie Davis followed with a double to right over Maris' head, and three batters into Game Two, Los Angeles already led, 2-0. The Dodgers won the game, 4-1, sending the Series to Los Angeles with a 2-0 advantage.

In Game Three, the Dodgers again drew first blood, scoring a run in the bottom of the first. After a Wills ground out, Gilliam worked a walk against starting pitcher Jim Bouton. An out later, Gilliam took second on a wild pitch. He scored when Tommy Davis bounced a bad-hop single between second and short. The lone run was all Don Drysdale needed for Los Angeles. Drysdale limited the Yankees to five base runners and struck out nine en route to the 1-0 victory. The Dodgers were one game away from a four-game sweep of their nemesis.

Game Four took place on October 6, a sun-splashed Sunday afternoon featuring a rematch of Game One's starting pitchers, Ford and Koufax. Frank Howard smacked a solo homer in the fifth for Los Angeles, but Mickey Mantle's home run in the top of the seventh tied the game at one apiece, setting the stage for more heads-up base running from Gilliam. Just 2-for-12 in the Series, Jim hit a Ford pitch that took a high bounce to third baseman Clete Boyer, whose throw to first was perfect except for one thing: Joe Pepitone, the first baseman, lost the white ball in the bright sunlight and white short-sleeve shirts from the crowd. The ball, free of any leather glove, took off down the right-field line. Gilliam alertly raced to third. Willie Davis hit a sacrifice fly on the next pitch, scoring Gilliam with the go-ahead run. Los Angeles now led 2-1.

Koufax held the Yankees off in the final two innings as the Dodgers swept the Series, four games to none. Los Angeles's pitching dominated, limiting the Yankees to a .171 batting average and .207 on-base percentage. The Dodgers used only four pitchers in the Series, as Koufax threw two complete games while Don Drysdale threw another. Ron Perranoski relieved Johnny Podres in the ninth inning of Game Two. Defensively, the Dodger infield was static, with Moose Skowron at first, Tracewski at second, Wills at short, and Gilliam at third. Eleven of the 25 Dodgers on the roster did not play in the Series. "We were very good defensively and we could pitch like hell," Tracewski said. "We caught them when they weren't hitting and that happens a lot."[28]

The Dodgers' World Series triumph netted Gilliam, and his teammates who received a full share, a $12,974 bonus.

A SURPRISING 1963 MVP VOTE

Twenty members of the Baseball Writers' Association of America cast ballots for each league's respective Most Valuable Player. When the results were released on October 30, half of them had Gilliam's name on their ballot, placing him sixth in the league vote, behind winner Koufax, Cardinals shortstop Dick Groat, Braves outfielder Hank Aaron, Dodgers reliever Ron Perranoski, and Giants outfielder Willie Mays. First-place votes were divided among Koufax (14), Groat (4), Aaron (1), and Gilliam (1). One writer omitted Koufax's name on his ballot altogether. Dodger outfielder Tommy Davis placed eighth in the final tally, giving Los Angeles four of the top eight vote earners. Koufax would also win the league's Cy Young Award, joining teammate Don Newcombe, 1956, as one of first pitchers to have won both awards in the same year.

Bob Hunter, a long-time sportswriter for the *Los Angeles Herald-Examiner* and *The Sporting News*, acknowledged he was the one vote for Gilliam. "That one vote was mine," Hunter wrote in *The Sporting News* on January 11, 1964. "Yes, I'm of the old school that would separate the pitchers from the regulars and Sandy Koufax was a shoo-in for the Cy Young Award. As it turned out, he swept them both."[29]

Speaking to Sid Ziff of the *Los Angeles Times*, Koufax stated, "I am amazed Junior didn't finish higher. Gilliam never gets what he deserves. He deserved to be higher." In typical fashion, Jim deflected his teammate's praise. "That was nice of (Koufax), but I doubt if I deserved more. I am pleased as it is."[30]

Ziff called Gilliam's 1963 season "perhaps his finest," noting that "every spring for the past three or four years they've been expecting some kid to chase him out of a job." Gilliam, who had turned 35 in October, responded to Ziff, "Some day that young fellow won't be back to the farm. I know I can't go on forever, nobody can. And the Dodgers can't afford to stand pat. They want to stay up there for years. They got to bring in the kids. I realize that."[31]

Former Yankee first baseman Bill Skowron, who joined the Dodgers for the 1963 season and won his fifth World Series, paid Gilliam the highest compliment after the season. "For years, I've known Jim was a pro, but I didn't really appreciate his value until I got to play alongside him."[32]

Gilliam's age continued to be a hot topic entering the offseason. "I don't know how old he is," Alston claimed. "But that never enters my mind. You can count the mistakes he's made in his major league career on your fingers."[33]

Despite his sixth-place finish in the MVP race, national sports writers were already dismissing Gilliam's productive season. The Dodgers' "infield, where Jim Gilliam alternated at second and third base with Dick Tracewski (2b) and Ken McMullen (3b), could stand bolstering,"[34] wrote Herbert Simons in the December 1963 *Baseball Digest*.

Even Hunter acknowledged the person he voted for as MVP in 1963 might not have a job in 1964. "Gilliam's work in the championship drive was recognized by enough votes to give him sixth place among the N.L. stars, but still the 35-year-old pro doesn't know whether he will be playing second or third or as a utilityman. It was the same last spring and the spring before and the spring before that."[35]

14

A BRIEF RETIREMENT

On April 10, 1964, four days before the Dodgers opened their season, the Baseball Writers' Association in Los Angeles held its seventh-annual awards dinner, in what Brad Pye characterized in the *Los Angeles Sentinel* as the champions of entertainment saluting the champions of the baseball world. The star-studded party, held at the venerable Hollywood Palladium on Sunset Boulevard, attracted more than 1,400. Entertainment was provided by Nancy Wilson, Frank Sinatra, Dean Martin, and Sammy Davis, Jr., among others.

Gilliam, one of several Dodgers attending along with their wives, received the Charles DiGiovanna Memorial Trophy as "the player who most typifies the Dodger spirit,"[1] the second time Jim had received the award. "It's a great honor to win this award for the second time. It just goes to show you what can happen in this great country. I just hope we can win the title again,"[2] he said. A photo credited to Murphy Ruffins in the *Los Angeles Sentinel* shows Jim standing behind a smiling Edwina, who was six months pregnant at the time. She would give birth to Darryl Gerrard Gilliam, an eight-pound, five-ounce son, three months later on July 2, 1964 at Cedars of Lebanon Hospital.

MAURY

For many fans of 1960s baseball, Jim Gilliam's name is inexorably tied to that of his Los Angeles teammate Maury Wills. Many recall the one-two punch at the top of the Dodgers order scratching together a run when the team needed it most. Wills often led off with a bunt single or walk. Gilliam would work the count deep, fouling off pitches or allowing borderline pitches to pass by without offering at them, in order to give Wills a chance to swipe a base. Once Wills was in scoring position, Gilliam would often hit behind Wills, frequently giving himself up as an out in order to get Wills closer to home.

The 1962 season was emblematic of this process. Wills played in all 165 games, swiping 104 bases, a Major League record, and scoring 130 runs, all National League highs, to win the league MVP award. Gilliam, playing his unselfish role, finished with 93 walks, second in the league, and a league-high 15 sacrifices. Tommy Davis often cleaned up the chaos that Wills and Gilliam had wrought, driving in 153 runs, the most in the National League since Hack Wilson had driven in an absurd 191 for the Cubs in 1930.

Wills authored three different autobiographies in the 1960s and 1970s, including an as-told-to, *It Pays to Steal*, following the 1962 season. In that book, Wills was effusive in his praise for Jim, stating he "owns a piece of the new stolen-base mark."

Wills writes, "(Jim's) role in the No. 2 position in our batting order was one of the keys to my success. I told Jim at the beginning of the season not to take any unnecessary pitches, not to do anything that would endanger his own personal record to help me steal bases....I know Jim sacrificed his own personal gains many times to help me. I can't think of another player in baseball better suited to follow me in the batting order."[3]

In recalling the 1962 season, Dodger teammate Ron Fairly wrote, "Maury received a lot of publicity for that feat, deservedly so. But Jim Gilliam, the man who paved the way to second or third for his illustrious teammate on many occasions, should have been given more credit for helping Maury. Batting behind him in the No. 2 spot, Gilliam spent much of the season batting with two strikes on him. Time and again, he wouldn't swing at good pitches in order to give Maury more opportunities to steal. Gilliam was the epitome of a team player, doing so many little things that never make the headlines, but win games."[4]

Gilliam maintained a team mindset when recalling 1962. "We were winning games and that's what we were paid to do. If Maury could steal second and I could move him to third and someone score him with a fly, that was what we wanted. With our pitching, one run often is a big run,"[5] Gilliam told Bob Hunter in the spring of 1964.

While Gilliam's public comments connoted a selflessness and "company man" approach to his role as the number-two batter in the Dodger order, Jim was occasionally frustrated with taking so many pitches. Dick Tracewski, a key member of the Dodger teams from 1962-1965, remembered, "Maury kind of demanded that he take a lot of pitches. Jim, he did it, for the good of the team, and let Maury run the bases. There were times with men on base that he would take a pitch that he didn't want to take. There was some problems there."

Indeed, as years passed, Wills became less complimentary toward Gilliam and their relationship appeared strained, particularly in the early 1970s as both players were reportedly being considered for managerial positions.

"The No. 2 man can be the weakest hitter on the club, but he had better know how to bunt with dependable, unfailing skill. I believe the first two hitters in a lineup set the style for the entire batting order. They are players who can jump on the pitcher, get a runner to second base, and, with the best long-ball hitters on the club up next, take control of the game away from him," Wills wrote in one of his two autobiographies published in the 1970s.

"Confidence at bat is one of the prime ingredients I would demand in my No. 2 hitter. He must feel confident he can get a hit no matter what the count since a large part of the job is taking two strikes to give the lead off man a chance to steal. He has to have a feel for the precise dimensions of the strike zone, and he has to be able to put solid wood on the ball on a hit-and-run play. Jim Gilliam, on the Dodgers of my era, was just about perfect in knowing exactly what to do when a runner was on base."[6]

It is possible, in hindsight, to read Wills' comments as a sort of backhanded compliment to Gilliam, praising Jim as "just about perfect" while simultaneously characterizing him as "the weakest hitter on the club."

Although Wills and Gilliam mostly complemented each other, their approach to their roles differed. Wills was fiery and vocal. Gilliam was quiet and reserved. That occasionally presented a problem, particularly when the competitive nature of each of them rose up in an important situation.

Tracewski recalled an incident one year, he could not recall which year it was, where "Maury wanted him to take more pitches and there were a few games when Jim swung the bat early in the count. Maury didn't appreciate that, and he wanted him to take more pitches and Jim answered back. It was a brief encounter, and it didn't amount to anything. I think Walter Alston laughed when he heard about it. They were two premier players."

Wills recounted a different disagreement in his second autobiography,

How to Steal a Pennant. During a game at Dodger Stadium, Wills was at first with Gilliam at bat. Wills contends that after the pitcher threw to first several times, Gilliam was becoming impatient. With two strikes on Gilliam, Wills took off for second as Gilliam was called out on strikes. Wills says Gilliam threw his bat down in disgust and returned to the dugout, glowering at Wills, who was ultimately stranded as second. It was Gilliam returned to the field that, according to Wills, things got heated.

> "'You do that again, and I'll stomp you right through the ground,'" I said.
> "'Up yours,'" Gilliam said.
> "'When this inning's over, I'll see you in the runway,'" I said.
> "'A pleasure,'" Gilliam said.
> "When we were in the runway that leads to the dugout inside the stadium, Gilliam pointed his finger in my face. In my neighborhood that was the gesture of challenge."[7]

Wills responded to the purported challenge by grabbing Gilliam by the collar and pressing him against the wall, at which point 6-foot-6 Frank Howard intervened.

"Frank grabbed both of us by our collars. 'What are you guys doing?' he demanded. 'You can't fight. We're all on the same team,'" Wills wrote.

"He held us in the air for a few seconds, and then he dropped us."

Wes Parker, who joined the Dodgers in 1964, Howard's last season with the team, did not recall the incident. "I never saw them argue or get upset. Jim was a quiet professional. Maury was more passionate, emotional," Parker said. Wills does not specify in what year the alleged incident took place, so it is possible the incident occurred prior to Parker's debut.

Dodger opponents were simultaneously frustrated and respectful of the Wills-Gilliam tandem. "Maury Wills wasn't as fast as all the base-running specialists for whom he paved the way. But he was smart. He introduced the art and science of stealing bases. I can't remember throwing him out," former Cardinals catcher Tim McCarver told Danny Peary in 1994. "Wills was made a more effective baserunner because Jim Gilliam batted behind him. Gilliam was one of the most underrated players of the era. He could do everything well—bat, field, the intangibles. He knew how to play the game."[8]

McCarver's teammate, first baseman Bill White, attempted to slow the Dodger run-producing duo down by using some rough tactics. "I would slap Wills around when he dives back to first. Tag him hard. I beat the hell out of him," recalled White, who became National League president in

1987. "One time I even played behind him so I could see what he was doing. We just couldn't keep them off the bases."

Gilliam's impact on Wills and the 1960s Dodger teams left such an impression that 15 years after Wills' record-setting 104 steals, *Los Angeles Times* columnist Jim Murray still marveled at Jim's unselfishness. "Maury stole 100 bases but Gilliam took 1,000 pitches for him to do it," Murray wrote. "You're 'expendable' in this spot. You're the kind of guy who shows up in the late movie saying to the platoon leader, 'Let me do it, sir' because the hero is too valuable to be risked in this situation. You're the 'give-up' hitter. The hero-maker. The headline the next day say 'Wills Steals Four More,' not 'Gilliam Takes 12 More.'"[9]

1964 SEASON: MORE UNCERTAINTY

As spring training began in 1964, the Dodgers, and particularly Gilliam, were flying high. The team had swept the rival Yankees in the 1963 Series in convincing fashion. Gilliam was a star contributor, having finished sixth in the league's Most Valuable Player voting. And, for the first time since the days in Brooklyn, he appeared as the team's top second-base option. Gilliam made 110 starts at second in 1963, the most at the keystone position since the team had moved to Los Angeles. Alston's percentage plays, however, limited Gilliam to only 67 complete games at second.

When the 1963 World Series rolled around, Gilliam was the team's third baseman, where he had started just 27 games during the regular season. The smooth-fielding Tracewski started all four World Series games at second, and figured to again share the reps with Gilliam and second-year player Nate Oliver in 1964.

But, as had become the norm since 1956, the team's starting third-base position was up for grabs. The Dodgers used a different starting third baseman in each of the team's previous six seasons in Los Angeles, and the club was destined to use a seventh different player. Ken McMullen, the Opening Day starter in 1963 who made 66 starts at the hot corner during the season, was away at military training and did not report until late in spring training. Despite McMullen's absence, Gilliam was not considered the odds-on favorite to retain the position he occupied the previous year. In fact, like so many springs before, he did not have a clearly defined role on the team.

"HE'LL BE IN THERE SOMEPLACE"

Twenty-six-year-old rookie Johnny Werhas came to Vero Beach with designs on being the 1964 phenom to take Gilliam's place in the lineup. A former USC Trojan teammate of Dodger outfielder/first baseman Ron Fairly, Werhas had spent the previous two full seasons at the team's Triple-A affiliate in Spokane, where he demonstrated plate discipline, ability to hit for power, and more than adequate fielding. In 1963 he led the minor-league Indians with 694 plate appearances, 95 runs scored, and 96 runs batted in. His 17 home runs and .294 average were second to outfielder Al Ferrara's 19 homers and .321 average. He also walked 67 times, finished with a .815 OPS, and was named a Pacific Coast League All-Star.

Media hype on Werhas began in February, prior to the team moving east to Vero Beach. The *Los Angeles Times* reported a crowd of more than 25,000 "poured" into Dodger Stadium on Sunday, February 23 to watch an exhibition of sorts as the "Dodger varsity" staged a public workout, and the championship of the Southern California Winter League was decided. The *Times* reported, "third base hopeful Johnny Werhas and first sacker-outfielder Ron Fairly, both former Trojans, topped the batting practice show as both laced homers into the stands."[10]

As the Dodgers settled into Vero Beach, *Los Angeles Times* writer Frank Finch explained Alston's thinking regarding both Werhas and Gilliam. "By a process of elimination," Finch wrote, "it soon becomes apparent that there's only one regular job on the ball club that's wide open—either second or third base."[11] Finch would quote Alston, "I don't know whether Jim will play second or third, but he'll be in there someplace."[12]

The inference from Alston's quote was that Gilliam's role on the 1964 Dodgers would be determined, as in so many previous seasons, by the actions not of himself, but by the ability and consistency of his teammates.

In Vero Beach, Werhas was assigned to room with Sandy Koufax, a clear indication of the team's optimism that he would be a permanent contributor to the 1964 club. Werhas spent a lot of time with Dick Tracewski and backup catch Doug Camilli, so much so that Koufax dubbed them the "Three Stooges."[13] Instead of being awed by the super-star, Werhas assumed the unlikely role of rookie-turned-Stooge, by teasing Koufax about his stardom. Writing in *The Last Innocents*, Michael Leahy quoted Werhas, "Sandy, you haven't mastered the art of walking through a crowd. You need to work on that. Hey, just watch me. Nobody bothers me at all."[14]

The Dodgers flew to Mexico City in mid-March to play a series of exhibition games against professional teams in Mexico, before settling into the rhythm of Grapefruit League games. It was there that Werhas seemingly seized the third-base job, getting five hits and knocking in five runs during the three-game series. Although Werhas struck out five times, Finch reported in the *Los Angeles Times* that Werhas "came up with one good defensive play after another and got his hits in the clutch."[15] Werhas told Finch, "I've been too anxious. I've got to relax. I don't mean to sound boastful, but I don't have any defensive problems. However, when I first joined the Dodger organization I had a reputation as a poor fielder—and I guess I was."[16]

Nearly 60 years later, Werhas remembers his Cuban-born Spokane manager Preston Gómez, who would coach third base for the Dodgers from 1965-1968 and again from 1977-1979, repeatedly hitting ground balls to him in the minors in an effort to improve his fielding and confidence. "I got to the point where I could throw to second for a double play with my eyes closed," he recalled.

Within two weeks of returning from Mexico, Finch was writing that the Dodgers Opening Day lineup was set, with "that spry guy, Jim Gilliam" at second and Werhas at third.[17] "I'm ready and I'm eager, but not apprehensive," Werhas said at the time. "Sure, I'll be nervous when I take the field at Dodger Stadium, but I think it'll wear off the moment the first ball is hit to me. It's just like in football or basketball; you settle down once you've made contact with your opponent."[18]

1964 SEASON OPENER

The Dodgers opened the season on Tuesday night, April 14 at Dodger Stadium with an 8 p.m. tilt against the eventual World Series champion St. Louis Cardinals. Fans were so excited to see the defending champion Dodgers that a "major traffic jam" delayed the start of the game "for at least five minutes to accommodate" a late-arriving crowd.[19] Perhaps this was the origin for the reputation Dodgers fans have for arriving after the game has started. The *Los Angeles Times* reported about 40,000 spectators were in the stadium at 8 p.m., 10,000 fewer than the 50,451 recorded in that night's box score.

Koufax opposed Cardinals righthander Ernie Broglio, an 18-game winner in 1963. The lineup card made out by Alston looked remarkably like one he would have made multiple times in 1963, with Wills leading off at shortstop, followed by Gilliam at second. It was only the third time in the seven years since the team moved to Los Angeles that Jim started Opening Day.

When Werhas saw his name in the eight hole, directly above his Vero Beach roommate Koufax, he became anxious. It was Gilliam who helped calm him. "I was nervous and excited, everything a young man would feel," Werhas recalled years later. "The atmosphere was great. My mom and dad were both able to be at the game. I got to the ballpark early and got dressed. I was pacing around, and walking around. I just couldn't sit down. Junior pulled me aside. He was actually sleeping on the training table and he told me to settle down. He said, 'It is easy to make the ball-club, but it is not easy to stay. You just do what you do that got you here and you'll be ok.' He was always very kind. He never failed to be a friend."

In the bottom of the third, still tied at 0-0, Werhas batted after Johnny Roseboro had popped to third. "I got jammed a little bit but hit a bloop single over second base," Werhas remembers. "I stood on first base thinking, 'I am leading the National League in hitting.'"

The Dodgers scored single runs in the sixth and the seventh, the latter coming on a two-out Gilliam RBI single to right, scoring Roseboro from third. Frank Howard put the game out of reach with a two-run home run in the bottom of the eighth, making it 4-0 heading into the ninth. With Bill White on first and Charlie James at bat, all of Preston Gómez's extra ground-ball work paid off as James grounded to Werhas, who threw to Gilliam at second to force White. Gilliam's relay to Fairly completed the routine 5-4-3 double play. For the game's final out, Ken Boyer grounded out to Werhas to complete Koufax's 4-0 shutout victory. The Dodgers were 1-0, and both Gilliam and Werhas had factored into the game's outcome.

Optimism abounded for Werhas and the Dodgers after the game. John Hall wrote in the *Los Angeles Times* the next day that Werhas "looks like he may be here to stay, and the Dodgers all gave him the big hand. Every old pro on the club stopped by to congratulate John on his poised performance."[20]

A MEDIOCRE SEASON

In many ways, April 14 was the highlight of the Dodger season. After the Opening Day win, the club lost nine of its next 10 games to fall to 2-9 and the cellar of the National League after play on April 25. The offense was struggling mightily. Gilliam was batting only .178. Werhas was only slightly better, hitting at a .229 clip.

On June 13, the Dodgers got as close as 4.5 games of first place, good for a tie for fifth place before a 5-10 stretch dropped them to eighth place, 11 games out. Los Angeles finished 80-82 and in sixth place in the National League. Alston and the Dodgers were befuddled by their struggles. The team was essentially the same as in 1963 when they swept the Yankees in the World Series, but they could never find a consistent lineup, especially at third base, where seven different players started games. Gilliam led with 62 starts, followed by rookie Derrell Griffith with 35, Dick Tracewski with 25, Werhas with 24, Bart Shirley with 11, Maury Wills with four, and Ken McMullen with three.

After Werhas and Gilliam struggled offensively, Los Angeles turned to Griffith, a 20-year-old rookie from Anadarko, Oklahoma, who had risen rapidly in the Dodgers minor league system. He hit .313 at Class-C Great Falls as an 18-year-old. He followed that with a .286 average at Double-A Albuquerque in 1963, and was batting .318 at Triple-A Spokane in 1964 when he was summoned to Los Angeles.

Griffith hit well, stroking a .290 average in 238 at bats in 1964. But his problem was in the field, where he committed 21 errors in 91 chances, a woeful .769 fielding percentage. The Dodgers also played Griffith in left and right field in an effort to keep his bat in the lineup. A shoulder injury hampered Griffith and forced him to retire a few years later, appearing in a handful of games in both 1965 and 1966.

"I think the team was trying to figure out what was the difference. We thought we were playing the same type of ball. We were playing the same players and the same teams. Things just didn't gel that year," Griffith recalled.

NO-HITTER #6

A bright spot for the Dodgers in 1964 was the continued excellence of Sandy Koufax.

Throughout his career, Koufax pitched nearly as many innings at home and on the road. His ERA, however, was a half-run better at home, 2.48 to 3.04 on the road, and he recorded 26 shutouts at home, compared to 14 away. The largest crowd of the season at Connie Mack Stadium, 29,709, attended the June 4 matchup between National League-leading Philadelphia and eighth-place Los Angeles. It featured a duel between two lefty stars, Koufax and the Phillies' Chris Short, who had beaten the Dodgers in five straight starts.

The teams traded zeroes for six innings, with the Dodgers scratching out three singles, while the Phillies batters had managed only a Dick Allen walk in the fourth. After picking Allen off, Koufax still had only faced the minimum 18 hitters. Gilliam, playing third base and batting third in the order behind Willie Davis and Maury Wills, opened the seventh with a ground-ball single to center. Tommy Davis followed with a single to right, moving Gilliam to third. Frank Howard slugged a three-run home run off the Oldsmobile sign to break the zero-zero deadlock.

Cookie Rojas opened the seventh by flying out to Tommy Davis in left. After Johnny Callison grounded back to Koufax, Dick Allen hit a slow chopper toward Gilliam at third. Jim charged the ball, fielding it on a short hop on the infield grass and rifled the ball to Wes Parker at first to retire Allen. "It was no tougher than the one I booted last night," Jim told John Dell of the *Philadelphia Inquirer* after the game. He was referring to an error he committed in the bottom of the 11th inning the day before, allowing Philadelphia to win, 1-0.

"He played it right," Koufax said. "If he had laid back I think it was hit slow enough for Allen to have beaten it out. And even if he hadn't come up with the ball, I would have given Allen a hit if I had been official scorer."

Phillies' manager Gene Mauch admired Gilliam's defensive play. "Jim Gilliam played the ball like the good player he is. He either gets the out or he gets an error and he didn't even think about getting the error."[21]

Koufax retired the last six batters, four by strikeouts, to complete the one-walk, 27 batters faced, no-hitter, the third of his career. In so doing, Koufax tied Cleveland's Bob Feller as the only pitchers to hurl three career no-hitters in the modern era. For Gilliam, it marked the sixth time he had played in a no-hitter. There would be one more.

THE FIRST RETIREMENT

The headline ran across the entire width of the *Los Angeles Times* sports section on Friday, October 2, 1964, "Dodger Shake-Up: Leo Out, Gilliam In." Dodgers general manager Buzzie Bavasi made the announcement that Leo Durocher would be replaced on next season's coaching staff with Jim Gilliam prior to the team's October 1 game against the Chicago Cubs. That the Cubs would beat Drysdale and the Dodgers that night, 4-3, mattered not. This had been a disappointing season for a team that swept the mighty New York Yankees in the World Series nearly a year earlier.

Attendance at Dodger Stadium had fallen as the season drew on. Fewer than 13,000 were in the stadium on Friday, October 2. The Dodgers were mired in seventh place, playing the eighth-place Cubs, 13.5 games back of front-running St. Louis. The Cards would hold off both Philadelphia and Cincinnati to win the National League pennant by one game.

The 1964 season was largely forgettable for the reliable Gilliam, who did not play that night. His batting average dropped 54 points from 1963, when he hit .282, to a career-low .228 batting average. That dip marked the third largest decline in baseball in 1964 behind Albie Pearson of the Los Angeles Angels (81 points) and future Hall of Famer Willie McCovey (60 points).

"I've been at bat about 250 times less than any other time in my career and I'm a guy who has to play regularly, although I have hit the ball well," Jim said as the season was winding down. "However, it has been right at someone. All you can do when that happens is try to do better next time. I've had seasons like this before."[22]

His comments reflected the wisdom of a veteran ballplayer and contained some measure of the truth. He had gone through stretches in his career where he struggled offensively, but had usually righted the ship by the end of the season. In 1961, his previous worst season, he hit .244 in just 439 at bats. Over the course of his 14 career seasons with the Dodgers, Jim would average 508 at bats, even with a final three-year average of 314 at bats.

As a result of his struggles, and those of the team, Gilliam had started only one game since mid-September. In this final week of the season, Gilliam had appeared in only one game, in the bottom of the ninth and the Dodgers trailing the Cubs, 4-3, on Sept. 29. With no one out and Tommy Davis on first, Gilliam lined out to right field as a pinch hitter for Bart Shirley. The Dodgers lost.

Gilliam rode the bench in both of the next two Dodger games against the ninth-place Houston Colt .45s. But as he checked the lineup card for what would be his final game as a Dodger player on October 4, Gilliam found himself in his familiar number-two spot, behind Maury Wills. The Houston starting pitcher that day was right-hander Don Bradey who, at nearly 30 years old, made his Major League debut nine days earlier against the Dodgers in Houston. He pitched one inning in a 7-2 Colt .45 victory that day. October 4 would be Bradey's only career start, and his third and final Major League appearance.

The Dodgers welcomed Bradey as if it were 1963 all over, with Wills reaching on a single and Gilliam moving him to third with an opposite-field base hit to left. Willie Davis drove home Wills on a sacrifice fly, and Los Angeles had its 1-0 lead. After Tommy Davis flew out, Derrell Griffith moved Gilliam to third on a double to right. John Roseboro followed with a two-run single to right. After Dodger rookie pitcher John Purdin singled home Ron Fairly, Bradey's day was complete: two-thirds of an inning pitched, four hits, two walks, and five runs allowed. The Dodgers coasted to an 11-1 victory, saddling Bradey with the loss, his second in three career appearances.

"Lum Harris (Houston manager) didn't say anything when he took me out. Some guys on the bench patted me on the back and said hang in there. It was probably one of the worst games I ever pitched," Bradey said. "At that time, it was more embarrassing than anything. Looking back now, it is kind of something—a lot of people don't get to play in the major leagues."[23] He finished his career with an 0-2 record and a 19.19 ERA.

Gilliam strolled to the plate to lead off the bottom of the fourth inning and singled to Rusty Staub in right. Alston sent Nate Oliver into the game to run for Gilliam. The 13,824 fans in attendance on the sunny, warm fall day in Los Angeles rose as the public address announcer explained to the crowd that this was Gilliam's last game as a player and that he will return in 1965 as a coach. As Gilliam walked toward the home third-base dugout, his teammates lined up to shake his hand, slap his back, and wish him well. "It was the most gratifying thing that has happened while I have been with the Dodgers,"[24] expounded Bavasi.

For Jim, coming after recent comments he was not thinking about retiring, the announcement was unexpected, suggesting an almost forced retirement. "This new job took me by surprise," he told Frank Finch of the *Los Angeles Times*, smiling. "I didn't know a thing until I came to the park this afternoon. I know the players and they know me and things won't be any different between us. The Dodgers could have traded me several times in the past, but didn't, and it is gratifying to know that they still want me at this stage of the game."[25]

Underscoring the idea that Gilliam as coach was not his idea, *Los Angeles Times* columnist Sid Ziff quoted him two days later saying, "I still think I could have played one more year."[26]

Coach Gilliam Brings Baseball Step Closer to True Integration

By BRAD PYE JR.

Baseball came a step closer to complete integration this week

General Manager Buzzie Bavasi of the Los Angeles Dodgers named versatile veteran Jim Gilliam as the first Negro baseline coach in the history of the major leagues Thursday.

Two other N e g r o e s — Buck O'Neil of the Chicago Cubs in 1962 and Gene Ba-

the third baseline in the sixth inning. A post he will most likely command next season as one of Manager Walt A l s t o n's four new coaches for the 1965 season.

Inasmuch as the Dodgers were the first to break the color line on the playing field in modern times by signing J a c k i e Robinson back in 1947, it was expected they would go all

open up some more doors for us,"

Beaming with pride and joy, Mrs. Gilliam explained her reactions to Jim's new position to the SENTINEL this way:

"I think it's just wonderful and we are very happy over it."

The entire Dodger team virtually concurs with Mrs. Gilliam.

Here are some reactions

have to cut Jim loose now. He can't run around with us any more."

Almost immediately one of the white players hollered: "Hey, Jim, I guess I can't beat you in Gin anymore. I guess I will have to let you win on purpose now."

From the foregone versatile Jim won't have any trouble coaching with the Dodgers, no matter what

color their skin might be.

On this score, Jim declares: "I've always got along with everyone as a player. I see no reason why I shouldn't as a coach. As a coach, I have a job to do and they have a job to do and I'm going to see it's done."

Since 1953 Gilliam has been a mighty man in the Dodgers success. He has played on f i v e NL and

three World Championship clubs. Jim e n j o y e d his greatest season in 1963 when he helped the Dodgers win the pennant and wipe out the New York Yankees in the World Series in four straight. He batted .282 in '63.

If Jim Gilliam can be half the coach he was as a player, the Dodgers should be back in the thick of the pennant chase in '65.

PROUD AND HISTORY MAKING day for Jim Gilliam and the Los Angeles Dodgers came Thursday night when the club named him as one of Manager Walt Alston's coaches for the 1965 season. In

the first photo Leo Durocher (l) is shown congratulating "Gentleman Jim," the man who is replacing him. In the second photo Manager Walt Alston (c) is shown welcoming Gilliam (R) and Harold "Lefty"

Phillips (L), another one of his 1965 coaches, aboard. Jim Gilliam, a solid family man, is pictured standing tall with his proud family. From left are Jim, his wife Edwina, his daughter Katherine,

14, and son, Malcolm, 15. Mrs. Gilliam has her arms around daughter, Yvette, 3.
—Murphy Ruffins photo

Reprinted with permission from the Los Angeles Sentinel Newspaper.

REACTION TO RETIREMENT

The October 1961 issue of *Ebony* magazine dubbed former Negro League star and Chicago Cubs second baseman Gene Baker, "The Most Important Negro in Baseball," a title bestowed upon him as a result of him being named player-manager of the Pittsburgh Pirates' Class-D minorleague affiliate in Batavia (New York) during the summer of 1961. "I know if I do a good job, other organizations will follow the Pirates. There are a lot of colored ball players who would make good managers,"[27] Baker said without identifying any of those players. Baker lasted one season as manager before being named player-coach of the Triple-A Columbus Jets in 1962. He spent 1963 as a coach for the Pittsburgh Pirates, where he made history at, of all places, Dodger Stadium.[28]

Pirates manager Danny Murtaugh and coach Frank Oceak were thrown out for arguing an out call at first base in the top of the eighth inning after Pittsburgh had taken a 3-2 lead and chased Sandy Koufax. Baker took over, managing the next inning and a half until the Dodgers' Willie Davis lined a three-run home run to right field, giving Los Angeles the 5-3 win.[29]

Negro Leagues star and Hall of Famer Buck O'Neil would experience a similar career path after being hired as a full-time coach of the Chicago Cubs in June 1962 following a long-standing role as an "unofficial coach" at the Cubs' spring-training facility in Mesa, Arizona. National League clubs would complain to umpires about O'Neil's presence in the Cubs' dugout during games, so the team hired him as an "official coach" to solve the problem.[30] "I didn't think it was that big a deal at the time," O'Neil wrote in his autobiography, *I Was Right on Time*. "But suddenly I was in *Sports Illustrated* and *Ebony* and all the papers. At the age of fifty, I became the first Negro to coach in the major leagues."[31]

Baker and O'Neil competed against Gilliam in the Negro Leagues as members of the Kansas City Monarchs in 1948 and 1949. Baker and Gilliam were among the seven players at the Haines City, Florida tryout for the Chicago Cubs in March 1950. Although Baker, who was four years older than Jim, would be signed by the Cubs that spring, he would not make his debut with the Cubs until September 1, 1953,[32] the year Gilliam won the Rookie of the Year.

After the 1963 season both Baker and O'Neil transitioned from the dugout to the role of scout, leaving Major League Baseball once again bereft of Black coaches. Baker managed Batavia again in 1964 before transitioning to full-time scout in the Pirates organization for the next 23 years.[33] O'Neil would serve as a scout with the Cubs until 1988, signing, among others, Hall of Fame pitcher Lee Smith.[34] It was against that backdrop that O'Malley saw an opportunity with Gilliam toward the end of the 1964 season.

"There have been few better-liked men in baseball—by teammates, the opposition, the fans and the press—than Gilliam," wrote Bob Hunter in *The Sporting News*. "It was a master O'Malley stroke that made Gilliam a coach and his work in this capacity is bound to be reflected in the success of future Dodger teams."[35]

In the 1963 *Jet* magazine article referenced earlier, A.S. "Doc" Young asked Bavasi about the potential for a Black coach in the near future. "The current player closest (to a coaching job) with ability is Gilliam. Gilliam might make a major league coach some day."[36]

In a sense, Jim had already reached that point. "Junior Gilliam was essentially the manager on the field," Nate Oliver, a member of the Dodgers from 1963 through 1967, said years later. "He had no problem taking on that role. If a pitcher was in trouble out there and something was going awry, Gilliam would step up immediately and act as the manager. Our pitching coach Red Adams would only come running out if he saw something mechanically wrong with the pitcher. If a pitcher fell behind, if he was wild or his concentration level wasn't there, it would be Gilliam that would call time and walk over to the mound. All our manager Walter Alston had to do was sit there and push buttons."

The sports page of the *Los Angeles Times* made no mention of Gilliam's final game in the next day's newspaper, choosing instead to focus its attention on the NFL matchup between the Baltimore Colts and the hometown Rams, as well as the Cardinals' pennant-clinching victory over the New York Mets. The Tokyo Olympic Games also competed for column inches.

The baseball world's attention on Gilliam was immediate, and mostly positive. Longtime rival manager Casey Stengel and current Colt .45s general manager Paul Richards both offered praise during interviews on the eve of the Cardinals-Yankees World Series. "That ball club should be mighty proud of Jim. He knows all the plays and seems to be standing in the right place most of the time," Stengel said. Richards added, "if Gilliam has the ability to teach the players 50% of what he knows about this game he will be a great coach."[37]

Perhaps the people most excited about the news of Gilliam as a coach were his teammates. "Jim is the most dedicated man to baseball I have ever seen," Tommy Davis said. "When you first meet him he gives you a hard impression. He looks mean. I used to be scared of him. It's going to be a help to everybody. There's nothing he has to learn."[38]

"Doc" Young's syndicated column in the October 8 *California Eagle* summed the excitement, and hope, of the Black press that this appointment would represent meaningful change. "Jim's promotion could be the important break-through many of us have been waiting, and asking for; Jim, according to the announcement, will be a full-fledged member of the Dodgers' on-field brass. He'll work out in the open, coaching at first or third base. Unlike O'Neil, who (sic) duties were limited, despite his great managerial history in Negro baseball; and unlike Baker, who was more unseen than seen, more anonymous in his role than famed, Gilliam will work with everybody on the club, will be an integral part of each game."[39]

15

"A $3,000 PLAY"

To fill Gilliam's spot on the roster for the 1965 season, Buzzie Bavasi engineered a massive offseason trade with the Washington Senators on December 4, 1964, acquiring third baseman John Kennedy, pitcher Claude Osteen, and $100,000 for Frank Howard, Ken McMullen, Phil Ortega, Pete Richert, and Dick Nen.

Kennedy was a defense-first infielder who showed little offensive pop as the Senators primary third baseman in 1964, batting just .230 with 7 home runs and 35 runs batted in over 148 games. His .604 on-base plus slugging (OPS) and 0.0 wins above replacement (WAR) suggest he would be a replacement-level offensive player at best for Los Angeles. His value, it seemed, was as a defender.

Following the 1964 season, *Baseball Digest* selected one Kennedy web gem as the Senators' defensive play of the year, reinforcing that bias. The play occurred during the second game of the year on April 15, 1964 at District of Columbia Stadium (later renamed Robert F. Kennedy Stadium). With the Senators holding a 6-4 lead, Joe Adcock of the Los Angeles Angels batted with two out and a runner on first. Adcock "hit as wicked a drive between Kennedy and third base as has ever gone off a bat. The ball actually seemed past Kennedy when, somehow, he speared it with an unbelievable backhand grab" and threw Adcock out at first. Senators general manager Bucky Harris, in his 46th year in baseball, implied it was the best play he had ever seen.[1]

Kennedy was immediately inserted in the lineup, starting the first 10 games of the 1965 season at third base, and 16 of the first 45, while utility infielder Dick Tracewski started 29. But neither player was hitting. The Dodger offense suffered an additional blow when Tommy Davis, the National League batting champion in 1962 and 1963, broke his ankle sliding into second base on May 1. Dodgers trainer Wayne Anderson sprinted on the field when Davis went down and told the *Los Angeles Times* after the game, "When I got there, the bone was sticking out at a right angle, and I popped it back into place."[2]

Henry Aaron (44), Jim Gilliam, and Willie Davis (3) at spring-training camp in West Palm Beach, Florida. Photo by Kenneth Davidoff.

The *Times* reported the Dodgers were immediately taken off the board as National League favorites in Las Vegas. Shortstop Maury Wills tried to make the most of it. "We were dead is what some people said. Dead. The first thing you tell yourself in that situation is you're not dead. And that's how you deal with it; it's your only chance."[3]

The next day, Davis and struggling second baseman Nate Oliver were replaced on the active roster by Derrell Griffith and journeyman outfielder Lou Johnson. Griffith hit .290 in 254 at bats as a rookie in 1964, but began the 1965 season in Spokane as the club had wanted Griffith, primarily an infielder, to work in the outfield.

Los Angeles Times columnist Sid Ziff authored a piece two days after Davis' injury, intimating Gilliam had "plenty to do" and did not suggest Gilliam would be activated. "You just don't stand around there," Gilliam told Ziff. "I try to pick up some move by the pitcher that will help us to steal a base. I'm responsible that the base runner gets the signal. It's my fault if he overlooks it. I can let the batter know on a hit to left field whether he can go for an extra base, because he can't see the ball himself. There are all sorts of things to keep you on your toes."[4]

But desperate times soon called for desperate measures, and, on Friday, May 28, 1965, the 36-year-old retired Coach Gilliam was activated and Griffith was sent back to Spokane after batting just .125 in 32 at bats. Griffith, who was installed in left field, started strong enough, going 4-for-10 with a home run, but suffered through an 0-for-22 stretch before being sent down. Fifty-five years later, Griffith remembered struggling with a sore arm. "I didn't tell anyone but it hurt to make throws. I guess my hitting suffered as well."

At the time, however, Alston did not envision Gilliam playing much beyond pinch-hitting duties. "I don't intend to play Jim at third base very much, but there will be times when he will finish up the game there, after pinch-hitting,"[5] Alston said. Danny Ozark, who had joined the Dodger coaching staff at the beginning of the season, subbed at first base when Gilliam was in the lineup.

Gilliam's first game action on May 29, 1965 came as a pinch hitter for pitcher Bob Miller in the bottom of the ninth with Tracewski on first, no one out, and the Dodgers trailing the Milwaukee Braves, 5-4. Gilliam, who struck out just 368 times in 7,617 big league at bats, did just that. After missing two bunts, Gilliam went down swinging. To add insult to injury, Tracewski was thrown out stealing for a double play. Transitioning from retirement to coaching to playing might not be as easy as Gilliam thought.

DOG DAYS OF SUMMER

On June 30, the Dodgers played a doubleheader at Chicago with the outfield situation, after Davis' injury, more or less resolved. Johnson was settled in left with speedy Willie Davis in center, and left-handed slugger Ron Fairly in right. That triumvirate would start 32 of 33 straight games in their positions between June 28 and August 2 as the club maintained a narrow hold on first place over Cincinnati and San Francisco.

But Alston found himself once again seeking more offensive help for the infield. Gilliam, who had made starts at third base, left field, and even right field, was hitting .320 with a .902 OPS following a June 29 game against the San Francisco Giants at Candlestick Park. But the rest of the infield was struggling. Rookie Jim Lefebvre had started all 75 of the team's games at second but was batting just .222 with a .633 OPS. Tracewski logged in with a .221 average and .637 OPS while playing all over the infield. Kennedy, hitting .175 and carrying a .511 OPS, had been relegated to the role of late-dinning defensive replacement.

The Los Angeles staff reasoned, and rightly so, an additional offensive-minded infielder would be critical as the calendar flipped to July and August, the so-called dog days of summer. Early season options Griffith and Oliver had been returned to the minors. So, the team turned to a 31-year-old career minor leaguer from Pennsylvania, Don LeJohn, to make his big-league debut.

LeJohn, signed by former Brooklyn Dodger outfielder Jim Russell—who had watched him on a Pennsylvania sandlot—had batted 5,510 times in the minors since the Dodgers signed him as a 20-year-old prior to the 1954 season. The back of LeJohn's 1966 Topps baseball card reads like an atlas, with big towns like Atlanta and Omaha listed alongside smaller communities like Great Falls and Wichita Falls. At the time he was called up, LeJohn was batting .395 with a .503 on-base percentage in 292 plate appearances for Double-A Albuquerque Dukes, where he was a player-coach.

LeJohn was incredulous upon hearing the news he was being called up to the majors. "How did I feel? After playing 12 years in the minors you just don't have much hope left...so I guess I was sort of shocked. The most I ever expected, and what I actually was hoping for, was a job as a minor league manager or coach,"[6] he said.

Alston inserted LeJohn in the lineup for the second game of the June 30 doubleheader in Chicago, a move that paid immediate dividends for the Dodgers. With Los Angeles trailing 2-0 in the top of the second, LeJohn, batting with two out and Lou Johnson at third and Lefebvre at first, lined an RBI single to right field off the Cubs' Bob Buhl in his first career at bat. Later, with the Dodgers now trailing 3-2, LeJohn led off the top of the fourth with a ground-ball base hit to left. He moved to second on a sacrifice and took third on a groundout before Wes Parker doubled him home to tie the game. Though LeJohn would go hitless in his final two at bats, he finished 2-for-4 with a run and an RBI in a 4-3 victory. He was replaced in the bottom of the eighth by Kennedy, who committed an error on the first ball hit to him. LeJohn started the next four Dodgers games at third base, collecting a hit in each, good for a .375 average. But as fate would have it, LeJohn would miss nearly a month after jamming his left ankle sliding into second base in a July 4 game against the Houston Astros.

As the calendar rolled to August, LeJohn was healthy enough to regain the starting third-base job, seeing his name on the lineup card 11 times in the month. But, like Kennedy, Griffith, and others before him, LeJohn stopped hitting. After a 2-for-4, 2 RBI performance on Aug. 7 at Cincinnati —boosting his average to .341—LeJohn finished the season, and his career, in a 6-for-37 slump, dropping his average to .256 for the season. He never reached the majors again.

LeJohn's presence on the roster afforded Alston flexibility in his lineup, particularly in early July when he sat Lefebvre and moved Gilliam to second, and again in early August when Gilliam shifted to left field so Lou Johnson could spell Willie Davis in center. It also freed Tracewski to conform to a utility role. The additional rest benefited everyone, especially Lefebvre, who raised his average from .222 on June 30 to .250 for the season, a performance worthy of recognition as the 1965 National League Rookie of the Year.

With LeJohn slumping and Kennedy still not hitting in late August, Alston was left with no other choice but to make Gilliam the everyday third baseman. Throughout his career with the Dodgers, Gilliam was the player Alston could always count on to perform whenever and wherever he played. From 1958 to 1965, Jim started more Opening Days on the bench, five, then on the field, three. Yet, Gilliam still averaged nearly 600 plate appearances and 140 games played per year during his 14-year career with the Dodgers. Gilliam was Mr. Reliable—someone Alston could turn to in a clutch situation with the knowledge that Gilliam would do what his manager expected.

VIOLENCE IN WATTS

As the Dodgers took the field at Dodger Stadium against the Mets on the evening of Wednesday, August 11, twenty-one-year-old Marquette Frye was pulled over by a California Highway Patrol officer near the community of Watts, suspected of drunk driving. Frye, a Black man, reportedly failed a sobriety test administered by the officer as Frye's brother and mother watched. As more police showed up, so, too, did members of the largely Black neighborhood. Initially, the crowd numbered 1,000 and violence ruled that evening and into Thursday morning. By Thursday evening, the crowd grew to an estimated 7,000. Over the course of the next six days—all Dodger home dates—the rioting persisted, with 34 people killed and 250 buildings destroyed. Martial law was enacted.

Although the rioting was less than 10 miles from the Gilliam household in "Black Beverly Hills," the reality was it might as well be in another state. But that was not the case for his Black teammates, especially Lou Johnson and John Roseboro, who lived much closer to Watts. The players carpooled to the stadium, taking different routes to avoid the impacted areas, and even wearing their Dodger uniforms to avoid being mistaken for rioters.

Future Dodger Derrel Thomas was 14 years old and lived further from Watts than Gilliam. He recalled athletes being afforded special treatment. "During those times if you were a professional athlete, even though the riots were going on, they still kind of looked up to the players. Respected them enough to not show too much bias. What we experienced then and I'm sure what Jim experienced along with Tommy Davis and Willie Davis were the same things. The rioters always looked up to the players and respected the players," Thomas said.

Wally Moon, Jr., the son of the Dodger outfielder, remembered talking to Gilliam during this time. "I had a chance to listen to him, Tommy Davis, and Johnny Roseboro talk about things. I learned so much about race relations in that clubhouse. When I asked him about it, Junior said, 'Little Moon, being a Black man in this world is hard sometimes, and sometimes it's just too much for some folks. We all got to do better in this world.'"

The stress of the riots and the pennant race boiled over for Roseboro during the last of a four-game series at Candlestick Park against the Giants a few days later. After a Dodgers 6-4 win on Saturday, August 21 gave the Dodgers a half-game lead on Milwaukee and 1.5-game lead on San Francisco, Roseboro felt uneasy. As author John Rosengren put it, "Danger portended. On the Dodgers' bus ride back to the hotel Saturday night,

Johnny remained on edge. The stress of the series, following the previous week's riots in Watts, had spiked his natural competitive spirit. Talking with Lou Johnson and Jim Gilliam about facing the Giants' ace the next day, Johnny said Marichal better watch himself 'because I won't take any guff from him.'"[7]

The game should have been remembered as a rare pitching duel between two future Hall of Famers in Koufax and Marichal. The two only faced each other four times, with Koufax winning the first two and Marichal winning the last two. Instead, the day is widely remembered as one of the uglier incidents in baseball history, culminating with Marichal hitting Roseboro on the head with his baseball bat. Video of the altercation shows Gilliam running in from his position at third base, glove still on his left hand, but he did not get into the fray. He was the seventh or eighth person to arrive on the scene in front of home plate. Koufax, home-plate umpire Shag Crawford, and Giants third-base coach Charlie Fox attempted to separate the combatants. Tito Fuentes, the Giants' on-deck hitter, pulled Roseboro off as off-field friends Willie Mays and Gilliam arrived.

Roseboro missed several games, even though X-rays showed no fracture. Marichal was suspended eight playing dates by National League President Warren Giles and fined $1,750. Dodger Ron Fairly felt the punishment was too lenient. "He should have been suspended 1,750 days and fined eight dollars. Using a bat is the same as going out with intent to kill. If I'd done something like that on the street, I'd have been arrested. He should be arrested, too."[8]

A SUCCESSFUL PENNANT PUSH

A smallish crowd of just 29,139 entered Dodger Stadium on Thursday, September 9, 1965 for the game against the Cubs. Sandy Koufax, with a 21-7 record, started for Los Angeles. The Dodgers finally broke a scoreless and hitless game in the bottom of the fifth when Lou Johnson walked and was sacrificed to second by Ron Fairly. With Jim Lefebvre batting, Johnson stole third and raced home when catcher Chris Krug's throw sailed past third.

The game remained 1-0, with both team hitless, until the bottom of the seventh when Johnson blooped a double over first base. Through seven innings, Koufax was perfect. Gilliam started the game at third base and had successfully fielded the only chance hit his way, a weak grounder off the bat of Don Kessinger in the top of the sixth. Gilliam had been playing up as a defense to the bunt, in position to field it cleanly and throw Kessinger out. "I thought I had a chance to beat it out," Kessinger said. "I got thrown out by half a step."[9]

As was Alston's preference, he lifted Gilliam for defensive purposes heading into the top of the eighth. When the manager made the switch often depended on when Gilliam would bat. Having just hit in the bottom of the seventh, Gilliam's turn in the order would not likely come up again, so the timing seemed right.

It did not matter. Koufax retired the final six Cubs via strikeout to throw the sixth perfect game in Major League history. It was the fourth time in four years that Koufax had hurled a no-hitter. Although he was not on the field when the game ended, Gilliam became the first player in baseball history to play in two perfect games. And, it was the seventh time Gilliam had played in a no-hitter.

Despite the performance, Los Angeles still had not nailed down a playoff berth. In fact, Gilliam and the Dodgers found themselves reeling just a week later.

On September 15, they were beaten, 8-6, by the eighth-place Cubs in front of just 1,886 spectators at Wrigley Field. The loss dropped Los Angeles to 82-64 on the season and into third place for the first time since mid-April. To compound matters, the team's workhorse starting pitcher Don Drysdale was removed after one batter in the second inning, having taken a line drive hit by Ernie Banks off his right ankle. The Dodgers led 3-0 at the time, but the bullpen could not hold the lead. Just 16 games remained in the season, and the Dodgers trailed first-place San Francisco by 4.5 games. The Giants had just won their 13th straight.

In a show of desperation the next day, and with his club nursing a 2-0 lead over the Cubs, this time in front of a mere 550 fans at Wrigley Field, Alston called on Koufax to pitch the bottom of the ninth in relief of starter Claude Osteen, who had walked future Hall of Famer Billy Williams to open the inning. Koufax, who had pitched six innings in Chicago two days earlier, calmly retired Ron Santo, Banks, and Harvey Kuenn to earn the save, his second of the season. Los Angeles would reel off 13 straight wins of their own, and 15 out of the final 16, to overtake San Francisco and win the pennant with a record of 97-65, two games ahead of the Giants.

The day the Dodgers tied the Giants for first—Sunday, September 26—was a microcosm of the team's recipe for success in that era. Wills, who broke the Major League record for steals when he swiped 104 in 1962, opened the bottom of the first for Los Angeles by beating out a bunt fielded by the St. Louis Cardinals pitcher, Ray Sadecki. As he was asked to do so often while batting with Wills on first base, Gilliam waited patiently for Wills to run. Sadecki, a lefthander, picked Wills off but Cardinals first baseman Bill White threw high to second and the ball sailed into left field. Wills wound up on third after swiping his 89th base of the season.

Gilliam, a switch-hitter batting right handed against Sadecki, executed perfectly, lining a single to right field and scoring Wills. The single run was all Drysdale needed, as he scattered five hits and did not walk a batter on his way to a 1-0 win. Los Angeles clinched the pennant less than a week later. Gilliam had indeed helped spark his club to the pennant, batting .277 with a .361 on-base percentage in the season's final month. He was at his best in 1965 in games in which the Dodgers won, hitting .344 with a .904 OPS. While it is true star pitchers Koufax and Drysdale combined to win 49 of the team's 97 games in 1965, Gilliam's offensive production in those games certainly helped propel the team to the World Series.

1965 WORLD SERIES

Game One of the 1965 World Series was scheduled for Wednesday, October 6. It was also the date of the Jewish holiday Yom Kippur, which meant Alston's star pitcher, Sandy Koufax, would not pitch until Game Two. Don Drysdale got the call in Game One, setting him up to also start Games Four and Seven, if necessary.

Drysdale would be the ace of nearly every other Major League staff, but Koufax's performance in 1965 was other-worldly. Koufax went 26-8 for a team that averaged just 3.8 runs of offense per game. Only the lowly Houston Astros and New York Mets averaged fewer runs per game. He struck out 382 in 335 innings. He received all 20 first-place votes for the National League Cy Young. Compiling a 1.043 OPS, only San Francisco Giants star Willie Mays' incredible season prevented Koufax from winning the MVP. Having Koufax available for three starts in the World Series would give the Dodgers a distinct advantage, but the Jewish calendar dictated otherwise.

Game One started well enough for Drysdale as he retired the first five batters, three by strikeout, before Don Mincher touched him for a solo home run in the bottom of the second, matching a solo shot from Dodger Ron Fairly in the top of the second. But the wheels came off quickly in the bottom of the third. Frank Quilici opened with a double and took third when Twins starting pitcher Jim "Mudcat" Grant sacrificed. Grant was safe when Lefebvre could not handle the throw at first. Zoilo Versalles, American League MVP in 1965, homered to left. It was now 4-1.

Drysdale would surrender four more hits and a walk before being lifted for Howie Reed. When the dust settled, the Twins were ahead 7-1. Drysdale had gone 2.2 innings, yielded seven hits and seven runs, only three earned. When Alston came to the mound to get him, Drysdale said, "Hey, skip, bet you wish I was Jewish today, too."[10] Minnesota cruised to an 8-2 win.

Koufax was on the hill to begin Game Two. He was opposed by lefty Jim Kaat, who was dominating early, not allowing a hit until Fairly opened the fifth with a single. Koufax, though not as dominating, was in control, limiting the Twins to three singles and a walk through five innings.

Versalles, who would be a thorn in the Dodgers' side throughout the Series, led off the bottom of the sixth with a hard-hit ground ball to third that bounced off Gilliam for a two-base error. He scored the game's first run, an unearned run, when Tony Oliva doubled Versalles home two batters later. Harmon Killebrew's single plated Oliva, putting Minnesota up 2-0, en route to a 5-1 win and a two-games-to-none Series advantage. Gilliam committed a second error in the sixth inning, but it did not result in a run.

After Game Two, Gilliam, who had committed just one error at the hot corner in his previous 31 games covering 108 chances, was visibly frustrated. "Just stay away from me," he initially snapped at reporters in an uncharacteristic display of emotion. Later, he explained the play, "The ball was a shot and I had one chance to short-hop it. But it didn't bounce like I figured and it went through me."[11]

Columnist Charles Johnson, writing the day after Game Two in the *Minneapolis Star* under a headline, "Twins can be 12th club to sweep four," proclaimed, "To add to the losers' miseries, their defense has fallen apart with Jim Gilliam showing his age at third base."[12]

Los Angeles Times writer Frank Finch was more forgiving than the Minnesota writers, alleging, "Uncharitable scorers charged Gilliam with an error when Versalles led off with a smash that hand-cuffed Gilliam, and might well have done the same to Pie Traynor. The ball rolled into left field as Zoilo reached second base."[13]

Minnesota media were also playing up the angle the Dodgers could not win in Minnesota, possibly due to the weather. Prior to Game Two, and similar to the night before Game Seven, it had rained heavily. Game Two was played on a "damp, dull, and dreary" day, the "kind of day that Minnesotans have come to love." It was so dreary that Minnesota Governor Karl Rolvaag, battling "both political and nasal problems," opted not to throw out the first pitch.[14] Gilliam did not discuss whether the rain affected the infield and the bounce Versalles' ball took.

Staked to a 2-0 lead and having beaten Drysdale and Koufax, the Twins were understandably confident heading to the sun and warmth of Los Angeles. "We thought, 'Gosh, we may have a chance to sweep the Series here," Hall of Famer Harmon Killebrew said years later.[15]

Perhaps only Ralph Belcour of Melrose Park, Illinois truly believed the Series was headed for a Game Seven. The *Minneapolis Star* found Belcour, who had waited "145½ hours in order to be first in line for Wednesday's World Series opener," outside Metropolitan Stadium in a heated trailer. Described as a "short, pudgy man with a weatherbeaten face," Belcour told the paper, "The Series is going a full seven games. The Dodgers will win three straight at home."[16] Belcour's prediction, it would turn out, was correct.

In a seemingly must-win situation in Game Three, the Dodgers gave the ball to Claude Osteen, the lefthander acquired along with John Kennedy from Washington during the previous offseason. Overshadowed by Koufax and Drysdale, "Gomer," as his teammates called him, had turned in a consistent 15-15 season with a 2.79 ERA. Described by Jack Mann in *Sports Illustrated* as "a small man for a big-league pitcher, unprepossessing, moderately endowed with talent and singularly unlucky,"[17] Osteen now was asked to do what the aces, Koufax and Drysdale, could not; beat the Twins.

The Twins left Minnesota with thoughts of a four-game sweep in their head, and Game Three certainly started as if that would be the case. Versalles pulled the game's first pitch for a ground-rule double down the left-field line. Two batters later, and with Versalles now at third, Killebrew walked. Earl Battey came to the plate ,and Twins manager Sam Mele played hit-and-run, but Battey missed the sign and took the pitch.

Dodgers catcher Johnny Roseboro threw to second, but Killebrew had stopped halfway to second and Wills alertly caught the ball in front of second base, throwing home to Roseboro. Versalles, caught in a rundown, was eventually retired Wills to Roseboro to Gilliam, who applied the tag near the third-base bag. Osteen settled down and allowed only five baserunners over the next eight innings, and Los Angeles cruised to a 4-0 win. Kennedy, as he had done so many times during the regular season, replaced Gilliam defensively, this time in the eighth inning after Jim hit in the bottom of the seventh. Kennedy booted the first ball hit to him, a Frank Quilici grounder with one out in the eighth. But the error would not cost the Dodgers.

Game Four was a rematch of Game One, with Drysdale on the mound for Los Angeles, opposed by Mudcat Grant for Minnesota. The Twins' Tony Oliva had slugged a solo home run to deep right field, drawing Minnesota to within 3-2 going to the bottom of the sixth, with Gilliam due to lead off. Over the course of his career, Jim was known to have a great eye at the plate. He walked 1,036 times in his regular-season career, an average of once every eight plate appearances. In 172 career World Series plate appearances, his rate was nearly identical, walking once every 7.5 plate appearances. Now, with his team clinging to a 3-2 lead and him leading off the bottom of the six, Gilliam did just that, working a walk off Grant.

Willie Davis batted next, stroking a single to Oliva in right. Nearly 37 years old, "retired" Gilliam raced around second with his head down, steaming for third. Rather than take the conservative play and throw to second—keeping a double play in order but conceding third to Gilliam—Oliva threw to third, where Gilliam slid in safely. Davis took second on the throw. Like so many instances in Gilliam's career, it was a play that did not show up in the box score or on a stat sheet. But Gilliam's ability to draw the throw to third base allowing Davis to take second would loom large a few minutes later. After the game, Oliva, who wished he had kept Davis at second, commented about Gilliam's first-to-third scamper, "That guy can fly."[18]

Sinkerballer Al Worthington relieved Grant and the Twins brought the infield in, but Fairly was able to sneak a ground ball up the middle for a two-run single, scoring Gilliam and Davis, giving the Dodgers a 3-run cushion. They would even the series with a 7-2 victory.

Once again, Gilliam was replaced by Kennedy late, this time, ironically, as a pinch runner in the bottom of the seventh after Gilliam was hit by a pitch. Kennedy would redeem himself defensively from his Game Three miscue in the top of the eighth by backhanding a grounder off the bat of Versalles—who else?—down the third-base line, turning a potential double into a force out.

After winning Games Three and Four to even the Series, the Dodgers jumped on Kaat early in Game Five, touching him for six hits and four runs in 2.1 innings. In that game, the Dodgers came out swinging. Wills opened the first with a ground-rule double to deep right field. Gilliam followed with an RBI single to right center. Willie Davis bunted to third but second baseman Frank Quilici, who was covering first, lost sight of Killebrew's throw in the white-shirted, sun-splashed crowd at Dodger Stadium. As the ball headed to the outfield, Gilliam, the player whose skills were supposedly diminished, sped all the way home from first to give Los Angeles a 2-0 lead.

With Los Angeles up 4-0 in the bottom of the fourth, the Wills-Gilliam combination struck again. Wills opened by beating out a dribbler to short. Twins reliever Dick Boswell became preoccupied with Wills. As Mann described in *Sports Illustrated*, "Gilliam was at bat for almost 20 minutes while Wills belly whopped back to first ahead of Boswell's throws."[19]

Wills eventually stole second and scored on another Gilliam RBI single to right center. Twice Gilliam had come to bat with no out and Wills on second. Twice Gilliam had hit to the right side in an attempt to move Wills to third. Twice the at bat resulted in an RBI single.

The Dodgers were cruising, ahead 5-0 with Koufax in charge. He had faced the minimum number of batters as the game headed to the top of the seventh. The only Twins base runner, Harmon Killebrew, was erased on a double play in the fifth. As was Alston's wont, Gilliam was replaced defensively by Kennedy, this time in the seventh inning, and watched the rest of the game from the clubhouse. The Dodgers coasted to a 7-0 win and a 3-2 series advantage.

Game Six was all Minnesota. The Twins, playing back in their home ballpark, rode a pair of home runs and dominant pitching by Grant to smother the Dodgers, 5-1. Bob Allison knocked a two-run shot to deep left off Osteen in the fourth, while Grant contributed a three-run blast of his own in the sixth off Dodger reliever Howie Reed for a 5-0 advantage. A solo homer by Fairly in the eighth was all that prevented a shutout. The stage was set for Game Seven. The question for Alston: who to start on the mound, Koufax or Drysdale?

A ONE-SIDED GAME SEVEN

Walter Alston stared down perhaps the most important decision of his managerial career after Game Six, whether to start Sandy Koufax or Don Drysdale on the mound in Game Seven. In fact, Alston titled a chapter about his decision in his 1966 autobiography (the first of two he would write), *The Toughest Decision*.[20] Drysdale was on more rest, having started Games One and Four, while Koufax started Games Two and Five, the latter just three days prior—meaning Koufax would pitch on just two days' rest.

Alston's thought process was articulated the same in both his autobiographies, written ten years apart. In his second, *A Year at a Time* (published in 1976), Alston reflected on the decision. "If we started Don, Sandy would have to be in the bullpen. Because of the arthritis in his arm it took

Sandy longer to warm up," Alston wrote. "I didn't tell (the media) or anyone else either that I had whispered to Koufax during the ninth inning of the sixth game that if everything was right—conditions, his arm, etc.— that I'd probably start him. I asked him at the same time to say nothing to anyone. But I wanted Sandy to know."[21]

By choosing Koufax, Alston was setting up a rubber match of sorts between his ace and the Twins ace, Jim Kaat. The Twins had roughed up Koufax and reliever Ron Perranoski for five runs in Game Two in Bloomington exactly one week before.

Official in-stadium attendance for Game Seven was announced at 50,596, one thousand more than had witnessed Game Six the day before. Millions more watched the NBC TV broadcast, delivered in color, featuring both Ray Scott, voice of the Twins, and Vin Scully, voice of the Dodgers.

The Dodgers strung three straight hits together—on three consecutive pitches—to open the top of the fourth and chase Kaat. Dodgers left-fielder Lou Johnson opened the inning with a line-drive home run that hit the left-field foul pole, silencing the partisan Twins crowd. "You could hear a cat pissin' on cotton after I hit it,"[22] recalled Johnson in Michael Leahy's 2016 book *The Last Innocents*.

For Johnson, the moment and the whole season must have felt like an out-of-body experience. A Black southerner from Lexington, Kentucky, Johnson began the 1965 season as he had most of the previous 13 seasons —in the minors. Making his pro debut at age 18 in 1953, Johnson's minor-league passport included cities like Burlington, Iowa; Olean, New York; and Ponca City, Fla. He had just over 200 Major League plate appearances for three teams on his resume when the Dodgers recalled him from Spokane on May 2, after three-time All-Star and 1962 MVP Tommy Davis broke his ankle.

Fairly hooked Kaat's very next pitch down the right-field line for a standup double. Then, with the infield playing up in anticipation of a Wes Parker bunt, Parker hit a high chopper over first baseman Mincher and into right field for a single, scoring Fairly. This play would be a source of contention after the game. Mincher was playing in, anticipating a bunt, a common weapon in Alston's offense. Parker already had two sacrifices in the Series and, in the pivotal Game Five in Los Angeles, the Dodgers racked up six infield hits, including bunt singles by Wills, Davis, Parker, and Johnny Roseboro.

Alston was asked after Game Five if he thought his team's bunting had made the Twins apprehensive in the field. "In some cases bunting and running might have an effect on some players and not on others. You should ask that question in the other fellow's room,"[23] he said. Parker was less evasive. "I think Mincher would've caught my ball if he wasn't playing in for a bunt,"[24] he said.

Twins manager Sam Mele was not taking any chances, once again summoning Al Worthington from his bullpen to end the rally, which he did by retiring Tracewski on a popup, bunted naturally. He then got Koufax on a grounder to the pitcher, and Wills on a foul out.

While the fifth inning might be considered early to make a defensive substitution, when Alston would call on Kennedy varied by game. Kennedy appeared in each of the three previous Dodger victories in the Series, entering as a defensive replacement for Gilliam as early as the seventh inning. Kennedy's lone at bat came in Game 5 at Dodger Stadium when he flew out to left fielder Bob Allison with two on and two out in the bottom of the seventh and the Dodgers ahead, 7-0.

In Game Seven, Alston had a lot to consider in the fifth. His team held a slim 2-0 lead with a struggling Koufax on the mound. The Dodgers held leads of four or more runs in each of the previous three wins when Alston made the defensive switch. Now, Alston weighed the better offense of Gilliam against the better defense of Kennedy. Gilliam was 1-for-3 on the day and assured of at least one more at bat, so Alston stuck with his trusted veteran.

The inning started innocently enough, with Mincher hiting the first pitch for a pop up to Gilliam in foul ground. With the count 2-1, Quilici lined a fastball to left center. The ball hit the fence on one bounce before Lou Johnson fielded it. Quilici glided into second with a stand-up double. Rich Rollins, batting for pitcher Worthington, walked to put two men on with only one out. Due up was the top of the order which, of course, meant Zoilo Versalles.

A native of Cuba, Versalles made his Major League debut in 1959 as a 19-year-old. Now, at the age of 25, he turned in an MVP season for the Twins. He led the American League in runs scored, doubles, and triples while batting .273 with 19 home runs and 27 stolen bases. He also won a Gold Glove in 1965. He could hurt a team in any number of ways. Alston strolled out to the mound where Gilliam joined Roseboro, Koufax, and the Dodger manager. Although Drysdale was warming in the bullpen as he had done previously in the first and third innings, the mound conversation did not involve taking Koufax out.

Versalles had hit Koufax hard in Game Two, handcuffing Gilliam at third for a two-base error. In Game Three, Versalles hit Osteen's first pitch down the left-field line for a ground-rule double. In Game Four, Versalles hit a hard grounder to third off Drysdale, which Kennedy backhanded to prevent a double and get a force out. It was clear that he was seeing Dodger pitching well. Prior to the first pitch to Versalles, Scully, who had taken over television play-by-play duties in the bottom of the fifth, observed, "Gilliam guarding the line to cut down the chance of an extra base hit at third." Given Versalles' previous at-bats in the Series, this seemed a smart strategy.

The first pitch was a high fastball, which Versalles chased and swung through. The second pitch was also a high fastball, but Versalles laid off it to even the count at 1-1. After fouling off a low-and-away fastball and another fastball over the middle of the plate, Versalles finally timed Koufax. He hit "a blistering rounder along the third-base line."[25]

Gilliam took a step to his right, moving slightly backward with his right leg, turning his toes perpendicular to the baseline. He did not have time to move his left leg as the ball was on him so quickly. Reaching with his gloved left hand, he fell to one knee near foul territory and backhanded the ball. He popped up quickly and beat Quilici to the bag by several feet for the force out.

A five-photo sequence of the play, credited to the Associated Press, ran in newspapers across the country, including the *Minneapolis Star*, an afternoon paper, on page 4D of its Friday, October 15 issue with the headline "Here's Play That Stopped Big Twins Bid."

The first photo showed Gilliam reaching toward the third-base line with his left, gloved hand, the ball nearly past Gilliam and on its way to the corner. The second photo showed him on his hands and knees, straddling the chalk line. His face is looking toward the outfield, his rear end is pointed to the bag. In the third photo, Gilliam is scrambling to his feet, completely in foul territory. He is looking at Quilici coming down the line. The fourth photo showed Gilliam beginning to run toward the bag, ball in his glove. The fifth photo captured Gilliam looking down as he steps on third base with his left foot. The ball is now in his bare right hand, his throwing hand. Quilici is beginning his slide, but still several feet from the bag.

A photo by John Croft in the *Minneapolis Tribune*, taken from a different angle, showed Gilliam crouched just across the third-base line in foul territory, with his back to the base. He is six to eight feet from the bag. His glove is on the dirt, with the ball in it. Gilliam's eyes are looking toward second base, presumably checking how much time he had to beat Quilici to the bag for the force out. The headline, above the photo, stated simply, "The Play."

"I didn't even have time to think about (the play). It was about a foot from the bag and as I grabbed it, I slipped to one knee," Gilliam told Associated Press reporter Mike Rathet. "But I saw the runner and knew I had time so I got up and stepped on the bag."[26]

On the Met Stadium mound, Koufax hollered, "Helluva play, Jim."[27] After the game, Koufax told the media, "That was my roughest spot, but then Gilliam fixed everything."[28]

From his position 90 feet away at home plate, Roseboro also marveled at the play, writing in his autobiography, "The Devil dove, backhanded the ball, got up and tagged the base for a force play. After that, Koufax was in complete control."[29]

Despite all of the adulation, Gilliam was typically nonchalant about the play and its magnitude. "It was my best play of this Series. I have been in six World Series and I find it hard to classify thrills or great plays."[30] After the game, Koufax acknowledged the play was the key defensive performance of the game. "Everybody on the club made great plays, but if that one had gone through the Twins were sure to get one run might have tied it up."[31]

In some ways, Gilliam would be remembered more for that play than anything else he did in baseball. "I think he was proud of it, most certainly. He made a defensive play that choked off the rally and preserved the game. I don't think he hung his hat on that. It was just a play that he expected to make himself and he did," said said future Dodger third baseman Ron Cey.

Gilliam's grab not only cost Versalles a potential extra-base hit, but likely a brand new Corvette as well. Al Silverman of *Sport* magazine, which presented the World Series Most Valuable Player with the new ride was quoted afterward, "If Versalles gets that hit, that ties the game and knocks Koufax out of the box. I'm sure Zoilo would have received the car."[32] Instead, the keys were given to Koufax.

WATCHING FROM THE CLUBHOUSE

It is not known how Kennedy, who passed away in 2010, reacted while watching Gilliam's play from the Dodgers bench. Perhaps it evoked memories of his own similar play in April 1964, which garnered him end-of-year attention in *Baseball Digest*. Or, perhaps he didn't see it at all. As Kennedy told Paul Hirsch for a biography on the Society for American Baseball Research website, "I had a lot of respect for who (Gilliam) was and the career he had had with the Dodgers. Plus, he was a nice guy. I knew when I would go into games, and I would get ready by going into the runway to throw and then stretch in the dugout."[33]

Batting in the seventh after Wills had grounded out, Gilliam singled on a ground ball to right off reliever Johnny Klippstein. He moved to second when Willie Davis was hit by a pitch, then taking third on Johnson's infield grounder. But Fairly flew out to right with Gilliam, an insurance run, stranded ninety feet away. As Scully told the national television audience during Gilliam's at-bat, the bottom of the seventh would have been a logical time to replace Gilliam: "Seems strange after his great play but this might be his last appearance in the Series. Normally late in the game he gives way for defensive purposes. And isn't that ironic." Listening to Scully, one can almost infer from his voice inflection he is placing a set of air quote marks around "defensive purposes."

Once Koufax retired Joe Nossek in the fifth, he settled down, inducing the Twins to go in order in each of the next three innings, keeping any potential tying run in the on-deck circle. Perhaps Alston's thinking would have changed had a runner reached base, but for whatever reason he stuck with the veteran into the ninth inning when Gilliam, who already had two of the team's seven hits, was due up third.

As Gilliam came to bat in the top of the ninth with one out and Wills on first base, Scully noted, "Jim Gilliam. Two singles; flied to right; grounded out. And the coach who became a player again is a big man today." Wills attempted to swipe second on the first pitch, a fastball high and tight that Gilliam could not check his swing on, but was thrown out. Jim continued his final at-bat of 1965, a ground out to shortstop, with Scully remarking to the television audience, "So Gilliam, who was retired officially at the end of '64, and then brought back as a player in '65, one of the big reasons why the Dodgers are here at all." Gilliam's at bat was his 28th of the Series without striking out, tying a record set by Charlie Gehringer of the Detroit Tigers in 1940.

With the bottom of the ninth set to begin, NBC moved Scully down to the Dodgers clubhouse and turned play-by-play duties back over to Ray Scott. Scott announced the change Alston had made in each of the three previous Dodger wins in the series, inserting Kennedy in at third base for defensive purposes, and removing Gilliam from the lineup. "A defensive change for the Dodgers in the last of the ninth. John Kennedy replaces Jim Gilliam, who came up with what might well have been a game-saving play for the Dodgers."

Koufax faced the heart of the Twins' order, as Drysdale was once again throwing in the bullpen. Oliva, a .321 hitter on the season, opened with a slow ground ball to Kennedy for the first out. Killebrew followed with a single to the hole between third and short. As is the custom late in a close game, Kennedy was protecting against a double. "I put myself almost right on the third-base line. I wasn't going to allow an extra-base hit,"[34] he told Leahy in *The Last Innocents*.

Gilliam, now watching and fretting before the television in the Dodger clubhouse, thought, "He is pitching on instinct now. Pure instinct."[35]

After Earl Battey, a .297 batter on the season, struck out, two men were down with Bob Allison, a powerful high-fastball hitter, stepping in as the tying run. Osteen remarked he felt Koufax was outthinking the Twins' hitters. "It's like Sandy was saying to (Allison), 'Okay, here are some fast-balls *up* and a little more *up*. See if you can hit them.'"[36] Allison struck out swinging, and Los Angeles was again the World Series champion.

A front-page *Minneapolis Tribune* photo by John Croft taken immediately after the last out shows four Dodgers converging between the mound and home plate: Koufax, Roseboro, Parker, and Kennedy. Gilliam witnessed the proceedings in the Dodger clubhouse, having already removed his number 19 jersey, but in sight of Vin Scully. When the NBC production threw it to Scully in the Dodgers clubhouse for postgame reaction, Scully stood above the revelers "high atop the safety of a trunk," waiting for "a little calm [to prevail]." Scully noted "One of the toughest parts of the World Series was played right here in the dressing room, and maybe next time we will have a camera here, as Jim Gilliam, who was so important in the victory, sat and watched the ninth inning on television."

Speaking to newspaper reporters after the game, Koufax had his left arm wrapped in ice. George C. Langford, a young United Press International reporter who would later become sports editor of the *Chicago Tribune*, captured an exchange between Koufax and Drysdale, who had a date to play golf the day after the Series ended. In the clubhouse, Drysdale reminded Koufax, "You know I pitched a shutout in the bullpen."

"I was a little shaky on purpose. If you and I are going to play golf tomorrow, I want you to be as stiff and sore as me," Koufax replied.

"Are you going to bring Junior along too?"[37] Drysdale asked, a reference to Gilliam's stop of Versalles' ground ball, which Koufax had admitted was the game's turning point. The Dodgers had plenty of reasons to joke and celebrate at the end of a long 1965 season. In addition to welcomed relaxation and golf outings, the performance of Gilliam and Koufax brought financial benefits.

"Yessir," Gilliam said immediately after the game. "That was a $3,000 play. It was just a reflex play. You see it and you go."[38]

When the final dollars were counted a couple of weeks later, the play turned out to be more like a $3,600 play. The Dodgers garnered a $10,297.43 bonus check as Series winners while the Twins, as losers, earned $6,634.36.[39]

So impressive was the play, and not just for its pecuniary value, that the Baseball Hall of Fame requested Gilliam's glove. Today, the 9-inch-high by 11.5-inch-wide Rawlings XPGS glove with a handwritten "19" in black ink on the back of the thumb can be found in the Hall's Museum Collection Storage in Aisle L. A picture of the glove is also available on the Hall's website. Fittingly, the glove is stamped "Anchored Web" on the inside of the webbing.[40] Truth in advertising prevailed in 1965.

16

A BALL PLAYER'S BALL PLAYER

FOR GILLIAM, 1965 MUST HAVE SEEMED SURREAL. HE BEGAN THE YEAR AS A retired player and first-base coach. He was activated two months into the season and performed well enough to finish third in the National League Comeback Player of the Year voting, behind Vern Law and Eddie Mathews, and 30th in the Most Valuable Player voting, just the fourth time in his career he had earned MVP votes. In December, recognized as a World Series hero, he was set to be honored in his birth hometown of Nashville and he was adored in his adopted hometown of Los Angeles.

Beverly Briley, the Democratic mayor of Nashville, declared December 10, 1965 as "Jim Gilliam Day" in his city. Jim and Edwina arrived at the airport shortly after 9 a.m., greeted by the mayor and representatives from the Chamber of Commerce and the Nashville Frontiers Club, which planned the day's events. Members of the media were also on hand to capture the moment.

The motorcade from the airport arrived downtown to begin a parade heading north on Eighth Avenue from Broadway, before turning east on Union Street to Fifth Avenue. The procession then turned north to Charlotte Avenue, where it finally turned west and stopped in front of the Tennessee state capitol. At a ceremony on the capitol steps, Mayor Briley presented Jim with a key to the city, while Governor Frank Clement made him the first Black in state history to be named an honorary colonel, prompting Gilliam to quip, "I hope this means I don't have to go to Vietnam." The *Long Beach Independent* even ran a headline, "Viet Nam for Col.

Gilliam?"[1] which, when read out of context, might have sparked fears in Dodger fans. A testimonial banquet was held that evening in Jim's honor at the Municipal Auditorium.

The *Nashville Tennessean* devoted several pages of coverage to the day's events in its December 11 newspaper. "I have had many memories in the last 15 years, but this day and night will go down as the greatest thing that has ever happened in my life,"[2] Jim said.

The festivities continued on Saturday morning at 9 a.m. with Gilliam holding a youth program, also at Municipal Auditorium, with the Dodger answering questions from youngsters, many of whom received autographed bats and balls. The day concluded with Jim and Edwina attending the Grantland Rice Bowl in Murfreesboro between Tennessee State and Ball State.

Jim Gilliam, always an observer of the game, at a spring-training game at West Palm Beach's Municipal Stadium. Undated. Photo by Kenneth Davidoff.

ANOTHER UNRETIREMENT IN 1966

Once again, Jim's retirement did not last long. Less than a month into the 1966 season, with the Dodgers struggling to stay above .500, the team activated 37-year-old Gilliam on April 26. The Dodgers dropped three straight games by the same 2-0 score and were desperately in need of offense.

Gilliam sat the bench during his first game on the active roster, a 4-2 Sandy Koufax win against hard-throwing Bob Gibson of the St. Louis Cardinals. "I'm ready to go nine innings physically, but I haven't seen any pitching this season except in batting practice. It's a little different when you are up against a Bob Gibson or a Juan Marichal,"[3] Gilliam told the *Los Angeles Times*, grinning.

Gilliam's first game appearance came a few days later, April 29, against the Cincinnati Reds at Dodger Stadium. After Nate Oliver doubled to left in the bottom of the ninth of a 2-2 tie, Jim—batting for starting pitcher Claude Osteen—worked a walk, giving the Dodgers runners at first and second with no out. Maury Wills bunted into a force play at third, moving Gilliam to second. At that point, Derrell Griffith was inserted as a pinch runner for Jim. Three batters later, with the bases loaded and two out, Ron Fairly singled, scoring Griffith and giving the Dodgers a temporary share of first place.

As the season entered its final month of September, the Dodgers were in third place, three games behind Pittsburgh and San Francisco, who were deadlocked atop the National League. To that point, Gilliam had not had luck replicating his 1965 success. On September 1, Jim was batting a career-low .208 with an on-base percentage of just .296. And, shortstop Maury Wills, batting .274, was out of the lineup with a balky right knee. Walter Alston inserted Gilliam into the starting lineup at third base, moved John Kennedy to shortstop, and gambled his team could find offense.

The plan worked. Jim went 3-for-4 with a walk, two runs scored, and the go-ahead RBI in the top of the tenth, as the Dodgers beat the Pirates, 4-3 on September 1. Gilliam did most of his damage against Pittsburgh starter Vern Law—not a surprise, given Gilliam's .296 career average in 125 at-bats against the Pirate. Pittsburgh pulled a tiring Law in the 10th inning with Gilliam up and the bases loaded. Reliever Pete Mikkelsen issued a walk to Gilliam, forcing home Lou Johnson. One out later, Ron Fairly singled home Wes Parker and Gilliam, and the Dodgers held on for a 4-3 win.

Gilliam's reunion with the fountain of youth continued as the team moved to Cincinnati. He was 5-14 with two runs and three RBI as the club ran its win streak to four games—a stretch where Jim batted .444. Los Angeles returned home to face San Francisco on September 5 and won again, 4-1, moving the Dodgers into second place, 1.5 games behind Pittsburgh. Wills returned in that game, but Gilliam stayed in the lineup at third, going 1-4 with a walk and scoring the go-ahead run in the seventh inning. He had raised his average 20 points to .229 in just five games, all Dodger wins.

Unfortunately, Gilliam could not keep the momentum going. He went 0-7 at the plate during the next two games against the Giants, both losses. Following an off day on September 8, Gilliam did not start as lowly Houston came to town on September 9. Against the Astros on September 10, the Dodgers squeaked out a 1-0 win in 10 innings. Wills opened the bottom of the 10th with a single and was sacrificed by Gilliam. After a Willie Davis ground out, Al Ferrara stroked a pinch-hit single to left, giving Los Angeles the win.

Jim's single to left field off Mike Cuellar in the bottom of the fifth inning would turn out to be the last hit in his Major League career. That same day, September 10, the Dodgers acquired 31-year-old infielder Dick Schofield from the New York Yankees for minor-league pitcher Thad Tillotson and cash. Schofield had not played third base since 1962, but started the last 19 games at the hot corner for Los Angeles, becoming the sixth player to start at third in 1966. Acquired too late in the season, Schofield was not eligible for postseason play.

The Dodgers swept a doubleheader from Houston on September 11 to officially move into first place, a spot they would not relinquish. Gilliam started both games at third base, but was replaced in both by John Kennedy. In the second game, Jim struck out looking and, perhaps feeling the frustration of the disappointing season, voiced displeasure with umpire Bob Engel's call. Engel ejected Gilliam, marking the first time since June 23, 1963 that Jim had been tossed from a game. He started at third base the next day against the Mets, going 0-for-2 with two walks, in what would be the final regular-season start of his career.

A week later, long-time columnist Sid Ziff broke the news to readers of the *Los Angeles Times* on Sunday, September 18. "Jim Gilliam says this is absolutely the last season for him as a player," Ziff wrote. "Gilliam has been the Dodgers' 'Old Man River.' He just keeps rolling along."

Ziff quoted Gilliam's definitive stance, "I feel better some days than others. But time has run out. I've had it. This is the end of the line."[4]

Jim's final regular season at-bat came in a pinch-hitting role on Friday, September 30 against the Phillies at Connie Mack Stadium. Batting for starting pitcher Claude Osteen to open the top of the fifth, Gilliam grounded out to short off the Phillies' Chris Short.

ONE LAST RUN: THE 1966 WORLD SERIES

Los Angeles reached the World Series for the fourth time in the nine years since the team relocated from Brooklyn. In each of the previous Series— 1959, 1963, and 1965—the Dodgers were victorious. That would not be the case in 1966, as the team met the Baltimore Orioles and seemingly forgot how to hit and field. Los Angeles scored a total of two runs the entire Series as Baltimore's pitching aces of Dave McNally, Jim Palmer, Moe Drabowsky, and Wally Bunker held the Dodgers to an anemic .142 batting average in the four-game sweep.

Despite not having started a game for Los Angeles since Sept. 12, Walter Alston inserted Gilliam in the Game One lineup playing third base but batting seventh, not his customary second spot. Jim's appearance in the starting nine warranted its own sidebar in the *Los Angeles Times* with the headline, "World Series Old Hat to Gilliam—His 7th!" The article, penned by Al Wolf, suggested Gilliam's seventh World Series in 14 seasons for the Dodgers was "the most any National Leaguer has played with the same club." The problem with that declaration was that three of Gilliam's former teammates—Pee Wee Reese, Gil Hodges, and Carl Furillo—had also played in seven World Series for the Dodgers. Reese appeared in the 1941, 1947, 1949, 1952, 1953, 1955, and 1956 Series. Furillo and Hodges both played in the 1947, 1949, 1952, 1953, 1955, 1956, and 1959 Series.

Gilliam's participation on four World Series champs set a franchise record that still exists today. Sandy Koufax was on the Dodger roster for six World Series but did not make an appearance in the 1955 seven-game victory over the Yankees. So while Koufax was also part of four World Series champs, he only played in three World Series. The same is true for Johnny Podres, who was also on the roster for four World Series winners (1955, 1959, 1963, and 1965) but did not appear in the 1965 Series.

With the Dodgers already trailing 4-0, Jim drew a walk off McNally in the bottom of the second but would be stranded on first. Batting with the bases loaded in the bottom of the third, and with the Dodgers now trailing 4-1, Gilliam again worked a walk, forcing home Lou Johnson from third and narrowing the gap to 4-2. But that was as close as it would be. Baltimore won the game 5-2 and would sweep the Series.

In Game Two, notable both as Gilliam's last MLB game and the last game Sandy Koufax would pitch in his career, the Dodgers committed six errors, including three unfortunate miscues by Los Angeles center fielder Willie Davis. Battling bright sunshine, Davis muffed two fly ballparks and added a poorly thrown ball to third in the top of the fifth, allowing Baltimore to take a 3-0 lead. Gilliam booted a ball off the bat of Brooks Robinson in the top of the fourth, but the mistake did not cost the Dodgers a run.

Gilliam was 0-4 at the plate against Jim Palmer in Game Two, and did not appear in Games Three and Four, played in Baltimore.

Wolf's October 6 article noted that Jim's appearance in Game One of the 1966 World Series was his 38th World Series game. Gilliam finished with 39 World Series games played for the Dodgers, tied with Furillo for third in club history, behind Reese's 44 and Snider's 40. "If they ever build a Hall of Fame for World Series performers, one prominent pedestal should be reserved for Jim Gilliam,"[5] Wolf wrote. Two days after Wolf's article ran, on Saturday, October 8, the writer died of an apparent heart attack at his hotel in Houston, where he was covering the UCLA-Rice football game. He was 62 years old.

That Jim Gilliam's professional baseball career was ending in the city, Baltimore, where it started was not lost on Los Angeles Times writer Frank Finch, who wrote an ode to Gilliam and his career published October 9, the day of Game Four. Finch summarized Gilliam's life in baseball, from breaking in with the Baltimore Elite Giants of the Negro Leagues to acquiring the nickname "Junior" to his failed tryout with the Chicago Cubs to his evolving role on the Dodgers, including hitting behind Maury Wills. Finch singled out Gilliam's play in Game Seven of the 1965 World Series as "the biggest defensive play of this versatile fellow's career."

After rattling off the statistical artifacts of Gilliam's career with the Dodgers—1,961 games played, 1,889 hits, 1,163 runs scored, 558 runs batted in, and 203 stolen bases (Finch omitted Jim's 1,036 walks against just only 416 strikeouts), Finch wrote, "Reluctantly we say hail and farewell to Jim Gilliam who, in every sense, was a ball player's ball player."[6]

A BALL PLAYER'S BALL PLAYER

Finch's words in the Los Angeles Times accurately summarized how Gilliam's teammates and management assessed his personality and contributions to the Dodgers as a player. Walter Alston managed Jim for 15 seasons, including the minors. Wherever Alston needed him was where Gilliam would play. If he needed Jim to bunt, he bunted. If he needed Jim to hit behind a runner, he gave himself up. "He was probably the closest thing to the perfect ballplayer I ever saw. In all the years, he never missed a sign. He played anywhere I wanted him to. He was a manager's delight."[7]

Former teammates and opponents alike recalled Gilliam in the same fashion. He was remembered as an intelligent baseball player who shared his knowledge with others. He was not a flashy player, seeking to grab headlines. He was an unselfish teammate, willing to put the good of the team in front of his own individual successes.

"He was a team player. He thought more about the team than himself. I don't ever recall hearing or getting an impression or signal that Jim was unhappy. He enjoyed what he did. He enjoyed the responsibility we gave him," remembered Peter O'Malley, who served as Dodgers president from 1970-98, and as owner from the time of his father's death in 1979 to 1998. "He did everything so well that he had the respect of everyone. He had to know that on a team whether you are a coach or a player you have to know that your teammates respect you. You can't miss that, and it was pretty obvious with Jim."

Bart Shirley recalled lining up alongside Gilliam and having him as a coach. Shirley's big-league career had few highlights, as the utility player bounced around the Dodgers infield in 1964, 1966, and 1968, batting just over .200 in career 162 at-bats. He remembers Gilliam's transition from player to coach as seamless. "He didn't try to do anything different. He came across as always himself."

Although he appeared in only 12 games during the Dodgers' 1966 National League championship season, Shirley was voted a one-third share of the team's postseason money, the equivalent of $2,730. To this day, he credits Gilliam for helping lobby for that on his behalf.

BASEBALL IQ

Perhaps the singular reason Alston trusted Gilliam was his high level of baseball IQ. Throughout his playing career, Jim repeatedly excelled in making the right play at the right time, reacting to the situation with ease. His play in Game Seven of the 1965 World Series was evidence of that trait. He positioned himself in just the right location to field Zoilo Versalles' ground ball. He did not try to make more of the situation other than getting the out in front of him at third base. His decision to try, successfully, for third base following an error in a tied Game Four of the 1963 World Series paved the way for him to score the go-ahead run. In hindsight, the decision was as much about knowing how the ball would travel in foul ground as it was about his speed.

Gilliam's ability to know precisely what to do in any situation, offense or defense, provided Alston an on-field manager whom he could trust. Players and teammates of Gilliam's repeatedly praised his knowledge of the game, particularly little things, that helped his team win games. Jackie Robinson wrote in 1964, "Jim Gilliam is the quiet kind, keenly observant, with an inexhaustible fund of baseball knowledge."[8]

Nineteen-year-old Al Ferrara, then a rookie outfielder from Brooklyn, recalled sitting next to Gilliam at lunch in 1959 on his first day at Vero Beach for spring training. "Here was someone I had looked up to a few years earlier when I was living in Brooklyn. We didn't say much—he never did." The two would converse more years later as teammates on the Dodgers from 1963-68. One day in 1967, Ferrara was speaking to reporters after a game in which he had a couple of key hits, answering questions about the opposing team's pitcher. When the interviews ended, Gilliam pulled Ferrara aside.

"'What are you doing?' He asked me," Ferrara remembered. "'You don't tell writers what pitches you hit, that takes away your advantage.' You don't think about those things, but they help you as a player and they help the team win."

Gilliam used a similar approach with pitchers. "Jim would never tell you how to pitch. He never talked about opposing players. Instead he talked about what you did and why you did it," Al Downing, a member of the Dodgers' staff from 1971-77, said.

A few years later, after he had joined the San Diego Padres, Ferrara was talking with long-time National League catcher Chris Cannizzaro about which Dodger gave him the most difficulty. Jim Gilliam, replied Cannizzaro, who would join the Dodgers in 1972 and 1973.

"All the guys drove me crazy, but Gilliam had a habit with a runner on first of squaring to bunt and putting his bat in my eye line so I could not see where the runner was as I was trying to throw him out stealing," Cannizzaro told Ferrara.

Gilliam offered similar, nuanced baseball knowledge to Wes Parker. The two had won a World Series in 1965 while becoming part of the first all-switch-hit infield in baseball. During Parker's final season in 1972, he was struggling to hit the knuckle curveball of the Chicago Cubs' Burt Hooton. "Jim said I should look for it instead of reacting to it. He was right. I hit it a couple times and Hooton never threw it to me after that," Parker remembers. "When he said something it was dead on. I loved talking to him. He saw deeply into every situation."

"When I played first base and Gilliam played second, he let me know when off-speed pitches were coming to left-handed batters," recalled Ron Fairly, a member of the Dodgers from 1958-68. "The second baseman can see the signs a catcher calls, signs that are out of the line of sight of the first baseman. When the pitcher started his windup, if an off-speed pitch was coming, Gilliam would say, 'Ronnie' loud enough for me to hear but out of earshot of the batter or the first-base coach. That pitch would make it more likely that the ball would be coming in my direction. Gilliam's vocal tip prepared me. It was a simple signal that could have a big impact."[9]

Jim did not say much publicly about how he approached being a coach, other than to suggest he was always busy on the field. "As a coach I have a chance to observe more than when I was play," he told a United Press International reporter in April 1967. "When you're playing, you have to concentrate on your hitting and fielding. It is my job to watch others, see their problems, and help them out."[10]

His propensity to get on base led to praise about his eye at the plate, but Tommy Davis wondered about his eyesight while driving. "We'd be driving down the street in spring training, and he'd drive right through a stop sign and I'd say, 'Jim, what's wrong with you?' He'd say, 'Oh. I didn't see that.' Incredible. In a 14-year career, he averaged 74 walks because of how good his eye was, and yet he'd still drive right through a stop sign."[11]

Manny Mota played 20 years with the San Francisco Giants, Pittsburgh Pirates, Montreal Expos, and the Los Angeles Dodgers, and spent an incredible 34 years as a coach for the Dodgers. "Junior was one of the smartest I ever played against," said Mota, whose teammates also included Willie Mays and Roberto Clemente. "He was a prototype second hitter. Not afraid to take a pitch. He was a clutch situational hitter. He didn't strike out much."

Mota recalled not just Gilliam's knowledge but also his ability to help players become better. "He didn't say much, but when he talked, you better listen. He knew how to handle any situation and how to react. He was a one-of-a-kind teammate who would do everything possible to help you."

Pee Wee Reese played alongside Gilliam in the Dodger infield from 1953-58 giving him a first-hand view of Gilliam's abilities. "I don't know what Gilliam's career average was or how many hits or home runs or RBI he had," Reese said. "I don't know anything about his 'statics' as Dizzy Dean used to say, but I do know he was a great man to have on the ball field. He never complained. He had the greatest attitude I ever saw. He did so many things for you to win a game that you'll never be able to find in the 'statics.'"[12]

Gilliam's widow, Edwina, also saw him as an unselfish, team player. "He was a very self-sacrificing ballplayer. He would do anything for the team," she said. "He never really had the credit he deserved, I don't think."

Gilliam's standing in the Dodgers record books provides evidence to support the sentiment he is not often regarded with the same adulation as his more famous Hall of Fame teammate. Nonetheless, through the 2024 season, Gilliam was tied with Sandy Koufax and Johnny Podres for most World Series championships, with four. His seven World Series appearances tied him with Pee Wee Reese, Carl Furillo, and Duke Snider for most in team history. He was second all-time with 1,036 walks, third with 8,322 plate appearances, fourth in runs scored with 1,163, fifth in games played (1,956) and at bats (7,119), sixth in runs created with 984, and eighth in hits (1,889) and offensive WAR (37.7). Only Zack Wheat and Reese, both Hall of Famer players, reached base safely more times in a Dodgers uniform than Gilliam, who did so 2,958 times.

"SECOND LOVE"

Jim Gilliam's transition into a fully retired baseball player and full-time coach in 1967 began much the same way previous Januarys did, by playing golf. Baseball was his first love, but Edwina characterized golf as Gilliam's "second love." He played as often as he could. Kathy remembers her father, when he was not on the road, playing golf "every single day" during the period in which she lived with him on Valleydale. "I'd get up at six and he'd already left. Baseball players and golf go together. Every shot was money. He was a hustler. He didn't play golf just for fun."

Many of those early morning golf outings included fellow infielder Dick Tracewski. "I played a lot of golf with Jim," Tracewski remembered. "We had a rule about playing golf. We would play early in the morning. We said, 'listen. If you make two holes in one and I make three, don't ever mention it in the clubhouse. Our lips are sealed about golf.' Our manager, Walter Alston, frowned on us playing in the season."

Doug Rau, a Dodgers pitcher from 1972-79, could attest to the seriousness with which Gilliam approached golf. "I spent more time on the driving range hitting practice balls with him than I did anywhere," Rau said. "We would meet up at the end of the day and talk about how similar it (golfing) was to pitching with spin and placement. He was a tactician with moving the ball and knowing how the wind affects flight and movement of the ball."

As part of the Southern California Open at Los Coyotes Country Club in Buena Park, Gilliam and several former teammates, including Sandy Koufax, Don Drysdale, Willie Davis, and Johnny Podres, played in a pro-am event on Wednesday, January 4, 1967. Paired with Koufax, Bobby Knoop of the California Angels, and Deacon Jones of the NFL's Los Angeles Rams, Gilliam led the foursome with a round of 87, good for sixth place in the pro-athlete flight. Three days later, on January 7, Gilliam appeared at Courtesy Chevrolet at Western and 9th, near Koreatown, along with Baltimore Orioles MVP Frank Robinson and Dodger infielder Nate Oliver to talk baseball, sign autographs, and pose for pictures from 10 a.m. to 2 p.m. Robinson was presented with a new Camaro for winning the World Series MVP.

A month later at the American Airlines AstroJet tournament in Carlsbad, Gilliam played alongside sports luminaries Mickey Mantle, Mike Ditka, Brooks Robinson, and Willie Mays, among others. The athletes voted Jim as the athlete who could become competitive in any sport. "They said Gilliam was one of the best coordinated guys they had ever seen," said Fred Scott, a business representative of many athletes. "He was a good football player in high school and he's a good golfer. They figured they could put a tennis racket in his hands and he'd probably be a great player in a month."[13]

Unfortunately, Gilliam and his partner, NFL quarterback Norm Snead, finished 10th in the three-day event, despite shooting an opening-round 60.

In addition to spending time on the links, retired Jim became much more active in community appearances, particularly those that supported, or had a connection with, Black-owned businesses.

Toward the end of 1967, Gilliam began working for Golden State Mutual Life Insurance, one of the nation's largest Black-owned insurance companies, during the offseason. When he stopped working for Hiram Walker is unknown. His official title was "insurance consultant," although it is unclear what that meant. A January 1968 photo in the *Los Angeles Sentinel* depicts Cubs infielder Ernie Banks on a tour of the Golden State Mutual Life Insurance building, admiring a piece of art work held by Artie Wimsatt, a public-relations staff member for the agency. The Golden State Mutual Collection, as it is now referred, was one of the largest African-American art collections in the country. Los Angeles County purchased 124 items from the collection and now administers them through its Arts Commission.[14]

Jim also began a surface-level friendship with Muhammad Ali. On

January 15, 1970, Gilliam joined a host of prominent Black athletes, including O.J. Simpson, Elgin Baylor, and John Carlos, at a special banquet honoring Ali. Held at the Hollywood Palladium and sponsored by the Los Angeles Brother Crusade, the event was positioned as "'must go' for all citizens who are civic minded and have the welfare of the community at heart."[15]

Three years later, on February 16, 1973, Gilliam was in attendance, along with O.J. Simpson, John Carlos, Wilma Rudolph, Bill Russell, and Rafer Johnson, among others, as Ali attended an open house for Family Savings and Loan Association, another Black-owned business.

1968: RACIAL SETBACKS ON THE DODGERS

On March 24, 1968, writer Charles Maher of the *Los Angeles Times* published the first of a five-part series entitled, "The Negro Athlete in America." In the opening article, Maher wrote, "If the Negro's objective in sports was simply to achieve equality, he may have overshot his target. Off his performance to date, it is possible to argue that he has not become equal, but superior."[16] Maher estimated that in 1967, 33.75 percent of National League regulars were American Negroes, a percentage that would be higher if he included "Latin American players of obvious or probable Negroid extraction."[17]

At the beginning of the 1968 season, not only did the Dodgers not meet the 33 percent threshold, the franchise scarcely resembled the teams of 15 years prior, when front-office management was carefully considering how many Black players should be kept on the roster. Gilliam retired for good after the 1966 season, while Maury Wills was traded to Pittsburgh after a controversy involving the team's goodwill trip to Japan after the 1966 World Series. Tommy Davis had been shipped to the Mets in November 1966.

As a result, the Dodgers entered the 1968 season with just one Black regular player, Willie Davis, and one pitcher, Jim "Mudcat" Grant, whom the team acquired from the Minnesota Twins in November 1967 in a trade that saw long-time Black Dodger John Roseboro go to Minnesota. That same month, the team also dealt 1965 World Series star Lou Johnson to the Chicago Cubs. Nate Oliver was traded to San Francisco prior to spring training in 1968.

Sure, Gilliam was coaching first, but the days of Robinson, Campanella, Newcombe, and Gilliam in the mid-1950s or Wills, Roseboro, Tommy Davis, Willie Davis, and Gilliam in the early 1960s were long gone. The question posed by *Jet* magazine in 1963 of whether the Dodgers had a Negro problem could be viewed very differently in 1968. The lack of Black representation on the Dodgers would pose a problem for the team less than two weeks later when Martin Luther King, Jr. was murdered in Memphis on the eve of baseball's opening day.

While several National League teams—including the Cardinals, Giants, and Reds—had lineups highlighted by outspoken Black stars who could advise their teams on how to properly honor and respect King, the Dodgers had just Davis and Grant. Outfielder Willie Crawford would become a key contributor on the 1968 team and several years after, but he was only 21 years old and began the season in Triple-A Spokane. Assuming the role of an outspoken leader, particularly on issues of race, was not something befitting Gilliam and his personality.

In the wake of King's death, President Lyndon Johnson declared Sunday, April 7 a national day of mourning and all of baseball stopped, except for the Cleveland Indians and the Los Angeles Dodgers, who played a meaningless exhibition game in San Diego, a year before the expansion Padres. Gilliam, Grant, and Davis all refused to participate in the game that day, but many of their Black counterparts on the Indians did play. Dodgers general manager Buzzie Bavasi offered the decision to play was "nothing disrespectful. Our main idea is to give the people some sort of amusement when they need it most."[18]

The Dodgers, like much of Major League Baseball, were scheduled to open their season on Tuesday, April 9, the day of King's funeral, against Philadelphia. The Phillies, whose Opening Day roster included four Black players—including Dick Allen and Bill White—were refusing to play, a decision supported by their owner Bob Carpenter and general manager John Quinn. The Dodgers said the game would go on. National League president Warren Giles stated, "The decision is up to the Dodgers. Unless the two clubs reach an agreement, the Phillies must play or risk a forfeit if they refuse."[19] A showdown loomed.

Buzzie Bavasi defended the team's decision by saying he consulted with Davis and Gilliam and "they agreed it was best to play. Willie and junior (sic) told me they will do their mourning in church and that's where we all should do it."[20] Gilliam's widow, Edwina, said while she was a churchgoer, Jim was not, casting some doubt on Bavasi's statement. Neither Davis nor Gilliam were ever quoted directly in the media regarding their comments. The only attribution was Bavasi saying he consulted with them.

Bavasi continued to attempt to rationalize the decision, but his comments only served to antagonize the situation. He believed the tele-vised game "may help keep people off the streets and to forget their anger." He also reasoned the Dodgers were playing a night game while King's funeral was in the morning. "If we'd had a day game scheduled like the others, we would definitely have cancelled, too. But our opener is at night. It will be 11 p.m. in the East and 8 p.m. here, long after the funeral."[21]

It was his unsuccessful attempt to draw parallels between King's funeral and the 1965 World Series, when Sandy Koufax did not pitch because of Yom Kippur, that cemented Bavasi's position on the wrong side of the debate. Black author "Doc" Young told *Los Angeles Times* columnist John Hall, "Bavasi said he was willing to give Willie Davis and other Negro members of the team Tuesday night off, just as Sandy Koufax was permitted to observe Jewish holidays away from the team. This was a terribly poor analogy. Some Americans are Jews; other Americans are not. But, all Americans are Americans."[22]

Bavasi received a lot of criticism for his responses and inaction. As author Glenn Stout wrote, "Everything Bavasi said about the situation made him sound insensitive, and the organization appeared totally out of touch. The Dodgers were excoriated over the decision. On April 8, O'Malley and Bavasi met and finally backed down, but the damage to the team's reputation was done. Bavasi didn't help matters by saying after-ward, 'There's no sense bumping our heads against a stone wall,' as if the decision had somehow been correct and everybody else was wrong. They simply didn't understand that choosing not to play was a matter of respect."[23]

That Gilliam was caught in the crossfire of a negative public-relations story surrounding the Dodgers and race seems inconsistent with his personality. "He was disinterested in that (race and politics)," Tracewski said. "There was none of that in him. He didn't get involved in that and he didn't care about it."

Ultimately, the Dodgers and Phillies did postpone their April 9 game, opening the season the next day, April 10, in front of 28,138 fans at Dodger Stadium. Brad Pye, Jr. took the Dodgers to task in the April 11 *Los Angeles Sentinel* under a headline, "MLK pays supreme price: But do Dodgers really care?" Pye wrote, "Personally, I'm getting sick and tired of hearing what a great debt Negroes owe the Dodgers. History will show that the Dodgers' romance with Negroes has been mutually beneficial."[24] He cited the team's World Series titles and attendance records as benefits Black players had given the Dodgers.

1968: A SEASON OF TURMOIL

When the Dodgers did take the field on April 10, they did so without manager Walter Alston, who underwent surgery at Daniel Freeman Memorial Hospital to remove a kidney stone. Harold "Lefty" Phillips, the team's pitching coach since 1965, was designated as "coach in charge" during Alston's two-week absence from the team. Phillips, who lacked any professional playing experience, was a scout for the Dodger organization from 1952-64 before assuming the coaching role. When Alston finally returned on April 29, the Dodgers had gone 8-8 under Phillips, who would be named manager of the California Angels six weeks into the 1969 season. He led the Angels through the 1971 season, amassing a career record of 222-225, not counting the Dodgers interim stint.

In choosing Phillips to serve as acting manager of the Dodgers, the front office opted to bypass not only the more prominent name of Jim Gilliam, but also third-base coach Preston Gómez of Cuba and bench coach Danny Ozark. A headline in the April 25 *Los Angeles Times* decried Phillips' rise from "anonymity" to manager.[25]

Gómez was named manager of the expansion San Diego Padres for the 1969 season and managed three different teams over seven seasons in the Major Leagues, retiring from managing after 1980. Ozark led the Philadelphia Phillies from 1973-79, winning three straight National League East titles, before being dismissed in late August 1979. Gilliam never managed in the Major Leagues.

Even after the King funeral blunder and Alston's surgery, the Dodgers' 1968 season continued to be clouded by front-office turmoil. After nearly 18 years as the Dodgers general manager, Buzzie Bavasi resigned after becoming a part owner of the expansion San Diego Padres franchise on May 27, 1968. From a timing standpoint, the announcement could not have been worse, as the free agent draft was scheduled for June 6 in New York. Fresco Thompson, who joined the Dodgers front office in 1940 and was the club's current minor-league director, was a logical choice to replace Bavasi. However, newspaper accounts indicated he was also a candidate for the general manager's job with the league's other expansion franchise, the Montreal Expos.

As Michael Leahy describes in his book *The Last Innocents*, this was the same week as Robert F. Kennedy's assassination at the Ambassador Hotel on June 5. On the morning of June 6, Thompson, along with assistant Bill Schweppe and director of scouting Al Campanis, flew to New York for the draft. That afternoon, 66-year-old Thompson was officially named the Dodgers' general manager by Walter O'Malley.

That draft, under Thompson's direction, yielded the Dodgers perhaps the greatest group of Major League talent in any one draft. The team's two-day draft haul included Bobby Valentine, Steve Garvey, Ron Cey, Bill Buckner, Joe Ferguson, Tom Paciorek, and Doyle Alexander, among others. Davey Lopes was drafted in the January phase of the draft. Together, they rose through the Dodgers' minor-league system, playing under manager Tommy Lasorda. Those players formed the core of the Dodgers championship teams of the 1970s.

Unfortunately, Thompson would never see the fruits of work. He became ill with cancer in September and passed away on November 20 in St. Jude's Hospital following liver surgery. Pallbearers at his funeral on November 23 at St. Juliana's Church in Fullerton were Campanis, Schweppe, Walter Alston, Don Drysdale, third-base coach Danny Ozark, and Jim Gilliam. Campanis was named to succeed Thompson as general manager.

HELPING SNATCH COCONUTS

History remembers Al Campanis as the Dodgers general manager famously fired after making racist comments on ABC's Nightline on the 40th anniversary of Jackie Robinson's breaking the color barrier. Years prior to that, when Campanis was the team's Dodgers scouting director in 1954, he published *The Dodgers' Way to Play Baseball*. The book provided positional and situational details regarding how players in the Dodger organization should play.

In the chapter titled "The Coach or Manager," Campanis wrote in regard to selecting a team, "From my experience in baseball, I suggest you pick the nine best players and play them even if you must change a player's position. In the Dodger organization, we nickname the changing of a player's position, 'coconut snatching'."[26] The concept was simple in pre-free agency baseball: move players around internally to fill needs.

In many ways, Jackie Robinson and Jim Gilliam were among the Dodgers' original coconut snatchers. Robinson was a shortstop with the Kansas City Monarchs in 1945, but a first baseman in Brooklyn in 1947. He then played almost exclusively second base until Gilliam arrived in 1953, when Robinson was snatched to be primarily a third baseman or left fielder, and occasionally a second baseman, right fielder, and first baseman.

Gilliam played every position in his 14-year career except pitcher, catcher, and shortstop. Injuries to outfielders Lou Johnson and Willie Davis on June 4, 1966 forced Walter Alston to shift Wes Parker to center field and insert Gilliam at first base for the ninth inning, the first time he played the position in his career. With the Dodgers up 11-0 in the first game of a doubleheader at the Mets the next day, Alston again switched Parker to center and inserted Gilliam at first, this time in the bottom of the seventh. Sandy Koufax was dominating the lowly Mets, so Gilliam did not figure to get much action. New York's Dick Stuart opened the bottom of the ninth with a ground ball to Jim Lefebvre at second, who flipped to Gilliam for the out. It was the only fielding chance at first base in Gilliam's career.

The Dodger farm system in the late 1960s was stocked with baseball talent and ripe for snatching coconuts. Bill Russell, the team's shortstop during the 1970s, was drafted as an outfielder in 1966 and made his big-league debut there in 1969. Steve Garvey was a third baseman at Michigan State before transitioning across the diamond to become a Gold Glove first baseman. Davey Lopes was an outfielder before he was an All-Star second baseman. Bill Buckner regularly bounced between first base and the outfield.

Third baseman Ron Cey was another member of this core group of future Dodgers and remembered the emphasis on position flexibility. "Back at the time our group broke in and were aligning itself to be the future players for the Dodgers a lot of it was about versatility. They were pounding that theme to us as well."

Drafted as a shortstop, Billy Grabarkewitz remembered the frustration that came with constantly moving positions, "The Dodgers were always versatile, but I felt if you play one position, you get better at it."

After beginning the 1970 season on the bench, Grabarkewitz took over second base, replacing an injured Ted Sizemore, the 1969 National League Rookie of the Year. Once healthy, Sizemore regained his starting spot. With Garvey struggling at third, Alston inserted Grabarkewitz at a position where he was not comfortable. While Grabarkewitz started 95 games at third that season, he also recorded 18 starts at second and 37 at short.

"I remember Jim (Gilliam) saying, 'You're gifted. You can play there (third base).' It became easier and easier," Grabarkewitz recalled. "Gilliam was smart and savvy. When he gave you instructions, you listened to him because you knew he knew. He would always talk to me about situations."

On the second day of spring training in 1971, Campanis had Grabarke-witz and minor leaguer Marv Galliher return to the field at the end of the day for an extra hour of fielding practice, leaving both men with sore arms.[27] Gilliam caught wind of Campanis's intervention and immediately became enraged.

"Jim was so upset (we were out there). He told Campanis, 'that's BS. Those guys won't be able to comb their hair tomorrow,'" Grabarkewitz said. "Alston cussed out Campanis. He said, 'You get me the players and you let me manage them.' Alston hated Campanis."

Sure enough, Grabarkewitz said he could not raise his arm the next day and wound up missing much of the 1971 season with shoulder injuries. His on-field performance never came close to matching his 1970 season, when he hit .289 with 17 home runs. He was traded after the 1972 season, along with Hall of Famer Frank Robinson, Bill Singer, Mike Strahler, and Bobby Valentine for Andy Messersmith and Ken McMullen.

Valentine was another coconut snatcher. Originally drafted as an outfielder, Valentine played six different positions during the 1972 season for Los Angeles. He started 43 games at second base, 38 at shortstop, 10 at third base, and another eight in the outfield.

"In the minor leagues we had a guy named Monty Basgall. He did a lot of the fundamental work. When I got to the big leagues—and it was only really for two years that I was full-time in uniform with Junior—he then took over," Valentine said. "He taught me the double play from second base. I never thought about being a second baseman until Walt Alston decided to move me to second."

Although he only started another 53 games at second base in his big-league career, Valentine recalled the specifics of Gilliam's instruction. "He used to say that in all my movement I was just wasting time. Get it and give it as quickly as you can. I never saw him play. I can't really speak to how quick he turned the double play. I'm sure it was really quick. It was legendary."

Al Downing was traded from the Milwaukee Brewers to the Dodgers in the spring of 1971. That season, Downing went 20-9 with a 2.68 ERA and finished third in the National League Cy Young Award, as the Dodgers finished second in the National League West for the second consecutive year. The team was a unique collection of veterans and young, highly touted draft picks like Buckner, Garvey, Valentine, and Russell.

"The draft made it much more difficult to coach players," Downing recalled. "The team placed a premium on who they drafted; nobody looked at overall ability. Coaches couldn't tell them what to do. Guys would get upset. Jim had a high baseball IQ. You could make a mistake once, and he would make sure you knew what you did on that play. You didn't make mistakes repeatedly."

"WORLD'S GREATEST BRIDGE PLAYER"

Gilliam's competitiveness showed in any activity in which he participated, from baseball to billiards to golf. The long, idle hours players spend in baseball clubhouses and plane rides are conducive for developing competitive card games. It is not surprising that Gilliam was also an aggressive card player, particularly bridge and poker. Where or when he developed his skills is not known, but a 1950s-era photo shows Gilliam and Jackie Robinson engaged in a serious card game inside the Brooklyn Dodger locker room, as clubhouse manager John Griffin lingers in the background wearing a top hat and smoking a cigar.

Gilliam's playing partners often included his manager, Walter Alston, along with his 1960s teammates Wes Parker and Don Drysdale. Parker traveled to Hawaii after the 1969 season to compete in a regional bridge tournament, suggesting he knew a little something about the game.[28] "Jim was the best bridge player I ever encountered, hands down," Parker remembered. "He had great card sense."

It was during spring training in 1966 when Charles Goren, who literally wrote the book about how to play bridge, visited Vero Beach. Alston and Goren paired for a game against Parker and Gilliam which Goren later summarized in *Sports Illustrated*.

"The result was that we wound up on the short end of a blitz at the hands of Gilliam and young Parker," Goren wrote. "Our opponents' bidding technique was not exactly of championship caliber, but they weren't a bit flustered playing against their manager and me and before an audience that included National League President Warren Giles and Duke Snider."[29]

Alston remembered being the weak link during the game in one of his autobiographies. "I must have been pretty much of a liability for Goren because Parker, who is pretty good and holds some master points, and Gilliam beat us. They felt pretty good because Goren has a little card he gives to people he plays if they should win. It's the size of a calling card and says, 'I beat Goren.'"[30]

Dodgers road trips in the 1960s and 1970s were the envy of the rest of the league, thanks in no small part to the 720B jet with the blue "Dodgers" script painted on each side and a baseball painted on the tail. Christened the "Kay O' II" in honor of Dodgers owner Walter O'Malley's wife, Kay, the plane boasted four different card tables throughout the cabin to help players pass the time.

"The most aggressive (game) was in the back and I didn't go to the back too often," Cey recalled, chuckling. "They were the veteran players that would take your money and laugh at you. I didn't get involved with that too much."

Tracewski recalled those competitive card games as well. "Once in a while I would go back there and watch the card games. There was never any money exchanged on the planes, but they played for money and Gilliam was in the middle of it. I understand he took home a lot of money."

Indeed, the back of the plane was where Gilliam could often be found. So confident was Jim in his card-playing abilities that one time he ignored his actual title, preferring to respond to one emphasizing his prowess in the card game. During a 1977 summer road trip, pitcher Don Sutton grabbed the intercom microphone on the team's plane and requested, "Would the batting instructor please report to the front of the craft?" Gilliam, watching a poker game in the rear of the plane, did not respond. Sutton tried a different tactic while requesting Gilliam's presence a second time. "Would the world's greatest bridge player report to the front of the craft?" Sutton said. Gilliam smiled and headed to the front of the plane.[31]

"LIKE YOUR UNCLE"

Jim's influence on the Dodgers during this period was not limited to coaching or being a leader in the clubhouse. Nor did it merely encompass baseball strategy and knowledge. While perhaps it was not a formal role, Gilliam also served as mentor to young players, particularly young Black players.

Many African-American baseball fans were Dodgers fans because of the club's role in integration. One such fan in the early 1960s was a young-ster growing up in Riverside, a city east of Los Angeles, named Johnnie B. Baker, Jr., better known by the nickname Dusty. "The Dodgers were always special to me. Tommy Davis was my hero. That was the reason I wore number 12 then and why I still do now," Baker said. "My Dad (Johnnie B. Baker, Sr.) always loved Charlie Neal, John Roseboro, and Jim Gilliam. It was a thrill to be traded to them."

Baker joined the Dodgers prior to the 1976 season and immediately bonded with Gilliam. He explained the player's relationship with his coaches and manager. "A coach is like your uncle. You can tell him anything. A manager is like your dad," said Baker, recalling a time in early 1978 when he was struggling.

"Devil said to me, 'Boy, what's wrong with you?' I was missing pitches.

Me and my wife weren't getting along. Just talking to him made me feel better," Baker said.

Valentine's recollection of Gilliam supports Baker's "uncle" analogy. "He was a friend of the players. There was no doubt about that. He talked to us a lot more than Walt would. During those times, there were a lot of errors being made and a lot of positions being moved around. Not necessarily in the most willing fashion by most of us. He was always a steadying influence. I hate to say 'just a good guy,' but good guys are hard to come by and he was one of them."

While Gilliam did not often talk openly about his experience in the Negro Leagues, it was evident to all around him that he was proud of having been a part of its significant past and his place in history. Just as Jackie Robinson had served as a mentor to him, "Uncle" Gilliam believed it was his role to pass on baseball knowledge and mentor young Black players, such as Baker. "He would tell me about Jackie all the time. (Gilliam) told about how Lee Scott, the Dodgers' traveling secretary, would move the whole team from a hotel if Black players couldn't stay there and how Jackie went down to a hotel lobby and sat in a restaurant that refused Blacks. We all followed Jackie. It used to be in a more subservient role."

Gilliam also spoke about how Black players should present themselves on the road, Baker remembered, advising against drinking in the players' hotel room or lying awake watching television. The 1977 Dodgers team featured several Black players, including Baker, Reggie Smith, Lee Lacy, Glenn Burke, and Davey Lopes. Gilliam wanted to share his knowledge of the Negro Leagues with them.

"Jim took me to Cool Papa Bell's house in St. Louis (3034 Dickson Street, later renamed James Cool Papa Bell Avenue) for lunch one day. I was as quiet as a church mouse. They talked about the Negro Leagues all day. Jim was tight with Lyman Bostock and Double Duty Radcliffe. They would sit around and talk it up. The stories were endless. Half were lies," Baker laughed.

UNLIKELY FRIENDSHIPS

Gilliam's mentorship of young Black men was not limited to the clubhouse and the diamond. He developed meaningful relationships with individuals around the club, often helping them improve their lives. Longtime Dodgertown employee Ben Grier was the beneficiary of Gilliam's kindness. He began at Dodgertown in 1958 as a porter but added the roles of groundskeeper, scoreboard operator, bus driver, and concierge to Dodger players and their families. The two men became fast friends at Dodgertown, frequently eating lunch together.

"I was a poor boy when I started my job here," Grier said. "Jim was a fancy dresser. He would give me the clothes he didn't care to keep any longer. He would accompany me on my trips at night to keep me awake. We were like brothers. He also took me to restaurants I had never been in."[32]

So close were the two men, the Dodgers flew Grier from Vero Beach to Los Angeles for Gilliam's funeral. Grier remembered Gilliam as a quiet, noncontroversial figure. "He was very sensitive. He didn't interlude anywhere he didn't think he wasn't wanted,"[33] Grier told the *Palm Beach Post-Times* in October 1978.

James Mims, Jr. was another young Black man that Gilliam mentored. Mims lived about 10 minutes from Gilliam growing up and played Little League baseball with Darryl Gilliam. When Mims was 12 years old in 1975, he began working at Dodger Stadium, selling programs for commission. On an average night, Mims would take home $30-35. During the playoffs and World Series, he could make as much as $200 per game. While the money was nice, Mims was motivated more by the perk of watching the game after program sales died down.

To get to his "job," Mims occasionally took the bus, but mostly relied on his father, James Mims, Sr. to drop him off at the corner of Sunset Boulevard and Elysian Park Avenue (renamed Vin Scully Way in 2017), and James Jr. would walk up the hill to go to work.

One day in 1975, Mr. Gilliam, as Mims still calls him to this day, stopped and said, "You are a friend of my son. Hop in." Gilliam gave Mims a ride up the hill and asked him what he was doing at Dodger Stadium and how he got home. "You can ride home with me," Gilliam said. And so began a four-season friendship in which Gilliam would drive Mims to Gilliam's house after a baseball game, and James Mims, Sr. would pick him up there. James Sr. started a job at Dodger Stadium in 1980, working as a security officer outside the press box.

Mims remembers his car rides with Gilliam were never silent. They often replayed key moments of that day's game. Mims does not recall exactly which game it was, but he remembers Gilliam's frustrations one evening. "The conversation was always, 'if I were the manager,'" Mims recalled. "He would painstakingly break down the game. It was often way over my head as far as strategy."

Most nights, Gilliam was the first one to shower and leave the clubhouse in order to begin the 45-minute drive home with traffic. Mims would meet Gilliam at his car, a 1972 kelly green Cadillac Coupe DeVille with a white top, for the ride home. Gilliam did not use the player parking lot, opting instead to "park amongst the people."

"We would get in the car. He would start flying through the parking lot. People would try to stop and ask for an autograph, and he would just 'no, I'm trying to get home,'" Mims remembered. "It was never a quiet ride home. He would say things to me like, how did I do that night? After big games he would say, 'I know you have a pocket full of money tonight!'"

In the 1980s and 1990s, Mims founded Mimsbandz, a wristband business featuring the likeness of baseball players. He targeted Black major leaguers as customers, including Dusty Baker, Eric Davis, Barry Bonds, and more. The Mimsbandz that Baker wore during the 2022 World Series championship were sent to be displayed in Cooperstown.

17

"JUST SO I GET MY CHANCE"

As prominent Black players like Frank Robinson, Willie Mays, Roberto Clemente, Hank Aaron, and Ernie Banks approached the ends of their careers in the 1970s, conversation turned toward their potential as managers. This represented a Fourth Gate facing Black players: becoming a manager. Many column inches would be spent speculating as to who would be the first Black manager, and what team would be willing to hire a Black manager.

Writing in the July 1965 *Baseball Digest*, Sandy Grady intimated that, without evidence of from where the information came, Jim Gilliam, the Cardinals' Bill White, and the Yankees' Elston Howard had "been tabbed as managerial candidates."[1] Both Gilliam and Howard expressed interest in one day becoming a manager.

"It's bound to happen, just as it was bound to happen that Jackie Robinson or someone like him would break the color line in baseball," Gilliam told Grady. "Some day the right man will happen in the right situation to be a manager."[2] From that point forward, and for the better part of the next decade, the drumbeat about who would be baseball's first Black manager sounded in the media. The accompanying refrain, however, was always some version of the same song—when will baseball be ready?

"Very few clubs if any are ready for it," Bill Veeck told Grady. Veeck, the former owner of the Cleveland Indians and St. Louis Browns and future owner of the Chicago White Sox, had signed several former Negro Leagues stars, including Larry Doby, Satchel Paige, and Luke Easter.

"There would always be a segment of the population that would make a loud yell. Would players accept discipline from a Negro? I don't know. We may have to wait until we aren't so self-conscious about it."[3]

Timing would be everything, both for the team that hired a Black manager, and for the individual chosen to fill that role. An obvious former player to be the pioneering first Black manager might have been Jackie Robinson, whom Grady suggested "time passed by."[4]

After his retirement at the end of the 1956 season, Robinson sought to distance himself from baseball, and had become more vocal in his assessment of the role of Black players and their benefit to Major League teams. "Baseball uses the Negro to pack 'em in, but it doesn't care about the Negro when he's finished. I think they're as far behind as in 1946. Some say you can't hire a Negro manager because of the public image. What bull! There are certainly Negroes who are better spoken than some men managing today,"[5] Robinson told Grady.

Hank Aaron was as big a star as existed in baseball in October 1965. He had just completed the 1965 campaign with a .318 average, 32 home runs, 24 stolen bases, and a .938 OPS. *Sport* magazine approached Aaron with the idea of authoring a first-person story headlined, "Are you ready for a Negro manager? I could do the job." The story ran in the October issue, timed to hit newsstands around the Fall Classic between the Dodgers and the Minnesota Twins.

Aaron devoted much of the lengthy piece, co-authored by sportswriter Jerome Holtzman, lobbying for a shot to be the first Black manager in baseball. Toward the end, however, he offered his thoughts on who would be good managers, citing Jackie Robinson first and Bill White second. Immediately after his rationale for those two, Aaron commented on Gilliam. But, because Gilliam was not a standout player, Aaron stopped short of suggesting he possessed the right background to be a big-league manager.

"Why do I choose Jackie Robinson? Because he has the intelligence to cope with the different problems that I've been speaking about. The fact that he was the first Negro player in the majors wouldn't enter into it. He is the type of fellow who knows the game. He'd know how things should be run.

"So would Bill White. He can get along with all of the ballplayers, and this is the big thing that would be in his favor. He'd make a helluva manager and he'd make a helluva handball player. He'd make a good anything.

"Junior Gilliam would be another potential big-league manager. The Dodgers made him a coach this spring and this was supposed to be a big advance for the Negro in baseball. But do you know that no one ever mentioned this to me, white or Black. It was just a guy getting a job, keeping a guy who had done a lot for the organization.

"Gilliam wasn't a superstar and a lot of the things he was able to do he had to learn the hard way. He could teach others. He wasn't a natural."[6]

White, who would go on to become National League president, emphatically stated in 1965 he did not want a managerial job. "I don't want to stay in baseball. I see men sitting around lobbies looking for baseball jobs, great players once. I'd rather not depend on someone else for security."[7]

When he retired after the 1969 season as a member of the St. Louis Cardinals (White had spent the 1966-68 seasons with the Philadelphia Phillies), White was offered a position with the Cardinals' Triple-A team in Tulsa, but he turned it down. "By this time my family was settled in the Philadelphia area, and I just couldn't see myself managing a minor-league team until the Cardinals' front office saw fit to bring me up,"[8] he wrote in his autobiography.

While Major League Baseball slow-footed hiring a Black manager, the National Basketball Association embraced hiring a Black coach when Bill Russell of the Boston Celtics was hired as player-coach for the 1966-67 season. The agreement, announced in Boston on Patriots' Day 1966, was greeted with modest enthusiasm by the Boston media, tempered by the implied racism of the time.

Writing under the headline "Russell Quick, Alert, Sensitive" for the *Boston Globe*, columnist Roger Birtwell opined, "In the chill hills of ancient Sparta, they left their young to live or perish. Only the strong survived. From this came a physically superior band of men. From the jungles they'd inhabited for centuries, our American forbears took African natives by force....Only the strong survived. Have our slave-traders and slave holders of the past produced a physically superior race?

"And now for the first time in the history of our democracy—in one of the major professional sports which are a product of our economic success —a descendant of slaves will have complete charge of a team. Bill Russell —quick, alert, sensitive—is the new coach of the Boston Celtics."[9]

Reading that some 55-plus years later it is easy to see how Birtwell is positioning Russell as, in some ways, the opposite of the "physically superior band of men" taken from the "jungles" to work as slaves in the United States. While a star athlete, Russell was also "sensitive," a trait reinforced through select quotes from Russell's teammates regarding his leadership abilities. "He's very determined to further himself in life. Without basketball, he would have had the same attitude. His life hasn't been a bed of roses. He's as much of a fighter for himself and for his team as I have ever met,"[10] said teammate John Havlicek, a white player who attended Ohio State University.

Havlicek's description could represent any number of groundbreaking Black athletes of the era. Jackie Robinson could certainly make a case he was determined to further his life, even though it wasn't a bed of roses. Boston has a troubled history with integration in baseball. The Red Sox passed on signing Robinson in 1945 despite a tryout at Fenway Park, and they were the last team to integrate when Pumpsie Green finally suited up for Boston on July 21, 1959, more than 12 years after Robinson debuted for the Dodgers.

Aram Goudsouzian, author of the 2010 book, *King of the Court: Bill Russell and the Basketball Revolution*, noted that Russell did not believe his skin color was a factor in his hiring. Robinson broke into a white-only league. Russell competed alongside many Black players. Goudsouzian highlighted a Russell quote in Milton Gross' column from the same issue of the *Boston Globe* as evidence.

"This doesn't even come close to the Robinson case," Russell said. "At that time there were no Negroes in any big-league sports. Now there are so many you don't even know who they are. But this is part of the thing Robinson did. It is part of the same story. Now maybe there will be some more Negro coaches and managers in sports."[11]

It would be nearly a decade before baseball hired a Black manager. The question as to why it took so long would be asked repeatedly.

"WHY?"

Associated Press writer Mike Rathet took advantage of the mundane nature of 1969's spring training to write an article asking essentially a one-word question, "why?"—as in why were there no Black managers in base-ball. He offered three commonly heard reasons as rationale: 1) no Black person was qualified; 2) the time isn't right; and 3) discrimination.

Bill Russell had led the Celtics to the 1968 NBA title and in the process of repeating in 1969. Clearly, Blacks were qualified to lead sports teams.

Frank Robinson, star of the Baltimore Orioles, stole the headlines from the story saying, "There's only one reason a Negro has never been a manager—his color. The reason there hasn't been a Negro manager is that no one has ever given a Negro manager chance to be one."[12]

"Chance" would become the definitive word over the next decade.

Who would get the chance, and what team would give that person the chance?

Rathet noted there were four Black coaches at the time: Elston Howard of the Yankees, Satchel Paige of the Braves, Ossie Virgil of the Giants, and Gilliam. Rathet interviewed Howard, Paige, and Gilliam, and the general theme was not lack of qualification or timing, but blatant discrimination.

Not one to make controversial statements or take a public stand on social issues, Gilliam's response to Rathet expressed both honesty and frustration, without mentioning discrimination. "It has to be the color of the skin—because no owner has been ready yet. There definitely have been qualified men, but the owners aren't ready.

"The players are ready. I've worked with young players and when you work with them, it's just a matter of them getting to respect your ability. There wouldn't be any problems with the players. I see where they're taking it pretty good in basketball now."[13]

When asked about his personal aspirations to be a manager, Gilliam replied, "I've been in this game for 22 years. This is all I've ever done and all I ever wanted to do. I'm 39 and not ready to retire, but I don't want to be a coach all my life."

All three felt the day would come, and soon, when a Black man would be named a Major League manager. And while no one interviewed used the word discrimination, Rathet noted, both Robinson and Gilliam discussed skin color.

Rathet's story even struck a chord with, of all places, the middle of rural America. On Monday, March 17, 1969, the editorial staff of the *Times-Democrat* newspaper, serving the Quad Cities (Bettendorf and Davenport in Iowa, Rock Island, East Moline, and Moline in Illinois[14]), offered its editorial space to the topic. Referring to the AP story that no Negro has been qualified or the time isn't ripe, the editorial staff openly questioned whether the time was "overripe."

"Given the chance, the Blacks surely could operate ably at the top as they clearly have in lesser roles, and as the great Bill Russell has in professional basketball in guiding the Boston Celtics. It's hard to buy the contention that no Negroes have been qualified. Or that the time isn't ripe. As Gilliam contended, the barrier has to be skin color. No doubt, Negroes eventually will manage in the big leagues. Why not now?"[15]

"Why not now?" was a fair question. As Major League managerial jobs opened, teams bypassing potentially qualified Black candidates were frequently scrutinized in the media. John Roseboro, a long-time teammate of Gilliam's, coached with the Washington Senators in 1971 and with the

California Angels from 1972 to 1974. He wrote in his autobiography of the frustration facing Black players after retirement.

"If you're a white Christian, welcome to the club. The good guys get the good jobs up front while Blacks like Larry Doby, Willie Mays, Monty (sic) Irvin, Jim Gilliam, Jackie Robinson, Henry Aaron, Ernie Banks, and many more get paid off to stay on the sidelines, in the shadows, and do as they're told. If you're white you can be in baseball all your life, but if you're Black the time comes when you're just an ex-ballplayer."[16]

A FORGOTTEN MAN

As the 1971 baseball season wound down, baseball was no closer to hiring a Black manager than it had been before the season started. No more accurate headline could have been written in October 1971 when *Black Sports* magazine dubbed Gilliam "Baseball's Forgotten Man." Brad Pye, the long-time *Los Angeles Sentinel* writer, described Gilliam as "patient" and "quiet" when it came to Gilliam's managerial aspirations.[17] The article ran the same month as Gilliam celebrated his 43rd birthday, hardly too old to be named a manager. Yet, Gilliam's comments in the article suggested a resignation of sorts that his window to becoming a major-league manager might, in fact, be closing.

"I would like to manage if the opportunity presents itself. I don't know if I will ever get the chance, but I would like to," Gilliam said. "I think that baseball people know a man by his ability. Like I have always said, I don't care about being a pioneer, just so I get my chance."[18]

Gilliam remained pensive about his managerial prospects while speaking with Pye. "I can't say if it will be in the Dodger organization or what organization. I know Maury's (Wills) been in winter ball managing; Frank Robinson has been in winter ball for 20 years or more. I have been in this game, as I said, for 25 years. I have played it for about 18 or 19 years. I've been a coach for the last five years. And I have been under some good managers. If I don't know something about this game now, I will never know anything about it."[19]

Jim's tenure as a full-time Dodgers coach to that point, 1967 to 1971, was the club's most disappointing stretch since World War II. The club was in the middle of a seven-year postseason drought, finishing a distant 8th in the National League standings in 1967 and seventh in 1968. Expansion in 1969 and the division of the National League into East and West coincided with changed fortunes, as the Dodgers rose to West division runners-up each year from 1970 to 1973, before finally winning the West in 1974.

The Dodgers' longtime manager Walter Alston managed the club on a series of one-year contracts beginning in 1954. He and Gilliam had a trust, a friendship, dating back to Gilliam's first season in the Dodgers organization, 1951 with the Montreal Royals.

Always the company man, Alston, who turned 60 in December 1971, walked the middle of the road when it came to speculating on Gilliam's prospect to be a manager. "I'm sure Mr. Gilliam knows as much about baseball as any of the guys you mentioned. I think the problem is, how well you can get this knowledge over to your players too; that's something else. A guy can know a lot and not be able to pass it on to the other players. He's kind of a quiet sort of fellow. But I think Gilliam can do that,"[20] said Alston.

But Alston stopped short of suggesting Gilliam, with whom he had a relationship for nearly two decades, should be his replacement once he was ready to retire. "I don't think Gilliam would have any trouble getting along with anybody. I've worked with him 18 years here and a couple of years in the minor leagues and that's about 20 years Jim and I have been together. Certainly if there is anybody easy to get along with, it's Junior Gilliam. It's hard to tell how they will react once they become managers. There is no way to predict that. We will just have to wait, but there is no question that the guys you mentioned could do that job."[21]

By continuing to lump Gilliam with "guys you mentioned"—players like Jackie Robinson, Ernie Banks, Willie Mays, Elston Howard, Hank Aaron, and Maury Wills—Alston was failing to flat-out endorse Gilliam as a manager. Perhaps these comments foreshadowed the 1976 decision to hire another Dodger organization lifer, Tommy Lasorda, to replace Alston in 1977.

COMPETING AGAINST A TEAMMATE

In addition to the challenge of convincing a white baseball owner to hire a Black manager, the normally quiet Gilliam found himself competing against a longtime teammate, one with whom he did not always get along, for the privilege. Maury Wills was aggressively campaigning for a managerial role. In its January 9, 1971 issue, *The Sporting News* devoted nearly two full pages and multiple pictures to Wills' interest in becoming a Major League manager and his experience managing the Hermosillo Naranjeros in Mexican winter ball.

Dodgers vice president Al Campanis was given credit for getting Wills, still the Dodgers everyday shortstop, the winter-ball managerial gig—

something Gilliam had not been afforded, despite his five years as the Dodgers first-base coach. "You can't tell much just by following a manager for a few games," Campanis said. "But you already know that Wills knows the game and is a remarkably keen student. He seems to like it in Mexico, and the fans certainly like him. This experience will give him an idea of what managing is all about."[22] Given Campanis' stature with the Dodgers, one would think he had the ability to influence who received opportunities to manage teams in winter ball.

Wills unabashedly lobbied for the position to succeed Alston as Dodgers manager, stating simply, "I want to be the first Black manager in the major leagues. If Alston manages another five years, which I sincerely hope he does, I'll play another five years."[23]

The timing of Wills' comments, possibly coupled with the rather pedestrian finishes of the Dodgers in 1968 and 1969, led team president Peter O'Malley to downplay speculation that Alston may be forced out. "We haven't considered Maury—or anybody else, for that matter—for the Dodger managerial job. It's Walter Alston's as long as he wants it. Our staff is watching Maury's handling of the Hermosillo team very carefully. We will have a better opportunity to evaluate his managerial potential after he has run a team over a full schedule."[24]

That Gilliam was no longer mentioned as a possible first Black manager was telling, given that Wills was still an active player and Gilliam had been serving as a coach. Perhaps this was another instance where Gilliam's quiet demeanor worked against him.

Two months later, *The Sporting News* devoted far less space, and no pictures, to a small portion of a Dodgers notes column with the meager headline, "Gilliam Wants to Manage." Two columns to the left on page 52 of the March 13, 1971 issue was a larger story with a bolder headline: "Doby Climbing Toward His Goal of Skipper Job." Montreal Expos coach and former Negro League and Cleveland Indians star Larry Doby had just been named the team's hitting coach, and was already aiming for a managerial role.

Ross Newhan quoted the ever-optimistic Gilliam, "If I'm not the first, then I'll be the second or the third or the fourth. When baseball is ready to hire a Black manager, it won't stop at one."[25] In 1971, Black players and newspaper reporters had been enabling Major League Baseball to hide behind the "when it is ready excuse" for more than six years since the Henry Aaron *Sport* magazine article. Gilliam likely felt trapped between his desire to be a manager, and his quiet, behind-the-scenes personality. He was not the type of person, like Wills, to openly campaign for the position and potentially force the issue in baseball.

"No, it doesn't bother me," Gilliam told Newhan when asked about all of the publicity given to Wills and others. "Although I think I may be better prepared than any of the others. I've been in baseball for over 25 years and during that time I haven't just gone through the motions. I've studied and applied myself. I know I'll get the chance and I'll be ready."[26]

The competition between Wills and Gilliam persisted, eventually reaching a boiling point during spring training in 1973. Wills, who had retired and become a television analyst for NBC that summer, was interviewed by Pittsburgh radio broadcaster Bob Prince for NBC in Bradenton, Florida. Prince asked Wills about Black managers, and specifically about the prospect of Gilliam, his long-time teammate, as the first Black manager.

"Gilliam knows the game, but he doesn't have the ability to lead 25 players,"[27] Wills responded. Wills went on to say that he felt he had the qualities to manage but did not believe a club would hire him. He predicted that Alston would retire at the end of 1973 and be replaced by Tommy Lasorda, an action that would indeed occur, but not until the end of the 1976 season.

The *New York Daily News* elaborated on the context of the question, quoting Prince, "Wills said, 'No way.' Then we broke for a commercial and as I was shaking my head, we came back and Maury explained that 'Gilliam has the knowledge of the game but he doesn't have the leadership ability.'"[28]

Nearly a week transpired before the interview found its way into the *Los Angeles Times*, with a quote from an obviously hurt and confused Gilliam. "I don't see how he could say that. I was a leader as a player. I have never been a softy. It is my job as a coach to follow orders, not give them."[29]

Indeed, Dick Tracewski, who played in the same infield as both Wills and Gilliam from 1962 to 1965, suggested decades later that it was Gilliam who was the club's leader. "He was a complete player who could do it all. In a lot of ways he was the leader of our club. Quiet guy that made the final decision on a lot of different things. Jim Gilliam was the ultimate professional and he commanded a lot of respect from every player."

Pittsburgh Courier columnist Bill Nunn, Jr. defended Gilliam in his May 12, 1973 column, stating, "Because he's the kind of man he is, Junior Gilliam, a coach with the Dodgers, won't comment on the slap Maury Wills made about his ability to manage in the major leagues. Gilliam feels, however, that if he gets the chance to manage in the majors he could do the job. A lot of players feel the same way."[30]

Writing in *How to Steal a Pennant*, the second of his three autobiographies (this one published in 1976), Wills stated his desire to be a manager, noting it "has little to do with the color of my skin....How qualified am I? I know I'm certainly as qualified as any of the people whose names have appeared in the paper as managerial material, either Black or white."[31]

After mentioning Tommie Aaron, Larry Doby, Tom Lasorda, and Jim Gilliam, Wills wrote, "All are good men, yes, and as I compare our individual qualifications and backgrounds, I have to say I'm as good as any of them."[32]

Wills eventually got his managerial "chance" in 1980 when the Seattle Mariners named him to replace Darrell Johnson on August 4, with the team mired in a nine-game losing streak, eventually stretching to 12 straight losses. Wills finished with a 20-38 record as manager in 1980, enough to warrant being invited back for 1981. But, after getting off to a 6-18 start, Wills was dismissed, and his managerial career was over with a .313 winning percentage. As a manager, he was mostly remembered for his mistakes, such as calling for a relief pitcher without anyone warming in the bullpen.[33]

After Gilliam had passed away, Wills attempted to downplay any direct controversy, telling Dave Nightingale, "The only reason Frank (Robinson) and I were mentioned more as candidates for that first job was that we were more controversial."[34]

JACKIE'S FINAL WISH

During the Dodgers' Old-Timers' Day on June 4, 1972, the club retired the first three numbers in franchise history: Sandy Koufax's number 32, Roy Campanella's number 39, and Jackie Robinson's number 42, an event that also happened to recognize the 25th anniversary of Robinson breaking baseball's color barrier.

Four months later, on Sunday, October 15, 1972, bright sunshine splashed down from the sky onto the artificial turf of Riverfront Stadium in Cincinnati. It was shortly before one in the afternoon, and Game Two of the World Series, between the Oakland Athletics and the Cincinnati Reds, was set to begin. Robinson and his entire family stood on the green synthetic turf, just in front of the tan dirt circle marking the pitching mound. Red Barber, voice of the Brooklyn Dodgers when Robinson broke the MLB color barrier 25 years earlier in 1947, served as a master of ceremonies for an event to honor Robinson's legacy.

Robinson was to be introduced by Commissioner Bowie Kuhn, who would present Robinson with a plaque commemorating the 25-year anniversary of Robinson breaking the MLB color barrier. Robinson was to say a few remarks and throw out the ceremonial first pitch. No one would know it at the time, of course, but this appearance at the World Series would be the last public appearance, and the last public remarks, for Robinson.

As Kuhn welcomed Robinson to the microphone, Robinson used the opportunity to further express his thoughts on baseball still not having an African-American manager. "Thank you very much, Mr. Commissioner. I am extremely proud and pleased to be here this afternoon, but must admit I will be tremendously more pleased and more proud when I look at that third-base coaching line one day and see a Black face managing in baseball."[35]

Reflecting on that 1972 World Series ceremony 15 years prior, Kuhn wrote in his memoir, "Hiring Blacks for front-office jobs has proven difficult for baseball, due to the combination of a certain amount of management reluctance, the unwillingness of former Black players to accept management salary levels and the reluctance of qualified Blacks to take front-office jobs."[36] Kuhn's comments 15 years after Robinson passed away merely recycled the same talking points used in the early 1970s before a Black manager had been hired.

Jackie Robinson passed away in an ambulance en route to Stamford Hospital in Connecticut on the morning of October 24. His funeral was held at noon on October 27 at Riverside Church on 122nd Street in New York City. Reverend Jesse Jackson delivered the eulogy to approximately 2,500 mourners, including much of the baseball establishment. Robinson's biographer, Arnold Rampersand, reported that Bill Veeck, Larry Doby, Henry Aaron, Roy Campanella, Hank Greenberg, and Peter O'Malley were all in attendance.

Robinson's coffin, silver-blue and adorned with red roses, was carried out of Riverside Church by six former athletes: Bill Russell of the Boston Celtics, and Brooklyn teammates Don Newcombe, Joe Black, Ralph Branca, Pee Wee Reese, and Jim Gilliam.[37] Said Gilliam to the Los Angeles Times on the day Robinson passed, "He was one of the greatest all-around athletes I have ever known on any athletic field. I was very close to him, and I learned a great deal from him on the field and off. We're all very sad."[38]

In his eulogy, Jesse Jackson suggested Robinson "turned a stumbling block into a stepping stone."[39] An interpretation of this visualization is that Robinson used a stumbling block, the First Gate of integration, as a stepping stone for Blacks in baseball. In his final public appearance two weeks earlier, Robinson had talked about the final stumbling block, or gate, having a Black manager in baseball. Unfortunately, he would never get to see it.

SAN JUAN 1973

Gilliam finally received a chance to manage during the winter of 1973-74, returning to the islands to pilot the San Juan Senadores of the Puerto Rican Winter League. The Senadores were a charter member of the Puerto Rican league, dating back to 1938-39. Hall of Famers Roy Campanella, Monte Irvin, and Roberto Clemente had all played for the San Juan franchise, while Clemente also managed the club in the 1960s and 1970s. In 1962, the Senadores moved into newly built Estadio Hiram Bithorn, which would eventually host many Major League games and serve as a partial home for the Montreal Expos in 2003 and 2004. The Senadores moved west after the 1973-74 season and became the Bayamón Vaqueros (Cowboys) for the 1974-75 season, where they stayed until returning to San Juan in 1983-84.

Gilliam inherited a team long on Major League experience, but short on star power. Four members of the Cleveland Indians, the last-place team in the 1973 American League East, highlighted the roster: Chris Chambliss, Rusty Torres, Charlie Spikes, and Tom Hilgendorf. Montreal Expos pitchers Balor Moore and Tom Walker, Dodgers second baseman Lee Lacy, Milwaukee Brewers catcher Eliseo Rodríguez, Pittsburgh Pirates infielder Jackie Hernández, and veteran pitcher Orlando Peña made up the core of the roster. For Chambliss, the experience also served as his honeymoon following his wedding during the 1973 season.[40]

Hilgendorf became one of Gilliam's trusted golf partners, playing with PGA star Chi Chi Rodriguez at the Dorado Beach Hotel. When Dodger broadcasters Vin Scully and Jerry Doggett were in Puerto Rico, Hilgendorf and Gilliam would golf with them as a foursome at an exclusive resort, El Conquistador.[41]

Gilliam's baseball knowledge and ability to relate to all players, regardless of position or race, was evident to the team right away. "He didn't say a whole lot. He expected and wanted your best. Had a way of drawing it out of you," Walker recalled. "He was in tremendous physical shape. He would get out and work out with the team, take ground balls on the infield, throw batting practice. It was like he could still play, though he didn't."

While he wasn't a pitcher, Gilliam still aided pitchers by helping them with something he knew well: baserunning. "One thing I remember him working with me on was keeping runners closer at first base. He mentioned things to look for, like the runner getting jumping or looking across the diamond at coaches. He helped me get quicker in the set position, and encouraged me to throw over to first more," Walker said. "I ended up picking a couple guys off."

Early in the season, on November 25, San Juan was hosting the Ponce Lions for a Sunday afternoon doubleheader. The first game was scheduled for nine innings, with the second game shortened to seven innings. Balor Moore, scheduled to start the opener, showed up at Hiram Bithorn Stadium sick.

Prior to meeting Gilliam, Moore knew the reputation of Dodgers players. "You could always recognize Dodgers. They just had a little more class. They wore alpaca sweaters and white shoes," Moore recalled. "I was young (in Puerto Rico) and I didn't know who Junior was. I knew he was credited with helping Maury Wills get all of those stolen bases. I had heard he had taken strike three so Wills could steal and asked him about that. He said 'No way I would take strike three. I would take a strike, but not strike three.'"

Moore, a left-hander, had struggled in 1973 with Montreal, going 7-16 as a starter with 109 walks and 151 strikeouts in 176 innings. Even though he was employed by a rival team during the season, Gilliam did not shy away from helping the 22-year-old Moore.

"Junior said to me, 'You've got stuff like I have never seen before, and I have seen Sandy (Koufax). I'm going to call Sandy and get him down here.' It never happened. It was not the help I needed at the time. But the fact he was willing to do that meant a lot," Moore recalled.

On November 25, 1973, Moore, despite the illness, did not need Koufax's help. Gilliam had told Moore, "Oh my God. You look horrible. One inning at a time. If you start looking worse you are coming out."

Inning after inning, Moore retired the Ponce batters, including future All-Stars José Cruz and Phil Garner. Through six innings, San Juan held a 5-0 lead. Moore, throwing mostly fastballs, had retired all 18 batters. But, Moore was laboring, "I went in the tunnel between innings, where it was dark and cool. Junior would put a cold, wet towel on me."

Still, going into the ninth inning, Moore had retired all 24 batters. He was three outs from a perfect game. Garner opened the inning by flying to

Spikes in left field. Moore faced Edwin Pacheco, who would log 4,770 minor-league at-bats without ever appearing in a Major League game. Moore struck him out, his ninth. The final batter was Chicago Cubs utility infielder David Rosello, and Moore induced him to fly to right field. He needed just 81 pitches, 72 fastballs and nine curveballs, to record a perfect game.

"Hal Breeden, my teammate in Montreal, said to me, 'I kind of knew what was coming but it didn't matter. No one was going to hit it that day,'" Moore said.

Gilliam had now participated as a player, coach, or manager in nine no-hitters, including three perfect games. He would witness a 10th no-hitter on August 9, 1976, when John Candelaria of the Pirates no-hit the Dodgers, 2-0.

Despite the lack of recognizable names, and Gilliam's lack of managerial experience, San Juan fared well, finishing 36-34, good for third place. "It wasn't a good team, but he got us to make the playoffs. He was a good man, very knowledgeable. He got along with everyone, and he knew how to get the players to respond," Rodríguez said nearly 40 years later.

The Senadores lost in the semifinals to Caguas Criollos, four games to two. Caguas fielded future MLB Hall of Famers Mike Schmidt and Gary Carter and won the finals and the 1974 Caribbean Series. Among the teams Caguas dispatched in the Caribbean Series were the Dominican Republic's Licey Tigres, managed by Tom Lasorda.

"I think he could have been a good manager. He knew the game. He gained players' respect and got them to believe in themselves. That takes a special leader," Walker said. "There is no doubt in my mind that he could have been a significant manager in the Major Leagues if he had been given the chance."

The chance.

FRANK ROBINSON'S CHANCE

By the time the dog days of summer arrived in 1974, baseball still did not have a Black manager. This time it was sportswriter Gary Libman's turn to ask "why?" for the Associated Press, which he did in a nationwide article on Sunday, August 4. The protagonists in this story were largely the same as in Rathet's story five years earlier and Aaron's *Sport* magazine story a decade earlier. Names like Robinson, Aaron, Banks, Howard, Doby, Wills, and Gilliam all resurfaced. But Libman's article presented a new twist to the narrative: the Major League executive who asked that his name not be used. "How many Blacks have agreed to go down and manage in the minor leagues?" the executive asked. "The tendency among Blacks is to want to make the jump to the majors right away. But the old way of taking guys right off the playing field...that's not the practice anymore."[42]

That the unnamed executive believed a "tendency" existed among Black players to want to go directly to the majors demonstrated an implicit bias given that, to that point, no Black player had gone straight from playing to managing. Furthermore, the executive tried to rationalize why Blacks did not want to go to the minors, using the California Angels as a comparison. The Angels began the season with Bobby Winkles, a white man born in Arkansas who had built Arizona State into a college baseball power in the 1960s, as manager.

To the unnamed executive, this was all about compensation. "If you take a guy like Bobby Winkles and a Frank Robinson, what do you think they're paying Robinson? If they made Robinson manager he'd have to take a big pay cut, and I doubt he'd do that."[43]

Robinson's response to the nonsensical and inherently racist compensation quote was, "It would be ridiculous to think I am going to step out as a player and make as much as a manager. It took me 19 years to make this much as a player."[44]

Midway through September, the Angels traded Robinson, along with pitcher Ken Suarez and cash, to the Cleveland Indians for Rusty Torres. Robinson appeared on CBS's *Face the Nation* on October 13, 1974, 10 days after Indians' general manager Phil Seghi named Robinson player-manager of the Cleveland Indians for the 1975 season.[45]

Answering a question from Jack Whitaker, Robinson stated, "Every time a job would open up, my name would pop up in the papers that I would be considered for the job along with Maury Wills, Elston Howard, people like that, Larry Doby. But nothing ever happened."[46]

Whitaker inquired if that was a frustration for him. "Yes it was. Not only just for me, but for Black people period. They would tell you, 'There was no qualified Blacks around.' That was ridiculous as far as I was concerned. You don't really know if someone can manage in the major leagues or any place else until he is given an opportunity."[47]

After Robinson began as manager of the Indians, Gilliam was talking to Dick Young of the *New York Daily News* on the Dodger bench. "What happened to Doby?" Gilliam asked Young, inquiring about Larry Doby, a Cleveland coach passed over for the position.

"If you're asking what I think," Young replied. "They hired him to reach the Black ballplayers on the club, particularly George Hendrick, and they don't think he did it."

Gilliam was incredulous. "That's baloney. I'm the coach of all the players on this team, not just the Black players. It's one team. That's the only way you win."[48]

Robinson wrote in his autobiography published in 1988, "When I think of all the Black players who contributed so much to the game and then, with so much more to offer, left it only because they were given no chance to manage a team or work in a front office or even coach third base, I have serious doubts about the integrity of many of those who run our national pastime."[49]

ALSTON RETIRES

After managing the Dodger franchise for 23 years, Walter Alston retired on September 27, 1976, and conversations immediately turned to who would be appointed his replacement: third-base coach Tommy Lasorda or first-base coach Jim Gilliam? Lasorda's advantage, it appeared, was that he managed the core of the Dodger players in the minors. Steve Garvey, Davey Lopes, Ron Cey, Bill Russell, Steve Yeager, and more had competed for Lasorda.

Ross Newhan quoted Lopes in the *Los Angeles Times*: "Lasorda is the man most familiar with the players here, most qualified to take over. If someone else gets the job, it will be an injustice to Tommy Lasorda."

Lasorda and Gilliam were both quoted in the article, with both expressing a desire to serve in the role but both declining to name the other person. "Walt's retirement is a shock," Gilliam said. "I can't say enough about him. He has been wonderful to me. My father passed away when I was two years old. If there was anyone who took his place, who I envisioned my father being like, it was Walt.

"Do I want to manage? Yes, of course. The O'Malleys know where they can find me."[50]

Forty-five years later, Peter O'Malley admitted Lasorda had the inside track to the job. "Consideration was (given to Gilliam) but I can tell you Tommy was the leading candidate. It was never promised to Tommy. When he coached for Alston at the same time Jim did it was not promised to Tommy because of what he had done managing in rookie ball, AAA, and then a couple years coaching in the major leagues. So Tommy was the natural choice. I guess the honest answer is Tommy was the leading candidate," O'Malley said.

Two days later, on September 29, the Dodgers made it official, appointing Lasorda to become the team's first new manager since 1954.

Members of the 1970s Dodgers, most of whom had been managed by Lasorda in the minor leagues, agreed with the decision. "I think Tommy was well groomed for the position. He brought the nucleus of the players that represented the infield," said Ron Cey, the team's All-Star third baseman. "The Albuquerque team that we had in 1972, I think 10 of those players graduated to the Major Leagues the next year. As did Tommy as the third-base coach. I just felt that it was kind of in line. He had this relationship that was longer and deeper with us."

Doug Rau, a mainstay of the Dodgers rotation from 1973-79 and a member of that 1972 Albuquerque team, reinforced the narrative Lasorda was being groomed for the position. "It was obvious from the time Lasorda joined us in 1973 that he was pointing toward that job. He was talking about it really strong in '74," Rau said. "Given his relationship with Al Campanis—Tommy and Al knew talent. I think it was a foregone conclusion from conversations I heard."

When asked if he was disappointed in Lasorda getting the position, Gilliam, ever the company man, told the *Los Angeles Times*, "Not at all. I'm very happy for Tommy. We've been close for a long time. He's put in his dues. I still want to manage and this only means I will have to wait a little longer to get my chance."[51]

Lasorda took the reins with four games left in the 1976 season, a year the team finished second to the Cincinnati Reds. Gilliam coached the final four games from the third-base coach's box.

DISAPPOINTMENT IN 1977

Gilliam approached the 1977 season with a mixture of enthusiasm for the campaign ahead, but also a sense of disappointment that it was Lasorda and not him in the managerial role. He found himself, once again, playing the role of the company man in the Dodgers organization.

"I don't know if Jim would have wanted that position," said Ron Cey. "He seemed to be really comfortable doing what he was doing. I'm not real sure about that, if he was disappointed. Certainly he was a big asset to us and I think he fit in well where he did."

In fact, Jim did want at least the chance to manage, telling legendary sportswriter Hal McCoy of the *Dayton Daily News* in May 1977, "Sure I want to manage. I managed San Juan in the Puerto Rican League in 1974. I didn't have a very good club, we finished third. I satisfied myself that I can handle men. I'm very confident that I can do the job.[52]

"No, no...not even disappointed. Actually, Tommy has been in the organization longer than I have. He managed in the minors and handled most of the guys on the team somewhere along the line."[53]

While Gilliam was saying the right things publicly, in private the sentiment was mixed. In early 1977, Edwina and Jim celebrated their 18th wedding anniversary. She does not remember Jim being disappointed by not being offered the managerial role. "He never said he really wanted it, but he didn't say he didn't want it. I'm sure if he had been offered it he would have been happy to take it. That's all I can say. Jim never complained. He was glad when he was able to coach because baseball was his life," Edwina said.

"I'm sure he would have loved it (managing). I'm sure any baseball player would have liked to have a position like that. Probably had something to do with his race. Probably had something to do with his educational background. I really can't say."

Former Dodgers player and Major League manager Dusty Baker suggested Jim, despite his baseball knowledge, was indeed conscious about his educational attainment. "Jim was good with the press, but there were others who spoke better than he spoke. He didn't go for higher education. I think that impacted him," Baker said.

Most Major League managers today employ a bench coach, someone whose role is to assist with strategic thinking and advise the manager on decision making. Al Ferrara, who played with and for Gilliam on the Dodgers from 1963 to 1968, believed Gilliam would have been perfect for that role.

"Teams wanted fiery guys as managers. I believe Gilliam had a lot more baseball knowledge than Alston. He was always telling me about options in any given situation," Ferrara said. "He would have been an all-time bench coach. Winning was all he cared about."

COACHING SUCCESS

Lasorda took pride in elevating Jim to hitting coach, adding to his responsibilities as first-base coach, in 1977. He reportedly said, "Jim, all you've ever been around here is a first-base coach. I'm telling you right now, I want you to be my hitting coach. You know more about hitting than any of these sons of bitches we've ever had here. I played with you, I know it."[54]

Gilliam's first challenge was transforming catcher Steve Yeager back into a hitter. Yeager cemented his status as the team's top backstop during the 1974 season, hitting .266 with 12 home runs. But while the power remained each of the next two seasons, his average declined to .228 in 1975 and .214 in 1976.

Given the title of special consultant, Walter Alston was at Vero Beach in March when he was asked about Yeager. "If he listens to Jim Gilliam and hits the ball where it's pitched, he can hit .290 or even .300."[55]

For once, Lasorda was more reserved than Alston in his prediction. "He's one of our spring projects for Jim Gilliam, our batting instructor. Steve hit only .214 last year and I believe he can hit at least 30 points higher,"[56] Lasorda said after watching Yeager hit home runs in consecutive Grapefruit League games.

The advice apparently worked: Yeager began the season on a torrid pace, hitting safely in the first seven games he played. When April ended, Yeager had a .368 average, a 1.117 OPS, and 13 runs batted in. "I think what (Gilliam) said has sunk in," Yeager said. "I was swinging too hard, jumping at the ball. I can sometimes hear him yelling at me from the first-base coaching box with little reminders. If I can hit .270 with about 15 homers and 60 RBI, I will have a rewarding year...I might turn some people into believers."[57]

When the season concluded, Yeager had batted .256 with a career-high 16 home runs, and 55 runs batted in. Although Yeager would play through the 1986 season, his performance as a batter never came close to his 1977 season numbers.

1978 SEASON

As the 1978 season was set to begin, Gannett's *Florida Today* newspaper, published in Brevard County due north of Vero Beach, printed a non-bylined story profiling Gilliam at his 27th spring training in Vero. In describing the 49-year-old Gilliam, the article states, "He still looks like he could grab a bat and hit behind the runner like he did for 14 years. His weight is the same 180 pounds it's always been. The face is crisscrossed with the creases and wrinkles that accompany employment in the sun. But Gilliam just laughs at the thought and admits, 'I'm in shape to walk nine holes—barely.'"[58]

The profile served as a biographical introduction to the low-key Gilliam for those individuals not familiar with the Dodger coach. "Gilliam is not your basic dynamic personality. He's soft-spoken and wastes little energy when he gestures or talks. As a result he's always been overshadowed by some of his teammates and co-workers. Like Jackie Robinson and Maury Wills and, of course, Lasorda.

"'It's not that I'm not fiery or anything,' Gilliam says. 'It's just that I know when to talk and when to listen. Fellows like Jackie and Maury were always speaking for the team and I just never really bothered to pipe in.'"[59]

Reading the article nearly a half century later, it is difficult to not see the piece foreshadowing what would occur seven months later. The uncredited author asks Jim about his career, life at Dodgertown and race, the 1978 Dodgers team, and his aspirations.

"Oh sure, I always want to better myself. And I guess that means managing is the next step up. But I'm very happy doing what I do. And I'm content to wait until the opportunity comes along,"[60] Gilliam said.

Jim entered the 1978 season content, waiting, as always, for his chance.

At some point in the 1970s, Gilliam was prescribed blood pressure medicine by his doctors, though he did not like the physical side effects it caused. As a result, he was not consistent in taking it out of sight from his family. "I didn't know he wasn't taking it," his widow Edwina said. "I really wasn't aware that he had high blood pressure that bad. I had asked him about it and he said I get tested all the time at the ballpark. I'm ok. He never complained about blood pressure."

Gilliam did not cook. His daughter, Kathy, recalled a meal he prepared for her once consisting of hot dogs and beans. He did, however, like home-cooked meals, particularly soul food and meat. "He never cooked anything. He liked meat mostly. I don't know what he ate at the stadium. He just liked home-cooked food," Edwina said. Perhaps his eating habits contributed to his high blood pressure.

On September 15, Gilliam drove Dodger manager Tommy Lasorda to Dodger Stadium around 2 p.m., returning to his home on Valleydale Avenue.[61] The team was scheduled to open a home series against the Atlanta Braves that night and entered the game with a magic number of eight over second-place Cincinnati. Veteran Don Sutton was scheduled to start on the mound for Los Angeles on a night when the Dodgers might become the first team in Major League Baseball history to draw more than three million fans in home attendance in a single season. Why Gilliam returned home in the middle of the afternoon, when most players would arrive for pre-game routines, is not clear.

Nor is it clear when exactly Gilliam suffered a cerebral hemorrhage at his home or who found him and called in a medical emergency. Edwina was at work at the VA Medical Center in Brentwood. Yvette and Darryl were both in school. Kathy was living in Santa Barbara. Someone called Edwina—she does not remember who—and she immediately rushed south down the 405 from Brentwood to Daniel Freeman Hospital in Inglewood, where she found Jim in critical condition. Initial media reports listed the diagnosis as a stroke and labeled his condition as fair, but his condition quickly worsened.

Gilliam arrived at the hospital around 4:15 p.m. and shortly thereafter underwent surgery lasting close to midnight. He was then taken to the hospital's intensive care unit. The hospital switchboard reported receiving about one call per minute from friends and Dodger fans inquiring about Gilliam's condition.[62]

At Dodger Stadium, Lasorda called his team together to share the news about Gilliam. "I asked each of the players, in their own way, to pray for him,"[63] Lasorda said after the game. His troops performed admirably, winning the game 5-0. For Sutton, it was his 49th shutout as a Dodger pitcher, tying him with Don Drysdale for the most in team history. The crowd of 47,188 pushed the Dodger season attendance total to 3,011,368.

After the game, Sutton's reaction to the record-setting evening was understandably subdued. "I feel very fortunate to have pitched on a night when we have set an amazing record," he said. "But it was unfortunate Jim Gilliam was taken ill tonight because he was here long before I was. If it's possible, I would like to stand in for him and tell him how proud I am. This three million figure is something neither Jim nor I ever imagined possible."[64]

The report on Gilliam's condition the next day was not positive. By Saturday night, September 16, he had slipped into a coma. Larry Pilcher, a spokesman for the hospital, called his condition, "very critical and guarded."[65] Doctors expressed uncertainty about prospects for a recovery.

18

SAYING GOODBYE TO A BROTHER

THE *LOS ANGELES TIMES* RAN A BRIEF UPDATE ON JIM'S CONDITION EACH DAY from Monday, September 18, to Friday, September 22, which was to say there was no update to his condition. He remained in a coma and in critical condition, according to an unnamed spokesperson from Daniel Freeman Hospital in Inglewood. Edwina was staying at the hospital "off and on." After taking the weekend off, the paper printed an update on Monday, September 25, attributing to the unnamed hospital spokesman that Gilliam had neither improved nor deteriorated. "All we knew was the whole situation just came crashing down on us," remembered Ron Cey.

His condition was of interest outside of Los Angeles as well. Over the course of his life, Gilliam had acquired many friends in other sports as well as entertainment. World heavyweight boxing champion Muhammad Ali called to personally check on his status.[1]

Twenty-six-year-old Joseph Frank "Chico" Black was in his home in Phoenix on October 8 when he heard that Gilliam, his godfather, finally succumbed to the effects of his brain hemorrhage at 10:55 p.m., two days prior to the World Series between the Yankees and the Dodgers beginning at Dodger Stadium. Chico immediately called his father, Joe, Gilliam's longtime friend and teammate. "Uh oh," was all the older Joe Black could say before he became silent. "Call me later," he instructed his son. Two days later the two flew to Los Angeles to attend services.

Kathy Gilliam learned the news from the 11 p.m. evening news. Somehow, the information about her father's passing had made it from the hospital to the media in five minutes. His death was reported as front-page news in the *Los Angeles Times*, directly below a banner headline trumpeting overcrowded classrooms in Los Angeles schools.

"I don't think he ever changed," Walter Alston told Scott Ostler in the *Los Angeles Times*. "He was the same the first time I saw him as the last—a quiet, hard-working ballplayer and a great guy."[2]

Jim's death cast a pall over the entire Dodgers organization, but particularly in the clubhouse, where it was especially dark. "I don't recall a lot of conversation, players mourning internally. It just felt so wrong that he could be here in seemingly good health and then just gone. There were natural questions about how it could happen to him at that age, 49 as I recall. Jim had no known vices as I recall. It was just baffling to the players and his fellow coaches," remembered Los Angeles sportswriter Lyle Spencer. "I was personally devastated. We'd become close. I liked to sit with Jim on the team bus and he'd tell me about the great Negro League players, as Campy also did in the spring."

The Dodgers dedicated their division title and playoff series win against the Philadelphia Phillies to Gilliam. The team had black 19 patches sewn on the left sleeves of their jerseys in time for the start of the World Series.

"A lot of people think that is rah-rah stuff," Dodgers manager Tommy Lasorda said. "But we truly meant it when we dedicated those games to him."[3]

Gilliam's body was available for public viewing between 9 a.m. and 9 p.m. on Tuesday, October 10 at Angelus Funeral Home on South Crenshaw. That same night, 20 minutes north via Crenshaw Boulevard to the Santa Monica Freeway, east to the 110, and north through downtown Los Angeles, the Dodgers jumped all over their longtime nemesis, the Yankees, and won the opening game of the World Series, 11-5.

"GREATNESS AGAINST A HEADWIND"

October 11 dawned as a balmy fall day in Los Angeles. Early-morning fog gave way to midday sunshine, and temperatures reached the upper 80s. At 10 a.m. Pacific time, a little more than 12 hours after winning a baseball game, much of the Dodger baseball establishment filed into Trinity Baptist Church on West Jefferson Boulevard. Media estimates pegged the standing-room-only crowd at anywhere between 2,000 and 3,000 people, creating a stuffy environment where many took to hand fans to cool themselves. Traffic barriers closed streets for a block in any direction around the church.

In Loving Memory

Of

JAMES W. GILLIAM

WEDNESDAY, OCTOBER 11, 1978
10:00 A.M.

TRINITY BAPTIST CHURCH
2040 West Jefferson Boulevard
Los Angeles, California 90018

Reverend Jesse Jackson
Officiant

Interment
INGLEWOOD PARK CEMETERY

ANGELUS FUNERAL HOME
Directors in charge

Surviving members of the Brooklyn Dodgers poured in: Roy Campanella in his wheelchair, Duke Snider, Pee Wee Reese, Don Newcombe, Carl Erskine, Joe Black, and Walter Alston. So, too, did members of the current Dodgers, bleary-eyed after their Game One World Series victory over the Yankees the night before. Reggie Jackson represented the rivals, seated between Davey Lopes and Tommy Lasorda. Blue orchids covered a blue casket holding Gilliam's body. A "door-sized floral wreath" with the number 19 was displayed on an easel behind the casket, but the overall amount of flowers was modest; the family had requested contributions to a trust fund for the four children in lieu of flowers.[4]

Because national baseball writers were in town for the World Series, the throng of media covering the service was larger than would be normally expected. As a result, "the funeral was turned into a Hollywood media circus by the TV guys with their cameras and bright lights,"[5] wrote Billy Reed in the *Louisville Courier-Journal*. Dave Kindred, who feared the service might digress into a rallying cry for the Dodgers, described the scene in the *Washington Post* "as much a media event as a memorial, and yet, happily, dignity survived the assault."[6]

Joe Black, Gilliam's long-time friend and teammate in Baltimore, Montreal, and Brooklyn, spoke with high emotions. "They say a man ain't supposed to cry, but how do you say goodbye to a brother without crying?"[7]

Reverend Jesse Jackson, who had officiated at Jackie Robinson's funeral six years earlier, delivered an emotional and poignant eulogy built on the theme, "Greatness Against a Headwind."

"If you run downhill with the wind at your back, the time is unofficial. But if you run uphill, against the wind, the time is official, and it means much more. Jim Gilliam's life was against a headwind.

"His father died when he was six months old—headwind. His mother taught him how to play baseball with a stick and a rag ball—headwind. He rode the back of the bus and stayed in separate facilities from his teammates. He fought a double standard without a word of resentment. He was a first-class man and a second-class citizen—headwind.

"He would have been a manager when others had five or six shots. He should have been a manager. He had discipline, daring, and determination. But he was never a manager because of the color of his skin. No wonder he had an aneurysm. He had to smile to keep from crying—headwind.

"It is small wonder that Jim Gilliam died from internal bleeding. Any man who is denied the chance to achieve his best, who was to alter his dreams bleeds every day—headwind.

"There is no greater trauma than the death of a loved one. I said when I was young that I didn't want to preach funerals. But death is part of life. Not to know what death is, is to be immature. We die daily. Death says to the living, 'Get your house in order.' It brings unscheduled family reunions. It is an attention-getter. It says to neighbors, 'You're next.' Jim Gilliam still got to his base without having to slide."[8]

Order of Service

ORGAN PRELUDE .... Dr. Raleigh Bastine

PROCESSIONAL—"*Largo*" .... by Handel

SELECTION—"*My Hope Is Built*" .... by Church Choir

SCRIPTURE .... Reverend Richard Pate

PRAYER .... Reverend Richard Schleef

SELECTION .... Soloist, Ms. Pearl Whitlow
              "*I Did It My Way*"

ACKNOWLEDGMENTS

WORDS OF TRIBUTE:
    Mr. Tom Lasorda, Mr. Davey Lopes, Mr. Joe Black
    Mr. Walter Alston

SELECTION .... Soloist, Ms. Pearl Whitlow
           "*Suddenly There's A Valley*"

OBITUARY .... Mr. Don Newcombe

SELECTION .... Soloist, Ms. Pearl Whitlow
            "*I Know What God Is*"

EULOGY .... Reverend Jesse Jackson

RECESSIONAL—"*Come, Come Ye Saints*"

POSTLUDE .... Trumpet Voluntary by Purcell

Active Pallbearers

DAVEY LOPES - FRANK SMITH - PRESTON GOMEZ
HERMAN HENDRICKS - JOE BLACK - STEVE GARVEY
LEE LACY - SANDY KOUFAX

Honorary Pallbearers

Mr. Walter O'Malley	Mel Goode	James Crowder
Mr. Peter O'Malley	Don Drysdale	Pee Wee Reese
Los Angeles Dodgers	Cazzie Russell	Duke Snider
Baseball Club	Billy Eckstein	George Perry
Buzzie Bavasi	Dr. Wesley Groves	Al Durslag
Roy Campanella	Wes Parker	Jimmy DeVoe
Bill Russell	John Roseboro	

As powerful as Jackson's eulogy was, Erskine, who played with Gilliam from 1953-59, remembered the eulogy's focus was not on Gilliam's characteristics as a person, but rather on the systemic racism Gilliam faced in his life. "I remember the funeral vividly and Jesse Jackson. I thought he didn't give Jim enough credit in his eulogy."

Steve Garvey, a Dodger star first baseman in the 1970s, also believed Jackson's eulogy did not embody the person Gilliam was. "(Jackson) said that Jim Gilliam, throughout his life, had always been challenged. Because of his race, he had trouble achieving his goals, that it was a constant struggle," Garvey wrote in 1986. "I could have misinterpreted this, but I don't think I did. And I don't think Gilliam felt that way....That image of walking against the wind, that might be apt for some—probably it was for Jackie Robinson—but I don't think it fit Jim."[9]

Gilliam's personality did not lend itself to attracting attention. He did not grab headlines or campaign for anything during his career. Sure, he stated he would like to manage when asked by reporters, but he did not seek out platforms to lobby for change against any of the headwinds he encountered: losing his father, the education system, the segregated restaurants and hotels, or the challenge of becoming a manager.

His widow, Edwina, said this was who he was. "Jim didn't talk that much. He was very, very quiet," she said. "He was ecstatic to be with the Dodgers. He loved the Dodgers.

"He was a good father. A good husband. He was a very self-sacrificing ballplayer. He would do anything for the team. If somebody was on base and they needed somebody to move him to another base, he would sacrifice his own self for that. He contributed a lot. I think he was the best team player they ever had. He never really had the credit he deserved, I don't think."

Gilliam was universally liked by people he encountered, whether they were teammates, coaches, executives, or players he coached. "He was a good friend. I was pleased to play with Jim. He was very popular," Erskine remembered fondly.

Nate "Pee Wee" Oliver recalled the role Gilliam played in passing on the legacy of Jackie Robinson:

"Jim was like Jackie was to everyone else. He was the chosen mentor to us. We would get the same treatment that he had. There were a number of things he was responsible for in my development. He was one of the smartest players in baseball."

After the service, Gilliam's casket was carried out of the church to the waiting hearse to be transported to Inglewood Park Cemetery five miles to the southwest. Dodgers Davey Lopes, Lee Lacy, and Steve Garvey were pallbearers, as were former Dodgers Sandy Koufax and Black, along with fellow coach Preston Gómez. A good friend of Jim and Edwina's, Herman Hendricks, was also a pallbearer, as was Frank Smith, another of Jim's friends from Los Angeles. The long list of honorary pallbearers included Walter and Peter O'Malley, the Los Angeles Dodgers Baseball Club, Buzzie Bavasi, Campanella, Snider, Reese, Don Drysdale, John Roseboro, Wes Parker, jazz musician Billy Eckstine, PGA golfer Jimmie DeVoe, Gilliam family physician Dr. Wesley Grove, and NBA stars Bill Russell and Cazzie Russell. The list also included Mel Durslag of the *Los Angeles Herald-Examiner*; television journalist Mel Goode; James Crowder, a tenant of the duplex Gilliam owned on Redondo Boulevard; and George Perry, a friend of Jim's who Edwina did not know well.

"I remember clasping the handle of the casket and walking it out of the church," Garvey wrote in his autobiography in 1986. "I felt sad, because I wanted there to be some kind of gesture praising Gilliam and how he had lived his life. The Dodgers wore black armbands, and that was nice, but it wasn't enough....He was a man who loved competition and the outdoors —especially golf. That was what we should have done, created the Jim Gilliam Golf Tournament. But we didn't."[10]

Inglewood Park Cemetery dates back to 1905 and was originally advertised as the largest cemetery in the world. Today, it's billed as the "Soul of the City of Angels" and serves as the eternal resting spot for dozens of prominent celebrities, entertainers, and athletes, many of them Black. Former Los Angeles mayor Tom Bradley is buried there. Musicians Ray Charles, Etta James, Billy Preston, and Ella Fitzgerald are buried there, as are baseball stars Curt Flood, Lyman Bostock, Jr., and Sam Crawford. Bostock's father, Lyman Sr., played against Gilliam in the Negro Leagues from 1946-1949. Bostock, Jr., an outfielder with the California Angels, was tragically shot and killed in Gary, Indiana on September 23, 1978, eight days after Gilliam collapsed at his home.

Jim was laid to rest in Grave #10, Lot 58, Miramar Plot. His headstone reads simply, "In Loving Memory, Jim Gilliam, 1928-1978."

At around 5:27 p.m. on October 11, John Ramsey, the public address announcer at Dodger Stadium, introduced the starting lineups prior to Game Two, seven short, emotion-filled hours after Gilliam's funeral service began. Just as he had done the previous night before Game One, the announcer asked the fans to rise and respect a moment of silence "in memory of Dodger great Jim Gilliam, for whom this World Series is dedicated." The crowd of 55,982 spectators dutifully stood, removed their caps, and stared either at their feet or the flagpoles in center field, where flags flew at half staff. Television viewers had their screen filled with a picture of a smiling Gilliam in his Dodger blue hat and white uniform. Unlike prior to Game One, when an airplane could be heard overhead during the moment of silence, Dodger Stadium fell completely still for 26 seconds. It was a fitting tribute for a man whose nickname sounded imposing, Devil, but who lived quietly in the shadows of his teammates.

NUMBER 19

During Gilliam's funeral service, Don Newcombe announced the Dodgers would bury the number 19 with Gilliam. No one would wear the number in Dodger blue again, unless his son Darryl, then 14, would make the team. Fred Claire joined the Dodgers front office in 1969, working in public relations, before eventually becoming general manager in 1987 after Al Campanis' ill-fated racist remarks on ABC News's *Nightline* got him dismissed.

Claire remembers making the decision about Gilliam's number with Peter O'Malley, then the owner of the Dodgers, and other executives. "It was not a detailed discussion. We decided without calling upon anyone but our thoughts that it was an appropriate way to remember the passing of a great player and what he meant."

O'Malley remained steadfast in his decision to retire Gilliam's number. "It was a no-brainer. He never played for anybody else. We signed him. He played. He coached. And sadly he passed away. To recognize Jim for what he meant to the organization even though he was not being considered for the Hall of Fame. To me, that was enough criteria to make it happen. So I totally take responsibility for that and I am proud of it."

Writing in the *Los Angeles Times* on October 13, two days after Gilliam's funeral, columnist Jim Murray wrote that Gilliam was his all-time favorite athlete. Remarking on the black number 19 patches the Dodger players and coaches wore during the World Series, Murray opined, "It is not a reminder to win. It is a reminder to play well, to play fair and do your best at all times. The number '19' has always stood for that on the Dodgers. The number '19' has stood for a man who was my friend, your friend, base-ball's friend, humanity's friend—an American, a major leaguer, a class act all the way."[11]

No one objected at the moment, but time has a funny way of changing opinion about certain historical events. In October 1978, only Jackie Robin-son, Roy Campanella, Sandy Koufax, and Walter Alston had their Dodger numbers retired. Three of those—Robinson, Campanella, and Koufax—occurred at a ceremony in 1972. Alston's was retired in 1977, the year after he stepped down from managing. "I think the decision to retire his number needs to be evaluated in context. Jim Gilliam was a Dodger Hall of Fame-type player. I was pleased the decision was made at the time," Claire said.

Today, only 12 Dodgers have their uniform numbers retired. Gilliam and Fernando Valenzuela are the only non-Hall of Fame players to have a

Dodgers number retired, prompting many Dodger fans to wonder why the club has not extended the honor to other significant players, including Maury Wills, Steve Garvey, and others.

"I don't think when someone wants another player's number retired, I don't think that person is saying, 'Well, Jim doesn't deserve it.' That's a stretch that doesn't work. They may really believe Gil Hodges' number 14 should be retired. I respect that and I happen to agree with it. That person is not saying, 'Jim's number should have never been retired,'" O'Malley remarked 42 years later, prior to Hodges' induction into the Hall of Fame in 2022 and subsequently having his number 14 retired by the Dodgers. "I'm not apologetic that we retired Jim's number at all. I would do it again today."

19

EPILOGUE

From 1956-61, future Dodger first baseman Steve Garvey had a literal front-row seat to watching the Dodgers. As a 7-year-old on March 28, 1956, Garvey's father, Joe, who was the Dodgers' preferred bus driver whenever their spring-training games brought them to the Tampa area, asked young Steve, "Do you have any test tomorrow, and if you don't, do you want to skip school?"

Joe explained to Steve he had a charter to pick up the World Series champion Brooklyn Dodgers at the Tampa airport and drive them to Al Lang Stadium in St. Petersburg, and would Steve like to go? Would he? Indeed. Steve watched and chatted idly with players as Jackie Robinson, Roy Campanella, Duke Snider, and the rest of the Dodgers got off the plane and onto the bus. Steve was invited to serve as an honorary bat boy, something he would do as frequently as his schedule allowed for the next several years while his dad drove the bus. As Garvey wrote in 2008, "Even at my age, I knew history was standing before me, and it was much bigger than baseball."[1]

Six years of studying the mannerisms of Dodger standouts up close and personal left a lifelong impression on Garvey, who wrote of his vivid memory of Gilliam. "I remember him sitting on the steps of the dugout, his hat off, enjoying the sun. He would sit there during most of the game, chewing gum, watching the young guys on the field, watching the newest challenger out after his job.

"Then in the last couple of innings, he would put on his hat, pick up his glove, and go in there and play like it was the seventh game of the World Series. He'd hit the ball to all fields, steal a base, always be looking to take the extra base. He had an attitude, an approach to the game, that impressed me even as a kid,"[2] Garvey wrote.

HALL WORTHY?

In February 2019, then 92-year-old Bobby Morgan was living in his home-town Oklahoma City. The former Montreal Royals and Brooklyn Dodgers teammate of Jim Gilliam from the early 1950s, Morgan questioned why someone was interested in writing a biography of Gilliam. "You want to write a book about Junior Gilliam?" Morgan laughed. "That's strange. He's been dead for 40 years."

When presented with facts of Gilliam's career, including his omission from Hall of Fame consideration, Morgan declared gruffly, "He was a good baseball player and a good teammate. He is not a Hall of Fame ballplayer."

Gilliam's absence from Cooperstown is not unique among his Dodger teammates. Carl Erskine, Don Newcombe, Carl Furillo, Willie Davis, and Maury Wills all enjoyed sustained, productive years in the Major Leagues primarily with the Dodgers, and none of them are in the Hall. An argu-ment can be made that the contributions of players during that era are overshadowed by the star power of the roster. Names like Pee Wee, Jackie, Campy, and Duke are immortalized in pop culture through music and movies. Gilliam's mark on baseball, though, is not debatable. He ranks alongside the greatest players to play the game. Consider the following facts about Gilliam's career.

- Gilliam is the only player to hit a home run in both the Negro League East-West All-Star Game (1950) and the Major League All-Star Game (1959).
- Along with Hall of Famers Monte Irvin, Larry Doby, and Satchel Paige, Gilliam is the only player to win both a Negro League Championship and a World Series.
- Gilliam and Irvin are the only players to win a Negro League Championship, a World Series, and a Caribbean World Series.
- Gilliam played in seven no-hitters. Gilliam was also in the dugout as a coach for two additional no-nos, and managed a perfect game in the Puerto Rican Winter League, giving him a total of 10 no-hitters in which he participated.

- Through 2023, Gilliam is 11th in baseball history for both World Series games played (39) and World Series plate appearances (172). He is eighth in World Series history with 23 bases on balls.
- Gilliam is the only Dodger to play on four World Series championship teams (Sandy Koufax was on roster for the same four titles, but did not play in the 1955 Series; Johnny Podres was on the roster for four as well, but did not play in the 1965 Series). Gilliam is tied with Pee Wee Reese, Gil Hodges, and Carl Furillo with seven total World Series played, most in Dodger history.
- Gilliam is the Dodgers all-time World Series leader in bases on balls, second in World Series plate appearances and at bats, and tied for third in World Series games played.
- Gilliam ranks in the top 10 in Dodgers history in 10 offensive categories including fifth in games played (1,956) and at bats (7,119), third in plate appearances (8,322), 4th in runs scored (1,163), second in bases on balls (1,036), seventh in doubles (304), eighth in hits (1,889) and eighth in position player WAR (40.8).

National baseball writer Jay Jaffe published *The Cooperstown Casebook* in 2017. Using modern baseball analytics to assess historical player performance, the book purports to explain "who's in the Hall of Fame, who should be in, and who should pack their plaques." Relying heavily on the analytical formula JAWS (Jaffe WAR Score System), which he first created in 2004, Jaffe leverages the statistic "as a means to measure a player's Hall of Fame worthiness by comparing him to the players at his position who are already enshrined, using advanced metrics to account for the wide variations in offensive levels that have occurred throughout the game's history."[3]

While prevailing opinion may be Gilliam's career was not worthy of election to the Hall of Fame, that Gilliam never received even a single vote, despite nearly two decades of productivity in the Negro Leagues and the Major Leagues, seems inappropriate. Writing for *FanGraphs* in November 2018, Jaffe noted the oversight of not including Gilliam and his long-time teammate Willie Davis on a single Hall of Fame ballot represented "historically, the worst slights."[4]

Exactly when Gilliam might have been eligible for a Hall ballot is difficult to determine. The Baseball Writers' Association of America (BBWAA) considers players for a ballot five years after retirement. Gilliam first retired after the 1964 season but was activated early in the 1965 season and again early in the 1966 season. His last game played was in the 1966 World Series, making him eligible for the 1972 ballot.

Forty-six players received votes in 1972,[5] including eight former Boys of Summer: Sandy Koufax, Duke Snider, Pee Wee Reese, Gil Hodges, Don Newcombe, Carl Furillo, Preacher Roe, and Carl Erskine. Three players— Koufax, Yogi Berra, and Early Wynn—received at least the required 297 votes (out of a possible 396) to enter the Hall. Thirteen additional players, including Snider, Reese, and Hodges, would enter the Hall in later years. No record exists of Gilliam's name ever being included on a Hall ballot. It is likely the BBWAA, in selecting players for inclusion, simply looked at Gilliam's career and, as Jaffe said, "he hit .265 with 65 home runs. He is not a Hall of Famer, duh. He didn't reach 2,000 hits."

Shortstop Roy McMillan retired in August 1966 after 16 seasons with the Cincinnati Reds, Milwaukee Braves, and New York Mets. He was a career .243 hitter with 68 home runs and 200 fewer hits than Gilliam. Known primarily for his defense (he won three Gold Gloves), McMillan was twice selected to the All-Star Game but never played a postseason game. He was, however, featured on the cover of *Sports Illustrated* on September 9, 1957, and "earned the reputation of being the best defensive shortstop in the major leagues and the title 'Mr. Shortstop.'"[6] McMillan received nine Hall votes in 1972 and remained on the ballot for two more years. That McMillan's career accomplishments, during the same era as Gilliam, warranted Hall of Fame consideration, while Gilliam did not, appears misguided. Gilliam, after all, had a Rookie of the Year award, four World Series titles, and two All-Star game appearances on his resume.

"The BBWAA at that time was not an efficiently run organization. Gilliam doesn't scan as a guy who would be in the Hall of Fame, but he deserved the courtesy and honor of being on the ballot," Jaffe said.

In considering Gilliam's "case" for the Hall, several factors worked against him. First, he debuted in Major League baseball in 1953 as a 24-year-old having spent five seasons in the Negro Leagues and two in the Dodgers minor-league system. It is likely Gilliam's career stats would look different had he been in the Majors earlier. "I look at players who participated in the (Negro League's) East-West All-Star Game as Major League caliber," Jaffe said.

Two years after Jaffe's comments in 2021, Major League Baseball officially recognized Negro League statistics. Gilliam participated in the signature Negro League East-West All-Star Game three times, in his age 19, 20, and 21 seasons (1948-1950), giving him four total All-Star appearances, as MLB does not recognize 1949 and 1950 Negro League stats.

In the two years he spent with the Dodgers' minor-league affiliate in Montreal, Gilliam led his team to two International League titles and was named player of the year in 1952, hitting .301 with a .862 OPS, 111 runs scored, 112 RBI, and 100 walks against just 18 strikeouts. But his path to Brooklyn was blocked in 1952 by not just Jackie Robinson, the incumbent Dodgers second baseman, but also by an unspoken quota of Black players on the Dodgers, who had Roy Campanella, Don Newcombe, and Joe Black as well as Robinson in 1952. Only after the Dodgers moved Robinson to third base and left field in 1953 was there room for Gilliam in the lineup. It is not far-fetched to think Gilliam would have debuted in the Majors as early as 1951 or 1952 had a team other than the Dodgers signed him.

Also working against Gilliam was his position on the Dodgers was never truly defined. Most historians and baseball writers consider Gilliam a second baseman—and it is true that is where he made the most starts, 969. However, he also started 598 games at third base and 207 more in the outfield, giving him 805 career starts, or 45 percent, at positions other than second.

Another factor potentially hindering Gilliam's place in baseball history might be his selfless, reserved nature on Dodger teams loaded with stars and personalities. His Brooklyn teammates included Hall of Famers Jackie Robinson, Roy Campanella, Pee Wee Reese, Gil Hodges, and Duke Snider, as well as revered players like Carl Furillo, Carl Erskine, and Don Newcombe, all lionized in *The Boys of Summer*. Although the book was a remembrance of the 1952 Dodgers, the year before Gilliam debuted, many stories refer to years when he was on the team.

Peter Golenbock, author of *Bums*, the storied oral history of the Brooklyn Dodgers, believed a combination of factors, including race, contributed to Gilliam flying largely below the radar among his teammates. "Jackie, Newk, Furillo, Pee Wee, Campy, Duke, and (manager Charlie) Dressen. These were a lot of talkers. These guys were Hall of Famers. Tremendous players. Gilliam never opened his mouth. It is hard when you are not a talker and African-American. There was a lot of prejudice in the world."

Gilliam's Los Angeles teammates were among the most recognizable stars of the 1960s, led by two dominant pitchers of the era, Sandy Koufax and Don Drysdale, both in the Hall. Outspoken and speedy Maury Wills was the face of the offense, stealing 104 bases in 1962, often with Gilliam standing in the batter's box, taking pitches so Wills could attempt to steal. Bob Hunter profiled Gilliam for *The Sporting News* in April 1964 with a headline reading "Gilliam: Unsung, Unhonored—and Unsurpassed."

Hunter declared, "when the phrase 'team player' was coined, it was coined for Junior."[7]

"There's no use to look for any individualism in my story," Gilliam told Hunter. "There is no use to look, because it isn't there. I don't get paid to hit home runs or that sort of stuff. I get paid to score a lot of runs, knock in some and move the runner into scoring position. I would not rate myself a great ball player, but I think I do a lot of things well—things which beat the other team."[8] Gilliam's career may be largely overlooked because of his approach as a team player, or "company man."

At least one of Gilliam's teammates believed a Hall call should have arrived. Tommy Davis, a fellow Dodger from 1959-66, wrote in 2005, "All Jimmy could do was beat you. He did nothing fancy. He'd walk. He'd steal a base, he'd get a base hit late in the ballgame, and that's one of the reasons why we were a good ball club....I've said it before and I'll say it again: Jim should be in the Hall of Fame."[9]

JIM GILLIAM PARK

August A. Busch III announced around the time of the funeral he would spearhead efforts to raise funds to improve youth baseball fields in the View Park area of Los Angeles, where the Gilliams lived. Darryl, 14 years old at the time of father's passing, played in the Ladera Little League, the primary beneficiary of the improvements. "Jim Gilliam was inspirational as a player, coach and citizen for 25 years. We want to recognize his memory in a manner that is appropriate," Busch said.[10]

"This is a lovely gesture, and I'm sure Jim would be very proud," Edwina said in 1978. "The Little League has done so much for the youth in this community and this is very welcome."[11] And so was born the idea for Jim Gilliam Memorial Field.

After a little more than a year of planning and fundraising, on Wednesday, December 12, 1979, city officials gathered on land east of South La Brea Avenue, just north of the Baldwin Hills area and not far from the Gilliam home on Valleydale Avenue, to dedicate Jim Gilliam Memorial Field, part of a 17-acre park now known as Jim Gilliam Park. J.T. Stevens, a marketing manager for Anheuser-Busch, presented a check for $30,000 "seed money" to Los Angeles Mayor Tom Bradley. Several family members, including Edwina, Malcolm, Yvette, Darryl, and Jim's mother, Katherine, attended the dedication, as did former Brooklyn teammate Roy Campanella and current or former Dodger players Davey Lopes, Ken Brett, Dusty Baker, and Lee Lacy.

Edwina praised the generosity of everyone who worked to secure her husband's memory. "Jim is not with us today in body, but he is here in spirit," she said that day. "As his family, we want to extend our sincerest appreciation to Anheuser-Busch for spearheading this Jim Gilliam Memorial Park and want to give our thanks to all those people who have helped create this lasting memorial to Jim."[12]

Campanella also spoke at the dedication. "My hope is that one of the youngsters that plays on this field will one day grow up and play for the Dodgers."[13]

Forty-plus years later, Jim Gilliam Park is still operated by the City of Los Angeles Department of Recreation and Parks and now features a variety of green spaces, including playgrounds, baseball field, basketball courts, tennis courts, and an indoor recreation center with a senior citizen center and child care center. Edwina views its presence, and the city's continued improvements, as a proud reminder of Jim's life.

"Budweiser did most of that initially. It's a beautiful park. I was on the board for some time after he passed away," she said. It has a "tennis court, and a very nice area for senior citizens. They have a lovely basketball court inside. Wonderful Little League program going. It is a wonderful asset for the neighborhood."

HOMETOWN HONORS

Jim Gilliam was finally inducted into a Hall of Fame in 1995 when he was posthumously honored by the Tennessee Sports Hall of Fame as part of an eight-person induction class. The Tennessee Sports Hall of Fame honored its first class in 1966, the year Gilliam finally retired as a player. Why it took the Hall of Fame 30 years to recognize Gilliam is unclear.

When the city of Nashville and Davidson County opened a new ballpark on April 17, 2015 to house its Triple-A franchise, the Nashville Sounds, a campaign emerged to honor a native son. Then-named First Tennessee Park is situated between Third and Fifth Avenues. Jackson Street served as the stadium's north border, not far from the old Sulphur Dell site. The new ballpark features many acknowledgments to the city's history with Black baseball, including pictures of Nashville natives like Jim Gilliam, Henry Kimbro, Butch McCord, and Jim Zapp.

One year prior to the ballpark's opening, Fred Lee, a local attorney, authored an opinion piece in *The Tennessean* imploring the city to honor Gilliam in some fashion at the new park. "I can think of no person who is more deserving of recognition at the new Sulphur Dell ballpark than

Gilliam," Lee wrote. "Whether it be by local corporate sponsorship coupled with naming rights; by naming an adjacent street in his honor; or by the building of a statue or monument in his memory, let's honor Nashville's own James William 'Junior' Gilliam, 1928-1978."[14]

In early 2015, Nashville Mayor Karl Dean did just that, beginning the process of changing the name of Jackson Street between Second and Fifth Avenues north to "Junior Gilliam Way." After receiving approval from the Metro Planning and Metro Historical Commissions, the Metro Council approved the legislation in May 2015.[15] With the necessary bureaucracy in place, the team identified a July 28 home game as the day for the official ceremony.

Nashville's public address announcer asked fans in attendance prior to the game to direct their attention to the field, where Sounds owner Frank Ward, Nashville mayor Dean, Metro Council representative Erica Gilmore, and a "very special video guest" would dedicate 19 Junior Gilliam Way as the permanent address of the ballpark, since renamed First Horizon Park. Gilmore concluded her remarks by introducing a video from legendary Dodgers announcer Vin Scully, who immediately expressed gratitude to the Nashville organization for honoring "one of my all-time favorite players and gentleman who wore a Dodger uniform."

Scully reminisced, "when I look back over the players who wore the uniform, certainly Jim is a standout without a doubt." Scully recounted a banquet at which he was introducing members of the Dodgers team. "And then, for whatever reason, I said, 'and now here is Jim Gilliam, baseball player,'" he said. "And that just seems to blow the audience away. They thought that was the best tribute that I could give him, and, I guess if I think about it, I was glad that I did. He was a wonderful human being."[16]

AFTERWORD

B.H. "Pete" Fairchild grew up in the rural southwestern Kansas farming town of Liberal in the 1950s and, like most other boys his age, he played baseball and collected baseball cards. By his own admission, Fairchild was not blessed with innate baseball talent. "They put you in right field when you don't have abilities," he said.

Little League baseball was "primitive" in the rural town, with strong winds distributing a consistent cloud of dust around the field. As a result, Fairchild often took his baseball cards with him to look at during the down moments of practice. He noticed one player, Jim Gilliam, had the same birthdate: October 17. And, so, Gilliam became a favorite player.

Twenty-five years later, Fairchild was a budding poet who had not followed baseball closely since those adolescent days when he heard that Gilliam had passed away. "I walked into my room and the poem came on me so fast," Fairchild remembered. "Baseball players can be such idols."

Fairchild, who now lives in California, has enjoyed a distinguished career as the author of seven volumes of poetry. He is a past finalist for the National Book Award and winner of the William Carlos Williams Award, the National Book Critics Circle Award, and the Bobbitt National Prize.

For Junior Gilliam (1928-1978)
by B.H. "Pete" Fairchild

In the bleak, bleacherless corner
of my rightfield American youth,
I killed time with bubble gum
and baseball cards and read the stats
and saw a sign: your birthday was mine.

And so I dreamed: to rise far
from Kansas skies and fenceless outfields
where flies vanished in the summer sun.
To wake up black in Brooklyn,
to be a Bum and have folks call me Junior
and almost errorless hit .280 every year
and on the field, like you, dance double plays,
make flawless moves, amaze the baseball masses.

You would turn, take the toss from Reese,
lean back and, leaping past the runner's cleats,
wing the ball along a line reeled out
from home and suddenly drawn taut
with a soft pop in Hodges' crablike glove.
And we went wild in Kansas living rooms.

The inning's over. You're in the shadows now.
But summers past you taught us how to play
the pivot (or how to dream of it).
And when one day they put me in at second,
I dropped four easy ones behind your ghost,
who plays a perfect game.

ACKNOWLEDGMENTS

When I began researching this book in 2019, I really had no idea where the narrative would go, with whom I would interact, or, for that matter, how I would accomplish this. Perhaps that is why this published book is both satisfying and amazing now that it is complete. This was an endeavor I could not have completed alone, and I am forever grateful for the support of people, many of whom graciously gave of their time, expertise, and connections. That so many strangers would do this for me speaks to the universal regard with which people remember Jim Gilliam.

At the risk of unintentionally omitting someone, I would like to publicly thank and acknowledge the following people who aided this project.

Former Major League players and executives who shared their recollections of Gilliam with me included: the late Carl Erskine, John Werhas, the late Bobby Morgan, Derrell Griffith, Dick Calmus, Tom Walker, Eliseo Rodriguez, Balor Moore, Nate Oliver, Dusty Baker, Fred Claire, Al Ferrara, Al Downing, Billy Grabarkewitz, Bill White, Wes Parker, Manny Mota, Bobby Valentine, Peter O'Malley, Doug Rau, Bart Shirley, Derrel Thomas, Fred Kipp, Ron Cey, and Dick Tracewski.

Family members and close personal friends of Gilliam, or those whose relatives were close to Jim, and who spent time helping me understand my subject included: Edwina Gilliam-Higginbotham, Katherine Gilliam-Belway, Darryl Gilliam, James Mims, Jr., Martha Jo Black, Chico Black, Scott Brewer, Harriet Kimbro-Hamilton, Wally Moon, Jr., Gil Hodges, Jr., and Roger Dinwiddie.

Those who provided context or connected me with others included: Peter Golenbock, Enrique Zorrilla, Adam Darwoski, Jay Jaffe, Lyle Spencer, Danny Torres, Jorge Colon Delgado, Hal McCoy, James Kahler, Brent Shyer, Bryan Burns, Ted Reed, and Jack DeLance.

Cassidy Lent of the National Baseball Hall of Fame and Museum met with me via Zoom during the height of the pandemic and helped greatly with access to materials housed in the Museum. Skip Nipper is the foremost expert on Nashville baseball history and aided my understanding of Gilliam's birth home. Tom Van Hyning is the author of two books about Puerto Rican baseball including the authoritative book on the Santurce Crabbers. He provided detailed statistics about Gilliam's time in Puerto Rico. Kelley Sirko of the Nashville Public Library scanned old maps for me to review during the pandemic.

Many accomplished baseball book authors graciously shared their time with me as I was forming this narrative and the subsequent book proposal. To Andrew Maraniss, Brad Balukjian, Skip Desjardin, Michael Fallon, Bob Luke, John Rosengren, Luke Epplin, Steven Wagner, and Jason Turbow, I offer my extreme and eternal gratitude.

An early supporter of my project was the late Pete Cava, who is synonymous with Indiana baseball, and my roommate at the 2015 Special Olympics World Games. Thank you, Pete. May you be watching a baseball game each day in Heaven.

Social media can be both a blessing and a curse. But, without the benefit of being welcomed into groups devoted to die hard fans of the Brooklyn Dodgers, many of whom would ostracize me for mentioning Walter O'Malley's name, I would not have an appreciation for what 1950s baseball in Flatbush was like. Those who shared their recollection or merely responded to my inquiries included: Matt Perlstein, Dave Johnson, Stu Wantman, Peter V. Trunk, Sr., Lou DeSarno, and Claire Elizabeth Hall. Thank you for welcoming me to your community, and may it always be October 4, 1955 on your calendars. Social media also brought me to Jim Denny, Rene LeRoux, Mark Jent, Jason Schwarz, B.H. Fairchild, and Charles LaBonge, all of whom share a passion for baseball and, to an extent, the Dodgers.

A shared passion of the Dodgers, baseball history, and memorabilia connected me to Herbert Ross, whose collection of Jackie Robinson memorabilia is remarkable; Wade Carothers, who owns some of the most rare pieces of Jim Gilliam memorabilia around; and David Petersen, who welcomed me to his home which contains roughly 25,000 unique pieces of Dodger memorabilia, including several Gilliam items.

Much of the research for this was completed while I was employed by the University of Arkansas. The Interlibrary Loan staff on campus are magicians, finding obscure articles from the 1950s and 1960s with little information other than a year and a month. Thank you. Dr. Melody Herr, head of scholarly communication at the University of Arkansas, was an invaluable sounding board early in the development of my idea. She was extremely patient and challenged me to make the end result better. Laura Cameron helped me gain access to the *Los Angeles Sentinel* digital database, which proved an important resource in understanding how the black media covered Gilliam and the Dodgers in the 1960s. Jeff Brazil permitted the use of his turntable to play a 1966 promotional record featuring a conversation between Gilliam and Vin Scully. The interview represented a rare opportunity to hear Gilliam's words in his own voice.

Thank you to Kevin and the staff at August Publications for believing in this work and taking a chance on me.

Finally, I thank my family who, I suspect, thought I was crazy. My father and mother, Bill and Jane, and my uncle, also Bill, encouraged me along the way and read early iterations of chapters. My wife, Andrea, supported me throughout as I traveled to SABR meetings, barricaded myself in our home office for interviews, and woke up early on weekend mornings to write. We survived three moves and two states during this time. I could not have finished without you. My son, Andrew, and I spent many nights watching both Dodger Major League and Minor League Baseball during his adolescence. The memories of meeting future big league stars with you will always be cherished. Do big things in college and always pursue your dreams.

NOTES

1. THE FORGOTTEN DODGER

1. Paul Zimmerman, "Figures Tell Dodger Story," *Los Angeles Times*, Aug. 14, 1964, Part III, 2.
2. Sid Ziff, "Bruin win no fluke," *Los Angeles Times*, Sept. 14, 1964, Part III, 1.
3. Zimmerman, "Sandy's the Greatest," Oct. 15, 1965, Part III, 4.
4. Tom Briere, "Koufax Lauds Play That Saved Victory," *Minneapolis Tribune*, Oct. 15, 1965, 21.
5. Author interview with Derrel Thomas, February 2, 2023.
6. Ken Picking, "'Headwinds' Couldn't Stop Jim Gilliam," *Atlanta Constitution*, October 12, 1978, 1D, 11D.

2. NASHVILLE

1. Jackie Robinson and Charles Dexter, *Baseball Has Done It* (Philadelphia, PA; J.B. Lippincott Company, 1964), p. 161.
2. Although he is not often referred to as "James Gilliam, Jr.," his father was also named James.
3. "Nashville ranks as south's school center," *The Nashville Tennessean*, October 28, 1928, p. 1.
4. Axel C. Hansen, "George W. Hubbard Hospital, 1910-1961," *Journal of the National Medical Association*, January 1962, 54(1), p. 4-5.
5. "Will Gilliam top Jackie? They call him the boy with the magic eye. But can his magic equal Robinson's exploits," *Our World*, August 1953, p. 66. & Ralph Dawson, "Star Recalls Sad Days of Life Here," *Nashville Tennessean*, December 11, 1965, 1, 9.
6. "Death Notices," *The Nashville Tennessean*, June 13, 1929, p. 2.
7. Charles L. Fontenenay, "When Junior Comes to Bat, Clarksville Begins to Rock," *The Nashville Tennessean*, October 3, 1953, p. 10.
8. "Tennessee Deaths and Burials, 1874-1955," database, FamilySearch (familysearch.org/ark:/61903/1:1:F6R7-6S9 : 10 February 2018), Forster Gillem, 26 Jan 1908; citing Nashville, Davidson, Tenn., reference v Z rn 171; FHL microfilm 1,276,593.
9. *The Tennessean* printed her name as Catherine in 1953, as did her Tennessee birth certificate, but a Tennessee marriage certificate listed it as Katherine. Jim Gilliam's first-born daughter is named Katherine, so for the purposes of this book, it will be Katherine.
10. "Tennessee Deaths, 1914-1966," database with images, FamilySearch (familysearch.org/ark:/61903/1:1:NSLQ-8V8 : 26 August 2019), Tim Gilliam, 8 Feb 1929; Death, Nashville, Davidson, Tennessee, United States, Tennessee State Library and Archives, Nashville.
11. "Tennessee Deaths, 1914-1966," database with images, FamilySearch (familysearch.org/ark:/61903/1:1:NSVR-WG9 : 26 August 2019), James Gilliam, 11 Jun 1929; Death, Nashville, Davidson, Tennessee, United States, Tennessee State Library and Archives, Nashville.
12. Ralph Dawson, "Star Recalls Sad Days of Life Here," *Nashville Tennessean*, December 11, 1965, 9.
13. Jack Mann, "Gilliam Brings Three Gloves and Waits Around." *Sport*, January 1963, p. 68.

14. familysearch.org/ark:/61903/1:1:NSNN-T25
15. Fontenenay, "When Junior," 10.
16. Charles Dexter, "Seniority Awaits Junior: Despite his Midseason Slump, There's a Solid Future Predicted for Brooklyn's Young Gilliam." *Baseball Digest*, September 1953, p. 34.
17. Fontenenay, "When Junior," 10.
18. "Tennessee Deaths, 1914-1966," database with images, FamilySearch (familysearch.org/ark:/61903/1:1:NSFG-9GP : 26 August 2019), Richard Gilliam, 17 Feb 1944; Death, Nashville, Davidson, Tennessee, United States, Tennessee State Library and Archives, Nashville.
19. Kelley Sirko, email message to author, December 16, 2019
20. Robinson and Dexter, *Baseball Has Done It*, 161.
21. Billy Reed, "Death in October: Jim Gilliam basks, too late, in the limelight," *Louisville Courier-Journal*, October 12, 1978, 9D
22. Roscoe McGowen, "Gilliam Takes Long Lease on Second Base: Rated Better than Jackie at Keystone." *The Sporting News*, April 29, 1953, 3.
23. Brent P. Kelley, *Voices from the Negro Leagues: Conversations with 52 Baseball Standouts of the Period 1924-1960* (Jefferson, NC: McFarland and Company, 1998), 56.
24. Author interview with Harriet Kimbro-Hamilton, December 8, 2020.
25. Interview with Harriet Kimbro-Hamilton, December 8, 2020.
26. Robinson and Dexter, *Baseball Has Done It*, 161.
27. David Climer, "Field of Dreams," *The Tennessean*, February 10, 1995, 1C.
28. Harold Sheldon, "He's not 'Junior' Anymore. Baseball's Gilliam Attains Maturity," *Baseball Digest*, November-December, 1956, 72.
29. Fontenany, "When Junior," 10.
30. Bob Oates, "Ten Position" Gilliam Says—You Can Learn to be a Switch Hitter." *Baseball Digest*, September 1959, 41
31. Robinson and Dexter, *Baseball Has Done It*, 161.
32. *Meet the Dodger Family: Junior Gilliam Dodger Handyman* (Los Angeles, CA: Union Oil 76, 1960), 4.
33. McGowen, "Gilliam Takes Long Lease," 3.
34. Luke, *The Baltimore Elite Giants*, 102.
35. "History," Woolworth on Fifth, accessed January 4, 2020, woolworthonfifth.com.
36. "Meet Junior Gilliam!" *Our Sports*, June 1953, 20.
37. Robinson and Dexter, *Baseball Has Done It*, 161.
38. Dexter, "Seniority Awaits Junior," 34.
39. *Meet the Dodger Family: Junior Gilliam Dodger Handyman*, 3.
40. Mann, "Gilliam Brings Three Gloves," 69.
41. Fontenany, "When Junior," 10.
42. Hanna, 1978, 19, 21.
43. Bill Traughber, *Nashville Baseball History: From Sulphur Dell to the Sounds*, (South Orange, NJ: Summer Game Books, 2017), 4.
44. Traughber, *Nashville Baseball History*, 9.
45. Traughber, *Nashville Baseball History*, 10.
46. Author interview with Skip Nipper, January 24, 2023.
47. Traughber, *Nashville Baseball History*, 11.
48. Harriet Hamilton, "The Contributions of Tom Wilson: A Negro League Team Owner's Impact on the Nashville Community," in *Baseball/Literature/Culture: Essays, 2008-2009*, eds. R. E. Kates and W. Toomey (Jefferson, NC: McFarland & Company, Inc., 2010), 188.
49. Luke, *Baltimore Elite Giants*, 6.
50. Arthur Daley, "Sports of the Times: A Job for Junior," *New York Times*, May 24, 1953, 213.
51. *Meet the Dodger Family: Junior Gilliam Dodger Handyman*, 4.
52. Author interview with Skip Nipper, February 11, 2021.
53. Started as backstop, speed changed him to infielder, April 29, 1953, p. 3

54. Jeff Hanna, "Jim Gilliam—Most Famous 'Lamb'," *The Tennessean*, October 10, 1978, 19.
55. Fred Russell, "Nashville-born Junior Gilliam is Dodgers' most promising rookie," *Nashville Banner*, March 16, 1953, 22.
56. Hanna, "Jim Gilliam," 19.
57. Tom Powell, "Gilliam set for full-time coaching," *Nashville Tennessean*, December 11, 1965, 15.
58. Hanna, "Jim Gilliam," 19.
59. Hanna, 1978, 19.

3. "JUNIOR"

1. William J. Plott, *The Negro Southern League: A Baseball History, 1920-1951* (Jefferson, NC: McFarland & Company, Inc., 2015), 145.
2. Plott, *Negro Southern League*, 1.
3. Dexter, "Seniority Awaits Junior," 34.
4. Plott, *Negro Southern League*, 154.
5. Plott, *Negro Southern League*, 155.
6. Robinson and Dexter, *Baseball Has Done It*, 161.
7. Arnold Rampersand, *Jackie Robinson: A Biography*, (New York: Random House, Inc., 1997), 127.
8. "Meet Junior Gilliam!" *Our Sports*, June 1953, 57.
9. "Barnett Pilots Nashville Cubs," *The Tennessean*, March 31, 1946, 2-C.
10. "Zapp New Elite Bat Star," *Baltimore Evening Sun*, April 11, 1946, 36.
11. Bill James, *The New Bill James Historical Baseball Abstract* (New York: The Free Press, 2001), 183.
12. Robert Peterson, *Only the Ball Was White: A History of Legendary Black Players and All-Black Professional Teams* (New York: Oxford University Press, 1992), 231.
13. baseballhall.org/news/six-candidates-elected-to-hall-of-fame-as-part-of-class-of-2022.
14. Luke, *Baltimore Elite Giants*, 39.
15. Luke, *Baltimore Elite Giants*, 101.
16. John Holway, *Voices from the Great Black Baseball Leagues: Revised Edition* (New York: Da Capo Press, 1992, 333-334.
17. "George Scales: The Rifle Arm of Negro Professional Baseball," *Black Sports*, May 1973, 32.
18. "Meet Junior Gilliam!," 57.
19. Martha Jo Black and Chuck Schoffner, *Joe Black: More Than a Dodger* (Chicago, IL: Chicago Review Press, 2015), 107.
20. "Meet Junior Gilliam!," 57.
21. Bob Hunter, "Gilliam: Unsung, Unhonored—and Unsurpassed," *The Sporting News*, April 4, 1964, 3.
22. Raymond Johnson, "One Man's Opinion: Hard Work Made Gilliam an Excellent Switch Hitter," *Nashville Tennessean*, December 10, 1965, 59.
23. Holway, *Voices*, 274.
24. "Meet Junior Gilliam!," 57.
25. Holway, *Voices*, 335.
26. "Elites Due Back Today," *Baltimore Evening Sun*, April 30, 1946, 23.
27. "Elite Giants Defeated by N.Y. Cubans, 7-4," *Baltimore Sun*, May 27, 1946, 17.
28. Luke, *Baltimore Elite Giants*, 102.
29. Tiant's son, Luis Jr., amassed 229 Major League wins and was named All-Star three times in the 1960s and 1970s.
30. James, *Bill James Historical*, 183.
31. Peterson, *Only the Ball*, 230.

32. "Sammy Hughes," Seamheads, accessed January 4, 2020, seamheads.com/NegroLgs/player.php?playerID=hughe01sam.
33. James, *Bill James Historical*, 186.
34. Peterson, *Only the Ball*, 233-234.
35. "Willie Wells," Seamheads, accessed January 4, 2020, seamheads.com/NegroLgs/player.php?playerID=wells01wil.
36. "Gray, Elite Nines meet," *Baltimore Evening Sun*, June 14, 1946, 37.
37. Dick Clark and Larry Lester, *The Negro Leagues Book* (Cleveland, OH: Society for American Baseball Research, 1994), 162.
38. "N.Y. Cubans play Elite Giants here," *Baltimore Sun*, July 7, 1946, 6.
39. "Elite Giants defend loop lead against Cuban foe," *Baltimore Evening Sun*, July 16, 1946, 22.
40. "Elite Giants defeat New York Cubans, 5-3," *Baltimore Sun*, July 17, 1946, 15.
41. Jamie Smith, "Take me out to the Leon Day Park," *Baltimore Sun*, August 24, 1997, 17B.
42. "Elite Giants down Newark team twice," *Baltimore Sun*, August 19, 1946, 13.
43. "Charles England," Seamheads, accessed January 4, 2020, seamheads.com/NegroLgs/player.php?playerID=engla01cha.
44. "Meet Junior Gilliam!" 57.
45. Holway, *Voices*, 335.
46. "New York Cubans top Elite Giants by 5-1," *Baltimore Sun*, August 28, 1946, 14.
47. "Elite Giants defeat Cincinnati nine, 10-6," *Baltimore Sun*, September 14, 1946, 11.
48. Clark and Lester, *Negro Leagues*, 162.
49. "Elite Giants face All-Stars today," *Baltimore Sun*, September 22, 1946, 8.
50. Luke, *Baltimore Elite Giants*, 103.
51. Bob Luke, *The Baltimore Elite Giants* (Baltimore, MD: Johns Hopkins University Press, 2010), 100.
52. ibid.
53. "Elites Due Back Today," *Baltimore Evening Sun*, April 30, 1946, 23.

4. BLACK BASEBALL

1. Luke, 2010, p. 104
2. Neil Lanctot, *Negro League Baseball* (Philadelphia, PA: University of Pennsylvania Press, 2004), 308.
3. Giants sign 2, *Baltimore Evening Sun*, April 28, 1947, p. 22.
4. Sam Lacy, "From A to Z with Sam Lacy," *Baltimore Afro-American*, August 30, 1947, 12.
5. Luke, 2010, p. 109.
6. Campanella, 1959, p. 66-67.
7. Hirsch, 2010, p. 48.
8. Kelley, 1998, p. 59-60.
9. Kelley, 1998, p. 60.
10. Jim Gilliam Talks With Vin Scully, 1966.
11. Bob Hunter, "Gilliam: Unsung, unhonored—and unsurpassed," *The Sporting News*, April 4, 1964, 3.
12. Chris Rainey, "Henry Kimbro," sabr.org/bioproj/person/henry-kimbro/.
13. Luke, *Baltimore Elite Giants*, 2.
14. Larry Lester, *Black Baseball's National Showcase* (Lincoln, NE: University of Nebraska Press, 2001), 1.
15. Larry Lester, *Black Baseball's National Showcase* (Kansas City, MO: NoirTech Research, Inc., 2020), 5.
16. baseball-reference.com/bullpen/Bill_Powell_(Negro_Leagues).
17. Nunn, Jr., *Pittsburgh Courier*, August 28, 1948, p. 10.

18. West defeats East, 3-0, before 42,099 fans, *Chicago Defender*, August 28, 1948, 10.
19. Lester, 2001.
20. Garlington, *New York Amsterdam News*, August 28, 1948, 26.
21. Lanctot, 2011, p. 57.
22. Holway, 1992, p. 329.
23. Holway, 1992, p. 327.
24. Holway, 1992, p. 338.
25. Holway, 1992, p. 327-328.
26. James, 2001, p. 187.
27. Lacy, Sept. 4, 1948, p. 8.
28. ibid, p. 8.
29. Ibid, p. 8.
30. ibid, p. 8.
31. Holway, 1992, p. 335-336.
32. Lacy, Sept. 4, 1948, p. 8.
33. Holway, 1992, p. 328.
34. Tom Van Hyning, "Jim Gilliam - Baltimore Elite Giants, Aguadilla, Almendares, Minors, and Santurce (Part I)," Beisbol101.com, accessed April 19, 2020, beisbol101.com/jim-gilliam-baltimore-elite-giants-aguadilla-almendares-minors-and-santurce-part-i/.
35. Van Hyning, "Jim Gilliam (Part I).
36. "Meet Junior Gilliam!," 1953, p. 57.
37. Dan Burley, "Confidentially Yours: In 1948, Whither Negro Baseball?" *New York Amsterdam News*, January 3, 1948, p. 10.
38. Jackie Robinson, "What's Wrong with Negro Baseball," *Ebony* (June 1948), 16.
39. Neil Lanctot, *Negro League Baseball* (Philadelphia, PA: University of Pennsylvania Press, 2004), 333.
40. Lanctot, 2004, 335.
41. "Gilliam first in Elite fold," *Baltimore Afro-American*, February 26, 1949, p. 14
42. Luke, 2010, 120.
43. Thomas Kern (n.d.). Leon Day. sabr.org/bioproj/person/leon-day/.
44. Brad Snyder, "Day dies week after greatest honor," *Baltimore Sun*, March 14, 1995, 1A.
45. Russ J. Cowans, "East wins as 31,000, Happy Chandler watch," *Chicago Defender*, August 20, 1949, 1.
46. Wendell Smith, "Wendell Smith's Sports Beat," *Pittsburgh Courier*, August 13, 1949, 22.
47. Luix Virgil Overbea, "Slumping crowds at East-West game is a warning signal," *Pittsburgh Courier*, August 27, 1949, 22.
48. Smith, "Wendell Smith's Sports Beat," August 13, 1949, 22.
49. Oscar Ruhl, "From the Ruhl book," *The Sporting News*, January 6, 1954, 14.
50. Wendell Smith, "Wendell Smith's Sports Beat," *Pittsburgh Courier*, August 6, 1949, 22.
51. "Len Pigg captures NAL batting crown with .386," *Baltimore Afro-American*, September 17, 1949, 15.
52. Luke, 2010, 122.
53. Nick Diunte, "Butch McCord leaves behind a baseball legacy of a lifetime," February 2, 2011, baseballhappenings.net/2011/02/butch-mccord-leaves-behind-baseball.html.
54. Byron Bennett, "Bugle Field—Home of the Baltimore Elite Giants," October 6, 2013, deadballbaseball.com/?s=Bugle+Field.
55. Luke, 2010, 17.
56. Bernard McKenna, *The Baltimore Black Sox: A Negro Leagues History, 1913-1936* (Jefferson, NC: McFarland and Company, 2020).
57. Bennett, 2013.
58. Wayne Hardin, "Stadium Sites Recall Glory Days of Black Baseball," *Baltimore Sun Magazine*, July 24, 1994, 15.
59. https://chap.baltimorecity.gov/historic-districts/maps/baltimore-east-clifton.

60. Neil Lanctot, *Negro League Baseball* (Philadelphia, PA: University of Pennsylvania Press, 2004), 350.
61. Lanctot, *Negro League Baseball*, 362.
62. Luke, 2010, p. 124.
63. Lanctot, *Negro League Baseball*, 355.
64. Lanctot, Negro League Baseball, 335-345.
65. Sam Lacy, "From A to Z with Sam Lacy," *Baltimore Afro-American*, February 11, 1950, 17.

5. THE MAJORS CALL. TWICE.

1. Kathy Patron, "'Farewell to Yale Field' was a day to remember." *The Ledger*, June 29, 2009, Retrieved from theledger.com/news/20071007/mccheadfarewell-to-yale-field-was-a-day-to-remembermcchead.
2. Sam Lacy, "Marquez shows speed with Yanks' farm club," *Baltimore Afro-American*, March 26, 1949, 15.
3. Jim Reisler, *Black writers/Black baseball: An anthology of articles from Black sportswriters who covered the Negro Leagues* (Jefferson, NC: McFarland and Company, 2007), 28.
4. Edward Burns, "Cubs become happy family as Carlsen signs; All in fold," *Chicago Tribune*, February 23, 1950, F1.
5. "Cubs buy two Baltimore Elite players," *Chicago Defender*, March 4, 1950, 16.; "Junior Gilliam, Roy Ferrell sold to Cubs' farm club," *Baltimore Afro-American*, March 4, 1950, 17.
6. Sam Lacy, "From A to Z with Sam Lacy," *Baltimore Afro-American*, April 1, 1950, 16.
7. Dan Burley, "Dan Burley on Sports," *New York Age*, May 6, 1950, 22.
8. "Cubs' tan players quartered separately," *Baltimore Afro-American*, April 1, 1950, 17.
9. Sam Lacy, "From A to Z with Sam Lacy," *Baltimore Afro-American*, April 1, 1950, 16.
10. Lacy, April 1, 1950, 16.
11. Luke, 2010, p. 125.
12. "Meet Junior Gilliam!," *Our Sports*, June 1953, 57.
13. Martha Jo Black and Chuck Schoffner, *Joe Black: More than a Dodger* (Chicago, IL: Academy Chicago Publishers, 2015), 114.
14. "Thurman, Taborn Heading for Springfield Club Berths," *Baltimore Afro-American*, April 1, 1950, 16.
15. Jack Mann, "Gilliam brings three gloves and waits around," *Sport*, January 1963, 69.
16. "Elite Giants Win 4-3 Test," *Baltimore Sun*, May 8, 1950, 16.
17. Thomas Skinner, "Elite Giants defeat Stars in ninth, 4-3; Gilliam returns," *Chicago Defender*, May 13, 1950, 16.
18. Luke, 2010, 128.
19. Luke, 2010, 126.
20. Sam Lacy, "Dodgers May Buy Gilliam, Coleman From Elite Giants," *Baltimore Afro-American*, July 1, 1950, 19.
21. Sam Lacy, "From A to Z with Sam Lacy," *Baltimore Afro-American*, July 22, 1950, 17.
22. Wendell Smith, "West Captures 18th Annual East-West Game, 5-3, Before 24,614 Fans," *Pittsburgh Courier*, August 26, 1950, 10.
23. Larry Lester, *Black Baseball's National Showcase: The East-West All-Star Game, 1933 to 1962* (Kansas City, MO: NoirTech Research, Inc.), 492.
24. "Stars Beat Elites as Paige Pitches," *Baltimore Sun*, September 4, 1950, 10.
25. "Jackie Robinson, Campanella, Doby Play Here Tonight," *Baltimore Sun*, October 9, 1950, 14.
26. Peter Golenbock, *Bums: An Oral History of the Brooklyn Dodgers* (New York: G.P. Putnam's Sons, 1984), 251.
27. Tommy Holmes, "The Mahatma Walks Up Montague Street," *Brooklyn Daily Eagle*, October 27, 1950, 15.

28. Murray Polner, *Branch Rickey: A Biography* (New York: Atheneum, 1982), 212.
29. Red Smith, "Gaylord, Gilliam, and Joe Black," *New York Times*, September 7, 1979, 18.
30. Jimmy Breslin, *Branch Rickey: A Life* (New York: Penguin Group, 2012), 73.
31. Breslin, 2012, 73.
32. Buzzie Bavasi with John Strege, *Off the Record: Buzzie Bavasi* (Chicago, IL: Contemporary Books, Inc., 1987), 204.
33. William Brown, *Baseball's Fabulous Montreal Royals: The Minor League Team That Made Major League History* (Montreal, Canada: Robert Davies Publishing, 1996), 136.
34. Dick Young, "The Sports of Kings and Queens," *New York Daily News*, October 5, 1952, B10.
35. Yet another version, as reported by Harvey Frommer in *New York City Baseball: The Last Golden Age 1947-1957*, claims the three players were purchased for $10,000, meaning Brooklyn paid $6,666 for Gilliam and Black (p. 119).
36. Luke, 2010, 131.
37. Roger Kahn Papers, BA MSS 50, National Baseball Hall of Fame Library, National Baseball Hall of Fame and Museum, box 8, folder 6.
38. Black and Schoffner, 2015, 115.
39. Holway, 1992, p. 336-337.
40. John Wiebusch, "Jim Gilliam recalls tough times in Negro Leagues," *Baseball Digest*, June 1969, 38-40.
41. Thomas Van Hyning, *The Santurce Crabbers: Sixty Seasons of Puerto Rican Winter League Baseball* (Jefferson, NC: McFarland & Company, Inc., 1999), 25.
42. Van Hyning, *The Santurce Crabbers*, 7-9.
43. Van Hyning, *The Santurce Crabbers*, 25.
44. Letter found on eBay.
45. Van Hyning, *The Santurce Crabbers*, 35.
46. Van Hyning, *The Santurce Crabbers*, 35.
47. Van Hyning, *The Santurce Crabbers*, 37.
48. Thomas Van Hyning, *Puerto Rico's Winter League: A History of Major League Baseball's Launching Pad* (Jefferson, NC: McFarland & Company, Inc., 1995), 46.
49. Meet Junior Gilliam!, 1953, 57-58.

6. THE MINOR LEAGUES

1. "Royals open I.L. sked at Baltimore tonight," *Montreal Gazette*, April 18, 1951, 23.
2. Jackie Robinson and Charles Dexter, *Baseball Has Done It* (Philadelphia, PA: J.B. Lippincott, 1964), 162.
3. "Gilliam drives in six runs as Royals blast Baltimore in I.L. opener, 15-7," *Montreal Gazette*," April 19, 1951, 21.
4. "Meet Junior Gilliam!," 1953, 58.
5. "Meet Junior Gilliam!," 1953, 58.
6. "Gilliam drives in six runs as Royals blast Baltimore in I.L. opener, 15-7," *Montreal Gazette*, April 19, 1951, 21.
7. Jimmy Powers, "The Powerhouse," *New York Daily News*, June 14, 1951, 80.
8. "Brooks groom Gilliam on Montreal farm," *Brooklyn Daily Eagle*, June 15, 1951, 19.
9. "Royals win two from herd," *Montreal Gazette*, June 18, 1951, 20.
10. Raymond Johnson, "One Man's Opinion: Hard Work Made Gilliam an Excellent Switch Hitter," *Nashville Tennessean*, December 10, 1965, 59.
11. Jimmy Powers, "The Powerhouse," *New York Daily News*, July 29, 1951, 22.
12. Bill Nowlin, "Rudy Minarcin." Society for American Baseball Research, sabr.org/bioproj/person/rudy-minarcin/.

13. Roger Kahn Papers, BA MSS 50, National Baseball Hall of Fame Library, National Base-ball Hall of Fame and Museum, box 8, folder 6.
14. Van Hyning, *The Santurce Crabbers*, 38.
15. Thomas Van Hyning, email message to author, August 5, 2019.
16. Van Hyning, *The Santurce Crabbers*, 38.
17. Bill Nowlin, "Sam Jethroe," Society for American Baseball Research, accessed January 24, 2021 sabr.org/bioproj/person/rudy-minarcin/.
18. "Branch Rickey discusses the Negro in baseball today," *Ebony*, May 1957, 42.
19. Bryan Soderholm-Difatte, *The Golden Era of Major League Baseball: A Time of Transition and Integration* (Lanham, MD: Rowman & Littlefield, 2015), 142.
20. Soderhom-Difatte, 2015, 149-150.
21. Steve Treder, "The persistent color line: Specific instances of racial preference in major league player evaluation decisions after 1947," *Nine: A Journal of Baseball History and Culture*, 2001, 13.
22. Treder, 2001, 13-14.
23. Jackie Robinson and Alfred Duckett, *I Never Had It Made*, (New York: G.P. Putnam and Sons, 1972), 104.
24. John Roseboro with Bill Libby, *Glory Days with the Dodgers: and Other Days with Others*, (New York: Atheneum, 1978), 110.
25. Jack Mann, "Gilliam Brings Three Gloves and Waits Around," *Sport*, January 1963, 69.
26. John Roseboro with Bill Libby, *Glory Days with the Dodgers and Other Days with Others*, (New York: Atheneum, 1978), 113.
27. Brown, 1996, 139.
28. Dick Young, "Ghost of August, 1951, Haunts Harried Dressen," *New York Daily News*, August 10, 1952, 79.
29. "International League," *The Sporting News*, August 27, 1952, 32.
30. Lloyd McGowan, "Gilliam tabbed Robinson's successor with Brooklyn," *The Sporting News*, October 1, 1952, 38.
31. Mike Huber, "Billy Hunter," Society for American Baseball Research, accessed January 5, 2020, sabr.org/bioproj/person/4cc6e9de.
32. Van Hyning, *Puerto Rico's Winter League*, 34.
33. Len Pasculli, "Bobo Holloman," Society for American Baseball Research, accessed January 5, 2020, sabr.org/bioproj/person/ae6a6b08.
34. Pasculli, "Bobo Holloman."
35. Van Hyning, *The Santurce Crabbers*, 39.
36. Van Hyning, *Puerto Rico's Winter League*, 55.
37. Thomas Van Hyning, email message to author, August 9, 2019.
38. Van Hyning, *Puerto Rico's Winter League*, 55.
39. Van Hyning, *The Santurce Crabbers*, 41.
40. Van Hyning, *The Santurce Crabbers*, 42.
41. Van Hyning, *The Santurce Crabbers*, 42.
42. Thomas Van Hyning, email message to author, August 5, 2019.

7. MOVING JACKIE

1. Harold C. Burr, "Robinson praises Gilliam, Hails Club's Purchase of Meyer," *Brooklyn Daily Eagle*, March 1, 1953, 20.
2. Roscoe McGowen, "Gilliam rated 'most likely to succeed' on Dodger trial," *The Sporting News*, January 7, 1953, 15.
3. Dave Anderson, "Pafko is traded to Boston Braves," *Brooklyn Daily Eagle*, Jan. 18, 1953, 1, 22.

4. Roscoe McGowen, "Deck clearing deals bring Bums $200,000 over winter," *The Sporting News*, January 28, 1953, 6.
5. Jim McCulley, "Boston gets Pafko for player and 75G," *New York Daily News*, January 18, 1953, C36.
6. Harold C. Burr, "Surgery makes Flock outfield vulnerable," *Brooklyn Daily Eagle*, January 14, 1953, 19.
7. Joe King, "Kid crop backs Dodger flag dynasty," *The Sporting News*, February 25, 1953, 1, 4.
8. King, February 25, 1953, 1.
9. Roscoe McGowen, "Robinson arrives at Dodgers' camp," *New York Times*, March 1, 1953, S1.
10. Norm Nevard, "Watch those illegitimate rookies!" *Baseball Digest*, March 1953, 31-34.
11. Dick Young, "Gilliam good; can't chase me: Robby," *New York Daily News*, March 1, 1953, B20.
12. "8 major teams carry list of 30 tan players," *Baltimore Afro-American*, March 10, 1953, 15.
13. Martha Jo Black and Chuck Schoffner, *Joe Black: More than a Dodger* (Chicago, IL: Academy Chicago Publishers, 2015), 106.
14. Black and Schoffner, *Joe Black*, 115.
15. Harold C. Burr, "Dressen figures on Gilliam as infielder," *Brooklyn Daily Eagle*, March 6, 1953, 15.
16. Burr, March 6, 1953, p. 15.
17. "Thompson Marvels at Gilliam's Play," *Brooklyn Daily Eagle*, March 7, 1953, 9.
18. Harold C. Burr, "Dodgers smother Braves, 8-4," *Brooklyn Daily Eagle*, March 8, 1953, 24.
19. Roger Kahn, "Problem of Negroes in baseball unresolved," *New York Herald-Tribune*, March 21, 1953, 12.
20. Rudy Marzano, *The Last Years of the Brooklyn Dodgers* (Jefferson, NC: McFarland and Company, 2007), 125.
21. Peter Golenbock, *Bums: An Oral History of the Brooklyn Dodgers* (New York: G.P. Putnam's Sons, 1984), 333.
22. Milton Gross, "The inside story of trouble on the Dodgers," *New York Post*, March 23, 1953, 48.
23. "'No race problem on Bums'—Jackie," *Pittsburgh Courier*, March 28, 1953, 15.
24. Golenbock, Bums, 336.
25. Roger Kahn, *The Boys of Summer*, (New York: Harper & Row Publishers, 1972), 173-174.
26. Roger Kahn, "What white big leaguers really think of Negro players," *Our Sports*, June 1953, 11.
27. Kahn, June 1953, 64.
28. Bill Nunn, Jr., "Gilliam key to spat on Bums' team," *Pittsburgh Courier*, March 28, 1953, 1.
29. Nunn, Jr., 4.
30. Marzano, 2007, 99.
31. "Hodges to check with Flock medic," *Brooklyn Daily Eagle*, April 2, 1953, 18.
32. Bill Roberts, "Gilliam figures hitting slump just temporary," *Nashville Banner*, April 6, 1953, 22.
33. Harold C. Burr, "Dressen cures Gilliam's slump," *Brooklyn Daily Eagle*, April 4, 1953, 4.
34. Burr, April 4, 1953, 4.
35. Raymond Johnson, "One man's opinion," *Tennessean*, April 6, 1953, 16.
36. Grantland Rice II, "Bums trip Braves before 12,059 fans," *Tennessean*, April 6, 1953, 16.
37. Arnold Rampersand, *Jackie Robinson: A Biography* (New York: Alfred A. Knopf, 1997), 256.
38. "Will Gilliam top Jackie?" *Our World*, August 1953, 66.
39. "Meet Junior Gilliam!" *Our Sports*, June 1953, 56.
40. "Meet Junior Gilliam!" *Our Sports*, June 1953, 56.
41. "Meet Junior Gilliam!" *Our Sports*, June 1953, 57.
42. Golenbock, 1984, 332.

43. Danny Peary, *We played the game: 65 players remember baseball's greatest era, 1947-1964* (New York: Hyperion, 1994), 254.
44. Neil Lanctot, *Campy: The two lives of Roy Campanella* (New York: Simon & Schuster, 2011), 287.
45. Harvey Frommer, *New York City Baseball, The Last Golden Age, 1947-1957* (Madison, WI: The University of Wisconsin Press, 2004), 78-79.
46. "Meet Junior Gilliam!" *Our Sports*, June 1953, 57.

8. A STRONG MLB DEBUT IN 1953

1. Tommy Holmes, "Scouting report on the Dodgers," *Brooklyn Daily Eagle*, April 3, 1953, 13.
2. Harold C. Burr, "Black best Dodger hill insurance," *Brooklyn Daily Eagle*, April 15, 1953, 17.
3. Dick Young, "Position no. 4 for Robby, replaces Gilliam at 2d," *New York Daily News*, July 7, 1953, C20.
4. "Rest proves tonic Jr. Gilliam needed," *Brooklyn Daily Eagle*, July 18, 1953, 8.
5. Tommy Holmes, "Gilliam provided three-way help," *Brooklyn Daily Eagle*, September 10, 1953, 17.
6. Duke Snider with Bill Gilbert, *The Duke of Flatbush*, 222.
7. Harvey Frommer, *New York City Baseball: The Last Golden Age, 1947-1957* (Madison, WI: University of Wisconsin Press, 2004), 31-32.
8. Raymond Johnson, "One Man's Opinion: Hard Work Made Gilliam an Excellent Switch Hitter," *Nashville Tennessean*, December 10, 1965, 59.
9. "Gilliam figured Haddix would win rookie prize," *The Sporting News*, January 6, 1954, 18.
10. Dave Anderson, "Gilliam in line for Rookie of the Year," *Brooklyn Daily Eagle*, September 2, 1953, 14.
11. C.C. Johnson Spink, "Freshman honors to Kuenn, Gilliam," *The Sporting News*, October 1, 1953, 1.
12. Neil Lanctot, *Campy: The two lives of Roy Campanella* (New York: Simon and Schuster, 2011), 229.
13. Thomas Barthel, *Baseball barnstorming and Exhibition Games, 1901-1962: A History of Off-Season Major League Play* (Jefferson, NC: McFarland and Company, 2007), 225.
14. Barthel, 245-246.
15. "Junior Gilliam to be honored here tonight," *Nashville Banner*, October 12, 1953, 28.
16. Fred Russell, "'Gilliam had great year,' says Dodgers' Campanella," *Nashville Banner*, October 13, 1953, 24.
17. "Jim Gilliam to rest after finishing tour," *Tennessean*, October 13, 1953, 21.
18. John Holway, *Voices from the Great Black Baseball Leagues: Revised Edition* (New York: Da Capo Press, 1992), 350.
19. Carl Machado, "Newcombe just as good as ever; Hurls 3-hitter," *Honolulu Star-Bulletin*, October 21, 1953, 34.
20. Monte Ito, "Lopats beat Campanella All-Stars, 7-1," *Honolulu Advertiser*, October 19, 1953, 16.
21. Ted Reed, *Carl Furillo, Brooklyn Dodgers All-Star* (Jefferson, NC: McFarland and Company, 2010), 119.
22. "A big man conquers a big fear," *Ebony*, March 1958, 101-104.
23. Fresco Thompson with Cy Rice, *Every Diamond Doesn't Sparkle* (New York, NY: David McKay Company, 1964), 114-115.
24. Jack Mann, "Gilliam Brings Three Gloves and Waits Around," *Sport*, January 1963, 69.
25. "Jim Gilliam to rest," October 13, 1953, 21.

9. "THE NAME'S JIM"

1. Frommer, 2004, 111.
2. "Remembering Junior Gilliam," *Dodger Bazeball: Past-Present-Future*, July 13, 2016, youtu. be/F4X4XyJ6rZc.
3. Dave Anderson, "Gilliam casts solid vote for Alston," *Brooklyn Daily Eagle*, January 18, 1954, 12.
4. "Gilliam signs, gets increase of $5,000," *New York Times*, January 18, 1954, 18.
5. Roscoe McGowen, "Sophomore jinx? It's just lotta bunk to Dodgers' Gilliam," *The Sporting News*, January 27, 1954, 8.
6. Anderson, January 18, 1954, 12.
7. Anderson, January 18, 1954, 12.
8. Harold C. Burr, "Junior Gilliam too fast to execute double play," *Brooklyn Daily Eagle*, March 1, 1954, 15.
9. Dave Anderson, "Dodgers work to polish Gilliam's base technique," *Brooklyn Daily Eagle*, March 16, 1954, 14.
10. Dave Anderson, "Ex-Dodger raves about farmhand," *Brooklyn Daily Eagle*, March 13, 1954, 8.
11. Oscar Ruhl, "From the Ruhl Book," *The Sporting News*, January 6, 1954, 14.
12. Harvey Frommer, *New York City Baseball: The Last Golden Age, 1947-1957* (Madison, WI: University of Wisconsin Press, 2004), 79.
13. John Lardner, "The 50 per cent color line," *Newsweek*, May 10, 1954, 95.
14. Fritz Pollard, "Can ball stars saturate clubs?" *New York Age*, May 15, 1954, 19.
15. Jackie Robinson, "A Kentucky Colonel kept me in baseball," *Look*, February 8, 1955, 89.
16. Roscoe McGowen, "Hodges hit in 11th halts Milwaukee," *The New York Times*, July 18, 1954, S2.
17. Danny Peary, *We played the game: 65 players remember baseball's greatest era, 1947-1964* (New York: Hyperion, 1994), 254.
18. Thomas Barthel, *Baseball Barnstorming and Exhibition Games, 1901-1962: A History of Off-Season Major League Play* (Jefferson, NC: McFarland & Company, 2007).
19. "Campanella's Stars play at Dell tonight," *The Tennessean*, October 18, 1954, 20.
20. "Gilliam's 3-run homer leads Campanella All-Stars to win," *The Daily Advertiser*, Nov. 4, 1954, 18.
21. Louis Effrat, "Dodger phones A-Buzz for Bavasi," *The New York Times*, November 2, 1954, 35.
22. Dave Anderson, "Dodgers get Post, Landrith from Reds," *Brooklyn Daily Eagle*, December 4, 1954, 8.
23. Dick Young, "Gilliam goes to Reds unless Phils up offer," *New York Daily News*, December 5, 1954, 122.
24. Dave Anderson, "Dodger trade pot due to blow lid," *Brooklyn Daily Eagle*, December 7, 1954, 16.
25. Dave Anderson, "Dodgers left at Post in struggle to complete trade with Redlegs," *Brooklyn Daily Eagle*, December 8, 1954, 20.
26. Anderson, "Dodgers left at Post," *Brooklyn Daily Eagle*, December 8, 1954, 20.
27. Dave Anderson, "Reds may kill Dodgers sale of Gilliam to Phils," *Brooklyn Daily Eagle*, December 28, 1954, 14.
28. William J. Briordy, "Gilliam accepts 1955 Dodger contract for reported $12,500," *New York Times*, January 18, 1955, 34.
29. Joe Trimble, "Dodgers snare Gilliam—He's still trade bait," *New York Daily News*, January 18, 1955, C20.
30. Frank Graham, "The Dodgers strain for a championship," *Sport*, February 1956, 43.
31. Dick Young, "Phils beat Dodgers in arclight game," *New York Daily News*, July 6, 1955, 74.

32. Dana Mozley, "Doubtful factors make Series most unpredictable in years," *New York Daily News*, September 27, 1955, 21C.
33. "Gilliams get divorced, Junior gets kids, wife gets $14,500," *Baltimore Afro-American*, January 17, 1959, 13.
34. Glenn Stout and Richard A. Johnson, *The Dodgers: 120 Years of Dodger Baseball* (New York: Houghton Mifflin Company, 2004), 217.
35. *New York Daily News*, October 4, 1955, p. C14.
36. Joe Trimble, "Yanks square Series, win 6th, 5-1," *New York Daily News*, October 4, 1955, C27.
37. Dick Young, "Snider will play 'If I can walk;' Stengel staying pat on lineup," *New York Daily News*, October 4, 1955, C24-C25.
38. Young, October 4, 1955, C25.
39. Young, October 4, 1955, C25.
40. Young, October 4, 1955, C25.
41. Stout and Johnson, 2004, 217.
42. Young, October 4, 1955, C25.
43. Young, October 4, 1955, C25.
44. Maury Allen, *Brooklyn Remembered: The 1955 Days of the Dodgers* (Champaign, IL: Sports Publishing, LLC, 2005), 192.
45. Allen, 2005, 190.
46. Allen, 2005, 190.
47. Young, October 4, 1955, C25.
48. Allen, 2005, 190.
49. Young, October 4, 1955, C24.
50. Young, October 4, 1955, C24.
51. Zimmer with Madden, 2001, p. 12
52. Frank Finch, "Penniless Amorós gets chance at new life," *Los Angeles Times*, May 7, 1967, D2.
53. James L. Kilgallen, "It's a Cabana in Havana for Sandy," *Buffalo Evening News*, Oct. 5, 1955, Sec. VI, 84.

10. LEAVING BROOKLYN

1. James S. Hirsch, *Willie Mays: The Life, The Legend* (New York: Scribner, 2010), 302.
2. Thomas Barthel, *Baseball barnstorming and exhibition games, 1901-1962: A history of off-season major league play* (Jefferson, NC: McFarland and Company, 2007), 184.
3. Advertisement for Beech-Nut Gum, *Ebony*, September 1955, 5.
4. Advertisement for Lucky Strike, *Chicago Defender*, June 18, 1955, 7.
5. Richard W. Pollay, Jung S. Lee, and David Carter-Whitney, "Separate but not equal: Racial segmentation in cigarette advertising," *Journal of Advertising*, March 1992, 54.
6. Dick Young, "Gilliam Deserves Better," *The Capital Journal*, October 12, 1978, 5C.
7. "Overtown's Lord Calvert Hotel," MiamiArchives.blogspot.com, May 6, 2015, miami archives.blogspot.com/2015/05/overtowns-lord-calvert-hotel.html.
8. Buzzie Bavasi with John Strege, *Off the record*, (Chicago, IL: Contemporary Books, Inc., 1987), 74.
9. C.C. Johnson Spink, "The low-down on majors' big shots," *The Sporting News*, January 6, 1954, 2.
10. Tommy Holmes, "Writers analyze the ball players," *Brooklyn Daily Eagle*, January 5, 1964, 14.
11. Ryan Fagan, "Sporting News supports proposal to remove J.G. Taylor Spink name from BBWAA award," *The Sporting News*, January 27, 2021, sportingnews.-

com/us/mlb/news/mlb-taylor-spink-award-hall-of-fame-bbwaa-vote/8yaah8w0-tiq518ttbmom0fw4y.

12. "BBWAA Career Excellence Award," baseballhall.org, baseballhall.org/discover-more/awards/884.

13. Dick Young, "Phils seek Gilliam—'Nix' says Buz," *New York Daily News*, March 1, 1956, 65.

14. Dick Young, "The Sports of Kings and Queens," *New York Daily News*, February 13, 1955, 31B.

15. Young, February 13, 1955, 31B.

16. Ed Hurley, "Dodgers' Koufax, Neal are heroes," *New York Daily News*, March 14, 1956, C24.

17. Bill Dow, "Fernandez paved way as Tigers' first Latino position player," *Detroit Free Press*, August 1, 2015, freep.com/story/sports/mlb/tigers/2015/08/01/detroit-tigers-chico-fernandez-first-latino-player/31009435/

18. baseball-almanac.com/recbooks/rb_2bas.shtml.

19. Golenbock, 1984, p. 413.

20. walteromalley.com/en/dodger-history/international-relations/1956-Summary_Introduction.

21. Fred Kipp and Scott Kipp, *The Last Yankee Dodger: From Brooklyn to LA and the Bronx* (Self-published, 2018), 126.

22. Sam Haynes, "Jr. Gilliams on verge of splitting?" *Baltimore Afro-American*, April 27, 1957, 1.

23. Samuel A. Haynes, "Jim forces wife out, mother in," *Baltimore Afro-American*, February 15, 1958, 20.

24. "Sleeping pills down Gloria," *Baltimore Afro-American*, August 24, 1957, 3.

25. Samuel A. Haynes, "Gilliams leaning toward an early reconciliation," *Baltimore Afro-American*, June 29, 1957, 15.

26. "Mrs. Gilliam recovers from pill overdose," *New York Amsterdam News*, August 24, 1957, 19.

27. "Sleeping pills down Gloria," 3.

28. Neil Lanctot, *Campy: The two lives of Roy Campanella* (New York: Simon & Schuster, 2011), 362.

29. Neil Lanctot, *Campy: The two lives of Roy Campanella* (New York: Simon & Schuster, 2011), 362.

30. Don Zimmer with Bill Madden, "Zim: A Baseball Life," (Kingston, NY: Total Sports Publishing, 2001), 22.

11. HOLLYWOOD

1. Several authors have documented the Dodgers' relocation to Los Angeles and the circumstances surrounding the deal for the land at Chavez Ravine as well as the resettlement of the Mexican Americans who called the site home. To understand the financial negotiations by which Walter O'Malley acquired the land, Neil J. Sullivan's *The Dodgers Move West*, (New York: Oxford University Press, 1989) remains the definitive factual accounting of the deal.

Additional context from the team's perspective can be found in Michael D'Antonio's biography of O'Malley, *Forever Blue: The true story of Walter O'Malley, baseball's most controversial owner, and the Dodgers of Brooklyn and Los Angeles*, (New York: Riverhead Books, 2009). Jerald Podair updates Sullivan's work by providing an additional 25 years of perspective regarding the impact on Los Angeles in *City of Dreams: Dodger Stadium and the Birth of Modern Los Angeles*, (Princeton, NJ: Princeton University Press, 2017).

The displacement of Mexican Americans from Chavez Ravine is vividly described in

Eric Nusbaum's *Stealing Home: Los Angeles, the Dodgers, and the Lives Caught in Between,* (New York: Public Affairs, 2020). Nusbaum's work differs from other books in that it relies on my personal accounts and first-person interviews to paint a picture of Chavez Ravine and its residents in the 1950s. John H. M. Laslett's *Shameful Victory: The Los Angeles Dodgers, the Red Scare, and the Hidden History of Chavez Ravine,* (Tucson, AZ: The University of Arizona Press, 2015) is a good complement to Nusbaum's work in that it focuses more on the social and historical contexts of the "Chavez Ravine affair."

Finally, and most recently, two books focused on the 1981 World Series champion Dodgers team, Jason Turbow's They Bled Blue: Fernandomania, Strike-Season Mayhem, and the Weirdest Championship Baseball Had Ever Seen, (New York, NY: Houghton Mifflin Harcourt Publishing, 2019) and Erik Sherman's *Daybreak at Chavez Ravine: Fernandomania and the Remaking of the Los Angeles Dodgers,* (Lincoln, NE: University of Nebraska Press, 2023), provide the appropriate context to understand how one person, Fernando Valenzuela, single handedly helped the city finally embrace the Dodgers.

2. Michael D'Antonio, *Forever Blue: The true story of Walter O'Malley, baseball's most controversial owner, and the Dodgers of Brooklyn and Los Angeles* (New York: Riverhead Books, 2009), 257.
3. Frank Finch, "Dodgers play 35 home tilts at night," *Los Angeles Times,* November 21, 1957, Part IV, 4.
4. D'Antonio, 2009, p. 258.
5. Charlie Park, "Wes Covington rates Dodgers team to beat," *Los Angeles Mirror,* November 12, 1957, 26.
6. Al Wolf, "Lillis rated key rookie by Dodgers," *Los Angeles Times,* January 26, 1958, Part III, 4.
7. Frank Finch, "L.A. officials deny Gilliam on block," *Los Angeles Times,* February 28, 1958, Part IV, 1.
8. Curt Smith, *Pull Up A Chair: The Vin Scully Story* (Washington, DC: Potomac Books, Inc., 2009), 68.
9. Frank Finch, "Revolving lineup fails to give any click to Dodgers," *The Sporting News,* August 6, 1958, 8.
10. Samuel A. Haynes, "Jim forces wife out, mother in," *Baltimore Afro-American,* February 15, 1958, 20.
11. Haynes, "Jim forces wife out, mother in," 20.
12. "Gilliam's Divorce Case Up This Week," *New York Amsterdam News,* February 15, 1958, 16.
13. "Baseball? It's Kiddies who are Mrs. Gilliam's Problem," *Baltimore Afro-American,* June 9, 1956, 21A.
14. "Gilliams divorced, Junior gets kids, wife gets $14,500," *Baltimore Afro-American,* January 17, 1959, 13.
15. "Gilliams divorced...," 13.
16. "Gilliams divorced...," 13.
17. "Baseball stars settle marital differences," *Pittsburgh Courier,* January 10, 1959, 27.
18. Marion E. Jackson, "World of sports," *Alabama Tribune,* January 16, 1959, 7.
19. Tom Clavin and Danny Peary, *Gil Hodges: The Brooklyn Bums, the Miracle Mets, and the extraordinary life of a baseball legend* (New York: New American Library, 2012), 230.
20. Ernest Reyes, "Gil Hodges in 'The Geisha Boy,'" January 24, 2018, dodgersblueheaven.com/2018/01/gil-hodges-in-geisha-boy.html.
21. Paul Zimmerman, *The Los Angeles Dodgers* (New York: Coward-McCann Sports Library, 1960), 146.
22. "Junior Gilliam," *Los Angeles Sentinel,* February 5, 1959, B7-B8.
23. "Gilliam to be married here," *St. Louis Post-Dispatch,* April 14, 1959, 7C.
24. "Dodger teammates at Gilliam's wedding here," *St. Louis Post-Dispatch,* April 26, 1959, 1D.

25. Dan Daniel, "Second All-Star Game to Gross 500 Gees," *The Sporting News*, June 17, 1959, 5.
26. Frank Finch, "Drysdale seeks 5th in row today," *Los Angeles Times*, July 26, 1959, part III, 3.
27. Zimmerman, 1960, 148.
28. "Dodgers get $11,231 for record take," *Los Angeles Times*, October 16, 1959, Part IV, page 1.
29. "Series Loot Action," *Los Angeles Sentinel*, October 22, 1959, B6.
30. Edward Robinson, "Abie's Corner," *California Eagle*, March 6, 1958, 6.
31. Brad Pye, Jr., "Prying Pye," *Los Angeles Sentinel*, October 30, 1958, A13.
32. "Nat Diamond hosts LA Dodger stars Saturday," *Los Angeles Sentinel*, August 6, 1959, B8.
33. "Junior Gilliam will represent Hiram Walker," *California Eagle*, November 5, 1959, 11.
34. "Fans and friends salute baseball's unsung heroes," *California Eagle*, November 26, 1959, 3.
35. "Teamwork," *California Eagle*, December 24, 1959, 11.
36. Larry Douglas, "Theatrically yours," *Ohio Daily Express*, May 26, 1952, 3.
37. Brad Pye Jr., "Hill Toppers give NAACP 2G's," *Los Angeles Sentinel*, January 28, 1960, A1, A3.
38. Frank Finch, "Gilliam signs for pay hike; Salary $22,000," *Los Angeles Times*, January 29, 1960, Part IV, page 2.

12. BLACK BEVERLY HILLS

1. Frank Finch, "Sherry act lays Phils in aisle, 3-2," *Los Angeles Times*, May 8, 1960, Sec. H, 3.
2. George Lederer, "'Different' Bucs open 3-game series," *Press-Telegram*, May 9, 1960, D-2.
3. Brad Pye Jr., "Would Dodgers really trade D-Boys?" *Los Angeles Sentinel*, September 15, 1960, B7, C4.
4. Frank Finch, "Nats reported seeking Gilliam," *Los Angeles Times*, October 8, 1960, Part II, 3.
5. Frank Finch, "LA waits for word on Colavito," *Los Angeles Times*, December 2, 1960, Part IV, 4.
6. "Podres, Duke for Howard nixed by N.Y." *Los Angeles Times*, December 7, 1960, Part IV, page 1.
7. Brad Pye, Jr. "Will L.A. Angels hire Negro coach?" *Los Angeles Sentinel*, December 15, 1960, B7.
8. "Dodger star Junior Gilliam…" *Los Angeles Sentinel*, December 1, 1960, B10
9. "Batting 1000," *Chicago Defender*, December 24, 1960, 4.
10. Two weeks after Yvette's birth, Cedars merged with Mount Sinai to form Cedars-Sinai Medical Center, one of the largest medical facilities in the Los Angeles area.
11. Frank Finch, "Gilliam signs $25,000 pact with Dodgers," *Los Angeles Times*, February 3, 1961, Part IV, 2.
12. Jim Murray, "The patient Mr. Gilliam," *Los Angeles Times*, April 6, 1961, Part IV, 1.
13. Murray, April 6, 1961, Part IV, 1.
14. Jane Leavy, *Sandy Koufax: A Lefty's Legacy*, 100.
15. Tommy Davis with Paul Gutierrez, *Tommy Davis' Tales from the Dodgers Dugout*, (Champaign, IL: Sports Publishing LLC, 2005), 129.
16. Murray, April 6, 1961, Part IV, 1.
17. A.S. "Doc" Young, "Refreshing world of sports," *Los Angeles Sentinel*, August 10, 1961, B11.
18. Frank Finch, "Dodgers trade Neal for Walls and $100,000," *Los Angeles Times*, December 16, 1961, Part II, 1.

19. Jackie Robinson and Charles Dexter, *Baseball Has Done It* (Philadelphia, PA: J.B. Lippincott Company, 1964), 163.
20. Hadley Mears, "When Nat King Cole Moved In," December 20, 2018, la.curbed.com/2018/12/20/18140283/nat-king-cole-house-los-angeles-housing-segregation.
21. Mears, "When Nat King Cole Moved In."
22. Josh Sides, *L.A. City Limits* (University of California Press: Los Angeles, CA, 2003), 190.
23. L.I. "Brock" Brockenbury, "Tying the Score," *Los Angeles Sentinel*, July 19, 1962, A21.
24. "Jim Junior's idol is Mays, not Dodger," *Oakland Tribune*, March 9, 1965, 43.
25. Dick Miller, "Koufax goes for sweep tonight," *Valley Times*, July 18, 1965, 23.
26. A.S. "Doc" Young, "You sit on pins and needles," *Los Angeles Sentinel*, January 25, 1962, B11.
27. Jessie Mae Brown, "Busy ladies are 10 'Best Dressed,'" *Los Angeles Sentinel*, March 1, 1962, B1-B2.
28. Jessie Mae Brown, B2.
29. Jessie Mae Brown, B2.
30. "Young Dodger wives celebrate Mother's Day," *Los Angeles Sentinel*, May 10, 1962, B3.
31. Jim Murray, "Gilliam's big in little ways," *Los Angeles Times*, January 5, 1962, Part IV, 2.
32. Murray, January 5, 1962, Part IV, 2.
33. Bob Hunter, "$1,000 bargain—Burright blooming as star keystoner," *The Sporting News*, March 28, 1962, 33.
34. Sid Ziff, "Beating the jam," *Los Angeles Times*, April 12, 1962, Part III, 3.
35. Leahy, 2016, p. 58.
36. Michael Leahy, *The Last Innocents: The Collision of the Turbulent Sixties and the Los Angeles Dodgers* (New York: Harper Collins, Inc., 2016), 58.
37. Leahy, 2016, 59.
38. Ron Fairly with Steve Springer, *Fairly at Bat: My 50 years in baseball, from the batter's box to the broadcast booth* (Rancho Mirage, CA: Back Story Publishing, 2018).
39. "Wife strikes out Dodger star Gilliam," *Los Angeles Sentinel*, Nov. 8, 1962, A1, A4.
40. "Junior Gilliam 2nd wife sues," *Baltimore Afro-American*, November 17, 1962, 14.

13. BENCH TO MVP CANDIDATE

1. Will Michaels, *The Making of St. Petersburg* (Charleston, SC: The History Press, 2012), 106.
2. Bob Hunter, "Old-pro Dodgers face showdown tussle with kids," *The Sporting News*, February 9, 1963, 16.
3. Jack Mann, "Gilliam brings three gloves and waits around," *Sport*, January 1963, 68.
4. Mann, 1963, 34.
5. Bob Hunter, "Dodgers hope that ???? players turn into bumper crop of !!!!," *The Sporting News*, March 2, 1963, 11.
6. Frank Finch, "Dodgers 'stronger' if Koufax healthy," *Los Angeles Times*, April 2, 1963, part III, 2.
7. Walter Alston, "Alston visions wide-open race," *Los Angeles Times*, April 8, 1963, part IV, 2.
8. Alston, April 8, 1963, part IV, 2.
9. Frank Finch, "Dodgers blow decision, take it out on bus," *Los Angeles Times*, May 7, 1963, part III, 1.
10. Alston and Burick, *Alston and the Dodgers*, 119.
11. Finch, May 7, 1963, part III, p. 1.
12. Alston and Burick, *Alston and the Dodgers*, p. 119.
13. Alston and Burick, *Alston and the Dodgers*, p. 120.
14. Frank Finch, "Dodgers Rout Cards, 11-1; Koufax Sharp in Comeback," *Los Angeles Times*, May 8, 1963, part III, p. 2.

15. Frank Finch, "Dodgers triumph," *Los Angeles Times*, May 18, 1963, Part II, 4.
16. Alston and Burick, *Alston and the Dodgers*, 117-118.
17. Frank Finch, "'Big D' dwarfs Giants before 50,047," Los Angeles Times, May 11, 1963, part II, 5.
18. Frank Finch, "Sandy's finger, arm ok—and how!!!," *Los Angeles Times*, May 12, 1963, Sec. C, 5.
19. Melvin Durslag, "Perfecto Larsen Viewed Sandy's Classic Curving," *The Sporting News*, May 25, 1963, p. 5.
20. Author interview with Nate Oliver, January 9, 2020.
21. Milton Gross, "No Dodger dissension? How nice!" *Boston Globe*, May 9, 1963, 45.
22. A.S. (Doc) Young, "Do the Dodgers have a Negro problem?" *Jet*, June 13, 1963, 48.
23. Tommy Davis with Paul Gutierrez, *Tommy Davis' Tales from the Dodgers Dugout* (Champaign, IL: Sports Publishing, LLC, 2005), 127.
24. John Roseboro with Bill Libby, *Glory Days with the Dodgers and Other Days with Others* (New York: Atheneum, 1978), 192.
25. Frank Finch, "Howard's homer wins another, 5-4," *Los Angeles Times*, July 21, 1963, D4.
26. Author interview with Dick Tracewski, March 20, 2023.
27. Author interview with Al Downing, June 9, 2020.
28. Author interview with Dick Tracewski, March 20, 2023.
29. Bob Hunter, "Same old story: Where is Gilliam in Dodger plot?" *The Sporting News*, January 11, 1964, 6.
30. Sid Ziff, "Troy's man in between," *Los Angeles Times*, November 1, 1963, Part III, 3.
31. Ziff, "Troy's man in between," Part III, 3.
32. Frank Finch, "Dodgers Inspire Dozens of Prophets," *The Sporting News*, December 28, 1963, 19.
33. Bob Hunter, "Smokey, New L.A. Money Man, Fires 'Seven Winners' Warning," *The Sporting News*, December 14, 1963, 4.
34. Simons, Dec. 1963-Jan. 1964, p. 23
35. Hunter, "Same old story," January 11, 1964, 6.

14. A BRIEF RETIREMENT

1. John Hall, "Sandy (who else?) named top Dodger," *Los Angeles Times*, April 11, 1964, Part II, 2.
2. Brad Pye, Jr., "'The Clan' & 'Fancy Nancy' stars for BB," *Los Angeles Sentinel*, April 16, 1964, B1, D3.
3. Maury Wills as told to Steve Gardner, *It Pays to Steal* (Englewood Cliffs, NJ: Prentice-Hall, Inc., 1963), 71.
4. Ron Fairly with Steve Springer, *Fairly at Bat* (Rancho Mirage, CA: Back Story Publishing, LLC., 2018), 83.
5. Bob Hunter, "Gilliam: Unsung, Unhonored—and Unsurpassed," *The Sporting News*, April 4, 1964, 3.
6. Wills with Freeman, 1976, p. 97-98
7. Wills with Freeman, 1976, p. 44-45
8. Danny Peary, *We Played the Game: 65 Players Remember Baseball's Greatest Era, 1947-1964* (New York, NY: Hyperion, 1994), 569.
9. Jim Murray, "Take Two, Number 2," *Los Angeles Times*, April 12, 1977, Part III, 1.
10. "25,000 pour into Stadium to see Dodgers," *Los Angeles Times*, February 24, 1964, part III, 2.
11. Frank Finch, "'We'll be better—IF,' says Alston," *Los Angeles Times*, March 2, 1964, part III, 1.
12. Finch, March 2, 1964, part III, 7.

13. Leahy, 2016, p. 198.
14. Leahy, 2016, p. 200.
15. Frank Finch, "Werhas bolsters bid for job with Dodgers," *Los Angeles Times*, March 16, 1964, part III, 2.
16. Finch, March 16, 1964, part III, 2.
17. Finch, April 2, 1964, part III, p. 2.
18. Finch, April 6, 1964, part III, p. 2.
19. *Los Angeles Times*, "Traffic snarl causes delay," April 15, 1964, part III, p. 1.
20. John Hall, "Werhas rates raves in first game," *Los Angeles Times*, April 15, 1964, part III, 4.
21. John Dell, "Sandy disliked call, lost Allen and perfection," *Philadelphia Inquirer*, June 5, 1964, 37.
22. "No thought of retirement, says Gilliam, nearing 36," *The Sporting News*, October 10, 1964, 42.
23. David Raith, "Don Bradey," sabr.org/bioproj/person/don-bradey/..
24. Sandy Grady, "A Negro manager? Some day—it could be Gilliam or Howard," *Baseball Digest*, July 1965, 64.
25. Frank Finch, "Dodger shake-up: Leo out, Gilliam in," *Los Angeles Times*, October 2, 1964, Part III, p. 1, 6.
26. Sid Ziff, "Munson amazes," *Los Angeles Times*, October 4, 1964, Sec. C, 3.
27. "The Most Important Negro in Baseball," *Ebony*, October 1961, 59.
28. Charles F. Faber, "Gene Baker," *Society for American Baseball Research*, sabr.org/bioproj/person/gene-baker/..
29. Jorge Iber, "September 21, 1963: Pirates' Gene Baker becomes first African-American to manage in the major leagues," *Society for American Baseball Research*, sabr.org/gamesproj/game/september-21-1963-pirates-gene-baker-becomes-first-african-american-to-manage-in-the-major-leagues/.
30. Buck O'Neil with Steve Wulf and David Conrads, *I Was Right On Time* (New York: Simon & Schuster, 1996), 212.
31. O'Neil, et al., 1996, 212.
32. Charles F. Faber, "Gene Baker," sabr.org/bioproj/person/gene-baker/.
33. Faber, "Gene Baker."
34. Bob LeMoine, "Buck O'Neil," *Society for American Baseball Research*, sabr.org/bioproj/person/Buck-ONeil/.
35. Bob Hunter, "Dodgers go to market seeking help on hill, three other spots," *The Sporting News*, October 24, 1964, 13.
36. Young, "Do the Dodgers have a Negro problem?", 49.
37. Frank Finch, "Year ago today Sandy paced 4-game Dodger sweep of Series," *Los Angeles Times*, October 7, 1964, 4.
38. Ziff, "Munson amazes," October 4, 1964, Sec. C, 3.
39. A.S. "Doc" Young, "Salute to the Big O," *California Eagle*, October 8, 1964, 28.

15. "A $3,000 PLAY"

1. Herbert Simons, "The 23 greatest plays of the 1964 season," *Baseball Digest*, Dec. 1964-Jan. 1965, 15.
2. Frank Finch, "Dodgers win but... Tommy Davis May Be Out for Season," *Los Angeles Times*, May 2, 1965, Sec. D, 1.
3. Michael Leahy, *The Last Innocents: The Collision of the Turbulent Sixties and the Los Angeles Dodgers* (New York: HarperCollins, 2016), 257.
4. Sid Ziff, "A Jim Dandy," *Los Angeles Times*, May 4, 1965, Part III, 3.
5. "Gilliam back on active list for Dodgers," May 29, 1965, part II, 1.

6. George Von Benko, "LeJohn devoted most of his life to baseball," (Uniontown) *Herald Standard*, accessed April 23, 2020.

7. Rosengren, 2014, p. 110.

8. Rosengren, 2014, p. 128.

9. Jane Leavy, *Sandy Koufax: A Lefty's Legacy*, p. 147.

10. Leavy, 2002, 185.

11. "Turning Point? LA Said There Were 3," *Minneapolis Tribune*, Oct. 8, 1965, 27.

12. Charles Johnson, "Twins Can Be 12th Club to Sweep Four," *Minneapolis Star*, Oct. 8, 1965, 32.

13. Frank Finch, "No Joy in 'Mudville:' Dodgers (Alias Mets) Strike Out," *Los Angeles Times*, Oct. 8, 1965, Part III, 2.

14. Irv Letofsky, "Win-Twins Weather? It's Lovely," *Minneapolis Tribune*, Oct. 8, 1965, 1.

15. Fay Vincent, *We Would Have Played for Nothing: Baseball Stars of the 1950s and 1960s Talk About the Game They Loved* (New York: Simon & Schuster, 2008), 214.

16. "'Waiter' Expects Series Return: Predicts 3 L.A. Victories," *Minneapolis Star*, Oct. 9, 1965, 1A.

17. Jack Mann, "Dodgers Down-And Up," *Sports Illustrated*, Oct. 18, 1965, 31-32.

18. Mann, "Dodgers Down—And Up," 34.

19. Mann, "Dodgers Down—And Up," 35.

20. Walter Alston and Si Burick, *Alston and the Dodgers: The Autobiography of One of Baseball's Greatest Managers* (Garden City, NY: Doubleday and Company, Inc., 1966), 165.

21. Walter Alston with Jack Tobin, *A Year at a Time* (Waco, TX: Word Books, 1976), 186.

22. Michael Leahy, *The Last Innocents: The Collision of the Turbulent Sixties and the Los Angeles Dodgers* (New York: HarperCollins Publishers, 2016) 330.

23. Paul Zimmerman, "Dodgers Feel Twins All Shook Up By Bunting, Running," *Los Angeles Times*, Oct. 11, 1965, part III, 2.

24. Leahy, 2016, 331.

25. Lew Paper, *Perfect: Don Larsen's Miraculous World Series Game and the Men Who Made It Happen* (New York: New American Library, 2009), 218.

26. Mike Rathet, "'We Did It the Hard Way,' Says Calm Alston," *San Bernardino County Sun*, Oct. 15, 1965, C-2

27. Briere, "Koufax Lauds Play," Oct. 15, 1965, 21.

28. Bill Hengen, "'When I Snap My Fingers,' Koufax Told Drysdale," *Minneapolis Star*, Oct. 15, 1965, 2D.

29. John Roseboro with Bill Libby, *Glory Days with the Dodgers and Other Days with Others* (New York: Atheneum, 1978), 214.

30. Briere, "Koufax Lauds Play," Oct. 15, 1965, 21.

31. Zimmerman, "Sandy's the Greatest," Oct. 15, 1965, Part III, 4.

32. Sid Hartman, "Grant Calls Koufax, 'Best Pitcher Alive,'" *Minneapolis Tribune*, Oct. 15, 1965, 22.

33. Paul Hirsch, "John Kennedy," Society for American Baseball Research, retrieved at sabr.org/bioproj/person/John-Kennedy/

34. Leahy, 2016, 333.

35. Jerry Mitchell, *Sandy Koufax* (New York: Grosset Sports Library, 1966), 161.

36. Leahy, 2016, 333.

37. George C. Langford, "Ace LA Pitchers Plan Links Game," *Mansfield News Journal*, Oct. 15, 1965, 24.

38. Langford, "Ace LA Pitchers Plan Links Game," Oct. 15, 1965, 24.

39. "Dodgers pocket winners' $hare," *San Bernardino County Sun*, Oct. 28, 1965, D1.

40. "Jim Gilliam World Series Glove," Baseball Hall of Fame, accessed April 23, 2020, collection.baseballhall.org/objects/2145/jim-gilliam-world-series-glove.

16. A BALL PLAYER'S BALL PLAYER

1. "Viet Nam for Col. Gilliam?" *Long Beach Independent*, December 11, 1965, B-4.
2. Tom Powell, "'Best day of his life' thrills Gilliam, wife," *Nashville Tennessean*, December 11, 1965, 13.
3. Frank Finch, "Run-drought over as Dodgers score early, win 4-2," *Los Angeles Times*, April 27, 1966, Part III, p. 4.
4. Sid Ziff, "Schmeling disagrees," *Los Angeles Times*, September 18, 1966, Sec. D, 3.
5. Al Wolf, "World Series Old Hat to Gilliam—His 7th!" *Los Angeles Times*, October 6, 1966, Part III, p. 7.
6. Frank Finch, "Gilliam Starts, 'Ends' Career in Baltimore," *Los Angeles Times*, October 9, 1966, Sec. D, p. 6.
7. Harvey Frommer, *New York City Baseball: The Last Golden Age, 1947-1957* (Madison, WI: University of Wisconsin Press, 2004), 78.
8. Jackie Robinson and Charles Dexter, *Baseball Has Done It* (Philadelphia, PA: J.B. Lippincott, 1964), 160.
9. Ron Fairly with Steve Springer, *Fairly at Bat* (Rancho Mirage, CA: Back Story Publishing, LLC, 2018), 83-84.
10. "Jr. Gilliam sees more coaching, less action," *Chicago Defender*, April 8, 1967, 16.
11. Tommy Davis with Paul Gutierrez, *Tommy Davis' Tales from the Dodger Dugout* (Champaign, IL: Sports Publishing, LLC., 2005), 56.
12. Harvey Frommer, *New York City Baseball: The Last Golden Age, 1947-1957* (Madison, WI: University of Wisconsin Press, 2004), 79.
13. "Dodgers' Jim Gilliam is Mr. Versatile," *Los Angeles Sentinel*, February 16, 1967, B4.
14. "Celebrating Black History Month and the Golden State Mutual Collection." Los Angeles County, lacountyarts.org/article/celebrating-black-history-month-and-golden-state-mutual-collection
15. Eddie Burrbridge, "Brotherhood Crusade salutes Muhammad Ali on April 15," *Los Angeles Sentinel*, January 14, 1970, B8.
16. Charles Maher, "Sports: A world where blacks are just a little more equal," *Los Angeles Times*, March 24, 1968, D1.
17. Maher, March 24, 1968, D8.
18. John Hall, "A place for games," *Los Angeles Times*, April 8, 1968, Part III, 3.
19. Dan Hafner, "Dodgers may postpone opener," *Los Angeles Times*, April 8, 1968, Part III, 1.
20. Hall, April 8, 1968, Part III, 3.
21. Hall, April 8, 1968, Part III, 3.
22. John Hall, "Bavasi's Error?" *Los Angeles Times*, April 9, 1968, Part III, 3.
23. Glenn Stout and Richard A. Johnson, *The Dodgers: 120 Years of Dodger Baseball* (New York: Houghton Mifflin, 2004), 303-304.
24. Brad Pye, Jr., "MLK pays supreme price: But do Dodgers really care?" *Los Angeles Sentinel*, April 11, 1968, 4B.
25. Dan Hafner, "Phillips rises from anonymity success as leader of Dodgers," *Los Angeles Times*, April 25, 1968, Part III, p. 3.
26. Al Campanis, *The Dodgers' Way to Play Baseball* (New York: E.P. Dutton & Co., 1954), 209.
27. David E. Skelton, "Billy Grabarkewitz," *Society for American Baseball Research*, August 25, 2016, sabr.org/bioproj/person/billy-grabarkewitz/
28. Bob Oates, "Parker taking batting practice sitting down," *The Sporting News*, February 7, 1970, 36.
29. Charles Goren, "Good play by a first baseman," *Sports Illustrated*, April 18, 1966, 110.
30. Walter Alston with Jack Tobin, *A Year at a Time* (Waco, TX: Word Books, 1976), 100.
31. Loel Schrader, "Sneaking a look at a Dodgers (trip) diary," *Independent Press-Telegram*, July 3, 1977, S-3.

32. Rody Johnson, *Rise and Fall of Dodgertown: 60 Years of Baseball in Vero Beach* (Gainesville, FL: University of Florida Press, 2008), 125.
33. Anne Krueger, "Friend reveres Gilliam," *Palm Beach Post-Times*, October 15, 1978, E10.

17. "JUST SO I GET MY CHANCE"

1. Sandy Grady, "A Negro Manager? Some day—it could be Gilliam or Elston Howard," *Baseball Digest*, July 1965, p. 64.
2. Grady, 1965, 63.
3. Grady, 1965, 64.
4. Grady, 1965, 64.
5. Grady, 1965, 64.
6. Hank Aaron and Jerome Holtzman, "I could do the job: Are you ready for a Negro manager?" *Sport*, October 1965, 106.
7. Grady, 1965, 64.
8. Bill White with Gordon Dillow, *Uppity: My untold story about the games people play* (New York: Grand Central Publishing, 2012), 112
9. Roger Birtwell, "Russell Quick, Alert, Sensitive," *Boston Globe*, April 19, 1966, 56.
10. Birtwell.
11. Milton Gross, "Russell took job because he couldn't resist challenge," *Boston Globe*, April 19, 1966,
12. Mike Rathet, "Why no Negro Manager? A Black, White Question," *Miami Herald*, March 9, 1969, 6E.
13. Mike Rathet, "Why no Negro Manager? A Black, White Question," *Miami Herald*, March 9, 1969, 6E.
14. Yes, there are five cities in the Quad Cities.
15. "The Time May Be Overripe," *Times-Democrat*, March 17, 1969, 4.
16. John Roseboro with Bill Libby, *Glory Days with the Dodgers and Other Days with Others* (New York: Atheneum, 1978), 257
17. Brad Pye, "Baseball's Forgotten Man: Jim Gilliam," *Black Sports*, October 1971, 34.
18. Pye, 1971, 35.
19. Pye, 1971, 35.
20. Pye, 1971, 35.
21. Pye, 1971, 35.
22. Frank Finch, "Wills' Goal: To Step Into Boss' Shoes," *The Sporting News*, January 9, 1971, 41.
23. Finch, January 9, 1971, 41.
24. Finch, January 9, 1971, 41.
25. Ross Newhan, "Gilliam Wants to Manage," *The Sporting News*, March 13, 1971, 52.
26. Newhan, March 13, 1971, 52.
27. Charley Feeney, "Wills Nixes Gilliam as 1st Black Pilot," *Pittsburgh Post-Gazette*, March 12, 1973, 20.
28. Augie Borgi, "Bucs Blast Mets, 7-6," *New York Daily News,* March 13, 1973, 70.
29. Ross Newhan, "Durocher Rates Astro Outfield with Greatest," *Los Angeles Times*, March 19, 1973, Part III, 4.
30. Bill Nunn, Jr., "Change of Pace," *Pittsburgh Courier*, May 12, 1973, 10.
31. Maury Wills with Don Freeman, *How to Steal a Pennant* (New York: G.P. Putnam's Sons, 1976), 29.
32. Wills with Freeman, 1976, 29.
33. Glen Sparks, "Maury Wills," Society for American Baseball Research, sabr.org/bioproj/person/maury-wills/

34. Dave Nightingale, "Gilliam's Dodger Spirit Lives On," *Chicago Tribune*, October 10, 1978, Sec. 4, 1.
35. youtu.be/Pdg0WApbYjI.
36. Bowie Kuhn, *Hardball: The Education of a Baseball Commissioner* (New York: Times Books, 1987), 116.
37. Arnold Rampersand, *Jackie Robinson: A Biography* (New York: Alfred A. Knopf, 1997), 460.
38. *Los Angeles Times*, October 25, 1972, part III, page 4.
39. Phil Pepe, "His fans & famous put Jackie to rest," *New York Daily News*, October 28, 1972, 2 & 23.
40. Tom Van Hyning, *Puerto Rico's Winter League: A history of Major League Baseball's Launching Pad* (Jefferson, NC: McFarland & Company, Inc., 1995), 41.
41. Van Hyning, 1995, 41.
42. Gary Libman, "Blacks' Managerial Hopes Dim," *New York Daily News*, August 4, 1974, 99.
43. Libman, 1974, 99.
44. Libman, 1974, 99.
45. Maxwell Kates, "Frank Robinson," Society for American Baseball Research, sabr.org/bioproj/person/frank-robinson/.
46. youtu.be/kcWOhyCK3vM
47. youtu.be/kcWOhyCK3vM
48. Dick Young, "Gilliam Deserves Better," *The Capital-Journal*, October 12, 1978, 5D.
49. Frank Robinson and Berry Stainback, *Extra Innings: The Grand-Slam Response to Al Campanis's Controversial Remarks About Blacks in Baseball* (New York: McGraw-Hill Book Company, 1988), 112.
50. Ross Newhan, "Alston retires after managing 23 years," *Los Angeles Times*, September 28, 1976, Part III, 1.
51. Ross Newhan, "Dodgers get their man; It's Lasorda," *Los Angeles Times*, September 30, 1976, Part III, 1.
52. McCoy, May 29, 1977, p. 3-D.
53. McCoy, May 29, 1977, p. 3-D.
54. Tommy Davis with Paul Gutierrez, *Tommy Davis' Tales from the Dodger Dugout* (Champaign, IL: Sports Publishing, LLC, 2005), 49.
55. Don Merry, "Questions surround Downing signing," *Los Angeles Times*, March 15, 1977, Part III, 2.
56. "Yeager on a Home Run streak," *Los Angeles Times*, March 7, 1977, Part III, 6.
57. Don Merry, "Battery sparks Dodgers' 5-0 victory over Giants," *Los Angeles Times*, April 17, 1977, Part III, 4
58. "Gilliam: Low-Key Pro," *Florida Today*, March 10, 1978, 1C.
59. "Gilliam: Low-Key Pro," *Florida Today*, March 10, 1978, 4C.
60. "Gilliam: Low-Key Pro," *Florida Today*, March 10, 1978, 4C.
61. "Gilliam listed 'critical,'" *Los Angeles Times*, September 16, 1978, Part III, 4.
62. "Dodgers' Jim Gilliam in a coma," *Miami Herald*, September 17, 1978, 2C.
63. "Little joy in Dodger runaway," *Honolulu Star-Bulletin*, September 16, 1978, B1.
64. Chris Mortensen, "Over 3,000,000 fans served," *San Pedro News-Pilot*, September 16, 1978, A10.
65. "Gilliam slips into coma; Condition 'very critical,'" *Los Angeles Times*, September 17, 1978, Part III, 9.

18. SAYING GOODBYE TO A BROTHER

1. Brad Pye, Jr., "Prying Pye," *Los Angeles Sentinel*, October 5, 1978, B1.
2. Scott Ostler, "Spirit of Gilliam alive for Dodgers," *Los Angeles Times*, Oct. 10, 1978, Part III, 1.

3. Ostler, Oct. 10, 1978, 15.
4. Bob Quincy, "Dodgers Say Goodbye to Their Friend, Gilliam," *Charlotte Observer,* October 12, 1978, 7B.
5. Billy Reed, "Death in October: Jim Gilliam basks, too late, in the limelight," *Louisville Courier-Journal,* October 12, 1978, 1D
6. Dave Kindred, "Baseball, friends pay last respects to Gilliam," *Washington Post,* October 12, 1978, washingtonpost.com/archive/sports/1978/10/12/baseball-friends-pay-last-respects-to-gilliam/f013a70d-c3f6-4dbd-a192-caa5cdb64e3d/.
7. David Israel, "Jim Gilliam: Another of the Boys of Summer is gone," *San Francisco Examiner,* October 12, 1978, 66.
8. Ken Picking, "'Headwinds' Couldn't Stop Jim Gilliam," *Atlanta Constitution,* October 12, 1978, 1D, 11D.
9. Steve Garvey with Skip Rozin, *Garvey* (New York: Times Books, 1986), 120.
10. Garvey with Rozin, 120.
11. Jim Murray, "A Salute to Gilliam," *Los Angeles Times,* October 13, 1978, Part III, 4.

19. EPILOGUE

1. Steve Garvey, *My Bat Boy Days: Lessons I learned from the Boys of Summer* (New York: Scribner, 2008), 8.
2. Garvey with Rozin, 1986, 119.
3. Jaffe WAR Score System, Nov. 19, 2012, baseball-reference.com/about/jaws.shtml.
4. Jay Jaffe, "Slights, returns, and Hall of Fame ballots," Fangraphs.com, Nov. 20, 2018, blogs.fangraphs.com/slights-returns-and-hall-of-fame-ballots/. Though he was not a regular second baseman, Gilliam (No. 39) ranks above Bill Mazeroski (No. 51) in Second Baseman JAWS leaders.
5. baseball-reference.com/awards/hof_1972.shtml#all_hof_BBWAA.
6. Richard Miller, "Roy McMillan," sabr.org/bioproj/person/Roy-McMillan/
7. Hunter, April 4, 1964, p. 3.
8. Hunter, April 4, 1964, p. 3.
9. Davis with Gutierrez, 2005, 57.
10. "Busch remembers Gilliam," *Los Angeles Sentinel,* October 19, 1978, B1.
11. "Busch remembers Gilliam," October 19, 1978, B1.
12. "Anheuser-Busch remembers Jim Gilliam," *Los Angeles Sentinel,* December 20, 1978, B4.
13. "Anheuser-Busch remembers…" December 20, 1978, B4.
14. Fred Lee, "Honor Nashville baseball great," *Tennessean,* February 18, 2014, 12A.
15. Mike Organ, "Street name to honor city's best ballplayer," *Tennessean,* April 5, 2015, 2C.
16. Scully, 2015, youtu.be/-ieul7mGMQc.

INDEX

Made in the USA
Monee, IL
18 March 2025

14180468R00187